A BLURB
FOR THE BOOK

The cover of the May 15, 1950, issue of *Newsweek* announced: "IN THIS ISSUE: WHAT MAKES A MILLIONAIRE GO COMMUNIST?" An interesting question.

Under "National Affairs" the magazine ran a six-column, two-page story purporting to give its readers the answer. It didn't, but it did amplify the question into a dilemma:

> By most tests of heridity and environment, Frederick V. Field should have been a Wall Street broker, a railroad executive, a gentleman farmer, or simply an amiable young man with no particular purpose in life except mixing a tolerable martini; in fact, he should have been anything except what he really is—a member of the Communist Party, U.S.A., who appears to rank just below the very top layer in the rigid class structure of the American Reds.

A column in the same issue, signed "The Editors," deepened the mystery:

> Associate Editor Harold Lavine has been covering Communist activities for seventeen years but never before has he encountered the paradox involved in painting a portrait of a millionaire Communist. Lavine interviewed more than a score of people who had known Frederick Vanderbilt Field since birth, and all of them, even the most bitter political adversaries of Field, discussed him in terms of "gentle, kindly, generous, sincere, realistic, wonderful fellow." With this issue *Newsweek* publishes the first comprehensive story ever written of Commodore Vanderbilt's great-great-grandson, whose personality defies his politics.

Translated, that means you can't be a decent person and a Communist, too.

The *Saturday Evening Post* (September 9, 1950) and *Life* (July 31, 1950), among other publications, in long articles tried their hands at explaining what had happened to that nice boy, Freddy Field. *Life* managed to get a picture of me at my desk, smoking a pipe, with bank statement and tobacco pouch on the desk top, and behind me on bookshelves portraits of Chou En-Lai, Chu Teh, Mao Tse-tung and my eldest daughter, Lila, and eight one-pound tins of Dunhill's "My Mixture" #A11101. The *Saturday Evening Post* illustration showed me looking grim, carrying some papers into a hearing of a subcommittee of the Senate Committee on Foreign Relations. Neither article answered the question *Newsweek* posed, though they made some gossipy stabs.

Now, decades later, it's my turn.

Frederick Vanderbilt Field

FROM RIGHT TO LEFT

FROM RIGHT TO LEFT

An Autobiography

Frederick Vanderbilt Field

LAWRENCE HILL & COMPANY
Westport, Connecticut 06880

Copyright © 1983 by Frederick V. Field
All rights reserved

Published in the United States of America
by Lawrence Hill & Company, Publishers, Inc.
520 Riverside Avenue, Westport, Connecticut 06880

Library of Congress Cataloging in Publication Data

Field, Frederick Vanderbilt, 1905-
  From right to left.

  1. Field, Frederick Vanderbilt, 1905-
2. Communists—United States—Biography. 3. Millionaires
—United States—Biography. I. Title.
HX84.F45A34   1983   335.43'092'4 [B]   82-23407
ISBN 0-88208-161-6 (pbk.)
ISBN 0-88208-162-4

1 2 3 4 5 6 7 8 9

Printed in the United States of America

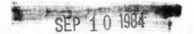

To my children and stepchildren, grandchildren and step-grandchildren, and
a great-grandaughter and a great-grand-
son—

* Lila, Gail, Lynn, Jorge, Leslie,
Nieves, Federica and Xochitl

* Myles, Kenneth, Lila, Douglas,
William, Elliot, Mark, Tania, Mara,
Cora, Niclaus, Marco, Marion, Leonardo
and Nievska

* Melissa, Dustin

CONTENTS

FROM
RIGHT
TO
LEFT

1

645 Fifth Avenue

M y parents, Lila Vanderbilt Field and William B. Osgood Field, maintained three homes. Two, the fancy ones, were my mother's, the third my father's. Our city house, one of the fancy ones, was where I was born on the thirteenth of April, 1905. That date, however, was withheld from me, and my birthday was celebrated on the fourteenth. In fact, it was not until fifty years later, when I needed a birth certificate to arrange for my residence permit in Mexico, that the date, the thirteenth, caught my serious attention. Before that I had paid it no heed or thought it a mistake on the part of City Hall. But when two further checks verified the thirteenth, I realized that I had come into this world not exactly when my mother had planned. She had her superstitions. She wouldn't walk under a ladder, there was something about black cats, she never sat thirteen at the dinner table and she had problems about Fridays. She changed my birthdate to the fourteenth so that I would get a proper start in life.

The New York house was at 645 Fifth Avenue, between 51st and 52nd streets, a block above St. Patrick's Cathedral. It took up part of the space later occupied by Best & Co., and after that by the Olympic Tower. In my childhood the house was flanked on the downtown side by the Union club, of which it goes without saying that my father was a member, and on the uptown side by another mansion, and north of that by Cartier. The latter two buildings are all that remain of the 1905 architectural landscape on either side of that Fifth Avenue block.

To the youngster Freddy Field, who spent much of his early life there, 645 Fifth Avenue was the center of the world. The house was not only in the dead center of Manhattan, and Manhattan was New York, for the other boroughs didn't count, but New York was the most important city by far in the United States, and the United States was without any question the

3

greatest country in the world. By some vague osmotic process this little shrimp soon realized that he lived not only in the center of the world but on top of it as well. Several of the largest mansions on the avenue, two of them taking up the whole block right opposite his house, belonged to his family. He was surrounded by servants who did everything for him but sneeze. The family had a country place and was building another. He was white, he was Episcopalian, he was rich. In short, he was privileged, he was superior, he was well above everyone else he saw in the street or in Central Park. Had anyone ever been so lucky?

It took Freddy Field a long, long time—it took school and college and travel and books and the people he had thought beneath him—to make him understand that the world was round and that it had no social or geographical center. Explaining how he came to that realization is the purpose of this book. And the story definitely starts at this elegant mansion at 645 Fifth Avenue.

My maternal grandparents had provided town houses for their children. Beside ours were two more, next to each other on 91st Street just off Fifth Avenue. These belonged to Mama's older sisters, Adele Burden and Emily Hammond. Aside from being practically in the suburbs, they boasted an elegant feature which our house lacked: a drive-in entrance so that you could walk into the house from your coach or automobile without exposure to the stares of the less privileged.

My mother's younger brother, Malcolm, was an exception to the normal propriety that the family maintained. The exception was underscored by my never going to his house or even knowing that he had one until I made some family inquiries while preparing this book. Malcolm was not talked about much in our home. I knew him only slightly, seeing him perhaps once a year when he made a formal call on my mother. Because the children were not supposed to overhear the little that was said about him, we naturally became all the more curious. Apparently, he had not only not made Skull and Bones, whatever that was, but he had not even had the inclination to finish his studies at Yale. Despite Uncle Malcolm's lack of a proper education, he could have had plenty of family jobs for the asking, but he seemed to prefer his leisure. It was obvious to us children that he was a disappointment. When he was still young, he fell asleep while smoking a cigarette, developed an infection from the resulting burn, and died. Or so we were told. I believed this story until, recently, my first cousin mentioned in his fascinating autobiography, *John Hammond on Record*, that although he was brought up with the same explanation he later found out that Uncle Malcolm drank himself to death. My mature conclusion is that my uncle was a near perfect example of a rich wastrel. In my childhood, however, he simply provided a reminder that the privileged were not necessarily good.

Opposite us, across Fifth Avenue, were those two enormous mansions, each of which took up half the block. One of them was occupied by Cornelius Vanderbilt, the other by his sister, my grandmother, née Emily Vanderbilt, married to William Douglas Sloane. I dutifully visited my grandparents whenever I was yanked across the avenue, perhaps once a week, either for a brief visit accompanied by my mother, or for a dreaded meal, though the latter event was postponed until I was old enough to behave myself. The meals and the house and its occupants were formidable.

We grandchildren were properly washed, dressed and coached if a meal was involved. Before leaving 645, we were checked to see if we had gone to the bathroom. The meals were an ordeal. A manservant wearing an operetta uniform and white gloves stood behind your chair. As the children were served last, by the time we had just begun shoveling food into our faces, but daintily, the adults would have finished and that man would quickly swoop forward and whisk our plates away. Whenever we were there, the horrible little Pekinese dogs, watchfully waiting on their satin pillows, must have enjoyed an especially tasty supper.

The talk was limited to safe and superficial subjects. A load of nectarines, peaches and grapes had just come in from the country estate's greenhouses and weren't they even larger than last year's crop? Wasn't Dr. Park's sermon last Sunday exactly what people must be told these days? And wasn't the music beautiful? What was it they sang? Usually there was talk about the children, in which we didn't participate. None of the conversations were at all serious, and I don't remember any heated discussions or anyone becoming excited at what was being said. Everything was formal, polite and banal.

I recall one occasion in that house when I more or less enjoyed myself. It involved my grandfather, who was the son of one of the founders of W. & J. Sloane, the Fifth Avenue furniture store. Grandpa's haberdasher had arrived on his annual trip from London. My older brother, Osgood, and I were summoned to the old gentleman's den. He was surveying the magnificent materials spread out before him and replenishing what already must have been an inexhaustible supply of shirts, socks, handkerchiefs and whatever else gentlemen in those days ordered from their London haberdashers. We could select what we liked, Grandpa told us. I have good reason to remember the handkerchiefs which were delivered a month or so later, because I managed to keep one of them for forty years or so, a beautiful piece of linen embroidered around the edges in what would now be called shocking pink and monogrammed with such a flourish that not even the FBI would have been able to identify the owner from that bit of evidence.

After we had made our selection, whoever had escorted us in instructed us to thank Grandpa and to take our leave. Our departure involved Grandpa's customary bussing us on the side of the face, which elicited our invariable complaint that his kisses were wet and the inevitable reprimand that we should wait until we were out of his sight before wiping our cheeks. That is my most vivid recollection of my grandfather until he died. Then all the shades in our house were drawn, and, dressed up, we crossed the avenue. I was not particularly sad, because my contact with him had been so formal and distant. I wonder how such a relation could have existed between a grandfather and grandchild who lived just across the avenue from one another. But at the time of his death I simply felt that I was participating in a dramatic family event that evidently meant much to my mother, and I did what I saw others doing. I stepped up to the coffin and peered inside. The waxen figure of my grandfather lay there, a horrifying sight. Although I have attended many funerals since, I have never again looked at the corpse. When I grew up, I felt strongly that my most recent physical memory of a dead person should not be of his embalmed body and cosmetically prepared face lying in a coffin.

My relations with my maternal grandmother, whom we called Nanan, were also formal. Usually visiting her with my mother, I gave Nanan a kiss on the cheek and stood before her for a moment while she commented on how much I had grown. Then I would rush off somewhere until it was time to leave, when the protocol was repeated. I never had a real conversation or even an informal chat with her.

She was a handsome woman, with beautiful red hair which faded gradually but never really turned white, even though she lived to be ninety-four. She was slight and erect and had perfect teeth. I do not remember ever seeing her sit on a sofa or a soft chair, only straight as a ramrod on a straightbacked chair. I suppose she judged her grandchildren by their manners, their dress and their looks. I, at least, never said anything to her except, "Good morning, Nanan" or "Goodbye, Nanan. Thank you very much." Many years later, when she was very old, I might add, "How do you feel, Nanan?" though there was no need for that, because she was never ill.

Her Fifth Avenue house was cold, austere and huge. On the ground floor was an enormous entrance hall, giving at its distant ends into a large, somber dining room and a formal living room. The marble hall housed an organ on which the organist from St. Bartholomew's Church, Mr. Gibson, performed during the "season." The walls consisted of alternate marble slabs and tapestry panels. The expensive, original tapestries had been purchased in Europe and then cut to fit the spaces between the marbles.

I never visited the second floor or beyond, nor the kitchen and pantry nor what must have been extensive servants' quarters. It was not a place in which a little boy could feel at home. When I came through the front door, no one said, "Freddy, run upstairs and find Grandma, tell her we're here." Instead, the butler said, "You will find Madam in the living room," or, "Madam will be down shortly." The visits to my grandparents were a duty, not something to look forward to.

Neither was our house a cozy place, although I do have pleasant memories of some of the rooms. My father was a book collector, and a truly magnificent library took up the whole width of the house and fronted on the avenue. Except for a large fireplace and windows, books filled shelves from floor to ceiling and overflowed on tables. Most of those books are now housed in the Harvard University libraries. Three French windows opened onto a balcony with a view up and down the avenue, where Osgood and I spent some of the more exciting hours of our childhood. Only a block away from the Cathedral, our location was a splendid one for the St. Patrick's Day parade. As World War I approached and arrived, numerous preparedness and farewell parades with fine military bands and heroic soldiers marched by.

I felt like a hero myself one day when I was eleven years old. I had joined a boys' training regiment which drilled with wooden guns in one of the armories and "manuevered" in Central Park. One day I was walking up Fifth Avenue in my khaki uniform with my weapon when I saw a large crowd in front of the Public Library. Curious to find out what was going on, I joined the crowd, which was being harangued by an orator with a British accent. The speaker was urging the men to come forward and enlist, a performance which I later realized was much like a religious revival meeting. The speaker was reaching pitch when he spotted me among a group of men who were not eagerly rushing forward to go to war.

"Come up here, young man," he yelled. Up to the stand I went with my wooden gun. He put his arm around my shoulder and began the most outrageous demogoguery about "this little fellow who is preparing himself for war while you so-and-so's stand there with your hands in your pockets." A few minutes later I was proudly strutting up the avenue toward 645 feeling that if the war were won I would largely be responsible.

My mother's boudoir was on the third floor of our house. Mama had her breakfast there, and when it was not a school morning, I joined her. That was where she kept innumerable notebooks to record menus (not recipes), dates, concerts and plays, social functions, gifts given and received, the servants' wages, years of service, Christmas presents, marital status and number and age of children, and goodness knows what other details of large-scale housekeeping. The room was just what a boudoir was supposed to be, very feminine, very French, with uncomfortable chairs, a marble fireplace and lots of panels and curlicues. I liked my mother and enjoyed being with her, and she liked me. We had an easy relationship. She laughed at my silly jokes; in a way I believe was respectful, I enjoyed teasing her. I spent quite a lot of time in that room and have good memories of it.

A small boy's impression of his mother, even of what she looked like, is likely to be indistinct. Only when we are considerably older do we achieve a clear visual and mental image of our parents. Mine of her is at her middle age before her life was cut off at fifty-six. Besides, I have photographs that remind me that she had fine blue eyes and brown hair and that she was rather short. She corrected her carefully watched figure once a year by a six-week fast during Lent. She was not as formal or as regal as her mother.

She was not at all like her sisters, Adele Burden and Emily Hammond, whom I knew only slightly. I was taken to the Hammond country home in Mt. Kisco once a year and have a vague recollection of spending a night there. Visits to the town house were even rarer. I may have been taken to the Burden summer establishment on Long Island as many as two times, only one of which remains clear in my memory. The visits to their 91st Street house were so few that I remember nothing about the interior. Although there was no animosity between my mother and her older sisters, nothing in my experience indicates anything more than a traditional sisterly affection. I had the distinct impression that his brothers-in-law disapproved of my father. He saw them only on rare occasions when family obligations required him to do so and always complained about it afterward. I therefore saw little of my aunts and uncles on that side of the family. What I knew about them was gathered from family conversations at home.

My mother was different enough from her sisters that they must be contrasted, not compared. Aunt Adele exploited to the full the social position to which she had been born and the privileges accompanying it. Aunt Emily devoted her inexhaustible energy to the minor ills of society. I think that part of her motivation for these good works was her feeling that because of the profligate nature of several of its members, the Vanderbilt name had fallen on bad times and needed rehabilitation. Strictly a reformist, she did not upset the social system, but worked within the Establishment to make it more palatable.

My mother devoted herself to her own mother, her husband and her children, all in a traditional, conventional way. She held lovingly to a limited, narrow view of life's possibilities. She was tolerant of anything she believed sincere. Sham, subterfuge, deceit, were the crosses God gave one to bear.

Although I didn't articulate it until a good deal later, I felt from boyhood that my mother was a simpler, less ostentatious person than those of her relatives whom I happened to know. She was simple in an atmosphere of very considerable luxury. Living mostly among high-society show-offs, vulgar spenders and pretentious autocrats, she had not a trace of vanity. While inheriting a fortune made by cheating, robbing, exploitation and egotism, as well as by guile and astuteness, she was a loyal friend, both to her social equals and to the people who served her. She was tolerant rather than haughty, democratic rather than autocratic.

In those early days of my life, the Vanderbilt clan was an awesome part of the American scene. With the passing of decades, other family names—the Rockefellers, the Mellons, the Fords, the Kennedys—have either endured in their prominence longer or more recently come on the scene to replace the Vanderbilts as household symbols of wealth, power and privilege. But that American classic, *The Robber Barons, the Great American Capitalists, 1861-1901* by Matthew Josephson, published in 1934, devotes considerably more space to the Vanderbilts than to J. P. Morgan, John D. Rockefeller, James J. Hill, Jay Gould, Andrew Carnegie or E. H. Harriman.

My family saga began at the close of the eighteenth century when an aggressive, astute and merciless sixteen-year-old from a family of Staten Island farmers bought a sailboat in which he carried farm produce and passengers to Manhattan. Seven years later, Cornelius Van Derbilt was the skipper of a steam ferry running between New York and New Jersey, and soon thereafter he earned the title of "Commodore" by developing an extensive trade with an expanding fleet. In the middle of the nineteenth century, he sold his boats and went into the railroad business. By 1873, he had a through line connecting New York and Chicago via Buffalo and over a hundred million dollars. He had become the richest man in the country.

His son, William Henry Vanderbilt, a law unto himself, a worshipper of money rather than people, greatly expanded the business and doubled the family fortune. Eight of his nine children survived childhood. Two of his sons inherited the larger shares of his fortune, but my grandmother didn't do badly. Her inheritance was estimated to have been just about equal to the New York State budget in 1885, the year in which her father died. Seven of these eight children multiplied themselves, not extravagantly, but to an extent today no longer fashionable. By the time I came along, the Vanderbilt clan was large, but because money multiplied faster than the family population, everybody still had stacks of it.

In my early years I met quite a few members of the clan but the only ones with whom I had more than a formal, distant relationship were some of my first cousins in the Hammond and Burden families. Apart from their exceptional wealth and luxurious scale of living, the Vanderbilts were pretty much like any other family. Some were attractive, intelligent and talented; others were not. I by no means met everyone in that extensive family that the Commodore dragged out of the obscurity in which the common American dwells, but it was quite evident that, take away the Rolls Royces, the palatial mansions, the huge retinues and the enormous wealth, there was nothing to distinguish a Vanderbilt from anyone else. Except, naturally and of course, some were a bit more arrogant than the ordinary run of human beings. And who could be surprised? While I was growing up, Vanderbilt was a conspicuous name, and just about everybody knew it and envied those who bore it.

My mother, if a son may say so, was the nicest of the bunch. Even in our early get-to-know-each-other sessions in her boudoir, our fondness for each other was rarely if ever expressed emotionally, and our verbal communication was trivial and superficial. But the apparent formality between us gave a false impression, and we actually had a deep and sound relationship. I admired and respected her and never had the slightest doubt of her affection for and loyalty to me.

The children's floor was a flight of stairs, or elevator if you were lazy, from Mama's boudoir. At the back were two bedrooms and a bath, in the middle a large hall with plenty of space to lay railway tracks or march several regiments of soldiers, and at the front, facing the avenue, another bedroom and bath and the nursery, another room of which I have fond memories. It was there that we played, had our meals and did our homework. Most important, it was there my mother would arrive at five o'clock every afternoon to spend an hour with her children.

In our city life that visit was the only regular contact with my mother when we were small. The boudoir sessions came a little later and were less regular.

Because I have lived such a different kind of life, it is hard for me to realize that my mother never took me to the park, never pushed my baby carriage, never changed my diapers or helped me get dressed. All those fundamentals of my early life were performed by nurses. Surprisingly, Mama and I developed an important and pleasurable relationship.

Every so often Mama brought a friend to the nursery. One of these was Geraldine Farrar. Does anyone remember the Gerry Flappers? The Gerry Flappers were a few among the debutantes of the Four Hundred who either liked or thought it fashionable to go to the opera and who idolized Farrar somewhat as a later generation worshiped Elvis Presley, though in a manner infinitely more ladylike and strictly limited to a narrow upper-class clique. Mama was one of them. Farrar was the rage. A beauty on and off stage, she was the subject of romantic myths or not-so-much-myths that titilated her admirers. She had a glorious voice. It was rumored that while studying music with Lilli Lehmann in Berlin, Farrar had an affair with Kaiser Wilhelm. She was certainly much sought after by certain gentlemen in New York. When I was about five years old, none of these stories meant very much to me, but later when I heard her sing and realized for myself how beautiful she really was, I remembered the talk of my childhood. When Farrar visited the nursery at 645 and sat me on her lap, I even then realized I was in the presence of an exceptionally glamorous friend of my mother.

Our house at 645 Fifth Avenue had some terrible aspects. The quarters of the four menservants were below street level, actually tucked under the Fifth Avenue sidewalk. The only daylight came in through thick glass blocks cemented into the surface of the sidewalk and the ceiling of the rooms. The women servants fared better; they lived on the fifth floor and had their own elevator.

When I was old enough for day school, I sometimes stayed in the afternoons to play softball in the yard. When it rained, I invited my friends to my house, where the basement hallway was big enough for a modified game—to the consternation of the servants, who had to maneuver a precarious passage from one workroom to another. The doors of the servants' underground bedrooms were at one end of the hall, and I remember them as vividly as I do the ballgame. The contrast between the way the servants, who were my friends, lived and the way we lived upstairs, made a deep and lasting impression on me.

Parts of the house were so frightening to me that I can still feel the terror. The entrance consisted of two pairs of double doors below and above the marble stairs from the sidewalk level to the first floor. Once those doors closed, no natural light entered the huge hallway leading to a gloomy dining room that stretched all the way across the back of the house. Although little light penetrated the back of the house because of the buildings crowded behind it, the dining room was paneled in the darkest possible wood, as were the long table and the round "family" table and chairs. The curtains, rug and chair covers were of a blue that flirted on the edge of being black. The room was somber and depressing. To the left of the marble hallway was a reception room decorated, for some unknown reason, in Swiss chalet style, as well as the elevator and the pantry. On the right was a circular marble staircase leading to the second floor. At the front of the second floor was the library, which I liked, and at the back a cheerfully decorated but seldom used ballroom.

The stairwell was scary. It was two floors tall, and from the distant ceiling hung an elaborate chandelier that gave out about as much light as a match in a dark alley. On the way up the stairs were two recessed corners which, under the best of circumstances, lay in deep shadows, and in them stood two figures of ancient armor, visors and all. Every time I went up or down the stairs, those figures frightened the daylights out of me.

Another circular staircase led from the second to the third floor. This one was carpeted and uninhabited by armored ghosts and therefore less forbidding than the lower marble one. But it was still scary, for it was even more dimly lighted. To get safely to the third floor, I had to maneuver it at lightning speed. I scaled two steps at a time until I was big enough to do it three at a time. Looking back, I am amazed at how often I raced up those two flights of stairs. There was a perfectly good elevator, a rather friendly cubicle with mirrors in which you could admire yourself during the trip, but apparently I was usually too much in a hurry to wait for it to descend to the ground floor.

What makes a child afraid of the dark? As a small boy I had a severe case of that affliction. When I went to bed at night, I would half sit up, propped on one elbow, and peer into the dark until, exhausted, my elbow would collapse and I would fall to the bed sound asleep. Sometimes I screamed until the nurse appeared. But instead of easing my fears, she scolded me for being afraid of nothing. Much of that disagreeable experience I associate with 645; I felt much better when we got to the country. Was it those awful stairs that haunted me? Did those armored fiends really come to life? Were they really ready to grab me as I bounded up those marble stairs?

It was during the months at 645 that our family life was stiffest, and most formal. It was then that we children saw the least of our parents and most felt the presence of the servants.

Fortunately, the city house was the family's headquarters only from January to June. It was then smothered with moth balls and furniture coverings and left to hibernate. We moved to my father's ancestral grounds in Lake Mohegan, a few miles east of Peekskill.

2

Lake Mohegan

Lake Mohegan was a contrast to 645 Fifth Avenue as well as to our third place, High Lawn, not only in the relative modesty of the house but also in our style of living and the social status of our neighbors. It was not a wealthy community. There were dairy farms, a few summer houses of city dwellers, a small military school and the village, which was not more than two or three blocks long.

Our house was clapboard over a wooden frame, architecturally shapeless, with a large porch in which a great deal of living took place. It was surrounded by large trees and bushes and an odd-shaped lawn just big enough to play softball at the five-year-old level. My room looked out over the roof of the porch. Birds sang just outside the windows, the breeze blew through the room and often I went to sleep with the rain pattering on the shingles of the roof. The grandest piece of furniture in the L-shaped living room was a mere upright player piano. The dining room had a space for only one table, a round one. And the pantry and kitchen were next to it, not hidden far away as they were in New York and Lenox.

My parent's quarters were in a separate water tower around which climbed an outdoor staircase. From top to bottom, the water tower's four stories contained the water tank, my father's bedroom and bath, which connected interiorly with my mother's bedroom and bath on the next floor down, and on the ground level the water pump and tool house. Constant fears that the tank would one day fall through fortunately never materialized. I don't believe there were any leaks or cracks to give substance to our fears; just the idea of a huge water tank in a wooden tower right on top of your parents' rooms was worrisome enough.

One of the pleasantest aspects of life at Lake Mohegan was that the servants were not quite so conspicuous. We still had plenty of them, but fewer than took care of us and themselves at 645 and High Lawn in Lenox. That was because a platoon stayed in town to seal up that house and another then went to Lenox to prepare that mansion for our later arrival. I have found documentary evidence to refresh my memory of the Lake Mohegan servant situation in the form of a photograph taken by my father in 1908, when I was three. My brother, Osgood, and I have not been able to identify all thirteen servants who appear in that picture, but we recognize several members of the organization that maintained our standard of living. A butler and two other men took care of indoor duties. There were two chauffeurs who doubled as coachmen, two nurses for us little, helpless ones, a maid for my mother, and five other women for the kitchen, laundry and general cleaning. Probably because our way of living was less formal in Lake Mohegan our lives did not seem so overwhelmed by these people as in New York or Lenox. I would not, however, claim that we were camping out.

Our way of life at Westfield Farm, as the place was called, came somewhat closer to that of Tom Sawyer and Huckleberry Finn, though they might not agree, than the statistical count of servants would suggest. We were free to run around, climb trees, hang around the farm, help churn butter, pick cherries and burn tent caterpillars, and, when the moral pressure became strong enough, help my mother weed her flower garden.

Of course, a lot of other people helped ease our burdens. The cows and pigs and chickens, sheep and horses and cars were all suitably tended to by staff. As a result, several buildings and houses or apartments accommodated the help, so, all in all, it might be said that our life-style retained certain elements of feudalism—from the landlord point of view, that is.

At the distant end of the property, perhaps three-quarters of a mile away from our house, my father's mother, Augusta Curry Field, had her house, barns and garden. We called her Mia. She was a widow, well enough off, but modestly so in comparison with the Vanderbilt branch. Her husband, William Hazard Field, had died in my father's youth. A strong-willed woman, she dominated her daughter, Mary Pearsall Field, whom we called Marraine, to the ruination of the latter's life. But before I became aware of such matters, Mia met her match in my mother's well-hidden sources of strength. I saw much more of Mia than I did of Nanan, and our relationship was less formal. I do not, however, recall it as a warm one. She was my grandmother and I was usually—usually, I say—polite with her. However, we had our troubles; she accused me of being ornery and I felt her to be intolerant. She was an intelligent woman who had traveled and lived a great deal in Europe. She was well-read and had brought up a son who, whatever his faults, was charming and intelligent in an aristocratic fashion.

Between the two houses was a cottage, complete for living, with a fine piano in its small living room. I well remember the piano, because during the summers of 1908 to 1910, when I was three to five years old, Leopold Stokowski played it all summer long. He had come to this country from a Polish family in England, a very young man with little money, and, somehow or other, my family had decided to help him out. Somewhere mixed up in the motivation, and perhaps everywhere in it, were Marraine's romantic aspirations with respect to this dashing young musician. My aunt was musical. She had what I was later told was an extraordinarily fine soprano voice. She had studied singing in Italy, closely chaperoned by my grandmother, but Mia refused to let her carry out her ambition to make a career of singing, and thereby closed the door on any kind of interesting life that Marraine might have developed.

Osgood, fourteen and a half months older than I, has fortunately kept family records, particularly great quantities of photographs taken by my father and some by himself at a very early age. There are a number of Stokowski in jovial family gatherings. I cherish the ones that show the maestro leading the family band, if you can call it that. I appear, reaching up to my musical colleague's knees and thumping a drum. Many decades later, when I became an amateur recorder player, I performed in a baroque ensemble under various lesser conductors. Little did they know that I occasionally blew the correct note at the correct moment partly because of my early training under the baton of that distinguished musician at Westfield Farm.

It was not Stokowski or Marraine, however, who got me interested in music. My mother did that. As a small child I often accompanied her to the opera or to concerts. At the beginning, the motive was to accompany her rather than to listen to the music itself. I enjoyed doing things with her; when it came to attending the Metropolitan or Carnegie Hall I was usually the only one in the family willing to go. I found the *Ring* hard to take in those early days—I still do—but not the glamour of Caruso or Gigli or Farrar or Kreisler or Spalding or Emma Eames. Before I was ten, Mama took me to hear Caruso sing *Pagliacci*, a short opera that usually combined with *Cavalleria rusticana*, though in this case the latter made no impression on me. Caruso did, however. I went having heard that he was the greatest of the tenors, and I was interested to find out what happened when he blew his notes in the faces of his operatic colleagues. My father on several occasions had let it be known to whoever was listening that Enrico Caruso was a lover of garlic and had trouble with his leading ladies as a result. I failed to document that story, but Caruso, giving that showy and dramatic part all he had, left me with an unforgettable memory. Quite aside from technique and quality, I don't believe I have ever again heard anyone sing with such gusto, such enthusiasm, such obvious pleasure and confidence in what he was doing.

Emma Eames I knew and heard because she, like Farrar, was a personal friend of my mother and called on her once in a while. Kreisler I heard mostly on records, but he called on us one day. He had been riding in some sort of conveyance going north on Fifth Avenue, and it had almost collided with my mother as she was crossing the avenue on her way home from her daily visit to her mother. Kreisler had jumped out of the cab or whatever it was, assured himself that she was all right and then made this courteous visit. Albert Spalding, some of whose records I also remember playing, had a beautiful place on a hilltop in Great Barrington, only a few miles from Lenox, and for some reason I do not recall, his family and ours exchanged visits every so often. And so, as a small boy, I was exposed to music and musicians, and little by little the music itself became a motive, apart from the pleasure of accompanying my mother, for attending concerts.

For a time in my childhood I took piano lessons. I was not interested, poorly taught I suppose, didn't practice and got nowhere. Perhaps I learned where the notes were placed on or between the lines, but I was not able to shorten the distance between a sheet of music and my fingers. At some early date Osgood and I were given saxophones, on which I got as far as performing "Onward Christian Soldiers"—not a typical saxophone piece— inaccurately and so slowly that had there been any soldiers they would have fallen asleep whether they were Christians or not.

At this point I may as well record one of my earliest lessons in anatomy. Both my paternal grandmother and aunt were stoutish women. They were corseted in such a way that their entire torsos were pushed upward and their bosoms stood out horizontally right under their chins. Mealtime was lesson time. If a drop of wine or coffee slipped between cup and lip, as it invariably did, it landed on this shelf and, gravity being impeded by a horizontal surface, stayed where it dropped. A napkin was quickly dunked in a water glass, and an attempt made to remove the spot with a horizontal movement straight out from the chin. The process led me to wonder what under heaven produced this strange bodily formation that my own skinny frame showed no possibility of achieving. Other than this, I received no sex education at home.

Our home was the opposite of a nudist colony. Brothers and sisters, sons and mother and daughters and father, were always fully clothed in one another's presence, and when we swam in the pool, the bathing costumes made the females look as though they were preparing for a visit to the North Pole. Sex in any form or fashion was not a permitted subject of conversation, and not even the most rudimentary form of sex knowledge was passed on from parent to child. All I ever heard was, "Freddy, you must always respect your mother."

There was, however, plenty of education in reverse. I was taught, directly and by implication, that the body was something we had but ignored. I would, for example, be sitting in my father's bedroom, talking to him through the partly open door of his bathroom while he was shaving. We had not finished when he was ready to step into the tub for his bath. He told me I could come into the bathroom to finish our conversation if I did not look toward the tub and sat in a chair he had placed near the clothes closet facing away from him. This I did and, talk ended, left the room without turning toward where he was washing himself. Many years later, when I was in my teens, Osgood, my father, and I took a month-long pack trip in the Canadian Rockies. At night we bathed in the streams by which we camped. One such stream ran for some distance fairly straight in front of our tepees. My father walked far upstream and around a bend before taking off his clothes while Osgood and I washed right at the campsite. With this relation to my father's body, it can easily be imagined how I was brought up with relation to the women in the family.

A young boy doesn't get very far trying to figure out the mysteries of life by watching his grandmother and his aunt wiping stains off their bosoms. In my case, serious sex education began in prep school via dirty jokes plus a once-a-year lecture on the dangers of catching syphilis from a chipped drinking glass or by sitting on a dirty toilet. There was, of course, no reference to the danger of infection by direct contact with a woman, for, if I may say so, that would be getting into dangerous territory.

I was five and six years old when my two sisters were born. Although they were born in the house in which I was living, I was kept completely unaware that anything unusual was happening. I did not know my mother was pregnant or even what pregnancy was. I certainly was not told that a brother or a sister would be coming along soon. Our family relations were sufficiently formal—or would distant be a better word?—that I had no occasion to observe any physical change in my mother. I can remember only that shortly before one of the girls was born—this was at High Lawn— a buxom woman whose presence was not explained to me appeared in the household. Later, when I understood what had been going on, I supposed she had been hired to take care of the infant in its early stages.

My baby sisters were untouchable as far as I was concerned. I did not crawl around the floor playing with them, or tickle them, or make funny noises to amuse them. They were in the hands of their nurse, I of mine, and we kept pretty much apart. Once, at Westfield Farm, as I was standing next to the crib of one of the little girls while she was being put away for the night, I leaned over and put my hand on her. Marraine, who was standing nearby, scolded me severely, telling me that babies were so fragile that I could easily have hurt my sister. Well, I didn't try that display of interest and affection again.

I saw more of my father while we were at Westfield Farm than at any other time of the year. He had started out at Harvard, but upon the death of his father had transferred to Stevens Institute of Technology in Hoboken, New Jersey. After being graduated, he had worked for a while and had something to do with the construction of one of the railway bridges that until recently crossed the Harlem River. When an uncle died and left him a large sum of money, he entered into partnership as an inactive associate with a Stevens classmate, Morris Kellog. The firm, M. W. Kellog Company, Construction Engineers, in due course became one of the big ones. My father did very well by that inheritance. Thereafter, he was a gentleman of leisure.

He was a tall man, six feet one-and-a-half inches, and judging by his early photographs and from what I was told, a handsome person. By the time I was old enough to record his appearance in my memory, he was overweight and had become—or was he always that way?—physically lazy. Leisure and luxury are not the best regimens for physical fitness. He had, however, a great diversity of interests and an undeniable charm, though the latter was not always apparent. He conversed well on books, art, photography and travel; sarcastically on the Vanderbilt family, my mother's "finishing school" education, the Tammany rule of New York City; meanly about Jews, Negroes and other ethnic minorities; disdainfully about the poor and the uneducated; and, in my later opinion, wrongly on all political matters. His social position and wealth, added to his personal qualities, were sufficient to gain acceptance by his in-laws. He had all the expensive tastes and habits needed to move in the topmost social levels.

His accomplishments were considerable and followed interesting lines. He had spent some time in India, some of it with George Vanderbilt (long before he had any other connection with that tribe), and there acquired a lifetime interest in Rudyard Kipling. By the time I had become somewhat familiar with his library, he had one of the world's leading collections of that author's first editions, letters and other memorabilia, and his collecting had branched out to other authors, mostly English. He published—with an able assistant, Bertha Coolidge, doing the dog work—two splendid books on his collection, *John Leech on My Shelves* and *Edward Lear on My Shelves*. Leech was a famous cartoonist, etcher, illustrator and caricaturist during the mid-nineteenth century, who for twenty-four years drew for the renowned British humor magazine *Punch*. Lear, also a nineteenth-century artist, remains best known for the "nonsense" books he addressed to children and for his limericks.

But I did not become aware of those interests until I was into the years of my secondary education. In my childhood days at Lake Mohegan, however, I did find out about his do-it-yourself abilities. He had a workshop, a separate building housing a large room equipped with workbenches and an assortment of tools. I enjoyed hanging around watching him make birdhouses, some of them elaborate Swiss chalets. I tried my own hand at it, but the result was so shoddy in comparison that, long before I acquired any skills, I lost interest. I suppose we chatted while he worked and I hung around, but about what I haven't the least memory. I enjoyed this far more than the formal life we led in the city and even at High Lawn, where there was almost no easy-going contact between father and son.

Then there was photography, the almost incessant picture-taking of the life and customs of the Field family and friends. There was the excitement of seeing how the pictures came out and leafing through the growing number of photo albums of which Mama was editor and custodian. Still photography led to motion pictures, although this development took place years later, and this in turn led him to undertake, with medical friends at the Presbyterian Hospital of Columbia University, some of the earliest experiments in the filming of surgical operations.

At Lake Mohegan, I also had far more time with my mother. For one thing, we ate two meals a day with our parents, something that was not allowed in the formal atmosphere of 645. There were also games in which both children and adults participated, and the nurses did not shadow us incessantly. And we musn't forget the weeding.

3

The Elegance
of High Lawn

We occupied High Lawn in Lenox, Massachusetts, in 1909, when I was five years old. I was too young to have overheard anything about the planning of the house and grounds and farm buildings, and in spite of having at least once having seen them under construction, I don't remember any of it as new. High Lawn came into my consciousness full-blown. The house, the gardens, the long driveway through woods, the tennis court, the farm on the other side of a small valley—these had, to me, always been there. Much later I came to understand that the whole caboodle had been a gift to my mother from her father. He had made similar gifts, one in Mt. Kisco and the other in Syosset, Long Island, to his other two daughters. Such gifts were not taxable in those days and were a way of passing on the family fortune to the next generation.

High Lawn was and remains a beautiful place. The architecture is Georgian, as are several other mansions in Lenox. Red brick with shuttered windows, the house was an oblong three stories high with a full cellar and large porches on the ground and second levels. A low curving wall led on one side to a billiard room and on the other to the laundry. Later, the addition of a large wing doubled the size of the work end of the house. For the family and guests, there were thirteen bedrooms and eight bathrooms. On the ground floor were a huge living room, a library, a dining room, a children's dining room, a pantry, a boudoir, an office for my father and another for my parent's secretary and still another bathroom. All that and extensive servants' quarters existed for two parents and four children and their guests.

A hundred yards away was a so-called "playhouse," with enough rooms, including kitchen and bath, to accommodate an average-size family comfortably. It served various purposes, but I best remember the occasional

20

picnics. The picnic procedure never varied. In the middle of the afternoon preceding the outing, an observer would have seen the butler carrying a large tray of silverware, plates and linen from the big house. Sometime later, he would be followed by the "fourth man" carrying cooking utensils, eggs, cream, salt and pepper. We participants would then gather at the appointed hour around the electric stove, and the picnic would get under-way. An outstanding feature was that everyone was in good humor. I wonder if that was not because we were, for a change, relatively on our own, away from the servants for a whole meal. Another characteristic that graced these occasions was lavish praise for the outstandingly delicious scrambled eggs my mother had managed to serve. My mother, whose accomplishments did not include cooking, could, however, stir eggs to scramble them. They tasted better than eggs at the big house, because it was such fun to rough it at the playhouse. After the fiesta was over, our observer, if still observing, would have noticed a maid on the way to the playhouse to clean up and the earlier procession returning.

While we children were small, fifteen domestics lived and worked in the house. Two chauffeurs lived in the garage, which had two small bedrooms, a bath and room for many cars and a workshop, but they ate in the big house. As a result, the total for meals was a minimum of twenty-three, and if we had guests, as we often did, the count went even higher.

Two of the butlers stand out in my memory, one for the silly reason that he had a pimple on the end of his tongue. As he stood behind my mother's chair during meals, he would incessantly roll the protruberance around his mouth, thus diverting me for minutes at a time from my food and the guest next to me. The other butler, Charles Harris, had a splendid personality and the even disposition that the job required. He was considerably more attractive than most of the gentleman guests. He and my mother, both strong characters, got along famously and worked together many years. Early in their relationship, they had settled on a *modus vivendi* which thereafter served them well.

Right after Mama's breakfast, the two met in the great marble hall that bisected the house lengthwise. Their agenda was the day's events for the household, which Charles would then pass on to the appropriate underling. There would be so many for lunch and dinner. Guests would be arriving at either the Stockbridge or Hillsdale station and a car should meet them. Master Freddy would be playing tennis at the Blakes at three and should be picked up again at five-thirty. My mother herself wanted to go to England Brothers in Pittsfield for shopping and, on the return, should be left off at her mother's, and she would walk home from there. After dropping her off, the chauffeur should pick up a basket of fruit at the Elm Court greenhouses.

Another car could meanwhile take Mr. Field and three guests to the Stockbridge golf club and wait to bring them home. Mr. and Mrs. So-and-so would be coming from New York for the weekend, and Elizabeth should be told to prepare the large guest room. My mother had left a small package with Rose, her maid, which should be delivered to the wife of one of the cowmen who had just had a baby. Miss Peto, the secretary, had telephoned that she was not well and would therefore not have to be picked up in Lenox.

The meeting was regularly interrupted by Mama's sudden preoccupation with one of her favorite pastimes, sneezing. As everyone addicted to this habit knows, the instant the desire approaches the periphery of one's consciousness it must be nurtured, lest it drift away. In order to coax it to a successful explosion, one should look up at the sun or another strong light. The middle of the hallway where my mother and Charles conferred was about fifteen yards from the nearest window. In the middle of a sentence my mother would gather her skirts and rush, not run, to the nearest sunbeam and in a few moments return to resume the day's directives with a contented smile on her face. Having inherited this taste for one of the finer things of life, I write as an expert. I have enjoyed it all my life, often to the consternation of others. "So sorry, Fred, that you have a cold." "Fred, you must immediately get out of the draft." Now that I'm in my seventies, my pleasure has been slightly impaired. Not that I don't sneeze as well as I ever did; decades of practice have made me well nigh perfect and noisier than ever. The impairment comes from jealousy; one of my daughters, Federica, sneezes better and more often than I do.

Our nurses were important in our young lives because we saw more of them than of our parents. They housebroke us and taught us the basics of living with other people. Through them I learned to speak French before English. Alas, while I still can understand and read a little, I have forgotten the spoken language entirely. I visited one of them much later, when she was living comfortably on her savings and a pension in a small village on Lake Geneva. It gave me much pleasure to see that she was no longer a servant.

Other servants were also very real people during my childhood, more often than not of greater importance than guests or relatives. One, for instance, was Albert Spiller, a man well under five feet in height. He had been a jockey before joining our family as coachman, and with the passing of the horses and carriages, he became the family chauffeur, When the demand on the cars increased, he became the number one chauffeur, driving the family exclusively while his assistant drove the servants and ran errands. Albert first drove me in carriages and sleighs, later in town cars and country cars, and later still he taught me to drive myself. He made excuses for me with the local cops on the few occasions I got tickets, and when I had my own car, he never let it leave the family premises without a full tank.

John Burke, the "fourth man," was the downstairs of the downstairs, for he took orders from everyone. A lifelong bachelor, of Irish descent and a faithful Catholic, either devoted to or emotionally imprisoned by—we never knew which—a mother to whom he turned over his wages, he was an outstanding personality in the household. His duties—coal for the furnace, wood for the fireplaces, garbage and such—kept him in the cellar regions much of the time. At one period we were short a male servant for the upstairs duties, and John was given an unwanted promotion and put in livery to wait on table. It was a disaster for him and for my mother. He was ill-suited to play the role of flunky and John returned to the cellar. He wrote poetry; at one time or another I listened to a good deal of it. I have no idea whether it was any good or not, but it was his way of expressing himself. It couldn't have been too bad, for one of his poems won a contest run by the old *New York World*, the prize for which was one of those large box-like portrait cameras that you operate with a black hood over your head. With it John became a proficient photographer, and was allowed to set up a small darkroom for himself somewhere in the nether regions of 645. One Christmas he presented the family with a volume of eight-by-tens of the interior of that mansion, the best I believe that were ever taken. He was still around working the downstairs of the downstairs when some of my nieces and nephews were growing up. He won their respect and affection as he had, many years before, won mine.

I also respected other servants of my early days, but there is no need to name them. The important thing is that these men and women were individual personalities to me, people of pride and dignity. They were in all ways as meritorious as my parents' fancy relatives and friends who lived in the upstairs. These servants formed as much a part of my human environment as did those they served. They played a positive role in my life, and their class status, their "position" in our household, played a significant part in developing my understanding of the world. I am grateful to these early friends.

Of course, we had an unequal relationship. According to the ridiculous measurements of our society, I was their superior, they my servants. If I wanted a horse, my parents bought me one, and a coachman groomed and fed it and brought it from the barn to the front door whenever the young master felt like riding. We had a baseball team made up of the farm hands, some of the men from the house, and other employees. Osgood and I played with them. We had nice uniforms with "High Lawn" spread across the front. The pitcher threw a strike and I yelled, "Great, Jack, strike him out!" I got a base hit and the second houseman exclaimed, "Good hit, Master Freddy!" I didn't think that inequality made any sense. I didn't like it.

High Lawn was a large "gentleman's farm" in that it did not pay for itself and was not meant to. When taxes began to hit the upper classes, the losses helped. The farm's chief asset was a fine herd of Jersey cows that produced the richest milk in the world. After my mother's death, my sister Marjorie acquired the rest of our interests in the farm, and she and her husband turned it into a successful commercial venture.

In my early years, aside from the cattle at High Lawn, there were chickens, pigs, sheep and even bees. The farmland produced hay, corn, alfalfa and whatever else was required to feed the livestock. The house was supplied by the farm and a large vegetable garden. All this had to be manned by a staff under the direction of a superintendent. The setup was about as feudal as you could get back to in the first quarter of the twentieth century. It did not, however, function as well as a truly feudal unit where the help were serfs and the whole enterprise nearly self-sufficient. At High Lawn, wages had to be paid, employees moved in and out of the place, and father and sons had their clothes made in London from material woven in Australia. Nevertheless, High Lawn made a pretty good stab at keeping itself in an earlier century. In the twentieth, it was an anachronism.

It need hardly be said that, for a young boy, life at High Lawn was easy. There were no responsibilities whatsoever, unless you consider showing up on time for meals or keeping your fingernails clean responsibilities. Except when school made its unreasonable demands, I woke up in the morning whenever I pleased and pushed the bell button which connected with the pantry three times as a signal that I would shortly be down for breakfast. Then I paused to decide whether to wear white flannels or crash knicker-bockers, and another heavy day began. Tennis or golf might be on the morning schedule and tennis or golf on the afternoon schedule. According to the standards of those days, I got to be fair at tennis. I collected several cups in junior tournaments at the country club, a couple of which were for mixed doubles in which I teamed with Margaret Blake, who later went far beyond me to become nationally ranked.

I never got to be a good player. Had there been tennis camps in those days, I might have rounded out my game, perfected an unreliable backhand, done something with the second serve and learned more about volleying. But as it was, there was no one to teach me. I learned something by playing a great deal, and for a while I was a little better than most of the other boys. That was all, and after eighteen, I hardly played again.

My father gave me a .22 rifle at an early age, taught me to squeeze instead of jerk the trigger and to point the weapon toward the ground when not firing. I got up one morning at dawn and went into the woods that lined the long driveway to the house. There was a chipmunk on the branch of a tree. I hit it with the second shot. Its guts came out, but it stayed on the branch. It took two more bullets to knock it to the ground, and by that time I didn't want to look at it. After that, I shot at tin cans and bottles. From the .22 I graduated, at about eleven or twelve, to a light but effective rifle for big game hunting called a Mannlicher. I never got good with it or particularly enjoyed using it.

But a rod and reel were a different matter. My mother, strangely enough for both the times and her upbringing, was an avid fisher. Before Osgood and I were old enough to join such adventures, she and my father had several times fished for tarpon off the Florida coast. The early family albums were full of pictures of my mother hauling in one of those monstrous animals or standing next to one that had been caught and hauled up on the beach to be weighed. When we came of fishing age, the site for that sport had been shifted to the Little Cascapedia River on the Gaspé Peninsula in eastern Quebec. There, in September, just before school opened, we would spend two weeks casting for freshwater salmon and trout and living the simple life. Simple is a relative term. There was no plumbing in the camps; we experienced the joys of outhouses. But each of us had two guides because the river current was swift and there were rapids up which the loaded canoes had to be poled. And there was a special guide to do the cooking. Nevertheless, our life was pleasantly informal. We were relaxed with each other. We had a lovely time.

I have not mentioned reading books, stimulating conversations with the adults or an awakening of my intellectual life because there was nothing to report. I was too busy for such things. My father's intellectual interests hardly touched me in those early days. Yet I remember that it was considered a good thing to have interests and that reading was one of the most important of them. Although reading itself made little impression on me, the idea of reading did. The practice eventually caught up with the idea well along in my teens. In my younger days, one of my father's favorite stories made me conscious that the world was divided between those who read books and those who didn't, and there was no question which side I was expected to join. The story had to do with Nanan and Grandpa's library at Elm Court, their Lenox estate.

Elm Court was larger and more lavish than High Lawn, although it did not have a farm attached to it. It did have, however, extensive greenhouses and a whole wing of the main house just for guests. The huge library was used as a secondary living room on less elegant occasions or when only the family was present. Its walls were lined with shelves which were loaded with splendidly bound volumes arranged in so orderly a fashion that they appeared to be unread. According to my father, they were unread. At some point in my early childhood, the room had been redecorated, and Grandpa had asked my father to fill it with books. The latter turned to his friend Charles Lauriat, a well-known Boston bookdealer, and conveyed to him the only instructions Grandpa had given him: there were X number of shelf feet to be filled and the dominant decor of the room was pale green, a color to be matched and complemented by the bindings. Not a word was said about authors or contents. The instructions were faithfully carried out; the outward appearance of the books was exactly what my grandparents and their advisers had wanted. My father, however, enjoyed telling us that he and Mr. Lauriat had had a grand time, even though nobody would ever appreciate it, putting together a fine collection of the world's best literature.

I was brought up an Episcopalian in the upper social and ceremonial reaches of the Protestant church and, in my childhood, attended church regularly with my parents. My memories of it have to do more with non-religious than religious episodes. Mama loved walking and did so at a healthy four-miles-an-hour pace. She and I often allowed the rest of the family to be driven home after Sunday services while we walked the exactly three miles between the church and High Lawn. Inside the church, though this unfortunate habit characterized only my very, very early days, I was attracted to the footstools the way a dog is attracted to a fire hydrant.

As I approached adolescence, I took lessons in church lore in preparation for confirmation. I remember that ceremony not for its religious aura but because it was the occasion for my first sip of wine. I did not enjoy the lessons leading up to it because I didn't like the clergyman. Children can sometimes intuitively reach a correct impression where an adult fumbles either because the situation is too complex or unpleasant to face. I did not feel the minister was sincere. Anyway, he smelled bad.

I was not conscious of any poor people in the congregation either at the Lenox church or at St. Bartholomew's in New York, though I suppose some may have occupied the back pews. I noticed that our servants belonged to other denominations and went to other churches. At St. Bartholomew's in the city, my father was a vestryman, a position of considerable social prestige. "Ah! That's the W. B. O. Field pew up there in front. And that's his wife, a Vanderbilt, and the children. How elegant they look!"

Among other responsibilities about which I knew nothing, my father passed the plate. In a church of that economic standing it overflowed with folding money, not coins. The choir was composed of professional singers who were excellent. The organ and organist were the best that could be found. And then, as part of my church experience, I remember that one winter Sunday on our return to 645, a walk of only a few blocks, just as we were passing the Union Club a kid made a direct hit with a snowball on my father's silk hat. Very funny.

There was no talk or instruction at home about faith, the meaning of religion or the particular church service we attended. It was taken for granted that one went to church, and that, in our family, meant the Episcopal Church. It can be said that we were automatic Episcopalians just as we were automatic Republicans. Nevertheless, the teachings of the church were supposed to guide my thinking, and in the early years to some extent they did. All good came from heaven. The customs of high society were of course God-given, and for any breach of them God's forgiveness was to be sought. The rich had been blessed by God and the poor castigated for reasons not explained.

Christmas and the New Year ended our High Lawn season, after which we returned to 645. The family Christmas was elaborate and climaxed long months of fun, though a little schooling was thrown in from the age of six. I enjoyed so much being spoiled by our bountiful Christmas that I have done my best, though in a more modest way, similarly to spoil my own children.

The High Lawn winter holidays were marked, among other ways, by the visit of Sheila Burden and Adele Hammond, at that time my two favorite cousins. They were a little older, about two and a half years, than I, but they were extremely nice and seemed not to be concerned with that small age difference. The important thing was that they were girls. They were the only girls, aside from our much younger sisters and the tennis partner I have mentioned, whom I ever saw more than casually, talked with and played with. Those annual visits became more and more important as I grew up; by the time I reached my teens, they were occasions to which I looked forward for months ahead. At some early point, I got up enough courage to start occasional correspondence with Adele, and to my delight, she responded. For many years we were good friends; for many years I carefully concealed this first infatuation.

As I typed that last word I wondered if it correctly conveyed what I wanted to express, so I looked it up in the dictionary. My large *Webster's International* says that "infatuation" means the "act of infatuating, or state of being infatuated." Big help. Then, after a semicolon, it tells me that it means "folly." That worries me. Undaunted, I continue my research. I turn to *Webster's Dictionary for Every Day Use*, and it informs me that "infatuation" means "excessive and foolish love." Now I am really disturbed. None of these definitions is what I want to say about my adolescent adoration of Adele. So I look up the word in my dictionary of synonyms. I don't find it, but I do find "infatuated," which is just as good. That gives me several choices: "fascinated, doting, fond, foolish, beguiled, captivated, silly." At that point I rest. I conclude that my particular use of the word "infatuation" expresses a combination of all those synonyms put together into one splendid emotional concept. And this, I hope, sufficiently suggests the nature and quality of my early sentiments toward my lovely cousin.

There was a traditional way of doing things at Christmas. Early that morning the doors to the living room were closed, for we had first to eat a good breakfast. Then everybody had to go to the bathroom. By the time these preliminaries were over, we were already exhausted from nervous excitement. Finally, the doors were opened, and we walked through to the living room. There in front of the fireplace presents extended far into the room in a separate row for each of us. My father's row was always longest, because my mother, working in deep secret with his book agents in Boston and New York, would give him fabulous additions to the first editions of his collection.

One memorable Christmas got off to an unusual start. Osgood and I must have been eleven and ten and my sisters four and five. We felt that their belief in Santa Claus was getting shaky. Faint doubts had been expressed in the early weeks of December. Some pernicious outside influences were obviously permeating our home, for Osgood and I, the only possible internal suspects, had kept the faith. We decided once and for all to squelch any doubts that might exist. We carried out our diabolical plan—I give Osgood full credit for it—at dawn on Christmas morning. We went to the farm, put some specimens of fresh cow manure in a pail, returned to the house and crept into the forbidden living room. There we spread the manure around the fireplace, convincing proof to anyone except a zoologist that the reindeer had paid a visit. We than retired to our rooms and reappeared for the customary Christmas protocol that began with breakfast.

The surprise, as the reader may suspect, came a little before we had planned. It came when my parents ceremoniously opened wide the doors that led from the dining room to the living room. A stench turned us back from the joys that awaited us. Charles was quickly summoned, and he summoned John Burke. All the windows were hurriedly opened, the cause of the trouble removed, Osgood and I forgiven (the spirit of Christmas) and, after a few minutes' wait for the fresh air to do its job, the festivities resumed. My sisters? They believed again.

The most curious gift in my pile invariably came from my great-uncle, Nanan's brother, after whom I had been named, Frederick W. Vanderbilt.

I always meant when I grew up to find out how his gifts were chosen. Certainly not by him or his wife, Aunt Lulu, for it would have been impossible for anyone who knew me or had ever seen me to pick such unsuitable presents. When I was seven years old, for instance, it was a gold safety razor, with extra blades in their own gold container, all packed in a larger gold box with my initials. At five years old, it had been a standard-size typewriter!

I never had a chance to check how Uncle Fred's presents were chosen, because when I might have done so many years later, that proper gentleman no longer thought well of his great-nephew.

4

Trees, Branches and Twigs

U ncle Fred Vanderbilt rates attention for more than just his strange Christmas gifts; he played a strange role in my life. By all accounts and from my own childhood observations, he was a pleasant, gentle, overly shy person. As I saw him, which was when he was not running a railroad or augmenting the Vanderbilt fortune, he was quiet-spoken, in no way aggressive, in fact, notably timid.

Aside from my being his great-nephew, the unspoken situation between us was that he and Aunt Lulu had no children, and I had been hopefully named after him. It had been made obvious to me all my young life that I had been named after him in order to provide him with an heir, which was a nice way to put it. From my point of view, the emphasis was slightly different, and I had been named so that I would inherit a large fortune. He was to do me a favor, not I him. In our family, there was a comforting precedent; my father had inherited his fortune from a childless uncle.

Uncle Fred was the second generation of the rich Vanderbilts after the Commodore. Although the family had been in this country for several generations before the Commodore came along, and in the Netherlands for untold generations before they emigrated, their present descendents had the custom of pretending that the family began with that nineteenth-century tycoon. The Commodore had assured the family's survival by siring thirteen children. Of the latter, only eight had issue and of those eight, only one was a male to carry forward the name. He was William Henry Vanderbilt to whom I have already referred. He kept things going, as I have also noted, by producing nine children, of whom eight lived to be adults. Of these, the fourth by age was my grandmother, Nanan, and the fifth, my Uncle Fred. Seven of these eight produced among them thirty children, of whom my mother was one.

I belong to the fourth generation of direct descendents of the Commodore, some members of which, like the author, are not rich any more. Before our generation began to die off, there were no fewer than seventy-three of us, all coming down that direct line from Cornelius the Commodore, through William Henry and his children. I have no idea how many of the Commodore's descendants from his seven children-producing daughters exist in this fourth generation. I wonder if anyone knows. Finding out might be a worthy though not a very interesting project for a college senior thesis. More interesting would be a sociological study of the fifth generation, if its members could be located, to find out what kind of twigs, and there must be hundreds of them, have grown out of the original robber baron's trunk. To my personal life what has been most pertinent was that when Uncle Fred died in 1938, long after retirement from active business, he still retained directorships in twenty-two railroads and many other corporations, and he left more than $78 million.

Uncle Fred never told me he was going to leave all or anything to me. But there was circumstantial evidence that I was in for something, and something out of that pile would be a lot. There were those weird Christmas presents. Neither my brother nor sisters nor first cousins, all of whom were Uncle Fred's great-nephews or nieces, received them. Then there were unexpected events. When there was to be a total eclipse of the sun very early one morning, I was invited to view it with Uncle Fred and Aunt Lulu. After the Vanderbilt Rolls called for me before dawn, we picked up my aunt and uncle and went to Morningside Heights to get a clear view of the phenomenon. That was a pleasant, almost affectionate experience. I do not remember any personal warmth toward me ever being expressed verbally or physically by either of them, but that sunrise expedition came close to being a human contact between two older people and a little boy. In any case, my parents made it clear to me that there was some kind of understanding about the inheritance.

We visited the Vanderbilt mansion in Hyde Park on the Hudson River a number of times. It is just a short distance further up river from the Franklin Roosevelt estate in the same town. The places provided an interesting contrast between the homes of a family that lived well and loved books and one that lived luxuriously surrounded by pomp and circumstance. There were books in Uncle Fred's house, but I have a feeling that, as in the case of Elm Court, they were there for their bindings rather than their contents.

Uncle Fred's Hyde Park is now a National Historic Site under the jurisdiction of the National Park Service. The latter took it over primarily because of its magnificent trees, but the entire estate—the mansion, the pavilion where the Vanderbilts lived while the main house was under construction, the gardens, greenhouse, coach house, boat house, barns and residences for the coachman, gardener, dairyman, et al.—have been carefully preserved.

An information brochure given by the Park Service to visitors upon payment of a small entrance fee says that the mansion "is a magnificent example of the palatial estates developed by financiers and industrialists in the period between the Civil War and World War I—a time when the United States surged into world prominence as an industrial nation and the new age of machines created wealth that was almost untouched by taxation."

I have never forgotten some of my childhood experiences at Hyde Park. One occurred in Aunt Lulu's bedroom, which was a reproduction of the queen's bedroom of the Louis XV period. To supplement this piece of information from the brochure, I turned to the *Encyclopaedia Britannica* to find that the lady who must have occupied the original was Maria Leszczynska. As Louis XV spent much of his time and life with a series of mistresses, I read on to discover more about Maria and found this wonderful sentence with its irrefutable sequitur: "The queen for some time seems to have secured his affections, and she bore him seven children." No such luck with the Hyde Park reproduction. But to return from that irreverent parenthesis to my early experience, one day in Aunt Lulu'a absence, my father and mother took Osgood and me to see that room. I immediately noted something I had never seen before: the immense canopied bed was surrounded by a fence, an item which provoked the only ribald remark I ever heard from my father. He explained, to Mama's horror, that when Uncle Fred wished to visit Aunt Lulu he put a quarter in the gate to open it.

On another occasion, the Vanderbilts and my parents were to dine with neighbors. They collected in the entrance hall, and so did we, to bid them goodnight. Aunt Lulu was having trouble with her fur coat, so that little gentleman, Freddy, stepped up to help her get it over her shoulders. Giving an upward tug, his hand slipped and knocked her wig forward over her face. Blushing to the roots of his red hair, Freddy apologized, expecting to be banished from the earth. Instead, Aunt Lula laughed and told him he was a nice boy. From a nonperson, she suddenly became a lady worthy of respect.

In recent years I have visited Hyde Park several times. I was drawn to the place by my own possible connection with it and my desire better to understand my uncle and his living style. On my last visit I went with a niece who had telephoned in advance to announce our arrival. We were treated as VIPs by the curators and staff. They explained that members of the Vanderbilt clan hardly ever visited the place and that to find someone who had actually stayed there was indeed a rarity. They asked us as many questions as we asked them, and one of the top people, an intelligent young woman, Susan Brown, who taped those of my remarks that were discreet, took us on a three-hour tour from top to bottom of the huge house, much of which, closed to the public, I had never seen.

The servants' quarters were better than I had expected. They were large, airy and decently lighted, altogether unlike those miserable quarters under the Fifth Avenue sidewalk of my own city home. I spent several minutes gazing at the crowded detail of Uncle Fred's room, the walls of paneled tapestries, a ceiling of particularly ugly carvings, an ornate bed backed by a wall-hanging of some dark red material on which a solitary decoration stands out: a seven-pronged crown of gold, on either side of which, from floor to ceiling, spiral wooden columns hold up a canopy. The latter protected Uncle Fred from leaks in the ceiling, would you suppose?

That room, as well as the whole mansion—except for a very few fine items, such as a graceful curving staircase—is, in fact, ornate, showy, pretentious, absurdly overdecorated, uncomfortable and in atrocious taste. It is an example of the vulgarity of the very rich in the latter part of the previous century and the early part of the present one.

Years after my childhood, I realized that I felt sorry for Aunt Lulu. I then first heard a pathetic family story about how the Vanderbilts, it seems, had not entirely approved of Uncle Fred's choice of a bride. Aunt Lulu came from a family that was well-to-do, but apparently was not far enough up the social ladder. And bless us if Lulu wasn't twelve years her bridegroom's senior. The best method of ingratiating herself with the clan was to present it with an heir. She and Uncle Fred had, it goes without saying, a box at the Metropolitan Opera, where they appeared weekly on the fashionable evening. The public, including many of her relatives by marriage, began to notice a bulge in Aunt Lulu's dress, and it grew larger as the season progressed. She and Uncle Fred then took a trip to Europe. The proper number of months having elapsed after the bulge was first noticed, they cabled the family that an heir had unfortunately died at birth. The story is a sad one because it maintained that Aunt Lulu had not been pregnant, but had been stuffing her dress. And it is a telling story, because thereafter Aunt Lulu was accepted by the family.

I know more about the Field family background than I do about the Vanderbilts. Partly to overcome the ponderous weight of the Vanderbilt tradition, I think that all of us children, though this was long after we had passed childhood, gave the paternal background a special look. We found a Field family tree fully as proud as the Vanderbilt one. It was just that during the nineteenth century the latter had been more abundantly fertilized than the former. The Field family was well enough off, but was not among the conspicuously rich, and its numbers were very much reduced.

Fortunately, a genealogist among my ancestors in 1895 published a book called *The Fields of Sowerby* after the locality in England where the family had lived for many generations. The author's name was Osgood Field, the same one which my brother now bears along with a couple of others. The earlier Osgood was a Fellow of the Society of Antiquaries of London, Corresponding Member of the New England Historic Genealogical Society and several etceteras. He traced a direct family line as far back as 1240, when Roger del Feld was born in England, and he established that Robert Field, a direct descendant, settled in Flushing, Long Island, in 1645. A little further along in generations, Peekskill begins to be mentioned, and that is just a short distance from Lake Mohegan.

As a student of pre-Hispanic history in this hemisphere, I am impressed with that date 1240. That was a long time ago—two and a half centuries before Columbus. In 1240, the Aztecs had not been heard of, but the Field family was already making noises. Though according to Osgood Field, the genealogist, they were not very loud ones. "The author," he writes, "cannot claim that [the Field family] has ever been greatly distinguished; or held a very high position. On the other hand, the status of its members has always been respectable, and their marriages have been contracted with the best people of their respective neighborhoods. From the commencement of this history, they have lived independently on their own land, although their estates were rather small." The name Field indicates this country background, just as do the names Wood, Hill, Lane, Brooks, Rivers and Forest.

My genealogical ancestor is too modest. My father's great-grandfather was Major-General Samuel Osgood, a member of George Washington's Cabinet as the United States' first Postmaster General. I understand the author's position, however, for the Osgoods only joined the Fields by marriage and were not in the direct line from Roger del Feld. Even though he himself was named after the Osgood branch, my ancestor was too pure a scholar to let that influence his objectivity. I had the pleasure of making some notes for this autobiography on a desk now owned by my nephew, John Osgood Field, which once belonged to Samuel Osgood.

Among the many normal and odd characters in the Field background were Sir John Field, who, thirteen years after the death of Copernicus, and based on the latter's discoveries, published the first astronomical tables that ever appeared in England; a lady who married an American Indian chief whom no persuasion could ever induce her to abandon; and what appears to be a name-dropper who wrote a book titled, according to an 1874 brochure of Harper & Bros, "*Field's Memories of Many Men and Women: Being Personal Recollections of Emperors, Kings and Queens, Princes, Presidents, Statesmen, Authors and Artists at Home and Abroad, during the last Thirty Years.* One wonders why he had no memories of princesses.

I don't want to give the impression that we were brought up wearing this famous or infamous background, whichever way the reader wants to look at it, on our sleeves. There wasn't any undue amount of talk about it. We were not constantly reminded that there were important if not rich, or rich if not important, or both rich and important, people behind us. As a matter of fact, among the upper classes, as the books of etiquette tell us, those things are taken for granted, especially if the family has been able to maintain that status for a few generations. At least you pretend that they are. It is vulgar to bring them too much to the surface. One of our fine contemporary authors, John Fowles, refers to this characteristic as "that ultimate, vulgar modesty of the very rooted and assured" (*Daniel Martin*). Special people are supposed to be recognized as special without having to advertise it. On the contrary, what talk there was, was more likely to center on that lady who chose to be a squaw, or an ancestor back in England, whom I have not mentioned before, who was said to be a highway robber. We are such splendid, respectable people, was the attitude, that we can afford to joke about those rascals. Rattling the bones in the closet just shows how solidly established we really are.

I am often asked if we are related to the Chicago Fields. I always mutter something to the effect that I don't really know and that, in any case, if we are, it must be very distantly. To that unsatisfactory reply, I can add that I once had the pleasure of exploiting the possibility of such a connection with that famous Midwestern clan. In the late 1920s, before I had formed the habit of propelling myself cross-country on four wheels, I would take the 20th-Century Limited from New York to Chicago, spend the day in that city, and in the evening catch the Overland Express for San Francisco. I wish we could still travel that way. I have yet to find as favorable an opportunity to read eight-hundred-page books.

Upon arriving in Chicago on the trip in question, I somehow got the yen to equip myself with a set of suitcases, a luxury which this young man who had everything happened not to have. I went to Marshall Field's and selected three matching leather pieces graded from small through medium to large. They were a good buy as, naturally, is everything sold at Marshall Field's. I still have two of them; the third was mislaid, shall we say, by one of my children. As I informed the salesperson of my decision, I realized that I did not have nearly enough cash to cover the purchase. Thinking quickly, I suppose much in the manner that the Commodore would have when faced with a similar crisis, I said, "Oh! I'm sorry, I'll have to pay by check on my New York bank. That's the only checkbook I happen to have with me." I didn't bother to add that it was the only account I possessed anywhere.

Uncertain, the man hesitated. "May I have your name, sir?" "Certainly," I replied, "Frederick Field." That, the reader will understand, was one occasion when it was not advisable to use the Vanderbilt connection. In Chicago the Fields were big stuff, but the Vanderbilts just something out of history. In a few minutes I was bowed out of the store by the salesperson and the floor manager, initialed suitcases in hand.

I remember my father saying that there was some relationship between the Eastern and Midwestern Fields. Having already done too much genealogical research for my taste, I shall investigate the matter no further.

Even without that Midwest connection, we were a branch of what was then a prominent and conspicuous family. We were in the Social Register, easily one of the most snobbish institutions of all time. I myself was listed at a very early age—and dropped guess when. We lived in the most elegant spots, Fifth Avenue and Lenox—for these purposes Lake Mohegan didn't count—and we had the traditional retinue of servants, but we were not spectacularly social. My parents entertained, but not to the extent or in the manner of high society. The dinner parties were sometimes large but not lavish. We had a cook, not a chef. My parents did not seek publicity. The social pages of the newspapers were notified of births, marriages and deaths, never of mere social goings-on. My own unsought publicity, much later, offended my immediate relatives as much as it did me. My parents were not ostentatious people, and they did not behave with the arrogance of much of high society. Mama was democratic in her manner and tolerant of different opinions and customs. She was not condescending. She was born to a secure position; she did not have to show off and did not want to. She was as natural as a person who lives in the rarefied atmosphere of wealth can be.

The Mexicans have a good word for the arrogant, publicity-seeking rich. They call them *popoffs*, a word that sounds what it means no matter how pronounced. I do not know a similarly appropriate word in English; we need one to express that special type of vulgarity. In our home, my father ranted about the boorish rich, especially when he didn't want to accept a social engagement or go to the opera, which he considered a social rather than an artistic event. I must admit that when I was older, I had doubts about his sincerity in this matter, for he certainly relished the life of luxury and never lifted a finger, only his voice, against what he claimed to dislike. On the other hand, I think he was really bored in company that was intellectually illiterate.

As none of us twigs of the family tree were needed at home to tend the flocks or plow the fields or gather the harvest, we went off to school and college at the appropriate age. That event not only began the process of weaning us away from home but also separated us from one another. As children, we had not been particularly close. Perhaps the two girls were closer to each other, but Osgood and I were a squabbly pair of youngsters. Possibly the fact that he was only fourteen months older than I had something to do with it. At this date I find it difficult to analyze that situation. Perhaps its essence was that I was envious and probably jealous of his position as the older son, the eldest child, with the favors and privileges that went with that status. Perhaps this envy contributed to my rebellious behavior as I attempted to establish an independent position for myself. One way our conflict manifested itself was that we drove each other nuts about punctuality. Osgood was a few minutes late for whatever we had to do together, and I became so obsessed with being on time that I usually showed up early, the latter doubtless the result of the former and the former aggravated by the latter. To this day I drive some of my best friends, like my wife, crazy by being so punctual that I arrive early.

Osgood, moreover, was definitely favored by our nurses and also, I believed, by our parents, although I now realize that I thought so unjustly. That, to use an expression in the Spanish translation of some Dr. Seuss nonsense, I didn't like *ni una pizcuita*. In my late life, I must now admit that the troubles we had in our childhood might well have been caused by Osgood's having been a nicer child than I, and certainly an easier one. Fortunately, when childhood and for that matter most of adulthood were behind us and we reached our sixties, we began to see each other more frequently and developed an uncomplicated and pleasurable relationship.

The older of my two sisters, Marjorie, stayed home through high school, longer than we other three, then went through Bryn Mawr, married a West Point graduate, George Wilde, acquired High Lawn and settled down to a long life of cattle breeding and dairy farming. In 1977, while I was gathering material about our family for this book, she won two awards that accurately reflect the life she has led. The congregation of her church in Lenox acclaimed her churchperson of the year, an honor reported in the *Berkshire Eagle*. From the same source I also learned that the American Jersey Cattle Club at their annual meeting in Delavan, Wisconsin, had voted Marjorie their highest honor, the Master Breeder Award. I wrote congratulating her and in reply she sent me a copy of the full citation in which among the "currently widely-acclaimed bulls" of High Lawn Farm was mentioned one named H. L. Pompey Frederick, which my sister informs me was named after me. There are surprising ways in which one can contribute to the public welfare. This one cost me no effort.

My second sister, May, the fourth of the Field family twigs, went to Foxcroft, a so-called finishing school of which I, in my early twenties at the time, ineffectually disapproved because of what I considered its very upper-class, horsey reputation. She informs me that those things to which I objected about her school have changed for the better. Whether that means the school doesn't have horses or rich girls anymore, I don't know. May married my Harvard roommate, Henry Jackson, who has spent a useful and enjoyable life in and around Milton Academy, a prep school of splendid reputation, in later years pitching in to help Harvard's everlasting and extraordinarily successful fund-raising. During and after raising a family, May distinguished herself athletically in golf and curling, sports she continues to pursue.

I find it interesting that of the four of us, three, Osgood, Marjorie and I, married persons from the Middle West. Osgood's wife was the daughter of a professor of chemical engineering at Ohio State University. She died after their two children had grown up, and he then married Mary Losey of LaCrosse, Wisconsin, who had for a long time been associated with the World Health Organization. Marjorie's husband was born in Winona, Minnesota, and my first wife, Betty, started life in Duluth. May's husband's family were Bostonians but not among the legendary Brahmins. I don't think it was coincidence that we chose spouses from outside the circles in which our parents brought us up. Maybe our marriages indicated that there was more in common among the four of us than showed in the lives we thereafter pursued.

For years I was more or less out of touch with my brother and sisters. I was out of the country a great deal and for long periods, and my interests took me in directions, both social and intellectual, distant from those they chose. But we did not lose touch altogether. I was, for instance, best man at one of my sister's marriages, and we all would meet cordially enough on various family occasions.

When, a good many years later, I got into all kinds of trouble and was accused of the worst sorts of evil, it was clear that I had moved a long distance away from the rest of the family. My brother and sisters were caught with little or no understanding or knowledge of their own of what their brother was up to. It must have been trying for them; it was difficult for me. The ties were not broken, but they fell into disrepair. After the political atmosphere of the country cleared somewhat, following the Cold War and McCarthy days, and after I had been in Mexico for some time, we all made an effort to resume more normal family relations. We have succeeded quite well.

Osgood, who had left Harvard with a degree in geology, has meanwhile had a distinguished career as a glacial expert. In 1940 he became research associate of the American Geographical Society and, after an interruption for service in the Army during the war, head of its Department of Exploration and Field Research. Through extensive field work in Alaska, Western Canada and the U.S.S.R., he accumulated an immense amount of data on the variations in length and volume of glaciers, published articles in the specialized journals and organized numerous glaciological activities and projects. He was editor of a project for the American Geographical Society under contract for the U.S. Army, which was published in 1975 with the title *Mountain Glaciers of the Northwest Hemisphere.* It consists of two volumes of text totaling 1,636 pages and a third volume of forty-nine maps. His full record of research and exploration, which I hope he will complete and publish, will be scientific. His brother's written record is political.

On a recent visit, Marjorie was kind enough to give me a charcoal portrait that had been made of me when I was eighteen. I was glad to have it because it helped me to remember the young Fred Field, about whom I was writing, and also because it falls into the category of family heirlooms, of which I have none. This is no one's fault but my own. What had happened was that when countless pieces of gold, silver, portraits, paintings, rugs, furniture, pianos and other ancestral possessions were divided, I was either in London or China or absorbed in my journey leftward and unresponsive to queries as to what I might want.

That 1923 portrait reminded me of another that somehow found its way into the home of my second daughter, Gail. This one is of that boy, Freddy Field, at seven. It is done in colored crayons with due emphasis on my brick top. But more interesting than the historical proof that I once had a good mop of hair is the origin of the portrait. An expensive portraitist had been contracted to do my brother. Early photographs attest to the fact that he was a good deal prettier than I, which the family recognized. His hair was allowed to grow and coaxed into long curls that hung around his head while mine went relatively unattended. Yet I cannot understand how this injustice occurred, for Osgood's hair wasn't even red. In any case, as his portrait—a post-curl one—was nearing completion, I realized that the artist was getting ready to leave without so much as looking at me. This occasion was one of the first on which I was challenged to face the facts of life. I thought I was bravely doing so, but my sulking must have shown more than it should have—or perhaps that is just what I had intended in the first place—and the artist did a quick picture of me as a consolation prize.

On that same visit, Marjorie pointed out a large painting of our sister May, done when she was eighteen and had just announced her engagement to be married. Marjorie muttered something about this picture and added, "And what's more, she was wearing my dress." I then told her the story of my consolation prize, which made us both laugh. Our parents had not only hired an artist to paint May's portrait and not Marjorie's, but had added insult to injury by borrowing Marjorie's best outfit for the job. In that case, there had been no consolation prize. Such are the trials and tribulations of the upper classes.

5

The Best Education Money Could Buy

I
f I was not well educated at the end of my formal schooling—and I wasn't—it was my fault, by choice. My parents did their share of the job; they bought me the best education that could be found, though they didn't get me started as soon as they might have. In my early days I didn't even know that there were such institutions as kindergartens; I was not aware that anyone I knew attended them. It was not until I had passed my seventy-fifth birthday and was chatting with Adele about our respective childhoods and parents that she informed me that she and her sisters had begun their schooling at the age of three. This small social registrite, however, didn't begin work on his three R's or begin mingling with his peers until he was six years old.

From 1910 to 1918, I went to day school in Lenox for the fall term and in New York for the winter and spring sessions. I have no good memories of either of those schools, just recollections of silly, inconsequential things. The principal of the Lenox school, for instance, measured how tall I had grown by the buttons on her shirtwaist—I think that is the word which was used in 1911-12—which had Lord knows how many buttons from her chin to where they disappeared in a skirt. Although this measurement was taken year after year, I never thought of asking the teacher if that was the only shirtwaist she owned. I do remember that the school in Lenox had two rooms, two teachers and six grades. I enjoyed a special class in carpentry that was given one afternoon a week.

At the New York school, I was bored. To amuse myself during study hour, I used to peddle erasers under the desks, making a profit of one mill per box of twenty-four. If I had been the Commodore, I would have parlayed that profit into an eraser empire. Even as it was, it turned out to be the most successful commercial venture of my life.

My boredom spelled poor marks, and at one point I almost got into serious trouble. The headmaster mailed a letter to my parents giving me exactly one week to improve my grades, or else. My father's secretary, a young woman about whom I shall always have kind thoughts, intercepted the letter and told me of its contents. I managed to avoid the or else.

I was made to engage in certain extracurricular activities so ridiculous that it is hard to believe they constituted, as they did, required training for little would-be gentlemen in those days. One of these requirements was the Dodsworth dance school. There, once a week, I was obliged to appear in an Eton suit to learn ballroom dancing. I will describe the suit because it is as rarely worn today, at least in the western hemisphere, as a suit of armor. Armor, as a matter of fact, whether made of iron plates or chain-mail, has a much better chance of making a comeback than the Eton suit, which even in my boyhood days was an absurd outfit. To help me describe it, I can rely on a photograph of Freddy prepared to go to Dodworth's.

Under his carefully combed hair and well-washed face appears a Buster Brown collar. This was a stiffly starched contraption, the sharp edges of which chafed the neck and flanged out over the collar of the jacket much in the fashion that some men today wear a sport shirt. The jacket, of a formal, dark material, was cut short in the style of a waiter's white jacket in warmer climates. it was adorned in front with three buttons covered with black silk and had the usual decorative buttons on the sleeves. The vest, which was made of the same material as the jacket, boasted lapels, four silk-covered buttons and two small side pockets between which, in Freddy's case, hung a gold watch chain. The uncuffed pants were of a somewhat lighter material, and were prevented from falling to the ground by suspenders. The necktie was black and sported a gold stickpin in the shape of a flying duck. The whole outfit was bottomed off by black patent leather pumps having large black bows on the toes. Freddy's sweaty hands were protected by white gloves.

In this insane getup I walked a few blocks south from 645 to the Dodsworth establishment. Luckily, I was fairly safe from ridicule because common American boys were not likely to be found in that neighborhood. The parquet floor of the ballroom consisted of diamond-shaped pieces of darker wood inlaid in a lighter color. These diamonds were the home base of the class. Freddy and his suffering colleagues placed their feet so as exactly to border the outer edges of two adjoining faces of the diamond. When the piano started up, we performed our dance sets, ONE-two-three, ONE-two-three, always returning at the proper beat to home plate. These once-a-week sessions were bad enough, but the worst came at the final class of the season. On that occasion the girls joined us, and we were told to apply what we had been taught all winter and spring. There was no getting out of it. Freddy carefully placed his pumps on the edges of the diamond, looked up, and lo and behold, a girl was standing right opposite him, her pink slippers placed exactly on the edges of her diamond. Being of the same age, she was of course considerably taller and heftier than he. The music started, ONE-two-three, ONE-two-three. There was no choice, contact had to be made. And Freddy quickly discovered that the only thing he had in common with his partner was that she perspired and he sweated. We had been taught the steps all right but not what to do with a female.

I belonged to the Knickerbocker Greys and joined my fellow mini-soldiers two afternoons a week at the Seventh Regiment Armory to drill and learn the manual of arms. I regret not having a picture of myself in full uniform with medals dangling on the limited space of my chest, particularly when I became an officer and wore a plumed hat, sword and epaulets. A modest fiesta was recently thrown for the Greys at the "21" Club, a well-known gathering place in New York. The party was joyously reported by Ms. Jane Geniesse of the *New York Times*. It reminded me that in order to join the Greys, a boy had to be at least four feet tall and seven years old. In my day, though I do not believe this was written into the statutes, one also had to be mentioned in the Social Register. (This requirement no longer exists due to the democratizing influence of such events as the Vietnam War.) I don't remember whether I began my military training at seven or at the riper age of eight, but I was at it for four years. The medals which I remember winning were for neatness (with several bars indicating multiple awards) and for being runner-up in the annual manual-of-arms competition. Those in charge of the Greys today, according to Ms. Geniesse, believe that it promotes such values as discipline, leadership and patriotism. In later pages, the reader will learn the result in the case of Freddy Field.

One winter afternoon as I was walking up Madison Avenue to the armory wearing my officer's plumed hat, a boy behind me, doubtless a ruffian from the lower classes, caught the plume squarely with a snowball, knocking the hat forward and a little to one side. I quickly leaned forward and sidewise, which brought me around half facing my enemy, miraculously caught the hat by the visor and, realizing what had happened, converted the whole movement into a polite bow. Figuring they were up against an unusually adept WASP, the boy and his cronies turned on their heals and ran, instead of pursuing their prey. I continued my triumphant march to the armory.

The schools I attended must have been better than I remember, for I had no trouble getting into an excellent prep school, then called a boarding school, though in those days social position counted for more than intellectual achievement. The children of the rich were entered in the schools and colleges of their parents' choice soon after birth. Osgood and I were entered in Groton and Harvard long before we could turn over in our cribs. As it turned out, we didn't attend Groton but went to Hotchkiss instead.

Groton came in for some battering from my father, but that had nothing to do with whether the school was academically good or bad. In that respect and from an Establishment point of view, it has always had an excellent reputation. In my father's opinion the trouble with Groton was that a lot of my mother's relatives had gone there. I guess he thought we ought to keep better company. I began to suspect that he was not especially happy at home and expressed his discontent in irritable denunciations of this sort.

My parents' marriage, I came to realize, was not a good one, except in a purely social or society sense. When I was still a very small boy, I remember some evidence of affection between them. Once, in my baby sister's room, my father put his arm around my mother's waist and gave her a warm hug. Another time, when we were walking across the fields, he swung her over a fence. I would not remember such signs of affection had they not been so rare and virtually nonexistent after those very early days. What I do recall is much squabbling and many displays of anger. Their marriage was held together by tradition and, I suppose, the children. In my parents' generation, divorces were uncommon; in that of their children, they occurred much more frequently. In any case, my father lost no opportunity to fuss and fume about my mother's family while taking every advantage of the connection.

My father gained the courage of his "convictions" in the choice of school from some professors at Teachers' College of Columbia University, where he served on a supervisory board. When he spoke to them about his problems in chosing schools for his sons, they strongly recommended Hotchkiss.

There was nothing plebean about Hotchkiss, which Osgood and I entered in the fall of 1918. It had less of the social register and more of the industrial aristocracy than Groton. It was also newer and less tradition-bound. And it was a fine school academically. Some of the teachers whom I got to know well were more responsible for starting my mind to work than any other persons or influences at that time. When my mind finally started moving on its own, an invisible magnet somewhere off on the left kept pulling me in that direction.

The man to whom I was principally indebted for getting my mind out of its Lenox-645 Fifth Avenue rut was John McChesney. He influenced a whole generation of Hotchkiss boys. He never said, "Get going. Grow up. Spit that gold spoon out of your mouth before you choke on it. Find out what the world is all about. Get started on your own and your friends will do all we can to help." But without saying so in so many words, he conveyed that message. He made you feel that he liked you, that he saw promise in you, that he wanted you to move ahead. He paid attention to you, talked with you out of class, threw you some ideological bones to chew. His interest continued after you left school and went to college, after you left college and began your adult life.

When I was in school, Mr. Mac was a bachelor, a teacher of English and master of one of the dormitories. Although I didn't live in his dormitory, I often went there. I always found a welcome and, like as not, one or two of the other young teachers. They talked about things I had never heard of before. The conversation was not heavy, just good and stimulating. In the course of my school life, I slowly learned that there were people like Mr. Mac and a few of his friends whose values were quite different from those with which I had been brought up. It wasn't until I had been out of prep school for some time that I realized he was a socialist. I don't believe that while I was in school I ever heard him use the word "socialism," though it was clear he did not think that gaining power through wealth was a proper goal of our society. I don't remember whether he attended all the school's church services. He attended some, I know, because he sympathized with my efforts in the choir, but I came to realize that he attended with his fingers crossed. His gods were to be found not in the religious myths but in books and in the real world. And his interests as a teacher were in the youths he could influence to go to the books to learn where reality lay.

I came to this appraisal of my finest prep-school teacher long after my school days had ended. Only much, much later, perhaps even after I had joined the Socialist Party, when wondering how I had come this far away from where I started, I thought of Mr. Mac and the hints and suggestions and nudges with which he urged me to think things out for myself. He was no radical, mind you—unless you count an intellectual socialist a radical, which I don't—but simply a first-rate teacher. He will appear again in this book.

If the Connecticut countryside, with its green rolling hills and valleys, its woods and lakes, had been in Mexico, the site on which Hotchkiss stands would inevitably have been occupied either by a pyramid or a convent. Decades later I discovered that the pre-Hispanic priests and the Spanish colonial churchmen invariable chose the most beautiful sites to locate their important religious constructions. One could not imagine a more glorious physical environment than those slopes and the lake on which the school was situated. It was so exceptionally beautiful just outside Lakeville that it was not just taken for granted even by a bunch of adolescent boys. We walked in it, ran through it, went down the hill to the woods, built a tree house where we could occasionally find some much needed inward peace. Even in the turbulence of our young lives we were conscious of a serenity that comes from Mother Earth. Yes, of course, that is why we sometimes call her Mother Earth. She draws us to herself, she enfolds us, she gives back her strength.

When I entered Hotchkiss at thirteen, I was the smallest, puniest boy in my class. I am not perfectly certain that this was statistically the case. I am sure, however, that I felt it to be. I was woefully innocent, inexperienced and shy, with no self-confidence. I was scared to death of girls, with whom my experience had been limited to those wholly innocent Christmas visits of my cousins, Adele and Sheila, or strenuous, sweaty tennis with the Blake girl. I did not even have a clear idea what a female body looked like. All of the other boys seemed ages ahead of me on that score.

I went out for football the first week of my prep school life, I suppose because I was so totally unsuited for the game. I wanted to prove to myself that I could do something that everyone knew I could not. I did so successfully. Two or three days after practice began, I caught a ball on a wet field, was tackled and fell with the cleats of one shoe sticking in the mud and not turning with my body. The broken leg cut short my football career rather heroically.

I was successful in a more important way. I had begun to take German as an obligatory foreign language and immediately got into trouble trying to fathom the construction of a German sentence. The football injury caused a six weeks' hiatus in my studies, and when I returned to classes, the professor, a strict, uncompromising man, informed me that I would never be able to make up the time lost and had better plan to repeat the course the next year. I told him I did not wish to repeat the year and begged him to give me a chance to see if I could catch up. Whereupon, for the first time in my life, I learned to study and to concentrate. I worked on my German grammar and vocabulary in and out of study hour and even made some sense out of where to place the verb. That was the first academic battle I won. It convinced me that no matter how far behind I fell, I could always catch up. That lesson served me well ever after, though at Harvard I took too much advantage of my new-found self-confidence.

I entered Hotchkiss in September 1918, just two months before World War I ended. The war in no way affected our school lives or curriculum nor was it discussed. I had immediately gone in for German without a thought that it was the language of the enemy. I did gain a consciousness of the war at home, however. My father had gone to secondary school in Germany and had become sufficiently wedded to German—or should I say Prussian?—culture to have a difficult time during the first years of the war.

When I was nine or ten, a group of friendly Lenox ladies with unfriendly intent made a surprise visit to High Lawn and serenaded him with the Kaiser's martial music. I was embarrassed by his nonconformity because I disagreed with what I understood of the authoritarian reasons he advanced for his pro-German position. I began to join in the hot arguments which occurred at mealtime, between him and whatever guests were around. I argued heatedly, if not with adequate information, in favor of what Woodrow Wilson was saying. This was therefore an important period for me, the time that I developed my first fumbling interest in public affairs and had my first intellectual confrontation with my father.

This conflict resolved itself after the United States entered the war and my father became a major in Army Intelligence. The family rented a house in Washington, D.C., for the duration, as my father's military service took place at a desk just down the hall from the office of Newton D. Baker, the secretary of war. Fifteen years later, when Mr. Baker was my boss at the Institute of Pacific Relations, I reminded him that my father had introduced us. Although I went to Washington for occasional visits, I otherwise continued my normal school routine.

During my Hotchkiss years, I learned more about my father. He was anti-Semitic, hardly mentioned Negroes, considered Catholics to be uneducated, and the Irish to be political crooks. He also thought that just about everybody you could possible think of outside the social registerites and a few respected medical men, collectors and connoisseurs were well beneath us. All my young life, I was brought up hearing violent denunciations of Jews. I remember only one Jew among all the family acquaintances and he was thrown out of the family circle, deservedly enough, I suppose, considering the customs of the day: My father found in our friend's bathroom pills used to treat gonorrhea. His attitude toward blacks was similar, but hardly ever expressed, because our lives never came within shouting distance of them or their problems. Although lots of rich Jewish bankers and businessmen were right on or even within the periphery of our social set, no blacks were anywhere on our social or economic horizon.

I also learned something about his interests. I have mentioned his superb book collection. From his German experience came a first-rate collection of Dürer etchings, which also eventually went to Harvard. He also had a splendid coin collection, which, for example, contained two of the only three known specimens of a particular issue. There was also a collection of American Indian artifacts. And strangely, in spite of being anti-Catholic (it was a lower-class religion), he owned an extraordinary collection of crucifixes; they hung on the walls of his High Lawn bedroom and overflowed into other parts of the house. One could call my father a jack-of-all-collections.

That description would be misleading, however. Papa did not put these collections together superficially or only because he had enough money around to buy them. He was, in fact, a respected authority on each of these subjects. In 1904, he joined the Grolier Club, and there he found kindred connoiseur spirits. He served on its Council, and in the 1920s, while I was at Harvard, became its president. He was also a director of the Metropolitan Opera Association and of Sloane's Hospital. I learned all this about him while as a father and a friend he was still a long way away from me.

One of the proofs that I was indeed the smallest boy in my class was that it took what seemed to be forever for my voice to change. I was blessed or cursed, whichever way you look at it, with a fairly decent soprano voice and soon became soloist in the choir. I never once felt I knew the music well enough to be confident about performing it. Whenever I had to sing, the butterflies took over my stomach the evening before and fluttered until the final bar of the music the next morning. I suffered more anticipating a Sunday service in which I was to perform than over anything that I experienced later in life. If a thirteen-year-old could develop an ulcer, I would have had one in 1918.

In spite of my sufferings, I liked Denison Fish, the music teacher and organist. He selected beautiful pieces; many years later I realized he had introduced me to some of the great masters of church music. He was friendly and encouraging and frank. On a Sunday afternoon following one of those solos, he said to me, "I had an argument with Dr. Blank at lunch. He insists you were flat on the high notes. I don't think you were. How did it sound to you?"

Instead of courageously taking the opportunity to reply, "For the love of Mike, don't make me sing another solo, ever," I indicated how pleased I was that he had disagreed with Dr. Blank.

Fortunately, I played tennis decently; in this respect my Lenox training stood me in good stead. I made the school tennis team, competed against other prep schools and in the final year won the school championship. Early in my Hotchkiss career, tennis in some measure counterbalanced my canary voice.

Hotchkiss had a larger proportion of boys on scholarships than most schools. They were not poor, but they came from families which could not afford a high tuition and would have sent their sons to public high schools if the Hotchkiss scholarships had not been available. The father of one of my close friends was the manager of a vacation lodge, the family of another had lost its small business. The scholarship boys cleaned the classrooms and halls and waited on table. The rest of us, the paying customers, would have been better off had we also been put to work. The presence of these scholarship boys had a refreshing effect on the social atmosphere. In general, I remember them as more mature and better students than the rest of us, and with fewer duds among them.

I had led such a sheltered life that by the time I was thirteen, I really didn't know anything about people my age who were not wealthy. It was a fine experience for me to learn that the scholarship boys had used their early years to better advantage than I had. I had to catch up to them, not they with that well-brought-up Freddy Field. It began to dawn on me that my privileges had not been such great benefits after all; many had been obstacles to a normal development.

Fortunately, once you were in school, there was nothing much you could do with extra money. You might be able to swill a larger quantity down at the "Vil," and more often, but that didn't count for much, except increase the problems you had with your complexion. Within the school, the distinction between those who had a little more to spend and those who had less or none came to our notice only over such trivial matters that no one paid attention to it.

One exciting event in those days was, I believe, unique to Hotchkiss. The school had a pleasant custom of giving unexpected holidays in honor of graduates who had excelled in some sport or academic activity or in public life. There was one to celebrate the breaking of the world high jump record by an alumnus; another for someone who had earned a Phi Beta Kappa award; another for an athlete who had been elected captain of the Yale football team. No one knew when the holidays were coming. At early morning chapel the solemn headmaster would go through the daily ritual of prayers and a hymn and announcements and then, just as we were about to scatter to our classrooms, he would happen to remember that there was just one more announcement. He had almost forgotten: we would be free for the day until six o'clock. On such occasions Osgood and I would rush to the telephone and put in a collect call to High Lawn. In an hour Albert would arrive, and we and all the friends we could pack in the car would spend a carefree day.

The first year was a difficult one, and the second just a little easier. By the third I had some hope that I would make it, and by the fourth I felt, half the time, that I was on my way. I had just turned seventeen when I was graduated and felt strongly that I was not yet ready for college, even though I had passed my college entrance examinations handily and could have entered Harvard in the fall. Instead, I made my first important decision on my own. I would wait a year and use it to grow up. The family went along with the idea; they were willing to let me go abroad or do pretty much whatever I wanted. I decided to ask the school if I could return for a fifth year so that I could sit in on courses, participate in extracurricular activities and generally take advantage of the academic and physical environment. The school agreed. It was a wonderful year. One of those unexpected holidays made it even more so. The holiday was given in honor of a group, to which I belonged, that had broken some kind of record in the college entrance examinations.

The young man who finished that fifth year in 1923 was a different person from the puny boy who had entered in 1918. For one thing, he had grown fairly tall though he remained skinny. He had licked a few enemies, and he had begun to identify some others he would meet along the road. He was not as shy as he used to be, he no longer felt at a disadvantage because of his puny physique, he knew that in a crisis he could concentrate on his studies and he had become independent enough not to be overcome by the prospect of going, alone, to Harvard. Socially, he had done only passably; he had by no means become a popular boy or a leader but he had made good friends. And not of least importance, his soprano had finally become a tenor. He had still got nowhere with the girls. He had twice invited a girl to school dances, but each time it seemed that his friends and even some of the younger masters had had a better time with them than he. He had to overcome his shyness. It was obvious to him that he was missing the nicest thing in life. But how to go about it? What did you say to a girl? What did you do with her? When he retired to his room, all the answers came to him. But in her presence, there was nothing but confusion.

Among his good friends were Mr. McChesney and two or three other teachers. Through them he had had a glimpse of the real world. They had made him restive. They had given him no answers, but they had started him looking for them. That is what I call education. In that sense those years at Hotchkiss must be regarded as successful.

6

Extracurricular Harvard

I was the only member of my Hotchkiss class to go to Harvard in the fall of 1923. I was on my own—exactly where I wanted to be. That, indeed, was important to me. I still had a long way to go before I felt at all satisfied with myself as a person—a destination I never reached, of course. I didn't want to reveal my weaknesses or failures to anyone. I wanted to go it alone; that was what I was used to doing. We had not been a family in which personal problems were discussed, and I never turned to my mother or father for help or advice. I never discussed my difficulties with the nurses. No one ever said, "Freddy, let's sit down and talk about this problem. Let's see if we can straighten it out." And no one even offered the 1910 equivalent of, "Freddy, what's bugging you?"

We didn't have direct confrontations when I did something naughty. In the downstairs bathroom at High Lawn there was a small table for hairbrushes and things like that, and in it was a drawer that held a pair of dark glasses for motoring. One day I thought it would be fun to try them on to see what I looked like in the mirror. I dropped the glasses on the tile floor and broke the lenses. I carefully put the broken glasses back in the drawer and snuck out of the bathroom, certain that the deed had gone unnoticed. I was mistaken. Later that day, Charles found me and in a friendly way informed me that my father was very angry at what I had done and that I should be more careful in the future. I told him that I was sorry. My father never spoke to me about the incident but had taken the matter up with me via Charles.

The standards for my behavior were everywhere about me. There were customs, traditions, ways of doing things that were obvious to a child. One walked a straight path with just a small amount of leeway on either side. It was not so much that one should not or could not wander beyond those

51

boundaries, it was simply that it was unheard of to do so. I learned where those boundaries were empirically. I did not have to be told. And because of the lack of communication in the family, I learned to make decisions about whatever detours or confusing road signals I ran into by myself. Those were the behavior habits with which I entered Harvard, and they are the behavior habits with which I still operate.

Once in college, I set out to achieve my objectives with a vengeance. I had excellent health, an abundance of energy and an internal drive that surprised even me. I began the last chapter by saying that I still did not feel educated after five years of prep school and four of college, a failure for which I accept the blame. In my first few weeks as an undergraduate, I decided that I was going to be socially and politically prominent among my classmates. I would do enough academic work to stay in college, but I would deliberately devote the major part of my resources to becoming a well-known undergraduate. I did not consciously tell myself that I was going to postpone my education until after college, but that is what my decision amounted to. That's what it cost me.

As it turned out, I got this urge out of my system sooner than I expected. By my junior year I had had enough success to realize that I didn't need any more of that particular kind. I was becoming uncomfortable over my neglect of the academic side of college life and envious of some of my friends who were making praiseworthy headway in their studies. But by that time I was so caught up in extracurricular undergraduate activities that I did not think I could simply drop them and turn to the books—at least not without changing my environment. I wrote Professor Alexander Meiklejohn at the University of Wisconsin and asked if I could transfer to his Experimental College for the remainder of my college career. I had been told that it was one of the most intellectually stimulating centers of undergraduate teaching in the country. I had heard Meiklejohn speak and had read some of his articles. Madison might be exactly what I needed. Dr. Meiklejohn replied that my application had come too late and he would accept transfers only earlier in the college course. So I returned to the feverish pursuit of non-academic fame.

After the early months of my undergraduate days, I was engaged in activities more elevating than picking up jockstraps, but that is exactly the way I occupied myself from September to the end of November of my freshman year. I entered the competition to become manager of the fresh-man football team. Except for one project in which we had to use our heads, the requirements of the competition could have been handled with the brain of an oyster. We never had lunch, but after morning classes rushed down to the locker room at Soldier's Field to make sure the gear of all the potential football heroes was neatly laid out. After practice, when the gear was filthy with mud and sweat, our job was to pick it up off the floor, where of course it had been thrown, hang it up in the drying room and clean up the place for the next day. During practice, which fortunately took place in the open air, we ran errands for coaches, trainers and players, most of which they should have done for themselves.

The most responsible task I was given was to be timekeeper for a game against another freshman team. I was handed a stopwatch and told, "Keep time." No one told me how to carry out this important job; I had only the haziest idea of when to start or stop the watch. I flunked, but fortunately no one knew it except me.

We had to use our heads for a few hours at the end of the competition. We were told to write a detailed plan for transporting the varsity to and from the Yale game. This job was an interesting one which involved working out the type and cost of travel, housing arrangements and menus for the players' delicate stomachs, including special canteens of water so that there would be no change from Cambridge to New Haven impurities. I worked harder and did a better job on this report than on any academic paper of my undergraduate life.

I came out second in the competition, which meant that I became assistant manager and won the right to wear the class numerals on my sweater. Like any other big shot, I wore the sweater inside out so that, while the stitching of the numerals was plain as day, it appeared that I was modestly trying to hide my importance.

After Christmas came hockey season. I tried out for the freshman team because I thought that I was a pretty good skater. Hadn't I played with the bigger boys on the frozen-over swimming pool at High Lawn? And wasn't I on the hockey squad at Hotchkiss? They wouldn't know here at Harvard that I never got into a game at Lakeville. The coach apparently did not agree with my estimate of my prowess and paid no attention to me. When the squad was announced, I was not on it. It was my opinion that so many candidates had tried out for the team that no one had noticed me. It was just one of those unfortunate things—especially for the team. A star had been snuffed out at birth.

No sooner had the Harvard athletic authorities made this mistake than I read in the college newspaper that I had been appointed editorial chairman of the *Red Book*, a publication that chronicled the achievements of the freshman class. This marked a shift in my activities from the playing fields to the less muscular exercises of journalism, committees and bank accounts.

The latter came into the picture because I found myself treasurer of Phillips Brooks House, the religious-welfare organization of the university, and secretary-treasurer of my class. In my senior year I was elected permanent class treasurer. In my time at Harvard, and I suppose the custom has continued, there was no electioneering for such posts. I have often wondered how and why I was elected to them. Perhaps more of the thousand-odd members of my class had come to know my name better through my other activities than those of my opponents. But I have a sneaking suspicion that something else played a part.

About the time when I was becoming aware that something mysterious about girls attracted boys, my cousin Adele—with whom the reader may recall I was "infatuated"—gave me a woolen knitted hat that pulled down over the ears for winter wear. I wore it indoors and out, in hot or cold weather, until it could be worn no longer. The habit of wearing unconventional headgear at unusual times persisted. At Harvard I sported a peculiar, light-green version of a Tyrolean hat, minus the feather and yodel. Perched on my red hair, it seems to have made a lasting if not pleasing impression. I have often thought that it was the hat rather than my personality or accomplishments that made me known among my classmates. Maybe they voted for me simply because it was safer to put someone whom they could easily spot in charge of their funds. The hat trick was also utilized by Senators Hayakawa of California and Patrick Moynahan of New York during their successful 1976 campaigns, an association that may please them as little as it does me.

The financial duties were by no means arduous. I carried them out conscientiously during my undergraduate days. The "permanent" treasureship, however, I found impossible to fulfill. I was away from the country too much, and my interest in the responsibility flagged as it picked up in other directions. In any case, I was never likely to take up residence in the Boston-Cambridge area from which the activities of the class would have to be directed. So I asked my fellow class officers to relieve me, a request with which they were only too glad to comply. A left-winger is not the sort of person likely to succeed in persuading his classmates year after year to break new records in the amount of cash or stock certificates they turn over to the alma mater.

The most demanding and longest lasting extracurricular activity in which I engaged concerned the university's daily newspaper, the *Harvard Crimson*, known, naturally, as "The Crime." It involved a three-year competitive climb from the neophyte stage to get on the paper, through the succeeding ones to become assistant managing editor, managing editor and, finally, president, as the chief editor was called. I went up the ranks to the ultimate position by working hard, keeping late hours, learning a great deal of lasting value—like concentrating amid the everlasting racket and interruptions of a newspaper office—and gaining from it a little more of that sense of self-confidence that I felt I needed.

I spent one fall covering football for the paper and thereby became well acquainted with the game played in the 1920s. The job included being what was called "spotter" for the press. This involved identifying the player who carried the ball or made the tackle or was penalized. To do that you had to anticipate the play. I regret to inform the reader that that long-ago experience has not in the least helped my comprehension of the modern game, which I vicariously enjoy in a comfortable chair facing the television screen.

Our team lost to Princeton and I wrote a bitter article about the ungentlemanly conduct of the Orange and Black. I used their alleged unethical manners to press a campaign for the de-emphasis of football. I, who was almost totally neglecting my own studies in favor of journalism, cried out to the Harvard authorities that football and football heroes were taking altogether too much play from the college's intellectual pursuits and its unsung cerebral heroes. We on the *Crimson*—and of course there were other forces at work in the same direction—got results. Harvard broke football relations with Princeton (not to be resumed until 1934), and shortly thereafter intramural football competition started and has, I believe, flourished ever since.

A friend who rowed on the varsity crew introduced me to several of the other seven. The crew had not been doing well in intercollegiate competition, and my friends put the blame on the coach. They gave me the details behind their gripe and asked me to use the columns of the *Crimson* to get the coach fired. I agreed to do what I could but thought that there was a more effective and prudent way to go about it. I went directly to the director of athletics, a new position for which the paper had been partly responsible, informed him of the situation and suggested that the matter might better be handled without publicity. Within a week the coach was dismissed.

Charles William Eliot, who had been president of Harvard from 1869 to 1909 and under whom the college had become a great university, died in 1926, the year I became president of the *Crimson*. We published a special twenty-page supplement recording his accomplishments. During his term the physical plant and the curriculum had been vastly expanded, the elective system whereby students could select courses introduced, and the graduate studies reorganized and greatly enlarged. Our supplement was widely circulated and well received.

The experience taught me to be more careful about proofreading, and a new word. While preparing the supplement, I had written to the then president of the university, Abbott Lawrence Lowell, asking him to contribute some thoughts on the significance of Eliot's influence on American education. He wrote me a snippy reply, beginning: "Dear Mr. Field: It would be tautologous for me to comply with your request. . ." Many years later, my daughter Lila gave me one of those miniature calculators when they were a novelty and I spent the next several days searching for something to calculate just to have the pleasure of using the gadget. The same thing happened with the word "tautological." I sought every opportunity to use it.

The carelessness of the proofreader might well have led to derisive laughter instead of praise for our effort. In the lead article, which I had written, appeared the phrase, "That great can, Charles William Eliot. . ." Fortunately, I caught the error in time to correct it for the main press run.

During the period when I was managing editor and president, we introduced several innovations. Book reviews had previously appeared on an occasional one- or two-page spread; we now began an independent monthly supplement, the first of its kind in collegiate journalism. We had been paying irregular attention to plays and movies; we now began publishing a regular weekly playgoer section with its own editor. And our editorial department, formerly called to action only when the president had to keep a social engagement, was put in complete charge of writing the daily editorials.

My junior year was distinguished by an almost total absence of academic activity. I was working intensively at the *Crimson* and many other extracurricular affairs, and I was enjoying a social life which consisted largely of bending the elbow with my friends. New college rules came to my assistance. It was necessary as a minimum requirement to get C's but attending classes was not required. During that academic year of 1925-26 I attended exactly three classes—a performance I am recording, not recommending. The result of my absences was that I entered the examination periods with a zero or close to it in most of my courses. In a few instances I learned from classmates that a paper of some sort was due and prepared it with satisfactory results. But in general I had to get an A in the exam to average out at C. I have ever since suffered frightening dreams about midyear and final examinations.

In order to pass, I cancelled all other activities for ten days or two weeks prior to the exams and used the time in two ways: I copied extensive sections out of the notebooks of A-student friends, memorizing as I went along; and in certain subjects like literature I virtually memorized tertiary sources. I also had pleasanter ways of cramming. I took, for instance, a three-hour drive with Kate Middleton, the fiancée of one of my classmates. She had recently been graduated from Radcliffe with honors in literature. During the drive she repeated and repeated the plot and significance of *Macbeth* until I knew it cold—just long enough, that is, to do splendidly in the exam. As I left the examination room, *Macbeth* left me.

This method of work almost led to disaster. Just before a final in French literature, I had spent a long weekend in New Hartford, Connecticut, at the home of a classmate, Joe Barnes. Joe was an excellent student, but for some reason felt inadequately prepared on that particular subject. So we both devoured a tertiary source that vividly characterized the leading French writers and their works, and then we walked hours and hours through the lovely New England woods asking and answering questions.

Back at Cambridge we sat next to each other to take the exam. As usual, every major section in it gave the student several alternatives. We each got an A, which meant that I had once again managed to average out at C. But a day or two later Professor Andre Morize, a brilliant lecturer who gave that course (I had heard him once), called us to his office. In a most courteous manner he said, "Gentleman, I've asked you to come in to take up with you a rather difficult matter. You both have written excellent examinations, but there are certain circumstances which trouble me. Throughout the examination, wherever choices were given, you chose the same questions. Your answers, your choice of language, were closely parallel if not identical. And I noticed that you were sitting next to each other. I am not at present accusing you of any wrongdoing, but I thought we should talk about it."

We told Professor Morize just what had happened, how we had crammed for the examination and had virtually memorized the text. He replied that our explanation was satisfactory, that we were both well-known undergraduates and that when he invited us to his office he had hoped just such an explanation would be forthcoming.

I was astonished a few weeks after arriving at Harvard to receive an invitation, including dinner, to a Boston coming-out party from a family I had never heard of. During the rest of the fall, two or three arrived every week. My family had no Boston connections, except my father's bookdealer, Charles Lauriat, and I hardly expected him to be mixed up in the debutante world. Moreover, I was the only boy in my class to go from Hotchkiss to Harvard, so that on arrival I didn't have a single acquaintance, aside from Osgood, even among my classmates. I therefore found the invitation rather strange. Obviously, my name could have come only from the New York Social Register. I was being invited solely on that social-financial qualification. That struck me as downright stupid.

Harvard has an unfortunate system of "final" clubs. They are called "final" because they are mutually exclusive; you may join only one of them. In my time, at least, they were unfortunate because of the criteria by which one was deemed eligible. My social position and the fact that I evidently was not personally objectionable made me fully eligible. I was invited to join several of them and chose the Delphic Club (popularly known as the Gas House). I chose it because I found the group from my class that was being formed to join it more congenial than those going into other clubs. We had, it seemed to me, more members from outside the New York-Boston area, more pursuing extracurricular activities that interested me and even some who frankly intended to spend their college days getting educated. Those were, however, purely subjective opinions: the Gas House was no better and no worse than the others. It was an eating and drinking association of more or less wealthy students who were fairly congenial. I was also asked to join the group being formed to enter the Porcellian Club, the social pinnacle of Harvard undergraduate life, and turned it down because I thought I would be more comfortable somewhere below the social peak. I hope and trust that much of what I objected to about these clubs has in the long time since I was there changed in the direction of a much more democratic system of choosing membership. That shift would be a difficult one because membership in those clubs is expensive, and as far as I know they do not have the funds to provide the large number of scholarships that such an objective requires.

I ate and drank at the Gas House a good deal during my sophomore and junior years but hardly at all during my last year. The food was good and the illegal liquor we brought in to drink there as good or bad as at any other place; the company was pleasant. But in my senior year, I was becoming troubled by the inequalities of our social system and beginning to realize that my own Social Register qualifications for prominence were ridiculous. Harvard had other types of clubs as well, several of which I joined. Some had legitimate intellectual claims; others were just fun. I was a joiner. I overdid it.

Those four undergraduate years fell in the middle of the Prohibition Era. They were the days of bathtub gin, speakeasies, disregard and disrespect for that law and galvanized stomach linings for those who survived. I had a connection in Boston, a not-unattractive, hard young woman whose husband and brother ran whiskey and alcohol down from Canada. I was always able to get a gallon or two of alcohol from her, and, fortunately, it always turned out to be fairly decent stuff. I say always, but in fact there was a period when the lady could not attend her customers, inasmuch as she was recovering from a bullet wound. For this she blamed some agents who had fired at her husband's contraband truck one night in Maine. As it happened, she was taking the trip with him. My roommates and I actually mixed the gin in the bathtub. We would empty the alcohol into the tub, add juniper berries I collected on weekends in Connecticut, add water, mix and bottle.

On outings, we carried flasks. As a flask did not contain much liquid, when I went to a debutante party in one of Boston's fancy hotels, I would fill it with straight alcohol and mix my drinks at the water cooler in the corridor outside the ballroom. It is difficult for me now, as I write this, to understand that particular aspect of the young Fred Field. There are other things about him that I like better.

A group of about ten of us did a good deal of carousing. At any time of the evening or night—duties at the *Crimson* were an exception—four or five were usually available for a spontaneous party. It often took place in our rooms and sometimes ended in a speakeasy in downtown Boston. There we could find canned music, a postage-stamp dance floor, one-dollar drinks and a girl, a sort of hostess or bar girl, whom we all liked and with whom none of us ever did anything except talk—endlessly. On special occasions, we went to the downstairs room of Locke-Ober's, famous for its good food then as now.

Lucius Beebe was one of the gang—and always available for a party. He came from a shoe-manufacturing family near Boston, was invariably formally and elegantly dressed, and carried plenty of cash. As an undergraduate at Yale, he had published a volume of poetry which had deservedly attracted a good deal of critical attention. For some infringement of the rules, I forget what, he had been asked to leave, and while Harvard has never been famous for its hospitality to Yale rejects, he had somehow joined our class. Lucius was the epitome of the *bon viveur* and later became famous—or notorious— as a connoisseur of wines and gourmet food. He also published several fascinating volumes on American railroads. The rest of us were a little doubtful of his sexual preferences until one day he, aware of these doubts, proudly showed us a poison ivy rash on his knees and elbows. This he claimed he had acquired the previous weekend on a picnic with some nurses from one of the hospitals. We were never given the opportunity to corroborate this claim by examining the nurse's complementary anatomy.

Lucius and I were good friends for a number of years, until our roads parted both geographically and politically. Some years after college he became a writer for the New York *Herald Tribune* and wrote several far-fetched but amusing columns about our less responsible carrying-on. One was largely devoted to an evening when, as the mostly mythical tale went, Freddy Field, celebrating something or other, hired Freddy the cab driver and his horse, also answering to Freddy, from the carriage stand in front of the Copley Hotel in Boston and rode in style back to his quarters in Cambridge. The locale of the story could be shifted at will to the hack stand on 59th Street outside the Plaza Hotel in New York, where, according to Beebe, there could also be found a driver and horse called Freddy.

Fables like those were harmless enough. But one nasty story that Lucius recorded in his *Herald Tribune* column has been repeated and repeated with no one paying any attention to my denials. Here is the way it appeared in the May 15, 1950, issue of *Newsweek*:

> Lucius Beebe, the determinably elegant writer on railroads and the drama, tells us of a Christmas dinner at Locke-Ober's restaurant in Boston. It was a swank affair, the silver and crystal sparkled, the wine flowed. Yet Freddy Field felt that something was missing. Suddenly he rushed out into the snow, grabbed a dirty-faced newsboy, and gave him half a dollar to press his nose against the window and look hungry while Field and his friends ate.

Such is the willingness to accept any disagreeable anecdote about a radical that this story has been repeated, without attempt at verification, even in a supposedly academic study about the Institute of Pacific Relations. It has been used over and over again, and no one has ever had the decency to check its authenticity. I hated it when it was first published; I hate it today. It's a filthy story. Anyone who knows me at all well would agree that the episode was completely out of character and could not have taken place. It was one hundred percent fabrication, a vicious lie from beginning to end. And anyone not blinded by the fascination of slander would realize that Harvard students who had the money to buy a ticket home did not spend Christmas in Cambridge or Boston, and they might know that as fine a restaurant as Locke-Ober's is, one does not dine there surrounded by crystal and silver. And during Prohibition we did not drink sissy-stuff like wine.

For the last three years of college, I was on the executive committee of the student council. We enjoyed a certain amount of authority, both actual and advisory. We met regularly and took our responsibilities seriously. In 1925 a National Student Federation was being formed to represent and further the interests of students of all colleges and universities in the country. The organizing conference, held at the University of Michigan, was widely attended from all sections of the country. I was about to write "from the West, Middle West and East" when I remembered a good friend I made from the University of North Carolina. The Harvard Student Council elected me as its representative. Months afterward, there arrived by mail at my Harvard rooms a gallon jug of moonshine from Chapel Hill. How this extraordinary extra-legal service by the United States Mails was ever managed I never discovered. I didn't try very hard.

The Federation was duly formed. The Princeton representative, Lewis Fox of Hartford, Connecticut, was elected president and I vice-president.

Ed Murrow, the well-known CBS broadcaster, became the second president a year or two later.

For me, the association with the NSF was the cause of two events. The first and lesser one was that in the summer of 1926 I was sent as head of the U.S. delegation to an international students' conference in Prague. Of the other members of our group I remember only the Vassar representative, Emily Floyd, and I remember her especially because I thought we waltzed together so beautifully. I don't know what she thought.

The European student representatives were all considerably older, more experienced, more sophisticated, and more politically oriented than we. There were two political groups: one led by the British delegation and the other by Central Europeans. The issues were hotly debated; the rivalry was serious and deep. But I must confess that I cannot remember what the issues were. All I do remember is that we Americans received a great deal of attention because our vote was much sought after by both sides.

The leader of the British group was a delightful Scotsman, Ivison Macadam, whom I got to know well. He later became secretary of the Royal Institute of International Affairs, which in respect to its Far Eastern work became affiliated with the Institute of Pacific Relations, the American branch of which I became secretary.

The unforgettable climax of the Prague meeting was a banquet given in honor of the delegates by the foreign minister of Czechoslovakia, Edvard Beneš. We sat at a huge horseshoe in a baronial hall of one of the ancient palaces. The head of each delegation was asked to say a few words. When my turn came, I arose well-prepared to deliver a short speech which I had rehearsed a number of times. I thought it would be courteous to deliver it in French, a fair amount of which I still remembered. When I sat down, the interpreter stood and began the translation—which he delivered in French! There was such a sudden roar of laughter that he couldn't finish even the first sentence. The content of my speech was soon forgotten, but for years afterward I was to run into delegates who had been present and who unfailingly reminded me of my heroic effort at international courtesy.

The other event for which my association with the Federation was responsible was of far greater moment. At the Ann Arbor meeting the Bryn Mawr delegate was the most attractive young woman I had ever met. Her name was Betty Brown, and she came from Duluth, Minnesota. We seemed to agree pretty easily on matters of student policy, and we laughed together at the silly things that always happen at meetings of that sort. With much mirth, Betty also supported my efforts to quash our president's habit of opening every meeting, large or small, with prayer. That campaign took about a year. A more important campaign begun at the same time took longer. Betty and I got married in March of 1929.

7

The Direction Is Set

What we are is a complex result of what we biologically inherit from our parents and what we experience in our environment. In the early years of my adult education, the controversy between the hereditarians and the environmentalists interested me. I read the principal protagonists of the two schools, usually finding the arguments of the environmentalists the more persuasive. The latest information on the subject that has come to my attention is given in the following newspaper summary of *The Universe Within: A New Science Explores the Human Mind* by Morton Hunt: "Research suggests that our minds come equipped with highly efficient neural arrangements built into us by evolution; these predispose us to make certain kinds of sense of our experiences and to use them in that distinctly human activity we call thinking. It is the product of an interaction between nature and nurture; each is essential, neither is wholly controlling."

Certain things are plain—and important. On the biological side, it is beyond dispute that it is significant whether one is born female or male, physically strong or weak, short or tall. On the environmental side, we need not argue as to whether it makes a difference to be born and raised poor or rich, on the equator or near the north pole.

There is endless diversity in the relative importance of various elements in a person's environment. The latter includes material things like trees and mountains and seas and houses and tools; it includes other people of all sorts; and it includes ideas and thoughts in whatever way they are communicated: through books, conversation, movies, art, lectures; by parents, teachers, ministers. The role that books play varies greatly with individuals, as does the influence of other people. Some, like many poets, are deeply moved by their physical surroundings; others don't care whether they are on the seashore or in the mountains as long as they are with friends.

Our subject, Fred Field, was fairly tall and thin with red hair, some freckles and good health. He was white and his parents were rich. He was a WASP, born in the most elegant section of New York, raised in Lenox as well as in the city. All these factors doubtlessly shaped him. So did the places where he began his education and the people whom he liked and those whom he didn't like. So did whatever his recognition was then of what was happening politically, socially and economically around him.

But, frankly, I don't know myself well enough to sort out the multitude of influences that impinged on my young life, nor to determine exactly which were more important at any given moment. My general impression is that individuals were less important than were the things that were going on around me. I have mentioned Mr. McChesney. He, along with a very few other teachers, certainly played an important role in my youth. So, to a less well-defined extent, did my parents, some of the servants, and, in a more negative than positive way, some of the guests who used to come to the house and members of our extended family, of whom I saw a great deal but never got close to. I have not had my share of heroes, or if one or two did show up for a while, it was not long before I was disillusioned. I have loved—in fact, some people think I've done a little too much of that—but the objects of my sentiments have not had much to do with the direction my life has taken. I have always had friends, though not many close, long-lasting ones, and even those enriched rather than guided my life. The experience I had with Anna and Earl Barnes was therefore an unusual one.

Mr. Barnes came from a long line of hard-working upstate New York farmers, not poor and not rich. His life was devoted to intellectual pursuits and sharply divided into two parts. The first was academic. At Cornell, while still an undergraduate, he had helped the president, Andrew White, collect material for a monumental work, *The Warfare of Science with Theology*. Then he became professor of European history at Indiana University while completing his undergraduate work. Last, he headed the Department of Education on the original faculty of Stanford University. There he began the studies of child psychology that occupied him for the next ten years, the last several of which were spent in England, and resulted in two large volumes of *Studies in Education*.

His long-time friend and colleague on the original Stanford faculty, Edward Howard Griggs, wrote a short life sketch of Earl Barnes at the time of the latter's death in 1935. In it Griggs refers to Barnes's "conviction that education was a concern of the whole of life, and led him more and more into the field of carrying education beyond the academic walls, to the less privileged and to men and women in the business of life."

This conviction persuaded Mr. Barnes to sever his academic connections and devote the second half of his adult life to teaching in England and the United States as an unaffiliated lecturer. He was well along in this second career when I had the good fortune to meet him and to spend many, many weekends at his home, "Treetops," in a small New England village called New Hartford, just a little over twenty miles from the capital of Connecticut. This came about because his son, Joe, was my close friend and classmate at Harvard.

It was Anna Barnes who made it possible for me to absorb some of the riches this family and home had to offer. An early graduate of Stanford, she taught history in California high schools until she married. She loved poetry, knew much about it, and often read it to her family and friends in the evenings. She was a warm, intelligent, liberated woman who had that special genius for making the most unlike characters feel comfortably at home. She devoted much of her married life to her first child, a daughter who at an early age caught polio and then at the onset of adolescence had doubled the tragedy with spinal meningitis. Were it not for this misfortune, I felt, Anna Barnes would have continued teaching or begun some other formal intellectual activity.

I was anything but an intellectual when I first got to know the Barneses. I had had little contact with the great books or the great thoughts. I knew a lot about upper-class living, and I was good at that. I was polite, well-mannered, and, I'm told, agreeable. At first, I was completely lost in the evening conversations led by Mr. Barnes. The talk might turn to any subject—the Soviet revolution, the poetry of E.E. Cummings, Mont St. Michel, *War and Peace*, *Ulysses*. Tolstoy merited an evening, but in the 1920s James Joyce might occupy the entire weekend. I was never convinced that all the participants who made wise—or were they slick?—remarks about *Ulysses* had actually read the whole book or understood it. I tried to do so myself, and that only fortified my doubts. Granted, there was a good-sized intellectual gap between the other participants and Fred Field, but it hardly seemed reasonable to me that such a book could be totally intelligible to the others and so obscure to me.

Literature, avant-guarde and traditional, and politics, left to right, were not the only subjects to occupy our evenings. On one occasion there was among the guests a young and pretty woman whose first novel had just been acclaimed. The subject turned to feminism, and Mr. Barnes suggested that an attractive female leg was a perfectly proper subject for an intellectual evening. The author, who later became very successful in both literary and commercial senses, began the conversation by giving us a generous look at hers. That was the middle 1920s; I wonder what a feminist could do today to have an analogous effect.

Whether the topic was women's legs or the thoughts of Leopold Bloom, I listened intently and never opened my mouth. I had nothing to offer those evening gatherings, and I had the sense—or was it shyness?—not to make an ass of myself. These conversations taught me, however, to get into that fascinating intellectual current as soon as I could.

Griggs makes a comment about Earl Barnes's lectures which might well have been directed to our informal evening conversations. "Always he urged discussion, following his lectures. He loved an argument, delighted in the active play of minds, even when strongly antagonistic to the ideas he had expressed. His aim was to awaken his audience to think, not to tell them what to think." It was this quality which had such an influence on me. Some of the teachers at Hotchkiss had given me a shove in that direction; these New Hartford evenings pushed me further. Earl Barnes and some of the other participants embarrassed me by the quality of their intellectual experience and by their ability to express themselves. I had never before been part of such a group. I felt exactly as I should have, an intellectual dunce. Fortunately, instead of being floored by my backwardness, I was stimulated by the knowledge and ability of these friends.

Earl Barnes was a liberal, not a radical. In 1926 he visited the U.S.S.R. with his eldest son and wrote in his notebook, "Howard and I have been very sympathetic with Russia. While holding no brief for communism, we are not devoted to capitalism; on the contrary, we both recognize its gross unfairness and we have great sympathy for the underdog." He predicted that in the Soviet Union, "There will be a steady swinging back toward the mechanics of capitalism, and toward forms of government sympathetic to the general practices of Europe." He in no way pushed me toward socialism or communism. He taught me to look, to inquire, to find out for myself.

I would have been scared off after the first few visits if it had not been for the ever-present welcome of Mrs. Barnes. I was embarrassed by my intellectual backwardness, but I felt comfortable in their home. I washed and dried my first dishes. I made my first bed. I weeded my first garden—that is, since "forced labor" at Lake Mohegan. I found ways to make friends with these people who had read so much more than I and who conversed so much more easily. I learned that living simply was more rewarding than being smothered by servants. And, always, Mrs. Barnes said at the end of the weekend, "Come back as soon as you can." I did.

One lasting result of these New Hartford visits was that through Mrs. Barnes's encouragement—indeed, she arranged the transaction herself—I acquired forty-odd acres of unoccupied land, known as Red Hill, half a mile from her place. There, for the next twenty-five years, I regularly spent weekends and vacations. That piece of land and what I put into it and onto it became an integral part of my life.

There was another important result. Joe, with his parents' backing, had decided to go to the London School of Economics for the academic year 1927-28 to learn the Russian language and to sit in on various courses in political science and related disciplines. His father had made close friends with leading persons in labor and liberal circles and provided his son with letters of introduction.

It required very little urging to persuade me to go along. Mrs. Barnes was to join us as soon as we located rooms. We found an adequate two-bedroom flat in Bloomsbury. There was a gas heater in the fireplace that functioned so many minutes on a shilling, a hot-water heater in the bathroom that leaked enough so that to survive a washing the door had to be left open. The kitchen looked underequipped, but from it Anna Barnes produced splendid meals.

The day after occupying the flat we visited the YMCA and were given membership applications to fill out. One of the questions asked whether we believed in Christ or were Christians or something like that. Being by that time nonbelievers and proud of it, as well as young men of high moral principle, but anxious, too, to find some way to keep healthy without putting much time or money into it, we found ourselves in a quandary. We missed the first two weeks of exercise, for it took us that long to make up our minds that the result would warrant the sacrifice. In the end, ethical principles gave way to physical considerations. We signed the Y's loyalty oath.

Aside from a few concerts and a swim in the YMCA pool two or three times a week, our life revolved around the London School. We saw few people. I visited some members of my father's family who lived in England, and the Barnes family had friends who were members of the Liberal Party, and they were kind to us. But otherwise, when not walking to or from the LSE, we kept our noses in the books.

The LSE had an outstanding faculty and an international student body drawn largely from the British Empire, then still very much alive, and a reputation for liberalism. Its most noted teacher, at least to those of us from Harvard, was Harold Laski, a young political scientist. His principal claim to fame, as far as we were concerned, was that he had been fired from the Harvard faculty in 1919 for taking a prominent stand in the Boston police strike.

There were also Allyn Young, an American economist who had become prominent through the post-World War I Dawes Plan; L. T. Hobhouse, a notable authority in the fields of social psychology and philosophy; Graham Wallas, a political scientist who had been Laski's and Walter Lippmann's teacher; and Bronislaw Malinowski, the inspirer of the modern school of anthropology, who that year was giving a final series of lectures before retirement into research.

There was nothing wrong with the teaching faculty at Harvard. It was among the great ones in the world. I had not, however, taken advantage of it. I had become mired in the nonacademic life, through my own indulgence, and needed a fresh, stimulating intellectual environment to pull myself out of it. I had to get to work to understand why I was so disturbed by the injustices I found around me. Why had they occurred? The Sacco-Vanzetti case, for instance, had been in the headlines while I had been at Harvard. The two anarchists were executed the year of my graduation, and the president of Harvard had been prominently involved in denying them what seemed to me obvious justice. I had become emotionally involved. Something was wrong. But what? I had to begin to educate myself—right away. The LSE sounded as though it might be the place to start.

Joe and I went to England by boat, the only way to get there in 1927. Our cabin was tourist class which was comfortable enough, and the food, as far as we sampled it, good enough. Not great, not luxurious. Not quite the way I had traveled with my father a few years before on our grand tour of the European capitals and restaurants and museums. But definitely the right way to travel to where I was to begin to find out what the world was all about.

A pleasant surprise happened the second day out. I don't remember whether the passenger lists of those days included the names of those as far down the scale as tourist class, but somehow my Hotchkiss friend and teacher, John McChesney, found out I was on board and invited Joe and me upstairs. Mr. Mac, a bachelor when I had known him at school and a man of very modest circumstances, had married a wealthy and very wonderful lady from the nearby village of Salisbury. They were on one of their annual trips to Europe—traveling first class.

What an astounding coincidence that was. It was Mr. Mac who had stirred my mind at Hotchkiss. Now I was traveling with Joe, and it was his family that had been so responsible for rousing me out of the doldrums of my big-shot Harvard life. And here I was actually on my way to start my adult education.

We never got to know how the quality of the food down in tourist held out; we landed at Southampton well fed because we had several times been entertained in the first-class dining room. The McChesneys were the kind of people who feed you well, entertain you and put your mind in higher gear all at the same time. It was a good voyage.

Several times in this book I come around to the question, What is a good education? What is the process by which one first wants to learn and then learns? And my answer is always along the same line: the importance of stimulation, from within and without, asking questions of yourself and others and learning what questions to ask, learning where and how to find the answers. Those were the elements that made up that academic year in London. It was a year that gave direction to the rest of my life.

Here is an example of the way it was.

Harold Laski had a personality that irritated me. He was uncommonly articulate, brilliant, extraordinarily well informed; his memory seemed infallible. He made me feel like a worm. He grated on me. He angered me so much that I went to the books to see if I could find something to prove him wrong. I didn't, but in my endeavor to get something on him, I plowed through a lot of pages. That's good teaching, I think.

Laski was a man of small stature, flushed cheeks and eyes that seemed to radiate a fire burning inside him. When I read of his death at much too early an age, I remember thinking he had literally burned himself out.

We were invited to his house on a couple of Sunday afternoons. It was his custom to invite as many students as his living room would hold—and then a few more. He obviously loved teaching; he wanted to give us more of himself than he could fit into his university lectures. One of those Sunday sessions made a lifelong impression on me. Because so many students were crowded around him, and there were not enough chairs, I found myself sitting on the floor, literally at the master's feet. Someone brought up the subject of how to read, and Laski began talking about it. Except for doors and windows, the walls of the room were lined with books. Laski suggested that a small group select some volume on an obscure subject that we guessed he had not thought of for a long time and carefully read twenty pages at any place in the book so that we could remember facts and details on which to question him later. I wish I could identify the book but I remember only that it was an ancient treatise on some scientific discipline.

After these preliminaries we handed the volume to our host. He placed it on a lectern to begin reading the twenty pages we had selected. We watched, fascinated. His head turned to the left-hand page, made one downward motion, then to the right-hand page and another downward motion, and so on rapidly through those twenty pages. We soon realized that he was reading each page in two glances, grasping the contents of half a page in a single glance and then quickly adjusting eye and mind to the second half of that page. His reading finished, we asked Laski questions designed to trap him. There were no facts, thoughts or theories with which he had not made himself familiar. It was an amazing performance. He explained that he had put himself through an arduous period of training his eyes and mind to read first phrases, then clauses, then sentences, then whole paragraphs, until he reached half a page. The process had been both physiological and mental.

How does one respond to such a man? There are only two possibilities. Either you give up and resign yourself to living life on a low intellectual level, or you say to yourself, "I'll get to work and go as far as I can." This experience with Laski showed me that anger is an effective pedagogical goad—anger at the teacher for being so brilliant, and anger at yourself for being such a dope.

I didn't get very far that year. It took me most of it to get on track. But the direction had been set in terms of intellectual habits, in terms of where and how to look for social truths. I never went back on those habits.

Spring vacation broke the reading grind at the LSE rather dramatically. My father and I had arranged to meet in Berlin, which I had not visited before, and after a few days there to journey to Munich and then to Upper Silesia. We planned to spend an extended weekend there with Count Schertoss, the son-in-law of my grandmother's second husband, Henry White. That vacation was an experience in life rather than in lectures and books.

I reached the Hotel Adlon in Berlin a day ahead of my father. There, by prearrangement, I met Wilder Foote, a former *Crimson* colleague who was spending some time in the city. We had a couple of drinks at the hotel in the late afternoon before setting forth to see Berlin night life. We didn't undertake anything very high class, just hopping from one mediocre bar and dance floor to another. At some point we picked up two pleasant young women whose company made the rest of the night's adventure more entertaining. At an ungodly hour the next morning, we boarded separate cabs and dropped our respective companions where they lived.

My father arrived at midday, too early for my comfort, but a hearty lunch revived me sufficiently to enjoy some sightseeing in the afternoon. We were about to bathe and shave before spending a sedate evening when my telephone rang. Erika Segnitz, my guest of the evening before, was in the lobby, entertaining the notion that it might be nice to have a drink downstairs before doing another night on the town. Because I figured my father would enjoy meeting this young lady, I called his room to explain what had happened and to suggest he join us in the lobby. The three of us thereupon had an elegant and expensive dinner, found a highly respectable place for dancing and a champagne several grades above that which I had downed on my first Berlin outing. The young woman proved to be entertaining and quite capable of coping socially with both generations of Fields. We enjoyed ourselves. At the decorous hour at which we parted, it was agreed that

Erika would meet us at the Adlon early the next morning for a day's sightseeing. The three of us thus spent another instructive and amusing day, and in the evening repeated, though at different establishments, the dinner and dance of the evening before.

That night, my father and I took a train to Munich. Next morning, we met Osgood, who had just come up from Innsbruck, and did more sightseeing. But there was no dancing that day or evening. Early the next morning, the telephone woke us up. Osgood answered, then mumbled to me, "Some dame wants to talk to you; she says she's downstairs." Erika was in the lobby. The only thing to do was wake my father and announce the news, which I did with my voice reflecting a certain embarrassment. I felt matters were getting a little out of hand. "Perfectly all right," he said, "I'll call the desk and ask them to give her a room down the corridor." And so the four of us spent two or three days *lachen und tanzen* and doing a bit of sightseeing too.

Little did I realize then what a small part I was playing in what was developing. A few years after my mother died, my father married Erika, a marriage which ended in divorce in the middle 1940s. I became trustee of a fund which my father set up for her benefit, the income from which I still send Erika nearly forty years later.

The visit to Upper Silesia was by no means a time for laughing and dancing. It was, however, educational. It was another example of how not to live. I found nothing redeeming in the count's way of life. A Prussian aristocrat, he made his living and preserved his class superiority through a feudal estate that exploited and kept in a state of virtual bondage the large number of families living on it.

On the first day there the count showed us around. In several carriages we traveled dusty roads from one village to another. As we approached each, the head man of the village ran out to meet us. The carriages stopped for a moment as he greeted the count, bowing low before him and kissing his hand. I watched this procedure in astonishment and disgust. This was not a movie, this was real life. Outwardly, I remained the well-mannered young gentleman; inwardly, I burned. When I got back to our rooms, I blew my top.

We were told that a wild boar hunt was being arranged in our honor for the second day of our visit. I balked. I wasn't any good with a rifle—I had traded my own for a camera—but I felt that the family's reputation was at stake: skill with a rifle should have been a part of my familial training. (As a matter of fact, it had been, but I had not taken to it.) When I learned a little about what was in store for us, I didn't like it a bit. My father told me that to back out of an event that was being organized in our honor would be discourteous to our host. So I swallowed my objections.

Next morning, off we went. The carriages took us to an extensive flat field covered with brush where we, the guns, were positioned a certain number of paces apart. Osgood and I, the novices in the group, were told to face the direction from which the beaters were to approach, and as we heard them approaching to watch for boars. They would come crashing through just ahead of the beaters. We were not to shoot to either side, where the other guns were stationed, for fear of hitting another hunter, and we were to shoot low so as not to hit a beater.

After a while we heard the beaters as they moved toward us, thrashing the brush with heavy sticks. I was beginning to sweat and wishing it were all over when suddenly two boars appeared directly in front of me, running fast. I fired as rapidly as I could. The animals passed within a couple of yards of me and continued on in perfect physical condition.

Having missed an easy shot, I was disgraced. Those were the only boars seen that morning. The count gave me a look that showed his disapproval of the way young gentlemen were brought up in the United States. My clumsiness, he muttered, had caused him to lose face with his serfs. My father, perhaps as fed up with the count as I was, said, "Don't worry about it." We returned to the castle to feast on other forms of feudalism.

That was quite a vacation. It was worth a dozen of the lectures at the LSE and weeks of academic reading.

8

Socialist

The direction of my life was set during the 1927-28 academic year in London, and the road on which I was to travel was found soon afterward. When I returned to New York in the early summer of 1928, I got a job in midsummer and took a decisive political step in the early fall.

Harold Laski had given me a letter of introduction to Mrs. Belle Moskowitz, one of the most influential advisers to New York Governor Alfred Smith. For some months it had been evident that he was the leading candidate for the Democratic nomination for the Presidency. The English press, which I had been reading, considered him an outstanding liberal and had carried a considerable amount of background material on his career. Following a parochial education, he joined his father's trucking business and soon became active in New York City and state politics. He first became governor in 1918 and eventually served four two-year terms. He made a name for himself fighting with considerable success on a number of liberal issues: the elimination of graft and corrupt practices in elections, workmen's compensation, women's suffrage, optional municipal ownership of public utilities, home rule for cities, the minimum wage for women, health insurance for industrial workers, equal pay for women in the school system, a shorter work week for women and minors. The controversy over his candidacy arose less from this reformist record than from his membership in the Catholic Church. There was a widespread belief among Protestants, whether genuine or dishonest I then had no way of knowing, that Catholics were dictated to by their hierarchy and that Catholic office-holders could therefore not objectively represent the public at large. As the first Catholic to run for the Presidency, Smith had to bear this heavy burden. To me it constituted a prejudice which had to be eliminated from our politics.

Mrs. Moskowitz, a stout lady with a reputation as a brilliant political strategist, received me in her office, read the short letter of introduction, and, evidently considering me a nuisance rather than a useful pawn in her strategy, sent me "downstairs" in a matter of not more than two minutes to find something to do, without giving a hint of how I was to go about it or whom I was to see. "Downstairs" in this instance was to provide my exit from the Democratic Party. Someone gave me a batch of literature which when I got home I read carefully, with the sinking feeling as I read on that it represented not at all what I was looking for in the American political scene. My slender contact with the Democrats, held together by no effort on their part and disappearing motivation on mine, evaporated. There was no reason why they should have made an effort to put me to work. I was very young politically, and in other ways, too, and everyone was too busy, I suppose, to start me in some form of apprenticeship. My association with the Democrats thus ended as soon as it began. Strangely enough, it was with Alfred Smith's trucking business, not his politics, that many years later I did have an association—an unpleasant one.

Nevertheless, the fever that had been quietly smoldering in me for some time had, during those months in London, begun to flare up. It was not quieted by failure to make my first political connection in the United States. It was a presidential year, politics were in the air, I was full of beans and wanted to change society overnight.

As a result, I made one of the important decisions of my life. I applied to join the Socialist Party. I reasoned I was more likely to find something related to the ideas that were forming in my head there than with the Democrats. I have often wondered what discussions, if any, took place in the party regarding my fitness to be a member, for it took two weeks for the SP to accept me. And two weeks after that, in the middle of October, the newspapers got hold of the story.

Under the leadership first of Eugene V. Debs and then, from the early twenties, Norman Thomas, the Socialist Party had played a prominent role in the progressive life of the United States. In 1893-94, the country had suffered a severe depression, one of the outstanding events of which was the Pullman strike in Chicago in the spring of 1894. The employees of the Pullman works, led by their president, Debs, struck over a wage cut. The federal government broke the strike by asking the courts for a blanket injunction against the union's interfering with the U.S. mails. The courts accepted the government's tortured logic, and Debs ultimately went to jail. And there he became converted to socialism. While still serving his sentence, he was nominated for the presidency by the Socialists. They renominated him regularly through 1920, when he was again incarcerated, this time under the notorious Sedition Act of 1918 for opposing American involvement in World War I.

The successes and influence of the Socialist Party during this period are often forgotten today. There were strong local campaigns for public own-ership of municipal waterworks, gas and electric plants. In 1911 eighteen American cities elected Socialist mayors and two of the big ones, Cleveland and Los Angeles, almost did so. Upton Sinclair's Intercollegiate Socialist Society had chapters in the leading universities. Just before World War I, the party's membership reached just over 118,000; there were Socialist mayors in fifty-six cities and a large number of Socialists in city and state public offices. Following the war, Victor L. Berger of Wisconsin became the first Socialist to be elected to Congress. He, too, was jailed under the Sedition Act. Five Socialists elected to the New York State Assembly were shamefully expelled by a legislature carried away by the postwar anti-Red hysteria.

Fifty years later, it is difficult to put myself in the position of that restless youngster, the twenty-three-year-old Fred Field. I remember him pretty well, of course, but I have trouble putting myself in his place without all of my intervening experiences interfering. Fortunately, because of the pub-licity given his decision and the temporary prominence into which it raised him, he had to explain himself publicly at the time. In good part, then, the difficulty in looking back fifty years is overcome by my having an eyewitness to the scene. One thing, however, I would like to report from the distance from which I now view those events. I like what Fred Field did. I would like to meet him now as he was then and talk with him about it. I wish we two could have lunch together so I could tell him face to face how pleased I am with what he did. I wonder what he would have to say to me. Would he understand what I did in all those years between the age of twenty-three and seventy-five? Would he approve? Or would he ask why I had done so-and-so instead of what I did do at the next turning point, or the next, or the one after that?

In October 18-20, 1928, fairly long stories about what I had just done appeared in the New York papers. The fullest article and the most authentic, from my point of view, was a long piece I wrote at the request of the *Jewish Daily Forward*. It appeared as the main feature in its English-language edition of Sunday, October 28. Another authentic source is a letter that I wrote with Jack Herling, a Harvard classmate who joined the Socialists with me. We sent it to all the New York City papers, and it was eventually run in full in the *Herald Tribune* and quoted in news stories in several other papers.

The opinions then expressed about my young friend were mild indeed in comparison to the treatment he was to receive twenty-odd years later. There was nothing nasty in this first round.

The *New York Times* said that "he appeared to be anxious to stress the independent nature of his decision to affiliate himself with the Socialists, wishing not to 'involve' his family in the matter." The *New York World* had more to say:

> His Hoover-voting relatives may look upon him as a black sheep of the family but not even the most conservative or critical of them could describe the very earnest and very young Thomas enthusiast as red. . . . Mr. Field appeared exceedingly youthful, slender, blond and slightly bewildered at the attention he was receiving from the New York press last week. . . . It seems he's a "white collar" man and gets down to his desk on 52nd Street, via the trolley line, every morning at 9 o'clock. . . . Throughout the interview, which was a good deal of a struggle on Mr. Field's part to keep his family out of it, his valued job, and even himself, the newest recruit to Socialism seemed a very earnest young man. . . .

McAllister Coleman was asked by the *Evening Telegram* to interview me, which is surprising, as I look back on it, because Coleman was then running for the U.S. Senate on the Socialist ticket:

> You cannot talk to this tall, slim, blond youngster without discovering at once that he has very decided economic and political views. . . . Now what is he after? Publicity for himself? That's funny when you know the man and his real modesty. A new kick out of life? Unh-uh. Is it hero worship for the personality of Norman Thomas? Wrong again. No, he is after what a surprisingly large number of young men and women are after these days, a party of the producers and creators rather than the owners and exploiters. .

Coleman ended his article by saying:

> It's a long call from 645 Fifth Avenue to that Brownsville meeting of garment workers to which Field and I are going tonight, a long call, but an understandable one, once you get the mental set-up of this youngster, who like so many others, has awakened to a cry, "A plague on both your parties."

Everyone seems agreed that I was tall, slender and blond. I thought I was skinny and red-headed. In any case, I was not yet that "youthful-looking man in his forties with thinning hair" whom we will get to know further along in this book.

My decision, with one important exception, did not cause much of a flurry in the family, though no one came up and said, "That's great, Fred. It's high time one of us took a step in that direction." I'm sure quite a few were not happy about what I had done, but the Socialist Party was not that dangerous and Norman Thomas was respectable. No one, with one exception, got downright angry. One person who helped me in this situation, as well as in others, was my mother. She was an extraordinarily tolerant woman, and her tolerance was felt by those around her. It had the effect of at least modifying their own intolerance.

Cholly Knickerbocker, a well-known society columnist of those days, later wrote two long Sunday pieces about my mother. He reported, among other things, that

> the sensational exploits that have won newspaper notice for so many Vanderbilts never have intrigued Mrs. William B. Osgood Field, and one might almost classify her as among the "more tranquil of the great ladies provided by the Vanderbilt clan." Mrs. Field has never exploited her children socially, and she did not seem one whit surprised . . . when one of her good-looking sons, Frederick Vanderbilt Field, came out and expressed himself in favor of Socialism. Young Field shocked his Vanderbilt connections—but his mother understood—and said nothing.

(In the interest of accuracy, I should say that it was the custom for society columnists to call the sons of the rich handsome or good-looking and the daughters lovely or beautiful.)

Several family friends came to my rescue—or so they thought—with the old and meaningless bromide about being radical in one's twenties, liberal in one's thirties and conservative in one's forties. They had it wrong. I was going in the opposite direction. I had been conservative from zero to about thirteen and liberal through prep school and college. In my twenties I was beginning to move to the left—where I remain fifty years later.

The exception was my great-uncle Frederick W. Vanderbilt. Shortly after my initiation into newspaper publicity, I was summoned to his office, where I was received by his male secretary. The secretary announced in the briefest possible manner that my Uncle Fred was displeased with me and no longer concerned about my future. I asked to see Uncle Fred personally to discuss the matter with him. I thought that in a face-to-face conversation I could explain the reasons for my decision. "Your Uncle Fred does not wish to see you."

Before joining the Socialists, I had thought of the possibility that doing so might jeopardize whatever inheritance Uncle Fred had planned to leave me. But it was a thought that passed quickly. I was already getting a good allowance from my mother, I knew I would inherit a decent amount from her and I was about to go on a salary in my new job. One chunk more was not the most important thing in the world. What concerned me was the thought of what would happen to me as a person if I didn't take this step. In my journey from my childhood reactions to a pampered life to what I had so recently learned in London, the logical next step was for me to join my working American colleagues to see if we couldn't make things better. Not to take that step would be weak, cowardly, a shameful evasion of my responsibility to myself. It was characteristic of my mother's tolerance that she never mentioned to me Uncle Fred's decision to cancel something that to her must have been extremely important. It was characteristic of my father's evasion of the real issues of life that he never mentioned my joining the Socialists.

In the *Forward* article, I wrote about my surprise at the commotion my move had caused. I had no desire for that kind of publicity. I had hoped to go into political work quietly, learn from it, perhaps influence others during the 1928 campaign and gradually figure out where I then stood in relation to society. Instead, circumstances plunged me forward faster than I had any intention of going. They did not alter the direction in which I was moving, but they certainly changed the pace and in certain respects the way that I made my move. How absurd it was, I wrote, that of the eight newspapers to which Herling and I had sent our letter, not one paid it any attention for two weeks. Then an enterprising reporter by chance learned what the middle initial of one of the signers stood for. "There is no news value," I wrote, "in a letter about important issues, none in an appeal to first voters to become aware of the fact that there is a third party. But the fact that there is a 'V' in a signature to the letter gives it such news value that all the syndicates broadcast it. . . . How can one fail to be impressed by the triviality, the superficiality of a social system which makes such monstrous nonsense over a middle initial?" This may not have been a sophisticated reaction, but it was a healthy one.   ·

I lashed out at the two old parties, both of which, I said, represented the status quo. The status quo should not be tolerated because it perpetuated injustice and inequalities. The old parties had to be forced to change their policies or else be defeated. I did not think such a change was possible because the money that maintained the system was too powerful. There was a vicious circle. How could the Democrats and Republicans get the funds necessary to support their elaborate organizations unless they catered to those who had them?

When I was in college, I was puzzled by the way the standard organs of public opinion frequently avoided, or at least distorted, what I thought were the real issues. I slowly came to the realization that newspapers, industries, commerce, even the land itself, were in the hands of a wealthy minority which could dictate its own terms. I was concerned about inequality of opportunity before I knew anything about the problems of blacks and other minorities. I, for instance, was able to go to the best schools and colleges, to travel, to study and read and seek out brilliant lecturers while most others of my age were already driving trucks or digging ditches or standing behind counters.

At Harvard, I continued in the *Forward* article, I had found that the college system seemed devised to give those who were born to leisure more leisure and those who born to work even more work. Clubs with luxurious houses, good food, facilities for study and reading and other amenities catered to the wealthy minority. There were exceptions, of course, but that was the general rule. Nine-tenths of the students had to eat in cafeterias; many worked every hour they were not studying. If there were not enough dormitory rooms to go around, and there never were, it was the poor students who had to look for rooms where they could afford the board.

I turned to more philosophical subjects. "Probably it was Plato and Kant more than any other influence that made me lose interest in the so-called things of the spirit and turn my attention to concrete issues that can be handled by the mind of man with pragmatic proof of results." That, I concede, was a pretty fancy sentence. I know what it meant, though, for I am familiar with what developed later. I was becoming a materialist, moving away from the concept of God. Plato and Kant were in this respect an introduction to Marx. By 1928, when I joined the Socialist Party, I had left "the so-called things of the spirit" and was moving toward the firm belief that all things come from earth, not heaven.

I was doing a lot of reading. In the *Forward* article I mentioned Beatrice and Sidney Webb's *Trade Unionism* and *Industrial Democracy*, Graham Wallas's writings, Laski's *Communism* and *Grammar of Politics*, Lenin's letters before the revolution, Kropotkin's *Ethics*, and the works of Benjamin Kidd. I failed to mention—I wonder why—a book that I had read in London. At a young age it started me thinking about death, not in a morbid way, but rather as one of the most difficult of our inevitable experiences. There is no escaping it, that's certain, but is there not some way in which we can accept it? Cannot the end of life be understood as part of the natural course of living it? I suppose that what the book taught me was that even in my early manhood I had to learn to face the fact of death and that living in a culture which was nonsensical in its approach to the subject, I would have to work out my own philosophy with respect to it.

The book was *The Nature of Man* by Ilya Metchnikoff, a Russian who did most of his scientific work at the Pasteur Institute in Paris and is variously described as a zoologist, pathologist, biologist and bacteriologist. In 1908 he shared the Nobel Prize for physiology and medicine. The message of the book, one of his more popular treatises, was that toward the end of a natural life, the phagocytes, which are the white blood cells that fight off disease, become weary of their work and gradually cease to function. Metchnikoff sought out and interviewed as many octogenarians as were willing to talk to him, not many by modern computer standards, but enough to convince him that just as in youth one longs for life, so in extreme old age one longs for death. That theory made death, if it did not happen prematurely, sound like something very natural and normal.

But perhaps I didn't include *The Nature of Man* in my *Forward* article because at twenty-three the phagocytes were working and I didn't want to dwell on the weariness which was bound to overtake them.

I did write, however, that along with philosophy and sociology and political science, I was also reading in other fields. I asked myself the ponderous question, "What is the ultimate fundamental on which civilization and all its ramifications is constructed?" And I wrote that I thought I could find the answer in psychology and perhaps, for historical perspective, in anthropology. I read Gustave Le Bon, William McDougall, Max Mueller, John B. Watson, Gordon Allport, Robert Briffault and Havelock Ellis and listened to lectures by Malinowski.

I had concluded, I continued, "that for social issues the individual was the true point of departure." But "then came the question, what does the individual desire?" Undaunted, I answered, "Every individual seeks to satisfy his own desires, which are, chronologically, physical necessities, fundamental desires, derived desires, sometimes known as standards or ideals." And that, I said, leads to another question: in a society how can all this be measured; how can society be judged as successful or not? I offered to answer that too. A society can be judged by the measure to which each individual in it is given equal opportunity for the most perfect self-fulfillment.

In one section, I said that I had traveled enough to realize how interdependent everything and everyone were, how whatever happened in one place or to one person in some way affected all others. I didn't say in the *Forward* article—because I did not know it then—that this interdependence was a fundamental of dialectic materialism.

I ended the article with a political exhortation. I announced that I was going to cast my first vote for Norman Thomas and the Socialist Party. "It is the only party," I said, "which regards political questions from an objective, scientific point of view, which promises an intelligent basis for judgments, which uses scientific measurements of social accomplishments." Well, of course, the Socialist Party was not quite up to that claim. If it had been, it might have gone further than it did, and I might not have found it a weak vehicle for my impatient ambition to correct the world's ills.

I met Norman Thomas a number of times and went to his home on two or three occasions, but I never got to know him well. I did not become a member of the party because of him, although in the years immediately after joining I admired him. Rather I joined because the party seemed to embody a point of view and principles in which I believed. That I had no meaningful contact with Thomas during my Socialist days was unimportant. Neither during this period nor later, when I moved further left, was I following a "leader" or a personality. I was looking for a place where I could forward what I believed.

Some of my work for the party was fruitless because my work was inept. During the 1928 presidential campaign, I spoke on street corners, but I was so inexperienced at that sort of thing that I doubt I persuaded a single person to change his or her vote from the old parties. I never learned to be a good speaker, certainly not in that most difficult of all spots, a street corner.

My principal activities were with Socialist-front organizations—if I may call them that. For some strange reason, only the Communists are thought to have them. Actually, all political parties, church organizations, social movements have front organizations to advance their objectives among youth, women, industrial workers and ethnic groups. They could not extend themselves and their ideas through our complex society without these groups. The League for Industrial Democracy and Pioneer Youth of America, two organizations to which I gave a good deal of energy, were nothing if not Socialist Party outcroppings.

Pioneer Youth ran a summer camp in an attractive location for children who came mainly from families in the clothing trades. I was active in it for several years and for a time served as president of its board of directors. That camp was enjoyable and useful.

Among my other activities with the League for Industrial Democracy, I contributed a chapter to a symposium called *Socialist Planning and a Socialist Program*, edited for the LID by its director, Harry W. Laidler. Among the twenty-nine other contributors were Rexford G. Tugwell, later Secretary of Agriculture in Franklin Roosevelt's Cabinet, several university professors, and a few Socialist Party officials. In a concluding chapter, the editor summarized our findings. His synopsis merits quoting because it pretty well represented my own thinking in 1932.

Laidler wrote that the authors were in general agreement on the following:

1. In America at the present time we have natural, technical and human resources to feed, clothe and shelter every man, woman and child in decency, security and comfort.
2. The existence of poverty and of a vast army of unemployed facing want and starvation is due not to our lack of resources, but to our failure to inaugurate

a planned economy, the primary aim of which is service to the community rather than profit for the few.

3. Under capitalism, where the essential industries of the country are privately owned, and where thousands of concerns are engaged in a mad scramble for maximum profits, social planning, on the basis of full use of all our resources for the welfare and happiness of the community, is impossible.

4. Genuine social planning is socialist in character. It requires that the community own its principal industries and run them democratically in the interests of all. . . .

5. To bring about socialist planning requires the strengthening of the organizations of the masses on the economic, cooperative, educational and, above all, on the political field. . . .

6. The movement toward peaceful revolution will definitely be aided by a development among socialists of more specific plans and programs for the transference of industry from private to public ownership and for the operation of a cooperative system. . . .

My own chapter in this symposium appeared under the imposing title, "The Far East as Illustration of the Necessity of World Planning." On rereading it, I am inclined to agree with a memorandum that one of my colleagues at the Institute of Pacific Relations, Bruno Lasker, sent me shortly after the book was published. The memorandum concluded, "Of course, your paper is covering too much ground to deal adequately with any part of the subject assigned to you." Devastating, but nicely put: the assignment was to blame.

There was not much more to my years with the Socialists. I was not called upon to be very active. And, indeed, my impression became increasingly strong that the party itself was not doing much. There was little publishing or education or propaganda or even organizing to be seen. Aside from the presidential election campaign every four years, the party seemed to be a splendid shell of an idea without anything important growing inside it. And I drifted away.

9

A Job and Travels

The job I took upon returning to the United States from the London School of Economics occupied me for the next eleven years. The job came about in a strange way. In fact, I did not know the man who one day called me up to invite me to a lunch that he said might interest me. Because I had nothing special to do that day, I accepted.

Arriving, I was greeted by the caller, Edward C. Carter, a striking white-haired man of about fifty who introduced me to a younger Chinese man standing next to him and to a few of the perhaps twenty-five others who had been invited. We soon sat down to eat, this being no fancy function with cocktails and goodies—and to my surprise I found myself placed to the right of the Chinese. I then surmised he was the guest of honor, because Carter was sitting at his other elbow. By the time coffee was served, I had learned something about him. His name was Yen Yang-chu, anglicized to Y. C. James Yen, and his friends called him Jimmy. He was a north Chinese though, unlike many of those of conspicuously slight physique. He was in his middle thirties, a graduate of Yale who spoke perfect English and a man of unusual charm. He was visiting the United States as the representative of an organization known in English as the Chinese Mass Education Movement, which he had founded to eliminate illiteracy in China. During his stay in the United States, Yen's host was the Institute of Pacific Relations (IPR), of which Carter was the chief staff officer. Other than that, I knew nothing about Carter and less about the IPR.

After the meal, Yen gave an impassioned speech on the illiterate condition of the Chinese masses, on the impossibility of modernizing, to say nothing of democratizing, China unless this illiteracy was overcome, and on the particular methods his movement had developed to accomplish this herculean task. He explained that he was in the country to raise funds and asked us to contribute. We did. I did. It was my first contribution in a series of contributions to causes that caught my imagination.

I emerged from that noon gathering with my first job. I became an assistant to Carter, and was assigned for the time being as secretary to Yen. I was to travel across the country, arranging meetings, functions and interviews for Yen, in order to raise a half million dollars. The job was an introduction not only to China but to my own country as well.

Carter, with whom I was closely associated for the next twenty years, was an extraordinary man. He had been the chief YMCA secretary in India during World War I. He had then returned to the United States, where, in association with some academic people, mainly from Teachers College of Columbia University, and others interested in adult education, he had founded an organization called The Inquiry. The purpose of the organization, which was never well known, was to study how to improve face-to-face communication among leaders at both national and international levels. It was a small organization with a small budget, a small staff and a small mailing list to which its publications were sent. Some of those who followed its work were fortunately in key positions to spread its ideas. I believe that The Inquiry contributed more to the round-table method of developing purposeful discussion than did any other organization at that time. For several years, Carter was the chief executive of The Inquiry and the American branch of the IPR, which became the testing ground for The Inquiry's findings.

Getting me to that lunch for Jimmy Yen and signing me up two hours later for a job that was to last many years was typical of the way Carter operated. He had somehow heard that I had recently returned from London, that I had become interested in a general way in international affairs, that I wanted to work but had not yet found out how or where. I saw him do the same kind of thing hundreds of times with others, in order to get them to do something or just to provoke them with a new idea. Later, as I gained experience, we worked together at involving people in the IPR. He was more subtle and indirect in his approach than I ever became. If I were to invite some young person to a luncheon to meet a Chinese with the notion of signing him up for a job that very afternoon, I would be inclined to tell him first what the luncheon was all about. But then I might well lose my man before he became fascinated by the oratory of someone like Jimmy Yen.

Our travels, Jimmy's and mine, involved a lot more than arranging interviews and banquets. He happened to be a one-speech man. At the end of weeks of travel and the Lord only knows how many deliveries, only a handful of words of that speech differed from the first rendition I had heard.

Yet, before each banquet, he would deliver it to me in our hotel rooms for review and criticism; and when we returned to our quarters later that night, Jimmy's first question would be, "Fred, how did it go tonight?" and we would go over it once again.

We were both seeing the length and the breadth of the United States for the first time, and each of us absorbed what he saw and heard in his own way. Jimmy, I believe, saw the country as a model for his own in many ways. He particularly admired the democracy we had developed. At the same time, he revered ancient Chinese traditions such as the Confucian ethic. How many times did he explain to me the proper relation of children to parents, of parents to grandparents and of the family to the state? I had doubts about the perfection of our democracy; being thrown in with the richest citizens in one city after another nurtured those doubts. I was not swept off my feet by the elegance of the company we kept, which was not representative of most Americans. Yen spoke in over thirty communities, however, which permitted me to meet a great many people. When the travels ended, I was excited about the country, its marvelous and ever varied landscapes and its seemingly infinite prospects.

Jimmy returned to his home in Peking with a few bags of gold and lots of promissory notes. By then my close friend, he invited Betty and me to visit him as soon as possible. We were able to do so a few months later.

After Yen's return to China, I formally joined the IPR staff as an assistant secretary. Carter gave me every opportunity to develop whatever administrative and research abilities I might have. We began as close working associates; we grew to be confidential, trusting friends. He advanced me rapidly in my IPR career. He saw to it that I had every opportunity to study and learn. He also pushed me into positions of responsibility which forced me to develop initiative, and he arranged for me to have sole authority for many research projects.

I was always open with Carter about my extracurricular activities, particularly when a potential conflict of interest was involved. He was tolerant and understanding of my urge to apply what I learned within the IPR to the political world in which I lived outside that organization.

In all my varied experiences, I never had a closer or longer relation with a person much my senior. Carter had an enormous amount of energy, unshakable integrity, a missionary-like zeal to reach the goals of his work and a singleness of purpose which superseded every other consideration in his life. He depended on his staff and made us feel important to him. He stood behind us, and he expected us to be loyal to him.

I respected Carter, and being myself devoted to both his goals and strategies, I learned a great deal from him. We had disagreements, mostly on the political level, but never any run-ins. I saw things more politically than he did; he saw them more optimistically. In Carter's view, nothing could not be overcome by energy and intelligence applied to truth. Though much younger, I suppose I had less faith in the goodness of mankind, especially that part of mankind that owned and ran much of the world. Carter was an outstanding promoter and organizer. He was untiring and persuasive in his pursuit of an objective.

When I first knew him, he neither smoked nor drank. Under the influence of his young staff he took to both, mildly and awkwardly. And we broke down some other austere habits and characteristics acquired, I should think, in a lifetime of YMCA work. My female associates even coaxed him to the dance floor, where his performance was also awkward. Every so often we enjoyed seeing him relax. It was also partly because of us that little by little he turned to a greater reliance on the printed word. When I first knew him, he kept in touch with what was going on and amassed his information mostly through conversation. I'm not sure whether we influenced him toward the political left or whether we simply supported his own liberal tendencies, but just about always he was on what I considered the correct side.

Edward Carter was, in short, an outstanding personality in my life.

In 1929 the IPR was to hold one of its biennial conferences in Kyoto, Japan, and it was arranged that several of the delegates from the United States and Great Britain were to meet in Moscow and travel to Japan by the Trans-Siberian Railway. It would be an interesting trip, especially because most of us had never visited the Soviet Union and none of us had ever taken the Trans-Sib. The IPR was anxious to interest the Russians in joining the organization because the USSR was one of the important powers in the western Pacific, had a long history of involvement there and was, we thought, destined to play an even larger role in the future. The trip would also enable us to approach Japan via Manchuria, an area of immense agricultural and mineral importance.

For Betty and me the trip had special importance. It was to begin with a fairly large group of notables to whom we had work responsibilities as secretaries. And after that we planned to go alone on a long visit to China and the Philippines, a sort of postponed honeymoon. When we were married, in March 1929, I was still working a busy schedule of travel with Jimmy Yen. It seemed that it would go on forever, so Betty and I decided to get married before the assignment ended, regardless of the schedule. At noon we had a quiet wedding ceremony in the library of 645, presided over by a minister acquaintance of Betty's and attended by my mother and father, Betty's brother and my grandmother, Nanan. At six-thirty we boarded a sleeper for a distant city, occupying upper and lower berths while in the adjoining section slept our friend Jimmy Yen. It can therefore be understood that we were looking forward to breaking away from our colleagues and superiors, delightful, stimulating and remarkable as they were.

While I had been devoting my time to Yen's fund-raising campaign, Betty had been working on the staff of The Inquiry. She was as well prepared for the Asian trip and for participation in IPR staff work as I, and in certain respects, such as her perception of people's abilities and characters, better qualified. I was often surprised at how astutely she described someone with whom I was associated. "How in heaven's name did you figure that out?" I would think.

We arrived in Moscow only twelve years after the revolution that shook the world. The Czarists and aristocrats of the land had been overthrown and dispossessed. Power had been seized by the Russian people; a government had been organized; the counterrevolution, supported by the Western powers, including the United States, had been smashed; and the gigantic task of constructing a socialist society was under way. But this was long before the Soviet Union had become a world power through its extraordinarily rapid economic and military growth. It was a bad year for agriculture. Drought had stunted the crops, and food was short. Moscow was just beginning to modernize. The huge hotels and other tourist facilities that exist today had not yet been built or even projected.

The hotel to which visitors were then assigned was an old-fashioned one. Our quarters had a nineteenth-century elegance, which was an adequate substitute for a certain inefficiency. They contained an elaborately decorated grand piano which did not serve its primary purpose, for neither of us could play the instrument, but it made an excellent high table on which to place the large can of fresh caviar which had been our first purchase. The surprising thing to us was that the Russians could take care of us at all so soon after such a social earthquake. None of the negative factors could diminish the excitement of our visit. We knew that we were present at one of the great dramas of world history even though we had missed the curtain raiser.

I had little background in Russian history, and I had not yet read much Marxism-Leninism. However, I already felt uncomfortable about the class structure of American society, even though it was obviously a hundred times better than the society which had been overthrown by the Soviet Revolution. I was beginning to understand the urgency of a thorough cleansing of social and economic relationships. I read, I was told, and I believed that the Russians had been liberated from the oppression of their former rulers. They were in the process of forming a new social structure in which human dignity should replace serfdom. A great struggle to modernize the country in order to rise out of the abysmal backward conditions of life under the Czars was getting under way.

I, along with many others on the left, would be disillusioned by some things that were to take place in the Soviet Union, and I, again along with others, was slow to accept our disillusionment. Only many years later did I become aware of some of the methods the Stalin dictatorship was using to achieve rapid industrialization, methods that bore no relation whatsoever to any doctrine ever advanced by Marx or Engels. But neither disillusionment nor disappointment could ever displace my appreciation of the immense constructive accomplishments of the Revolution. In no more than a few decades the Soviet Union moved into the modern world with a form of social organization that was changing the lives of everyone who lived in it. The Soviet Revolution of 1917, and thirty-two years later the Chinese upheaval, have been without question the most important political events of this century.

The destiny of the world and of each national unit must remain in the hands of representatives of the people, not in those of ruling monopolies or minorities. If the latter refuse by adjustment and negotiation and compromise to give way to a more equitable organization of society, they become responsible for the violence which in those circumstances inevitably and necessarily accompanies the revolutionary process. I should add that if the new rulers make the same mistakes as those they replaced and develop into oppressive, power-hungry minorities, they will suffer the same fate as their predecessors.

One of the main currents of history in my lifetime lay in finding and achieving the changes needed to form a just society. In 1928-29 I was trying to find my way into that mainstream. My short visit to the Soviet Union and my longer and more intimate visit to China gave me a strong push in the direction that I have been sure is the correct one ever since. Whatever mistakes those countries have made in the difficult journey of their revolutions, their general movement toward a socialist form of society is where the future leads. I have not envied my contemporaries who remained in the eddies and backwaters of progress. And I despise those who have spent their lives trying to turn back the current.

We spent a week in Moscow gaining general impressions, many of the details of which I have since forgotten. There was a visit with Madame Krupskaya, Lenin's widow, and two evenings with young people our age, which included free conversation and the inevitable glass of tea. And, of course, there was the caviar, which had cost next to nothing and which we ate in heaping spoonfuls. Meanwhile, our principals were busy negotiating the Soviet Union's entry into the IPR with government officials. Betty and I, on the lower echelons of the staff, were not party to those discussions, which, in due course, proved successful.

The Trans-Sib was a once-in-a-lifetime experience. The tracks were still the original broad gage which enabled the sleeping cars to be wider and the compartments correspondingly large. The beds ran the width of the train and between each two compartments were the washbasin and toilet. This arrangement permitted us to have lectures every afternoon by one of the experts among us, the professor occupying the bathroom and sitting on the only piece of furniture made for that purpose. The doors opened on each side to the adjoining rooms crowded with the audience.

The food was neither plentiful nor good. There was a shortage throughout the country, and no favoritism was shown distinguished and undistinguished travelers alike. There were always eggs, however, and the cook made omelets that we ate several times a day without getting bored. The train stopped with some frequency to refuel both engine and passengers. The stations were often a distance from the nearest village—at times we couldn't even see one—but there were always women with baskets of dried fish waiting to meet the train.

Our group occupied all of one sleeping car. A few cars behind us was quarters for a German track team that was keeping in shape while traveling to some friendship meets in the Far East. The moment the train stopped, the athletes went out jogging in the direction of their destination. By the time the train got under way again, they were far up the track out of sight. Either through the kindness of the engineers or because it took that long for the train to pick up speed, the runners were still able to swing aboard by the time we overtook them.

A great deal of reading and studying had to be done in preparation for the conference, and it kept us busy. I had brought along several volumes of the early essays of the Fabian Society, the forerunner of the British Labour Party. The essays were concerned with the growth of the trade union movement, the morality of socialism and the need to take over the government gradually over a long period without resort to revolutionary methods. They were anti-Marxist-Leninist. Mild as were the doctrines preached by this material, it caused me some trouble when we reached Japan. We were held up well over an hour while customs officials turned over each page of each volume, frequently interrupting this exercise to talk to each other, about what I never knew. I could not understand a word of what they were saying, and they could not read a word of what they were examining.

Several days out from Moscow, we discovered that a dispute between the Chinese and Russians over the railway that ran from the Manchurian border to Mukden had provoked the Chinese to take up a section of the track.

We were notified that our train would therefore not enter Manchuria and drop us off at Mukden as planned but would instead keep north of the Amur River in Russian territory and take us all the way to Vladivostok.

The Chinese Eastern Railway, which crossed Manchuria and on which we were to have traveled, had been constructed by Russia under an agreement reached with China as far back as 1896. It remained in Russian hands after the Russo-Japanese War of 1904-5. There had been a period of confusion after the Soviet Revolution, but in 1924 the railway returned to *de facto* Russian control. In 1929, using the pretext of having found Soviet propaganda along the right of way, the Chinese seized the line, removed some sections of track and thus forced a change in our plans. A few months later, the row subsided.

Vladivostok, in 1929, was the dirtiest, most miserable place I had ever visited. The best hotel, to which we were escorted, was filthy. After nine days on the Trans-Sib, we ourselves were not immaculate. On our floor of the hotel there was just one bathroom. The tub was nauseating and crawling with cockroaches. It took Betty and me a full hour to clean the room enough so that we could take baths. The bedroom was little better. We sought help from a young man at the hotel desk. Somehow we made our strange plan known to him, and he guided us to a store. There we bought four large tumblers. We then did a thorough job of turning the bed inside out and getting rid of the livestock by either eviction or murder. We half-filled the tumblers with water and placed the bedposts in them. The only remaining way for the enemy to invade our bed was to find a path into the room by the crack under the door, which we had carefully stuffed, then climb a wall, make their way along the ceiling and from there drop on us.

We were doubly protected because Betty, anticipating troublesome nights on our voyage to strange Asian towns, had made us each anti-bug pajamas. I wish I had had my picture taken in my pair, which tied around the ankles and neck. We slept rather well.

When we arrived in Vladivostok, there was no boat in the harbor destined for Japan. We had to wait three days for a small Japanese freighter to show up. Meanwhile, the only diversion the town had to offer was the local militia, which did a great deal of drilling with wooden guns in case the trouble over the railway flared up.

The trip on the freighter was marked by one of those happenings you talk about for the rest of your life. On boarding the ship, we were shown to our cabin. It had been equipped, oddly enough, with three bunks. We soon learned that the third was already occupied. While we were unpacking, a pleasant-looking blond young woman knocked and came in. She spoke some English and politely informed us that she was the ship's whore. She would appreciate our making some arrangement about the use of the room. This we did by agreeing to vacate it during her working hours. She was one of probably thousands of white Russians who in those days plied the coastal ships, the principal Manchurian towns and the ports of the China coast, practicing the only profession open to them.

10

China and the Philippines

Because of the detour to Vladivostok, we were behind schedule. Before the Kyoto conference, we needed time in China to get some feeling for opinion there before returning to Japan. As soon as possible, several of our group took the train through Korea into Manchuria to Mukden. A short stay in that unappealing city was highlighted by a luncheon given us by the "Young Marshal," Chang Hsueh-liang, the son of the "Old Marshal," Chang Tso-lin. At the time of the overthrow of the Manchu dynasty, in 1911, Chang Tso-lin had been a chieftain in the northern pioneer areas of Manchuria. Later, he became a powerful warlord based on Mukden in the rich central territory of the region. He had never shown any respect for the Chinese government, either in Peking or Nanking, and had in fact played the game with the Japanese, who provided him with the necessary chips. In 1928 he perished in a mysterious explosion.

After the warlord's death, Chinese assertion of sovereign rights in Manchuria became more vigorous. Chang Hsueh-liang, his heir to the warlordship, adopted the policy of strengthening the Chinese political administration of Manchuria and of speeding up Chinese economic development. Under his administration railway lines and port facilities were begun with the intention of wresting the economic control of the region from the Japanese. Shortly after assuming power, the Young Marshal openly declared his allegiance to the Nanking government by flouting Japanese advice and hoisting the national flag over Mudken. There was some importance, then, to our luncheon with him.

We were picked up at our hotel by Chang's secretary, a young man who spoke good English and who offered us his calling card. His name was followed by a series of letters that gave the impression, as indeed they were intended to do, that he possessed several important degrees of higher learning. I don't remember the exact order of the letters but they went something like this: a.c.a.sch. ec.un.l. He was not quite as impressive as his credentials sought to make him. The letters simply indicated "attended classes at the School of Economics, University of London."

The Young Marshal's residence was surprisingly modest for a person pretending to fill such as important role. It was not large, and it was furnished in the usual aesthetically unsuccessful combination of Chinese and Western objects. He was off somewhere when we arrived, and the secretary undertook to show us around. The climax of the short tour, for there was not much to see, found us standing in the dining room, which was closed off from an entrance hall by a curtain. Glowing with pride at the statesmanlike qualities of his master, the secretary told us that, after the death of his father, Chang Hsueh-liang had trouble with several of his father's influential generals. They were hesitant to accept the new leadership. The Young Marshal had therefore invited them to a feast at his home to talk matters over. The feast had just begun when the Young Marshal was called out of the room. When the curtains parted again, it was not for his return but rather for his guards, who machine-gunned the guests to death. Thus were his political problems solved.

We were still awaiting the arrival of Chang—who turned out to be playing golf—and I found myself wandering in a rose garden outside the house. A particularly nice specimen a few feet off the path caught my eye and as I stepped in to examine it more closely, I heard a sharp cry behind me. Turning quickly, I saw someone rushing forward and urgently gesturing me to stop moving. No harm was done. But there might have been, had it not been for the ever-vigilant eyes of the guard. Just beyond the rose ran a line of electrified wires designed to protect the ruler from unwelcome intruders.

Chang finally arrived, greeted us cordially and we all moved into that terrifying dining room. We sat at a large round table in the center of which was placed the food. We realized that our behavior in high Chinese society was about to be tested and that leaving the path between the dishes and our plates clean would indicate that we had not liked the food. We passed the test. The food, which included the northern specialty of steamed bread, was excellent and sufficiently drippy to leave ample evidence of our appreciation.

The next day, we boarded a train for Peking, which we reached after a short stopover in the port of Tientsin. Everything in Peking was strange, interesting, exciting. I don't ever remember being so keyed up by a new experience. It was so exhilarating that I felt I could not absorb enough. The Forbidden City was then closed; I suspect that the interior was falling into disrepair under an administration that had no time for nor interest in such cultural luxuries. Nevertheless, a great deal of the city could be seen from the outside. Several times I arose very early in the morning just to walk around it. I had been to Paris, London, Berlin and Venice, but none of the palaces or castles I had seen approached the dignity and magnificence of this monument.

That first visit to Peking gave me a good political lesson. We were taken directly from the railway station to the Wagon-Lits Hotel, a comfortable place but situated within high walls and with an entrance protected from the rest of the city. I was aware of the reason for this, including the Boxer Rebellion and the antiforeign feeling, but I felt that those sentiments should be part of the long-ago past. In 1929 what kept running through my head was that some Westerners felt that they deserved to be isolated and quarantined from the inferior Chinese. I was embarrassed at living apart from the people I had come to visit. But as far as I knew, there was then no other way for a foreign traveler to stay in the city. I did better on my next visit.

After only a few days in Peking we returned to Japan to attend the IPR conference, which I will discuss in a later chapter, but for the moment I will stay with our travels, which next took Betty and me to the Philippines.

On the way our boat stopped off in Shanghai, where we picked up mail and messages. There was a cable for me: "Harvard won, love, Mama." It was obvious that Yale had once again bit the dust, but the message gave me a great opportunity to tease my mother. I cabled back: "Whom did they beat? Love, Freddy."

Paul Scharrenberg, the secretary-treasurer of the California State Federation of Labor, an active member of the IPR for many years, had brought to the organization's attention a potentially dangerous situation which was developing over the immigration of Filipino male workers into the mainland United States. He suggested that the IPR investigate the situation and publish the results so that the public would have the facts before trouble flared up. The crisis was close at hand because, in May 1928, Congressman R. J. Welch of California had introduced a bill calling for the exclusion of Filipinos from territories of the United States by the simple device of declaring them aliens, even though the Philippines were then an American colony.

The immigration had begun in noticeable volume a few years before World War I. It had started as a result of the alleged need of the Hawaiian sugar plantations to compensate for the loss to their labor supply caused by the Japanese government's voluntary restriction of Japanese migration to Hawaii. By the time our study started, there were about 75,000 Filipinos in Hawaii and about 69,000 on the mainland. Nine-tenths of the latter were young males.

A staff member of the American IPR, Bruno Lasker, was put in charge of the investigation and carried out the Hawaii and California portions. Betty and I were jointly assigned to cover the areas in the Philippines from which the migrants came. We were to look into their social and economic backgrounds and report on the incentives that were held out to them by the recruitors for the Hawaiian sugar barons as well as the dreams which grew from the often false and always exaggerated rumors of the quick riches to be found in the United States.

We reached Manila in early December 1929 and spent the next three months touring the island of Luzon. We visited the villages the migrants had left and wrote up our extensive notes in a fine hotel overlooking Manila Bay. This was the first piece of independent research that either of us had undertaken. As no one knew much about the subject, our instructions were no more specific than indicated in the above paragraph. We were on our own, not only in delineating our end of the work but also in finding out how to go about it.

We worked hard—and we also relaxed. A well-known archaeologist, Otley Beyer, soon befriended us and made some very helpful suggestions. His house was filled with artifacts; chairs, tables, and desks were covered with these archaeological remnants and the dust which they produced. Each object was carefully labeled with the stubs of trolley-car tickets as to type and provenance. Beyer explained that these stubs were the only paper he had been able to find which would survive the hot and humid climate for any length of time. But it was not in his house that he gave us most of his opinions and information. He did that sitting between us in the first row of the balcony of the leading vaudeville house, which he attended as regularly as a church-goer attends his place of worship. It seemed to be his one form of escape from his teaching duties at the university and his own investigations. That was fine with us, except that because the show changed only every six weeks, the ones we saw we got to know by heart. Betty had been to college with the daughter of Dwight Davis, the American governor-general of the islands and the donor of the Davis Cup. As a result, we enjoyed some country club favors from the Davises. They put us up over Christmas in Baguio, a resort town north of Manila. In those days it had nothing except a golf course, a modest wooden clubhouse, some bungalows and a village so inconspicuous that I remember nothing about it. That is the same Baguio where the world championship chess matches were played in 1978, a Baguio which, according to press accounts, now boasts fancy hotels and a convention center. Betty and I were the only outsiders in that "resort town" during Christmas of 1929. In Manila we were several times invited to attend parties at the officers' club on the American military base a short distance out of the city. From the attention Betty got, one would have thought she was the only attractive young woman to have visited the Islands in some time. After several of these parties, we dodged further invitations, because Betty didn't find dancing with the American generals and colonels at these bashes the pure joy they seemed to have found in her company.

We rented a car for the trip from Manila to the northern tip of Luzon and back. In those days one drove on the left-hand side of the road—the British imperialist had been the first and the most throughout the Far East—and that, together with the strange fact that the livestock preferred the paved highway to the green pastures, made the drive one thrill after another. The villages were interesting and the people, who spoke Tagalog with a little Spanish or English, were always cordial. School buildings were the newest and most conspicuous feature of the towns, a symbol of the American occupation replacing the church, the symbol of the previous Spanish rule. I don't know about the rest of the curriculum, but the English taught in those newfangled schools was wanting. It was explained to us that the original language teachers, from whom the present Filipino teachers had learned their English, were American soldiers who had remained after the seizure of the Islands at the beginning of the century. The vocabulary consequently included quite a few expressions not commonly heard in American living rooms.

The book which resulted from the investigations in California, Hawaii and the Philippines was published by the University of Chicago Press in 1931 under the title *Filipino Immigration to Continental United States and to Hawaii*. In the author's preface, Bruno Lasker wrote, "The field study was completed in the United States and Hawaii between November, 1929, and February, 1930; and significant additional data from the Philippines was contributed by Frederick V. Field, assistant secretary of the American Council of the IPR, and Mrs. Elizabeth Brown Field. . . ."

From the Philippines we returned to Shanghai. It was not a city in which to spend much time unless you had business there. It was a huge, crowded metropolis living off a large working class drawn from the countryside, living in slums, and paid literally starvation wages. I went back there two years later for another IPR conference, and having a job to do, I enjoyed it more, or perhaps I should say, I disliked it less.

We interrupted the Shanghai visit with a trip to Nanking, then the capital of China and 422 miles up the Yangtze River. We went armed with a letter of introduction to J. Lossing Buck, an expert on land utilization and a professor at the local missionary college. He received us cordially and filled us with information on the agricultural problems of the country. His wife was not downstairs to greet us, and he explained that she was busy in her study and would see us at lunch. At the meal, we learned that she had been working with her Chinese teacher, as she did every morning, over some writing she had undertaken. It was not until two or three years later with the publication of *The Good Earth* that I realized that Mrs. J. Lossing Buck was Pearl Buck and that she had been working on that very book when we made our visit.

That was my only visit to Nanking, though I very nearly had to make another on a delicate and sensitive diplomatic mission. In the fall of 1931, when I was in Shanghai with a large IPR delegation, it was suddenly brought to the attention of the officers of the organization that the annual celebration of the 1910 Revolution would take place in Nanking two days later. President Chiang Kai-shek would preside over ceremonies at the tomb of Sun Yat-sen, and distinguished foreigners were expected to attend. Our officers hurriedly made reservations on the night train to the capital while I remained at our Cathay Hotel headquarters in Shanghai. The next morning at breakfast I was handed a telegram from our chairman. Dated two hours earlier in Nanking, it said: "We have arrived but have forgotten to bring flowers to place on the tomb. As they cannot be bought here kindly purchase appropriate floral arrangement and get it to us by evening even if you have to bring it yourself." Buying the flowers was easy; getting out of making the trip myself was not. I had no desire to see Nanking again and even less to make the trip in the guise of flower boy. I could picture myself waiting some distance from the tomb with a huge bouquet in my arms until the band struck up "The Star-Spangled Banner" and then waiting for a signal from my chairman before rushing forward and handing him the offering. I figured that I was not being paid three hundred dollars a month, which in those days was a pretty good salary, to waste two days as a delivery boy. My Chinese colleagues fortunately came to the rescue. They found a young friend not only willing to make the trip but eager to do so in order to participate in the ceremony. The delegation thought the flowers very pretty.

It was on the earlier trip that Betty and I met George Sokolsky. He was editor of the *Far Eastern Review* and an advisor to T. V. Soong, the brother-in-law of Chiang Kai-shek and Chinese Secretary of the Treasury. The English-language journal was an authoritative reflection of British and American imperialist interests in Asia and was sponsored by the more important banks and commercial and industrial concerns. As an adviser to the financial cabal that controlled the country, Sokolsky was privy to the inside working of the Chiang-Soong-Kung group. That was an interesting family arrangement. President Chiang and Kung, who held various cabinet posts, were married to two of Soong's sisters. A third sister, the widow of Sun Yat-sen, broke with the plundering members of the family early on, became sympathetic to the revolutionary forces and after 1949 became Vice-President of the People's Republic.

For the few days of our stay in Shanghai, Betty and I put up at the Cathay Hotel, located a short distance from the Whangpoo River, which forms part of the great port. Between the hotel and the docks was the small park which became internationally notorious for the signs at its entrances: "No Dogs or Chinese Allowed." The signs might well have been put around the social life of visitors, for while the city was teeming with Chinese, foreigners came into contact only with the young "boys" who cleaned their hotel rooms and the young "boys" who served their meals or the human wrecks who pulled their rickshaws. Unless foreign visitors had some way to break down the barriers, they had no social contact with the Chinese. Betty and I were therefore greatly pleased to learn that Sok was married to a beautiful Chinese woman. He himself was round, whether viewed from the top, side or front, with a mop of tight curls over an intelligent if not handsome face. The couple made a striking contrast. During that visit, we began a friendship which was renewed a few years later when the Sokolskys left China and took up residence in the New York area.

That park with its "No Dogs or Chinese Allowed" sign was mentioned at a dinner party which I attended when I returned to Shanghai two years later. In Shanghai, like other colonies or semicolonies or, for that matter, wherever the class distinctions are great enough to allow the luxury of servants, the latter serve, among their other contributions, as a major topic of all conversations among their employers. At this particular party, the amahs—women whom foreigners hired to take care of their children—were spoken of in highly favorable terms. They took care of the white princes and princesses from the time the little ones woke up to the time they were tucked in at night and spent much of the daytime in that park with the offensive signs, where an exception was of course made for Chinese women caring for foreign infants. The hostess declared that her babies always seemed so content with the amahs. They never cried, never seemed restless. When she herself, due to some breakdown in the household, had to wheel the baby carriage to the park, the children were always whining and fussing. Several other mothers at the party chimed in, "How true, how true." At last, an elderly aunt or grandmother who had spent more years in Shanghai than the other women at the party, informed us that the cause of the amahs' competency had perhaps escaped the attention of the younger mothers; after all, they were extremely busy carrying out their housewifely duties, such as constantly negotiating in pidgin English with the "Number One Boys" who actually ran their households. The amahs, she explained, always carried with them a small pinch of opium. When the infants became troublesome, they would rub just a tiny bit of it under their noses. This kept the little darlings—and their mothers—quiet and contented.

The artificial life of foreigners in Shanghai, and in a few other ports of China, was politically based on the division of the city into two parts, the Chinese city over which the Chinese government exercised sovereignty, and the foreign concessions, where the foreigners held extraterritorial rights. Until 1943, when these rights were canceled, the foreign concession was subdivided into what was known as the French Concession and the International Settlement, the latter composed of what were formerly separate British and United States concessions. The great commercial enterprises, the broad streets, the transportation facilities, the urban services, the first- and second-class hotels were concentrated in the foreign concessions. The Chinese city was a jungle of filthy, narrow streets and hovels.

Again, as when we stayed in the Wagon-Lits Hotel in Peking, surrounded by high fences to keep unwanted Chinese out, I felt awkward and embarrassed in Shanghai. And my political education continued.

Betty and I began to feel that we were not seeing the real China. Living in a foreign compound in Peking and visiting international, foreign-dominated cities like Shanghai could hardly give us an accurate feeling for the country and its people. I sought out the American consul to ask his advice about traveling inland. He advised strongly against it, saying that the unsettled political situation in many parts of the country and the failure of the central government to exercise effective control made it dangerous for foreigners to wander outside the principal port cities. He warned especially against going west up the Yangtze further than Nanking. When I asked about the French railway that ran from Hanoi back into the province of Yunnan, he advised against that, too, but added that that particular area involved less risk than others if we insisted on traveling inland.

With that lack of encouragement, we took a ship to Hongkong and from there made a one-day excursion to Canton. There we bought a nice necklace of translucent amber and some decorated pewter, purchases which are still in the family.

Back in Hongkong, we arranged our trip to Indochina and China's southernmost province. We booked passage on a small French steamer that carried mail and freight down the coast as far as Singapore, stopping off at small ports as well as places that had no harbor and where passengers and cargo were unloaded by launch.

The ship offered three small cabins for passengers, the usual comfortable quarters for the captain, poorer ones for the lesser officers and squalid ones for the crew. We sailed late one afternoon and made our first intimate acquaintance with the ship a couple of hours later when we were served our first meal. It was excessively greasy and unappetizing and seemed even worse because only a few feet away the captain was enjoying what looked and smelled like a more than adequate supper. We were not the complaining sort, however, and continued to suffer by contrast throughout the journey. The second day we learned that the food for the captain's table was prepared by his own special cook, ours by someone who evidently had no culinary ambition.

We retired shortly after the first meal and went to sleep half-conscious that the boat had begun to rock and pitch. Not much later we were awakened by one of the weirdest noises I have ever heard, a persistent, agonizing, loud moaning or wailing. When we went out on the narrow deck corridor to investigate the source, we became acquainted with the ship's cargo. It consisted of as many water buffalo as could be fitted, like sardines in a can, but alive and standing up, on the open fore- and afterdecks one level below our quarters. They were seasick and complaining about it. They stayed with us until we left the ship at Haiphong; the poor animals never did adjust to life at sea.

At one of the stops we had several hours on shore. This was an island off Indochina on which the French maintained a penal colony. Although we did not enter the prison area, we got a long, close look at a hundred or so prisoners, with balls chained to their ankles, who were breaking up large rocks with heavy hammers. Surrounded by guards with rifles, they were working under a blistering sun on a slope that joined a beach to the higher land of the island. It is one thing to read about such penal colonies or to see them in movies; it is quite another to see one in real life.

Hanoi, a short train ride from the port of Haiphong, was a French town having its opera house, its hotel de ville, its plaza, fountains and flowers, its French hotel and smartly uniformed French officers walking the streets, followed at several paces by their betel-chewing Indochinese wives and a brood of children. That was the way the center of town looked at least. We were not, I suppose, intended to notice the chain gang cleaning the streets under the eyes and rifles of guards.

The outskirts of Hanoi were hovels and mud streets, open sewers and poverty. An imposing bridge had recently been erected to span the river that ran along the edge of the city. We stood for a long time at the town end of the bridge watching. Hundreds of peasants, nearly all women carrying heavy burdens on their backs, were crossing in our direction, and others, often men, were pushing or pulling larger loads on home-made carts. There were no cars or trucks. Upon reaching our end of the long bridge, the women put down their loads and, still standing, lifted their skirts and relieved themselves. We were told that before the bridge was built, the approach to the city was a much easier one over a low trestle just above the water. Now, however, the government forced everyone to use the bridge, and collected a tax from each.

The train from Hanoi to Yunnanfu (now Kunmin) ran on narrow-gauge tracks. It had no sleeping cars and no diner. The small cars were arranged with two rows of facing seats with a spittoon built into the floor between the seats. Four people thus occupied a set of seats, two facing two others, with the spittoon between them. At that time, white people were not very popular, whether in the French colony or in the interior of China. During the three days that Betty and I sat on one of those benches, the opposite one was occupied by Chinese or Indochinese who taunted us by spitting as close to our legs as possible while pretending to aim at that central receptacle. We felt helpless. We knew no Chinese. There was no way of saying, "Look, friends, we're on your side. We're not running dogs of imperialism."

In Indochina, the train ran only in daylight hours as a matter of security because there had been a number of night raids. Even for the daytime ride, the last car was filled with soldiers, just in case. We and the other bourgeois travelers spent the night in Indochina in a small French hotel within walking distance of the station. We were met at the train by a military escort and taken up a path fenced with barbed wire to the entrance to the hotel, the grounds of which were also protected by barbed wire. One got the impression, to put it mildly, that from the point of view of the natural inhabitants of Indochina, the French colonizers had not made a great success of things and were not popular. Anyone who visited the land when we did could not have been surprised at the subsequent history nor fail to be astounded at the utter stupidity of the American Establishment in trying to replace the French. John F. Kennedy and the others who were so responsible for getting the United States heavily committed must have been totally uneducated in the history, customs and beliefs of the people of southeastern Asia.

We spent the second night on the train, having by then crossed into China, and on the third day we reached Yunnanfu. The consul in Shanghai had told me that he would write the YMCA secretary, an American, in Yunnanfu telling him of our plans. On the train, Betty and I had decided that we would like to be on our own if that were possible, rather than find ourselves in another non-Chinese atmosphere. At the station we hired a conveyance—I don't remember whether it was rickshaw or carriage—and asked to be taken to an inn about which we had been told. Our language problem got in our way, and we found ourselves at the Seventh Day Adventists' compound instead. Someone there told the driver where we wished to be taken. When we finally arrived at the inn, Betty suggested that we unpack hurriedly to look convincingly settled before the missionary located us. By the time we had finished unpacking, Betty had found someone to take out our laundry. Immediately thereafter, the gentleman arrived, insisted we pack and accompany him to his house, where his wife awaited us. Not wishing to offend such kind people, we reluctantly gave up our plans for independence. A block from the inn, we passed my shirts already being scrubbed in the ditch, a combination of drain and sewer.

We spent several days sightseeing. One outing was unforgettable. On the outskirts of the city, we found ourselves looking into a long and wide valley, all of which was a glorious mass of color rising high on the mountains at either side. We had never seen such an extensive flower garden, nor have I ever seen one since. We did not need to be told what we were admiring. This vast acreage of poppies provided the economic basis of local power and corruption.

The evening before we were to leave, our hosts and ourselves got down to brass tacks about the missionary business. The YMCA man and his wife were sincere, unsophisticated people. They lived in a world that did not exist and were working earnestly toward a goal which they could not possibly achieve. The only way that the missionary had managed to attract and hold the attention of a handful of Chinese boys was through basketball. Years of effort and money had gone into building a headquarters and ball court which was occasionally used by a pathetically small number of local youth, after much persuasion. The ultimate purpose of the Christian missionary effort in China in those days was, as I observed it, to save Chinese youth from "godless communism"; and, of course, basketball under a foreign instructor who couldn't play very well himself built health, and health produced clean, unrevolutionary thoughts. It is extraordinary that the Chinese revolution succeeded against such odds.

We expressed our point of view that evening more delicately than I have here—at least I hope so. The next morning I woke up with a high fever, and instead of setting off for Hanoi, we stayed in the missionary's attic for several weeks. I had paratyphoid. The cause was not hard to determine. On our last day in Hanoi, I had stupidly drunk hot chocolate, which as everybody knows, or should know, can easily be made without boiling the water.

During our extended stay, our hosts, as a matter of courtesy and good politics and perhaps to keep a modest handout coming, received the local warlord, a nogoodnick, one of whose principal sources of income we had recently admired in that valley on the outskirts of the city. This annual event consisted of feeding him tea and cookies. Betty, who was eating with the family—there were also two small children—found herself listening in on the preparations for the visit. The conversation, some of which took place after the children had retired for the night, centered on whom the warlord would bring with him and what could be done about it. It was a conversation that must have taken place each year—with the same result. This ruler was an infidel, so far removed from being a Christian that he had a large number of concubines. Should a missionary and his wife, especially when the house was not large enough to keep the children away from the living room, welcome those loose women? If not, how could the warlord be informed that only he and his legitimate wife could be allowed to come? How could the good work continue if the warlord was offended?

The outcome was a complete surrender to local custom. The living room was arranged with the dining table in the center for the tea and cookies and an assortment of chairs lined up against the walls. The day came, the warlord arrived—and so did his wife and seven concubines. The latter, well-brought-up young ladies, demurely placed themselves on the chairs next to the wall, and there they remained. The guest of honor and his true wife communicated with the missionaries while Betty wondered what they said. In no time at all, the annual event was over.

The occasion was ludicrous and has to be reported in that fashion. But I have no wish to ridicule a well-meaning man and woman, for they were good people and generously took us into their home. They did not realize that their work was futile; they did not appreciate the absurdity of what they had been assigned to do. The fault and the blame lay not with them, but with the false concept of trying to convert people to ideas and practices completely foreign to their own cultures.

When my health improved, I started taking walks. I needed to get my leg muscles back in shape so that I could nimbly dodge the liquid darts that would be aimed at them on the return trip. I never felt so hated as in the streets of Yunnanfu. The people sicked dogs on us and shouted insults. On one walk that I took with the doctor, I asked him to translate what they were yelling. All of it was a variation on the theme of "running dog of an imperialist."

Weary of our overlong sojourn in Yunnanfu and of our pronounced unpopularity in its public places, we journeyed back to Peking.

11

More
of the Far East

Betty and I spent a month based in Jimmy Yen's home in Peking. It seemed to be a typical middle-class home with the rooms bordering a central patio. In order to enter the house, one first passed through the entrance gate and came face to face with a wall which was a little wider than the gate and blocked a direct line from street to patio. That wall kept out the evil spirits, which travel only in a straight line, unlike human beings, who can walk around a wall. On one side of the patio were the bedrooms, and opposite them the working quarters. Facing the entrance was a large family living room. Jimmy's wife, Alice, was the daughter of a foreign missionary and a Chinese woman, and she and Jimmy had three very young sons at the time of our visit.

They entertained us handsomely with sightseeing trips to the Summer Palace, Yenching University, the Peking Union Medical College, the famous "gates" or entrances to the city, an ancient Jewish synogogue and just the plain streets of this great metropolis. But we didn't visit the Great Wall. I am very aware of that omission because every visitor who has gone to China since the country has again been opened to foreign travel seems to have his or her picture taken at the Wall. On that visit it never occurred to us to go there, or perhaps a trip that far out of the city was then considered dangerous. We met some of the Yens' friends and colleagues, and on one special evening they invited musicians to play for us on ancient instruments with which we were completely unfamiliar.

I had never seen such poverty as was everywhere evident in Peking and the rest of China during that time. In fact, up to then, I had never been surrounded by poverty, smelled it, touched it, suffered because of it. As a child and a youth, I had seen it, without being too much aware of it, and it was not a subject that was discussed at home. Although everybody knew that it was nearby, we accepted it as part of the world we lived in. In my young days, there were no freeways or thruways or interstate highways in and out of New York City, so to get to Lake Mohegan or Lenox we drove through the center of Harlem. The buildings were old and unkept. The sidewalks and streets were littered with paper and garbage, and the tops of the buildings were lined with wash drying in the sun and soot. Women hung out of the windows just watching what was going on in the street below.

Harlem was a sharp contrast to the 645 Fifth Avenue area. Our sidewalks and the avenue were kept clean. Our laundry was dried—where? Nowhere that I ever went. My mother, Lord knows, never leaned over her windowsill to watch what was going on in Fifth Avenue. Nanan did not lean out of one of her windows to yell at my mother on the other side of the avenue.

Harlem was indeed a contrast, and obviously nearly all the people who lived there were poor. But I did not know then that many people lived in one room, that the plumbing hardly worked, that a great many were unemployed, that they leaned out of the window to turn their backs momentarily on what was behind them. I did not know much, if anything, about discrimination or segregation. I was not conscious of widespread malnutrition, of inferior schools, of police brutality or of rapacious landlords.

Poverty existed in New York, all right, but I lived far away from it. In Peking, or anywhere in the China of those days, you could not live remote from it. You lived with it and in the midst of it. And after a short while, you could not help but be constantly aware of it. Rickshaws were the basic means of transportation, but we were shocked by their inhumanity. The men, young and old, who pulled them until they became exhausted, were undernourished, sick human animals. When I had a chance to go to India a year or two later, I decided not to take the trip because I was horrified at the thought of seeing more poverty on such a scale.

One of the most interesting events of those weeks in Peking started out unpleasantly. Jimmy had told us that a dinner was to be given in our honor by a former prime minister of China under the dowager empress. two decades before, the last imperial court of the Manchu dynasty had been overthrown and with it the boy emperor, Pu Yi, and the elderly dowager empress, Tz'u Hsi, who actually exercised the power. In 1910 Sun Yat-sen, a liberal, socialist-oriented Cantonese who had been educated abroad, launched China on the road to independence and modernization, but his presidency lasted only forty-three days. He was succeeded by a conservative, opportunistic bureaucrat, Yuan Shih-kai. The decade from 1912 to 1922 was marked by political fragmentation of the nation under regional warlords. Chiang Kai-shek then emerged as leader of the Kuomintang, the revolutionary political organization founded by Sun Yat-sen. With financial and military help from the Soviet Union, Chiang partly subdued the warlords and unified the country to some extent. Before Sun died, in 1925, he had proclaimed the "Three Principles of the People"—nationalism, democracy and improvement of the people's livelihood—as the basic creed of the Kuomintang. But Chiang postponed, delayed and put off its implementation on one pretext after another while he and his colleagues in the central government ransacked the nation for their own benefit. That situation, worsened, of course, by the Japanese invasion and World War II, lasted until the success of what is known as the Chinese Liberation under Communist leadership in 1949.

The party in our honor was to be held in the Western Hills not far from the city. We left for the occasion by car and reached the hills just as dusk was falling. There we found waiting for us sedan chairs, one for each of us, and each manned by four carriers (they were called coolies). I didn't like the idea and told Jimmy that Betty and I were quite capable of walking up the hill; indeed, we would enjoy doing so. No, he explained, we were in China, and it would be misunderstood if we showed our disapproval of this custom. So we climbed into our chairs, and four attendants carried each of us up the long steep climb at a dogtrot. The surprising smoothness of the ride occupied my attention. There was hardly any motion inside the sedan. The carriers chanted a complicated rhythm that kept each out of step with the others, thus giving the passenger the feeling that he was gliding uphill. This is not as easy to accomplish as it sounds. Imagine that four friends go out for a walk and try to establish and maintain a rhythm whereby each puts his right foot down out of step with the other three. I don't believe it can be done without a chant that enables each walker to keep to his separate beat. On my next visit to Shanghai, I one day heard a loud commotion outside my room at the Cathay Hotel and looked out to see several score of men carrying a huge load of silver bullion. They supported this burden by a complicated system of interwoven poles which rested on their shoulders. They were jogging in such a complex broken rhythm that there was practically no motion to the cargo except for a smooth forward movement.

The former prime minister's party turned out to be a sixty-four course feast, which was the highest culinary honor that could be offered a guest. In old China feasts were built in multiples of eight, so that, depending on the importance of the event, eight, sixteen, thirty-two or sixty-four courses were served. No one was expected to eat all of them. A newcomer, especially if he was to be the guest of honor, learned that he should eat and enjoy the main courses, which fell on the multiples of eight, that he should at least nibble at the minor climaxes of the meal, the multiples of four, and that with the other courses he might do what he pleased. Keeping track of where you are during the meal is not as difficult as it might seem. Several courses are served at the same time; and numbers eight and twelve, for instance, are easy to distinguish from nine, ten and eleven, which are plainly side dishes. However, a sixty-four-course feast is undeniably a formidable undertaking, the staggering statistics of which are forgotten in the visceral joys of the world's most delectable cooking.

The feast given by the elderly former prime minister and his wife was something entirely new in my experience. Our host did us a very great honor because, he said, I had helped Yen Yang-chu on his recent visit to my country. Nothing like that had ever happened to me before. I had felt, as I still do, that having the opportunity to work for such an important objective and for such a fine man was an extraordinary privilege. The honor was unexpected, and I was deeply moved.

After that first feast in the Western Hills, Jimmy whispered to me that the host was going to present me with a small gift that I was to take back to the United States. The old gentleman made what sounded like a flowery speech. Jimmy translated, I should say, a tenth of it, and the prime minister handed me two large scrolls. They were superb examples of the portraits of provincial governors, ministers and other leading bureaucrats that were painted around the end of the eighteenth century. One portrait depicts a kindly looking, elderly man who, as indicated by the number of claws on the dragon which decorates his clothing, had the rank of provincial governor. The other picture is of a sharp-featured, domineering woman who must once have made the life of some high official miserable. (Experts who have examined the two portraits believe that the victim was not the amiable dignitary of the other portrait.) These fine paintings I had framed, contrary to the Chinese custom, and they now hang behind my chair in our dining room. I gave them, along with other Asian art, to Nieves, my present wife, when we were married. Her children by a previous marriage were then very young, and as a foreigner recently come to Mexico, I must have seemed very foreign to them indeed. Teasingly, I told the children that the old lady and gentleman were my grandparents, a bit of misinformation which confused them for some time. They still refer to the old Chinese bureaucrats as *los abuelos*.

This feast in the Western Hills was a sober occasion. A less sedate feast, at which I was again guest of honor, was given on my next visit to Shanghai by the young secretaries of the Chinese branch of the IPR. Staff members of some of the other IPR councils were also invited to this stag party. I remember a fairly long table seating, I should say, five on each side and two at each end; that is, some fourteen guests in all. While the food was straight out of heaven, what was particularly memorable about the feast was the wine with which we washed it down. It was on the table as we sat down, and it was replenished as rapidly as we spilled it down our throats. I was quick to learn what was expected of me. I had first to go around the table, greet each guest and *gam-bie* (bottoms up) with him. That amounted to thirteen drinks. Upon resuming my seat, I was expected to respond in the same manner to each toast offered to me. That friendly form of inter-communication lasted throughout the lengthy meal. Chinese wine is served in small porcelain cups that are lifted to the mouth with the thumb on the rim and the forefinger supporting the underside. (There are no handles.) Small the cups undeniably are, but when you multiply small by thirty, forty, or forty-five—though who could count at that stage?—the intake is considerable. I managed to uphold my honor and that of American youth—but only just.

Some distance from Peking the Mass Education Movement had an experimental center where theories and methods were tried out among a group of villages. Jimmy wanted to take us there. The five of us, Jimmy and two of his colleagues and Betty and I, boarded an early-morning train for the trip south to Paoting, in Hopei province, and from there went due west on donkeys. We dressed alike in long blue Chinese gowns, but there the likeness ended. The compactly built Chinese looked well and comfortable. And Betty looked as though the clothes had been invented for her. But as for the author of this tale! I was thin, long and gangly. I had red hair, and the color of my skin and eyes was all wrong, to say nothing of the contours of my angular New England head.

In a short time we were out of town and passing through flat, dry agricultural country occasionally interrupted by small, poor villages. Jimmy had explained to us that no missionaries or other foreigners had been in this part of China for at least a couple of generations. His warning was soon proved to have been not in vain. We passed through the first village and aroused nothing more than a great deal of curiosity and considerable laughter. But on approaching the next village, we noticed children's heads suddenly bobbing above the crops as they rushed to get there before we did. When we arrived, the one street, along which we were to pass, was lined with every adult who was not out in the fields and dozens of children. The latter were convulsed with laughter. It is fairly hard to keep one's dignity while riding a donkey in any case, and to do so under those circumstances was impossible. I have had a special place in my heart for Chinese children ever since.

Once we were on the other side of the village I began an inquiry I pursued relentlessly for the several days it took to get an answer. What, specifically, was there about me that had given those kids such fits? I assumed, I told them, it was all those qualities so un-Chinese which I exemplified. I was too tall, I had that ridiculous hair and skin, I was hopelessly awkward as a donkey jockey, and my eyes were blue. My friends were polite and evasive. I pleaded with them, in the interests of international relations, to tell the truth. Finally, after several days, they did, and the answer surprised me. The features I had mentioned were strange to our Chinese audience, it was true, but the particular feature that had set off the explosion of mirth were my eye sockets, which are set deep in my skull. Then I understood. To us the Chinese are conspicuous for what we call their slant eyes, though that is not really what we mean. The distinguishing characteristic is that their eyes are much nearer the surface of their faces. If a ruler is laid across the bridge of a Chinese nose, it will almost touch the surface of the eyes on either side. Our eyes, set in the hollows of our skull—often under bushy eyebrows—seem particularly strange to the Chinese. I must confess that, until that trip in Hopei, this had never occurred to me.

Another experience in a somewhat larger village, a sort of county seat, has been shared by travelers in every part of the world. Jimmy told us as we approached the village that we were going to stop for a while because the village elders wished to greet us. He said we would be offered tea and that it would be discourteous to refuse it. The water, however, was polluted, and there was no way to know whether it had been boiled sufficiently (or at all) in preparing the brew. Under no circumstances were we to drink it. With these contradictory instructions in mind, we were ushered into what must have been the town hall. The elders greeted us simply and politely and asked if we would not share with them a cup of tea to honor the occasion of our visit to their region. By gestures and smiles we conveyed our delight, and the tea was handed to us. Betty had meanwhile spotted a couple of potted plants and I an open window, and we maneuvered toward these disposal points. That, our friends assured us as we rode out of town, resolved the contradiction. We thus had our tea and didn't drink it.

During all this time, during our stay at the Yen home, during the journey we undertook, as well as while we were working together in the United States, Jimmy was educating me in the problems of the Chinese language, the central core of his work. While I never learned to speak Chinese or recognize more than a handful of characters, I did acquire some understanding of the immensity of the problem. A great many years later, when I was working on the identification of pre-Hispanic symbols, my acquaintance with Chinese characters helped me to approach the task with some foreknowledge, and, vice versa, what I learned from the Mexican symbols amplified my earlier contact with Chinese ideographs.

The Chinese written language contains some 50,000 characters. Some of these are pictographs, which are more or less recognizable depictions of the objects they represent. Others are ideographs, which are more abstract and represent ideas and concepts. Ideographs are not phonetic; they express no sound. According to *Webster's New International Dictionary*, they symbolize "directly the idea of a thing and not the name of it." There are also compound ideographs and phonetic compounds; one part determines the meaning, and the other gives a clue to the pronunciation.

Learning to read the Chinese characters requires the student to train himself to absorb instantly a complex of lines or strokes. The strokes seldom exceed twenty, but in at least one instance a single character involves sixty-four. If the student is to become a scholar he must also learn to read the different calligraphies which have developed over the ages. These vary from delicate to bold penmanship, from slanted to square handwriting and from clear, meticulous renditions of each character to a fast-running style. Fine calligraphy is a form of art; many of the most valued scrolls of the past preserve the writing of great calligraphers.

To further complicate the spread of reading and writing, there was only a vague relation between spoken and written Chinese. For something like ten centuries the spoken language continued to change, to develop in terms of vocabulary and pronunciation, with marked regional differentiation, while the written language retained its original form. The separation between written and spoken Chinese became more and more of a problem, for the written language remained virtually static and the spoken language developed regional differences of such importance that there was no longer one national language spoken by all Chinese.

Before the liberation of 1949 the Chinese masses had neither the leisure nor the opportunity to memorize the thousands of characters necessary to become literate in the written language. Only the sons—not the daughters— of the rich and powerful could devote the years required to learn to read and write. Government officials and scholars were therefore chosen from the ranks of those privileged few, and literacy became an important tool of the ruling classes. The perpetuation of illiteracy was, conversely, a means of prolonging the *status quo*.

Two of the major accomplishments of the People's Republic of China— long after my original visit there—have been virtually to wipe out illiteracy and to unify the spoken language. To facilitate the teaching of Mandarin or, as it is called in China, p'u-t'ung-hua, a latinized alphabet has been adopted to supplement the characters. The latinized written language has also facilitated scientific research and other modern pursuits requiring linguistic precision. The old characters, moreover, have been reduced in number—in much the same way that Yen's Mass Education Movement did so in the 1920s—and the number of strokes required to write many characters has been reduced.

When Betty and I were visiting Yen in 1930, I had absolutely no idea that a revolution would change the whole Chinese situation during my lifetime. But I had already begun to think about the language problem in political terms. I could not see much chance for the success of the Chinese Mass Education Movement in a country ruled by an unenlightened dictator who in turn was kept in power by a combination of foreign interests and the most reactionary and corrupt internal elements. Because it is much more difficult to exploit a literate population than an illiterate one, mass education is the enemy of oppression. A regime such as Chiang Kai-shek's thus found itself confronting a dilemma. A certain degree of industrialization and modernization was not only inevitable because of China's exposure to outside influences but also essential to the well-being of the ruling class. You have to feed a cow in order to milk it. Even corrupt officials starve unless there is economic activity from which they can steal their percentage. The other side of the dilemma was that a nation cannot modernize and industrialize without increasing the degree of literacy and other forms of education among its population. A complicated piece of machinery cannot be produced or made to run with ignorant labor. A modern banking system cannot be operated with illiterate clerks.

The compromise that is usually reached under such circumstances is to educate just enough to permit a certain amount of economic growth, but not enough to let the population get politically out of hand.

As the name of his organization implied, Jimmy Yen intended to take a massive step toward eliminating illiteracy. I believed that he would be allowed to set up a pilot experiment, to bring lots of dollars to China and to promote reforms that would impress foreigners and some of the Chinese intelligensia. But I did not believe that the movement would be allowed to spread far and wide or to gain more than token political and financial support from a regime like the one that then ruled China.

Although Jimmy and I disagreed on this issue, we never pressed our disagreement. He felt that the purpose of his movement was so obviously good that its growing circle of supporters was bound to prevail against the reactionary elements. I was skeptical.

My second visit to Asia, to which I have already referred, took place in the early fall of 1931 when the IPR was to hold another of its biennial international conferences. This one was to be in Hangchow, a famously beautiful city southwest of Shanghai. Because of the Sino-Japanese situation, the site was shifted to Shanghai at the last moment.

Edward Carter and a number of the delegates from the United States and Great Britain were again traveling via Europe and the Soviet Union while I was instructed to cross the Pacific with another group. We planned to meet on September 19 in Mukden and from there proceed to Hangchow. We could not have picked a more extraordinary date for our rendezvous.

The boat trip across the Pacific was then one of the world's greatest pastimes. Although the passenger ships were neither as large nor as luxurious as were those plying the Atlantic, they were comfortable and offered badminton and Ping-Pong, mediocre food and a well-stocked bar, and endless time. A passenger could end a trip better educated from a couple of hundred hours' reading, fully rested from long sleeps, far better acquainted with ship mates or a combination of the three.

The day before landing at Yokohama, I was given the task of preparing suitable remarks for my superiors to make to the Japanese newspaper correspondents who we supposed would board the boat when it docked. I put together a few fatuous sentences and passed them around. Sure enough, a number of reporters came on board and asked for the IPR delegation which was waiting for them in the lounge. The reporters looked around and not finding the one person for whom they were looking, asked, "Where is Mr. Johnson?" I found him in a corner talking to some non-IPR passengers and told him the newspapermen wanted to talk to him. They greeted him, "Mr. Johnson, sir, welcome to Japan. Would you be so kind as to compose a short poem for us expressing your feelings upon arriving in Japan for the first time?" They paid no attention to anybody else. They were interested only in James Weldon Johnson, the secretary of the National Association for the Advancement of Colored People, a well-known poet, and the only black among us. In a matter of minutes he gave them a few lines, very much in the Japanese-Chinese style, which appeared on the front pages of the Tokyo press the next morning.

One of the junior members on the trip was a young woman named Ellen Auchincloss whose name appeared in the Social Register. Although she did not actually belong to the IPR group, we included her in all our social activities. She was making her first trip to China to spend a year with Jimmy Yen as his English-language secretary. Needing an assistant to maintain and expand the contacts we had made together in 1928-29, he had somehow found this young lady to volunteer a year's work.

Just about all of Ellie's qualities were in her favor. She was able, an attractive companion, and eagerly looking forward to China and the job. The only problem—for me, that is—was that Ellie was traveling with a dog, or what she said was a dog. It was easier to believe her than to figure out what else the animal might be. It was about the size of a Chihuahua but also kind of shaggy. Looking back, I'm sure that it belonged to the canine social register.

The reason that I am still complaining about the dog at this late date is that, in those days before women's liberation, Jimmy had written to tell me about Ellie and to ask me to see that she reached Peking safely. He had not mentioned that there would be anyone or anything else in the party. I figured then, and still do decades later, that traveling is complicated enough without thinking up ways to make it more so. Be that as it may, we three social registerites got along famously and together observed the beginning of World War II in Asia.

The rest of the party was going directly to Shanghai by boat from Japan. Ellie and what's-his-name and I were headed for Mukden, where we were to join up with the Carter group and from there go by train to Peking. At that time, the way to get from Japan to Mukden was to ferry across from Shimonoseki, Japan, to Pusan, Korea, and then travel north-northwest through the length of Korea, which was then one nation, to the Manchurian border and then another hundred and thirty-five miles to Mukden.

We journeyed through Korea during the daylight hours of September 18, passed through the northern part of that county and into Manchuria during the night and arrived in Mukden on the morning of September 19. That same evening and night the Japanese army invaded Manchuria and seized Mukden. Historically, that date marks the beginning of World War II in Asia. It is said, and there is much evidence to support it, that neither Emperor Hirohito nor his civilian government knew their troops had invaded China's Manchurian provinces until they heard about it the next day. The Japanese Army apparently acted on its own and presented the Emperor and foreign powers with a *fait accompli* the following day.

Ellie, the mutt and I were certainly aware of what was going on. We hardly slept that historic night. During the early hours of the evening, the Japanese train officials had been getting messages from their military to check and recheck the train's passengers and contents. Since we were the only Westerners on board, we naturally got special attention. Ellie and I were sharing a compartment—most decorously I wish to point out—I in the upper and she in the lower berth. (I forget where Fido laid his cute little head.) Not a half hour passed without the officials, usually in pairs, entering our quarters to see if they could figure out why we were following so closely on the heels of the invading army.

I had a regular U.S. passport. It read "No. 72005—Passport—United States of America Department of State." On the next page appeared the seal of the Department of State and my name. Somehow or other the train bureaucrats got it into their heads that I was an official representative of the U.S. Department of State, and that could only mean that that clever Uncle Sam had known all about the invasion, even if Hirohito hadn't. Presumably I was a government agent, disguised as a dog fancier, already rushing in to put myself in the thick of it. A dirty, though ingenious piece of business. And very embarrassing to the Japanese military. So we never really got to sleep that night.

It is extraordinary that the train went through on schedule and that we remained on it to our destination. We arrived in Mukden at exactly the day and hour we had planned on months before in New York. The station was in turmoil. The people knew that the Japanese had taken the city and were rapidly spreading out through the region, but they didn't know why or exactly what was happening. Would the Chinese put up resistance? How and when?

Not knowing what we would find in the streets, Ellie and I and our colleague decided to sit on our baggage in the waiting room and see what happened. We didn't wait long. Carter and his group, having arrived earlier that morning from the north, showed up after first looking for us at the hotel we had previously designated.

Then we did something we all regretted later. The Carter party had in tow a Chinese who had some connection with the Young Marshal Chang Hsueh-liang, whom we had met two years before. This Chinese, in the military and political whirlwind of that September morning, hadn't made up his mind as to which side his bread was buttered on. Being an opportunist and aware that the Japanese army had taken the city, and seeing no Chinese resistance, he opted to tie Japanese flags to the windshields of the two cars he had hired for us. And so we ventured forth. Twice we were stopped by bewildered and angry students. We felt acutely embarrassed that we had mistakenly accepted the protection of the Japanese flag.

When word got to us at the hotel that a train would be leaving for Peking the next day and that reservations had been made for our party, we left.

The fact that our two groups had met on schedule, that we had encountered no major personal incidents during our twenty-four-hour stay in Mukden and that we had been able to leave for Peking on a functioning train was nearly unbelievable. As I look back on those events now, they seem even more so.

The events of September 18 had been triggered by an incident of incredible triviality. An explosion which had taken place a short distance north of Mukden had cracked the fishplate at the junction of two rails, damaged the rail flange for two feet on each side of the junction and knocked a few splinters off a wooden sleeper. The damage was so slight that shortly thereafter a train was able pass the spot at normal speed. The incident was obviously provoked by the Japanese themselves to give them the excuse to occupy the entire area in "self-defense." The Japanese aggression against China, which started that night in Manchuria, soon spread to Shanghai, then to all of North China and back again to the central part of the country. The bombing of Pearl Harbor spread it throughout southeast Asia. The aggression was not stopped until fourteen years after the so-called Manchurian incident, by which time millions of lives had been sacrificed.

On the return trip from the IPR conference in Shanghai, a large number of delegates from the United States, Canada and Great Britain stopped off in Tokyo for about ten days. Our visit happened to coincide with the Emperor's annual garden party, to which influential Japanese and foreigners were invited. Our entire IPR crowd, including their humble secretary, received elegant invitations, embossed with the imperial emblem, a sixteen-petaled chrysanthemum. Only the Emperor was entitled to use the emblem of a chrysanthemum with so many petals. But I never learned whether he grew in his garden special chrysanthemums having the same number of petals—I did not attend the party. The men in our delegation had instructed me to carry out the important job of renting them the formal wear required to gain entrance to the Emperor's garden. This I did with excellent results: sleeves and trousers were invariably too short or too long. I was later informed that several delegates were happy when the occasion and the discomfort ended. One, however, was pleased to discover that in the inside back of his frock coat had been sewn a large linen square on the top left of which was written "date" and on the top right "wearer." Several VIP names were filled in, the last of which was Charles A. Lindbergh.

That mission accomplished, I went off for a three-day holiday to Nara, one of Japan's famous resorts. I didn't like formal parties, I didn't like getting dressed up like a damn fool, and I didn't like wearing a rented suit, even if the Czar of All the Russias had worn it before me.

On the second day of my vacation, I was reading in the inn's beautiful garden when two uniformed men stepped up and asked to speak to me. After the usual identifications, they asked me if I would be so kind as to hand them my invitation to the Emperor's garden party. I explained that I couldn't because I didn't have it. Where was it? Flustered, I said I didn't know. I must have thrown it away or lost it.

Things looked quite bad at that point. My interrogators informed me that this was a very serious matter. Invitations to the Emperor's garden party were not exactly invitations, they were commands. If because of some unusual circumstance (what circumstance except death would keep anyone from such a privileged occasion?) the invited person could not attend, he was obliged to return the invitation. I apologized. I had not known the customs of the country, I said, and had no wish to insult anyone, to say nothing of the Emperor himself. I hoped they would forgive me. I doubt that they did, but they did not bother me any more.

I lower my eyes as I inform my readers that, on returning to Tokyo, I found the invitation in some luggage I had left behind, and by then, realizing I possessed a collector's item, I kept it. It remained in my files for years. I do not know how much continuity exists in whatever Japanese agency takes care of matters of this sort, but in case that invitation is still on some list of the missing—and in order to prevent a search being made of my house after my confession—I hereby declare on my honor that somewhere in my peregrinations the invitation was finally and forever lost.

12

The Institute
of Pacific Relations

When Jimmy Yen went back to China at the end of the 1928-29 winter, I began to work full time for the IPR. This job occupied me until the fall of 1940 and took me on the long Asian trips that I have described, although with only passing reference to the organization, in the two previous chapters. I must now describe the organization itself.

Until I began the IPR job, I had not experienced the discipline of office work, of regular hours, of finding my place among a small but well-prepared staff or of learning what was expected of me. I also did not know much about the outfit that had employed me. Can any one forget the nervousness and uncertainties of the first days of his first job? I was as jittery as any young person on his first regular job and worried that that nice man, Edward Carter, would suddenly realize that hiring me had been a mistake. I did not even know how to write a business letter, because I had never written one before. And although I had learned a little about the IPR during those months with Yen, I did not know enough to function responsibly. While the organization had only a few other staff members in those early days, they knew how to type and draft letters or how to research or write. What did they think of this inexperienced young man whom the boss had suddenly brought into the organization? Would they accept him, teach him the ropes and help him through those first weeks?

The job worked out well. I got all the friendly help and encouragement anyone could ask for. I was broken in to the routines of office work and the subject matter and methods of the IPR in the pleasantest possible way. Our small 1929 group became a closely knit staff that worked together for the next eleven years. It formed the nucleus of a constantly growing organization as the troublesome years of the 1930s came and passed.

I was an IPR staff member or member of the executive committee of its

116

board of trustees until 1947. It was through that organization and Yen Yang-chu that I became interested in and then acquainted with Asia. When the bad times of the McCarthy era arrived, I became a conspicuous figure in the controversy that engulfed the IPR and that eventually led to the organization's demise in 1961. I will always consider it to be one of the most extraordinary private institutions that existed in the United States during a good part of my adult life. It was the principal focus of my nonpolitical activity. In spite of the publicity given my political life, I can report that during the turbulent decade of the thirties I devoted much more time to the IPR than I did to all my political interests put together.

One grim consequence of my association with the IPR was that it brought into focus a strange aspect of my relation with my father. He never recognized that I had a job, perhaps because he didn't believe that a young man of my social position should work. The fact that for the first eleven years of my association with the IPR I was a paid employee and for the last half of that period the top staff officer of its American branch was never acknowledged by my father. He never telephoned me at my office; for all I know, he didn't even know where it was. He never spoke of my work or asked me questions about it. I took several trips to China and Japan, spent three months in the Philippines researching a book, wrote one myself and edited another, but not one of these subjects ever came up in our conversations. His notion of a suitable life for me, I imagine, was to follow in his tracks, skipping, of course, the few years when he worked as an engineer before his entrance into the Vanderbilt clan. He lost out by never becoming acquainted with my work, for I had a fascinating job.

The IPR deserves full and fair study by historians, which it has not yet received. There have been several doctoral theses written on aspects of the organization's work as well as on the treatment it got from hysterical red-baiters in and out of government. For a deliberately biased account, the inaccuracies and prejudices of which are a historical tragedy, the reader can refer to the 226-page report of the Senate Subcommittee on Internal Security of the Senate Committee on the Judiciary on its hearings of 1951-52. It is a disgrace to the Senate of the United States. It is a travesty of democracy.

In 1974 the University of Washington Press published *The Institute of Pacific Relations—Asian Scholars and American Politics* by John N. Thomas. The flyleaf calls it a "sober and sensible account," and I think that that was its aim. It has one nasty bit (Thomas repeats the filthy story about me that originated in that Lucius Beebe column to which I have already referred), and several nice passages about me. Although I can quarrel with a number of statements and assertions, Thomas's book is, on the whole, a decent academic attempt to analyze some of IPR history. It focuses on internal frictions which developed within the organization and on the attacks made upon it by outside political forces intent upon finding a scapegoat for the victory of the revolutionary forces in China. As the author is the first to admit, it is not a definitive history of the IPR. While it refers to the Institute's abundant research and educational output, it does not pretend to describe it.

The IPR also issued its own reports and publications. They are available in many of the country's larger university and public libraries. In 1977, thirty years after resigning from the organization, I found 547 entries in the New York Public Library card catalogue under "IPR."

The full history of the IPR has yet to be written. Before Asian centers were established in our larger universities, the IPR was virtually alone in stimulating research in the problems of the Pacific area. Every two years it brought together prominent scholars, businessmen and political leaders from all the countries of the Pacific and from those countries having interests therein for frank discussion of their mutual affairs. It also experimented with methods now widely employed in teaching Chinese and Russian and by every means within its grasp tried to overcome the ignorance about each other of the nations and peoples in and bordering the Pacific Ocean.

Its accomplishment in all these directions was impressive. In the United States alone, much of the current work of scholars and teaching and research centers in regard to Asian affairs has its origins in work done by the IPR decades ago.

In the unusually interesting history *The Rockefellers* by Peter Collier and David Horowitz, the IPR is twice referred to incorrectly as the Institute *for* Pacific Relations. While the IPR certainly hoped for peace, it was not a pacifist organization, as implied by the error. The correct name is the Institute *of* Pacific Relations, the word "pacific" referring to the area of and surrounding the Pacific Ocean. IPR was an unofficial body established to promote the cooperative study of their mutual relations by the peoples of and concerned with that area.

Perhaps it goes without saying that my autobiography is not the appropriate place for a history of the IPR, and I am certainly not the right person to write such a book. The Institute's story and my own were interwoven for a good many years because I was one of a number of persons who associated with it from its early days through its period of growth and influence. The same political factors which separated me from the IPR eventually caused its dissolution. Some doubtless think that I played a considerable role in its downfall. Someone who can stand off and take an architectonic look at the organization must write its history.

I began my IPR work a few months before it held its second biennial conference in Kyoto. One of the world's most charming cities, Kyoto had been the political capital of Japan for a thousand years, until Tokyo assumed that function in the middle of the nineteenth century. Although it is located only twenty-six miles from the huge industrial complex of Osaka, Kyoto remained the cultural capital. While I was there for three weeks, I was so occupied in conference work that I saw too little of its temples, palaces and crafts. I did manage, however, to get lost one night and thus indulged in some involuntary sightseeing.

One of the IPR's most pleasant aspects was the conviviality of the staff which came together during the conferences. We were all in our twenties and enjoying that age in the relative calm and prosperity of the 1920s. We were all exploring the world intellectually and physically, and perhaps it was natural that we found each other interesting and congenial. We had strong and curious stomachs for the gastronomic pleasures of other cultures and took delight in washing them down following local custom. It was not unusual, then, that one evening a bunch of us, Chinese, Japanese, British and Americans, should explore Kyoto, find a fine restaurant and relish several hours of pure joy. For some reason which I do not remember, I found myself alone some time after midnight in the nearly deserted streets of this large city. Because I knew that a trolley-car line passed near our hotel, I jumped on the first one that came my way. As it gathered an unbelievable speed in no time at all, I realized that I must have made a mistake, because no trolley ever moved so quickly. Instead of boarding a trolley, I had taken one of the rapid-transit vehicles to the neighboring city of Osaka. With a friendly assistance of some Japanese who spoke not a word of English, I somehow got back to the conference hotel in time to bathe and appear as a bright young secretary at next morning's breakfast.

My job as assistant to Carter put me in touch with every aspect of the organization's work. The conferences themselves were highly organized round-table discussions that lasted for two weeks. Elaborate preparations for them were required, and the Kyoto meeting would be the first test of the IPR's ability to fulfill those requirements, for it was still a very new organization. It had been founded in Honolulu in 1926 by a group of YMCA-oriented individuals financed by and dependent upon sugar-plantation wealth. Their original idea—a pleasant but ineffectual one—was that putting a bunch of well-washed people around a table to discuss Filipino contract labor or Japanese immigration into American territory or extraterritorial rights in China would result in something beneficial to mankind. The trouble with the idea was that many, if not most, of the participants in the discussion would be ignorant of the facts and opinions involved and would therefore simply speak their biases and prejudices. I don't mean to knock the idea too hard, because it actually developed into a very worthwhile project. I had the good fortune to come on to the scene just when this development was taking place.

Edward Carter, who also came out of the YMCA, pushed more than anyone else for a program that would provide round-table discussion with a foundation of pertinent research and fact-finding. Carter's views prevailed, although not without some long-lingering resentments on the part of the Honolulu brethren. In order to be closer to research facilities, including specialists in the various disciplines and areas involved and strong university centers, as well as the substantial funds that were needed, the headquarters was moved to New York.

As a result, we were busily engaged in the early part of 1929 in beginning a long-term research program, a shorter-term fact-finding program to serve as a foundation for the Kyoto discussions, recruiting distinguished personnel to attend the conference and a staff to take care of them, and collecting the considerable amount of money all of this required. By "we," I mean not only our small group in New York but also our colleagues in Japan, China, the Philippines, New Zealand, Australia, Canada, Great Britain and other countries bordering on or having interests in the Pacific area.

The studies intended to prepare conference participants for their discussions were called "data papers" and were therefore closely related to the conference agenda. The papers had theoretically to be complete and in the hands of the participants before they left their homelands so that on arrival they would be well prepared. Inevitably, some of the papers were not completed on time, and, inevitably, some participants did not do their homework as thoroughly as they might have. In general, however, the discussions proceeded from a foundation of very considerable factual information. The round tables were thus able to concentrate on what should be done, given the facts, rather than wrangling about the facts themselves.

Much thought and work had already gone into what could be called the technique of round-table discussion before I came to the IPR. An organization called The Inquiry, to which I have already referred, had for several years been quietly studying how to make discussion a process of group thinking rather than a stubborn repetition of already held opinions.

I had already participated in enough group discussions to have become discouraged by what seemed to be the futility of hashing and rehashing the participants' prejudices. The work that the IPR was doing to develop a technique that would avoid such pitfalls interested me from the outset. After three conferences—Kyoto, Shanghai and Banff—our staff collectively prepared a pamphlet in which a section called "Discussion Technique" summarized what had so far been achieved in this area.

Designed to avoid the constant reiteration of the same point of view, IPR discussion methods aimed at analyzing and solving the problems involved in the subject at hand. Discussions which could achieve this goal required the participation of people with different experiences and from diverse backgrounds. They also had to be capable of changing their opinions on the basis of new evidence introduced in the sessions. Many of the participants in the IPR conferences were individuals prominent in government, industry, banking or labor, and therefore normally reluctant publicly to change their opinions. Publicity was therefore given only to the findings of the round tables as a whole, not to the positions expressed by individual members.

These rules of the game permitted the IPR to avoid the inflexibility and red tape of officialdom. It often permitted delegates from one country to differ more among themselves than from those from other countries. In 1936, for instance, we held our conference in the Yosemite National Park, a magnificent site for an international gathering of some 250 people from all over the Pacific world. Among the Chinese delegates were Tung Pi-wu, who became president of the People's Republic of China after the 1949 revolution, and Liu Yu-wan, who at about the same time became one of Chiang Kai-shek's Taiwan representatives at the United Nations. A considerable contrast also existed between two of the staff members at the earlier Kyoto Conference. John D. Rockefeller III and I were both secretaries to the American delegation at Kyoto. While our lives touched at that particular point, our later careers took sharply different directions.

For a number of years, John and I were actually friends who enjoyed occasional lunches on the top floor of Rockefeller Center, dinners at each others' homes, and once in a while a game of tennis. When we were both in Japan in 1929, John was still living on what seemed to be a limited allowance from his father. He recorded every expense, no matter how trivial, in a small notebook which he kept in his pocket. Because we had been generously feted by our Japanese friends, I suggested near the end of our stay that it would be appropriate for us to give a joint cocktail party at the Imperial Hotel in Tokyo for those who had been so kind to us. John agreed, but the next day told me with some embarrassment that we had better give up the idea because he was running short of money and would not be able to pay his share of the bill. I assured him that I had enough cash left to pay it all. The party went off well. A few weeks after we returned to New York, I received a note from John enclosing a check for his half.

Through helping to prepare for my first IPR conference in Kyoto and then sitting in on the round tables, I learned an important lesson in foreign affairs: the interconnectedness of the domestic and external affairs of any nation. Even though the IPR concentrated on foreign relations, the organization recognized that external affairs are usually secondary to domestic concerns, growing out of and being conditioned by the latter. The relevance of certain domestic factors such as food supply, land and income distribution and population policies to international affairs had been accepted from the beginning of the Institute's studies. No problem of international relations could be divorced from the domestic situation that gave rise to it. A few years later, I edited a book for the IPR about the interrelations of the peoples of the Pacific. More than half of its contents concerned factors such as population, land use, food production and consumption, transportation and public finance, which at first glance appeared to be of only internal concern to each national unit.

Carter was an indefatigable and persuasive money-raiser. Because I accompanied him on many of his fund-raising excursions to the presidents of banks or oil or business-machine concerns, I should have acquired more skill at this indispensable adjunct of our work, but I never acquired the taste or temperament for it. Later, when I headed the American staff, I did a good deal of fund-raising but always regarded it as a necessary evil rather than an exciting challenge. My approach was apologetic instead of aggressive. Some of the important money-raising, however, especially with the Rockefeller and Carnegie people who supported us with large grants, was done through lengthy and detailed reports on how we had spent the last grant and what we proposed to do with the next. I drafted many of Carter's appeals and those that later went out under my own signature. I enjoyed that aspect of money-raising.

In reading an IPR report issued after I had left, I was astonished to discover that between 1926 and 1952, the organization had published 249 books, 696 conference documents or data papers, 60 monographs, 136 pamphlets and 46 items classified as educational material. These totaled a staggering 114,466 pages. The books alone came to 72,411 pages or an average of 291 pages per book. By way of comparison, my thirty-volume edition of the *Encyclopedia Americana* contains just over 23,000 pages.

Research, however, should be measured by quality, not quantity. In 1940 the Rockefeller Foundation, which, along with the Carnegie Corporation, had been the principal support of the research program, described the IPR as "the most important single source of independent studies of the problems of the Pacific area and the Far East." By that time, the long-term projects initiated in the early years were nearly completed and in great demand among the various branches of the American government about to become involved in a war in an area about which it knew little. The American armed forces purchased the research volumes, which provided useful background information, as well as 750,000 copies of a series of popular pamphlets based on the volumes.

The long-term projects were in the broad fields of population problems, land tenure, agricultural techniques, the industrialization of Far Eastern countries, the family, colonial administration, nationalist movements, labor organization, international politics, trade and investment.

After I had been working several years for the IPR and had made several trips to the Far East, I became conscious of my own lack of a basic requirement for the job. I could neither speak, read nor write Chinese, Japanese or Russian. This was not, however, as great a handicap then as it would be today. The 1930s was a decade still marked by the British Empire and the nearly universal use of English. Chinese, Japanese and other foreigners had learned to be polite about our ignorance and to compensate for it. The IPR also helped me to cope with my Asian illiteracy. Our corresponding organizations in China, Japan and other countries were staffed with bilingual personnel, and the international secretariat, located adjacent to ours in New York, always included able Chinese and Japanese.

Nevertheless, the assumption that the English language was enduringly dominant and that other people must adjust to it was pure and simple cultural imperialism. This principle was not only undesirable; it was also impractical. Anyone with half an eye open could see that with the world moving the way it was, our privileged position was not likely to last much longer. More important, the time was passing when so-called specialists in trans-Pacific relations like myself could hold research or educational jobs without a knowledge of the foreign languages involved. Both the United States government and the universities urgently needed Asian specialists who were trained from the ground up.

The American Council of the IPR accordingly went to work on the problem. In 1933, we organized an experimental, intensive summer course in the Russian language. We developed new teaching materials and methods and secured the cooperation of Harvard and in subsequent years that of Columbia and the University of California. The experiment demonstrated that in a ten-week period students could master the basic Russian grammar and acquire sufficient vocabulary to read easy material. A second such session could extend that through reading practice to a point where independent translation of current material with the aid of a dictionary was possible. The astonishingly successful results encouraged us to experiment with Chinese, which seemed to be more difficult.

In 1936, we obtained a three-year grant from the Rockefeller Foundation to set up a comparable experiment in the teaching of Chinese. The program was not designed to produce sinologists but rather to make Chinese available as a working tool for those engaged in studies and activities in which lack of familiarity with the language was a serious handicap.

The first summer session was held in 1937 at the Linguistic Institute of America at the University of Michigan. It lasted eight weeks and was limited to twenty students. Dr. George A. Kennedy of Yale was director. His preparation of teaching materials for the school reminded me of my earlier lessons from Jimmy Yen. Dr. Kennedy made a thorough study of the frequency with which particular ideographs occurred in Chinese. It showed that about half of modern Chinese prose contained no more than 150 different ideographs. Kennedy called these pronouns, signs of quantity, names of positions and directions "the joints in the skeleton of the language." With the addition of another 350 ideographs representing common nouns and verbs, about 75 percent of all Chinese prose could be covered. A total of 1200 ideographs covered over 90 percent of the same material. A familiarity with the patterns of the language was therefore obviously within reach of the students at an intensive summer school.

The first year's grant had been used for the preparation of material; the second and third financed two experimental summer teaching sessions. At the end of the three-year experiment, Dr. Kennedy was able to report that "whereas Chinese had traditionally been regarded as beyond the reach of the ordinary person, the language school project has indicated otherwise." "This," he added, "does not minimize the difficulty of the language, but rather suggests the improvements which are possible in teaching it."

The new teaching methods and materials in Russian and Chinese which the American IPR pioneered were then carried forward by universities. The IPR withdrew from active participation because our basic policy was to initiate ideas and projects and to sponsor experiments in order to pass the results on to existing institutions.

13

Politics
and the IPR

Why did I devote myself to this type of work for so many years? What attracted me so much to work which was, after all, academic and scholarly, rather than actively political?

While I did this kind of work, I was moving left politically. At the height of my involvement with the IPR, I became associated with the Communist Party. I wrote for left publications at the same time that I wrote articles, papers, reports and books for the IPR. No one has ever claimed that the writing I did for the IPR was not "objective" in the American academic sense. Thomas writes that I even often disagreed with some of my IPR colleagues in order to keep the organization on a "pure" academic path.

He notes, for instance, that at the time of the Soviet purge trials, "both Field and Carter accepted the Soviet version." While I have more to say about this in a later chapter, I will state for the moment that what Thomas writes is unfortunately true. He then reports that Carter felt that the American Council was in a good position to counter the adverse image of the Soviet Union created by the trials. "Field, however, parried Carter's suggestion that the IPR take an active role, saying that it did not have jurisdiction in that area."

Thomas also points out that in 1938 I vetoed a suggestion that the American Council set up an office in Washington, D.C., "on the grounds that it might lead to lobbying by IPR personnel."

The IPR was a scholarly organization financed by exceedingly conservative sources, operating in a capitalist environment, attempting to influence the academic and educational habits of a bourgeois society. What was I doing there?

I worked there because I firmly believed, as I still do, that the furtherance of knowledge is desirable in any society. Upon joining the IPR staff, I soon

decided that the organization's objectives and methods had universal validity. As my political development moved me to the left, I also became
more and more convinced that the way to destroy an academic organization
operating in a bourgeois environment was to inject controversial political
issues into it. I wanted to strengthen the IPR, not ruin it. The kind of
world I looked forward to would benefit from a strong IPR and large-scale
research and educational accomplishments. How, for instance, could an
effective radical movement be built without raising the general awareness
of all Americans to their relations with the people of Asia? How could
interest in the Chinese revolution be aroused without broadcasting both
the conditions which brought it about and its relevance to the American
scene?

The McCarthyites claimed that I was the organizer and leader of a "red
cell" within the IPR staff, and I was directly questioned about this several
times in Senate hearings. The accusation implied that within our staff there
was an organized unit of the Communist Party which met regularly and
carried out tasks on behalf of the Party. Such a group never existed, nor
did I or anyone else ever try to form one. If an effort of this kind had been
made, I certainly would have known about it. No evidence was ever presented to support this false charge, but it was nevertheless repeated over
and over again.

Some other staff members, besides me, were probably associated in some
way or other with the Communists. Considering the political temper of the
thirties, the fact that the staff consisted of recent college graduates and
men and women of unusual capability, I would not be surprised if some of
them sympathized with the Party. But I didn't inquire about their politics,
just as I never asked who were Catholics, Jews or WASPs.

We recruited our able staff by seeking out bright young people. One day,
for instance, I went to see Professor Parker Moon of Columbia University,
the author of *Imperialism and World Politics*. I told him we were in a position
to enlarge the staff and asked him to recommend one of his present or
recent students. A few days later he called me up to say he had talked to
the best student he had had in a long time. That was the way Miriam Farley
joined us. She remained with the IPR long after I left. After Joe Barnes
came onto the staff, he and I got in touch with the Bryn Mawr administrators
to see whether they could recommend a recent graduate. They reported
that a member of that year's graduating class, Harriet Moore, who just
happened to have the highest academic average in the college's history,
wanted to try her hand at the kind of work we were offering. William
Lockwood, who was a colleague for several years, later became a full professor
at Princeton. Russell Shiman, who edited *Far Eastern Review* and collab-

orated in the *Economic Handbook of the Pacific Area*, went from the IPR to the United Nations. Barnes went to the *New York Herald Tribune*, first as a correspondent, then as foreign editor, and later to the publishers Simon and Schuster as an editor.

It was because of the dichotomy of academic and political output that Phil Jaffe and I started a magazine independent of the IPR called *Amerasia*. Phil was a friend who was deeply interested in what was happening in China. He owned a greeting-card business that brought him a good income and a fair amount of leisure to pursue other interests. He was never on the staff of IPR or any of its governing committees, so that from the point of view of the Institute, it was my participation in our joint venture that was in question, not his.

Both Phil and I felt that a magazine devoted to the rapidly changing situation in the Far East would fill a large gap. The existing publications on Asian studies, *Pacific Affairs* of the international secretariat of the IPR and the *Far Eastern Survey* of the American Council, were both obliged to avoid making political conclusions from the information they published. As a result, a good many persons on the IPR staff, as well as friends and acquaintances in the academic world, needed a place to express themselves politically. When a study showed, for instance, the role played by old-fashioned, feudal Chinese landlords in support of Chiang Kai-shek's government, the author wanted to explain the significance of that datum. Within the IPR and the usual confines of academic work, a writer could say with impunity that *x* percent of the land of Kwantung Province was held by *y* number of landlords who held in serfdom the masses of Chinese living in the area. But an author got into trouble and made trouble for the IPR if he pointed out that the situation was bad and should be changed. Add that the system of ownership and production was bolstered by U.S. government support of Chiang and there would be hell to pay. My thoughts ran along the lines so well expressed by an old Chinese saying I later found in Nadine Gordimer's *Burger's Daughter*, "To know and not to act is not to know."

Our staff was not composed of ivory tower recluses but rather of young college graduates who were well aware that a holocaust was rapidly building across the Pacific. I think they agreed with me that political action was futile in the face of public ignorance and that our basic job was to contribute to the IPR research and educational programs as effectively as we could. By expressing our political conclusions outside the Institute, our academic work within the intellectual limits of the IPR would become all the more scholarly.

I discussed the idea of setting up an independent magazine with Carter and others in the IPR. I explained that such a magazine could help protect the IPR from political pressure from within. Carter agreed, and so did the others.

Phil and I thus went ahead and launched *Amerasia* in 1937, he as publisher and I as chairman of the board of editors. Our distinguished editors were mostly leading Asian scholars, including such personalities as Edward Carter and Owen Lattimore from the IPR staff. Stanley K. Hornbeck, chief of the Far Eastern section of the State Department, contributed the lead article to the first issue. *Amerasia* soon gained a healthy circulation, and a greater prestige than we had anticipated.

Later, when it became known that both Jaffe and I had engaged in Communist Party activities, some members of the editorial board resigned, screaming in horror that they had been duped. But they had not objected to any of the articles we had run nor complained about the magazine's policies. And they had been consulted right along about the journal's contents. Nevertheless, they said they had been duped. They complained that they had not known of our Communist affiliations. Well, I hadn't asked them about *their* affiliations when I asked them to join the board. I knew only that they were accomplished in their respective disciplines and that their political views deserved airing. All they knew about me, and it was enough to cause them to accept the invitation, was my IPR work. And they had known about it and had a chance to judge it for a quite a few years.

This business of affiliations was a one-way street in the days of the Cold War, and it still is, to a good extent. While affiliations on one end of the political spectrum were acceptable, those on the other were not. On the right side, you didn't have to reveal your ties, and no one asked you about them. On the left, the Establishment made it known that you were obliged to volunteer information about your affiliation, your friends, your reading habits and, for that matter, your sleeping habits.

I never went along with that hypocritical standard. Those professors who claimed I had duped them probably did so in order to ingratiate themselves with the Establishment. If they really, truly thought so, they were damn fools.

I did make one mistake with *Amerasia*, but I quickly recovered and corrected it. At one time I suggested that the American IPR take over the magazine and use it to present all sides of Asian political questions. By that time the Sino-Japanese War had reached such proportions and the Japanese intention of taking over all of China had become so obvious that I thought the IPR should stop ignoring the implications. A journal open to all points of view might, at this dangerous stage in Pacific relations, be a proper and useful thing. I asked for comments from all members of the board of trustees.

A majority favored the idea, but several important trustees, notably Carl Alsberg of Stanford and Philip Jessup of Columbia, opposed it. I decided not to go ahead with the proposal.

Later, I was glad I had been discouraged by a persuasive minority. With my suggestion I had trespassed on my own principle that the IPR should be kept clear of politics or even a hint of policy-making. The fact that I quickly conceded my error and never again pressed the issue indicates that my original belief was never far below the surface. While on the subject of *Amerasia* I should note for the record that I severed all connections with the magazine long before it became involved in the "Amerasia Case" at the end of the war, a case which involved possession and publication of supposedly secret State Department documents.

I resigned as secretary of the American IPR in 1940 to become executive secretary of the American Peace Mobilization, a Communist-front organization opposed to our joining what we then regarded as an imperialist war. I remained on the board of trustees of the American Council and on its executive committee until 1947, when Cold War pressures forced me to sever my last formal connection with the organization.

Although the Institute itself made every effort to defend my record as a staff member, the public gained its general impression from these resignations. Indeed, the record of my service with the IPR has largely been presented—and distorted—by those government and private bodies which in the postwar period set out to destroy the organization by, among other tactics, fouling my reputation. Therefore, though I would not otherwise think it in good taste, I am going to offer here some appraisals of that record—even though they read like an obituary.

The Thomas book, to which I have already referred, derives, as the numerous footnotes attest, from a thorough examination of the reports, private papers and correspondence of the IPR found in various libraries; personal interviews with fifteen persons closely connected with the IPR at the time I was associated with it; a minute study of the Tydings and McCarran subcommittee hearings and the record of Owen Lattimore's trial; and familiarity with a large number of pertinent books, periodicals and some unpublished theses and other material to which the author was given access. Thomas's book is an academic work and follows, I should think, although the published book does not say so, from the author's doctoral dissertation. It is generally anti-Communist in tone; and it assumes that Communists and their sources cannot be trusted. Nevertheless, by the standards of American academic scholarship, it is a "sober and sensible account."

The book contains two summary estimates of my IPR work. The first is very general:

Personable, hard-working, and a flexible administrator, Field was held in high esteem by his colleagues during his tenure as secretary of the American Council (1933-40). What later tarnished his image, and that of the IPR, was an increasing leftward political metamorphosis culminating in Field's open identification with Communist causes by the mid-1940's.

Thomas's choice of the word "flexible" is just, though I may interpret it differently from Thomas. The job was so varied that I never knew from one day to the next whether I was a fund-raiser, administrator, researcher, literary critic, buffer between the staff and the trustees, or a jack-of-all-trades and a specialist in none. When the unexpected happened, it did not interrupt a regular routine but simply altered the nature of that day's lack of routine.

Among the personages who at one time or another served as chairman of the international IPR was Hu Shih, the distinguished Chinese philosopher who was China's ambassador to the United States in the late 1930s. With the considerable effort involved in the organization of such affairs, I had arranged a large cocktail party at a private home in his honor. My objective, aside from bowing to the ambassador, was to interest the guests who would be attracted by the presence of Hu Shih in the work of the IPR. But when I went to his hotel to escort him to the party, I found his two worried and harrassed assistants frantically trying to summon a doctor. Hu Shih had suffered a heart attack a few moments before.

I telephoned the host of the cocktail party. He happened to be a well-known doctor, and he immediately called the Presbyterian Hospital for an ambulance, informing the staff of the importance of the patient. Forty-some years ago, traffic was not what it has become and the ambulance came quickly. I followed it in my car and remained at the hospital long enough to assure myself that the ambassador was in good hands. By the strangest coincidence, the intern on duty was the son of our family doctor in Lenox. Then I raced back to apologize to the guests, arranged for someone to talk about the IPR and rushed back to the hospital. The attack had not been severe and Hu Shih recovered well. He remained in the hospital a week or so, and when he was ready to leave, he confided in me that the embassy was broke and could not pay the bill. I did Chiang Kai-shek that one little favor. To no one's surprise, Chiang never thanked me, nor did anyone else. More important, I was never reimbursed. I really should have gone to Taiwan after the Kuomintang gang arrived there and presented my claim. Add forty years' interest and it would help tide me over in my old age.

One of Betty's friends and classmates at Bryn Mawr had been Katherine Hepburn. We had seen her every so often after we married and had, of course, followed with interest the beginnings of her fabulous career. She called me up one day at the IPR to ask me if I could drop over to her apartment because she wanted to ask a favor of me. When I did so, she explained that a good friend was going to have a birthday in a few weeks and that she wanted to prepare a present for him. She had a good idea, but didn't quite know how to carry it out, and asked if I could help her. She wanted a huge map of the Pacific area mounted on a roller which could be hung high on the wall and rolled out for viewing. She explained that her friend liked to fly and was particularly interested in that part of the world. I found a small map for her to be copied in large size. It was a rare map at that time because it centered on the Pacific Ocean with Canada and the United States on the right and the countries of the Far East (though in this case it was the Far West) on the left. I made a few technical suggestions about the mounting so that a spectator could view the whole map without crouching. Kate liked the suggestions and the map, thanked me and told me she was sure that Howard Hughes would enjoy having it.

Another day brought a telephone call from T. V. Soong, the minister of finance of the Chiang Kai-shek government, who was staying at the Waldorf-Astoria. He said that China was about to apply for a sizable credit from the American government but that his staff lacked a lot of the necessary statistics. He asked if we had a staff member who could help out with this urgent matter. A colleague and I collected a few documents for reference and hurried over to Soong's suite, where he greeted us personally and outlined the problem. We completed the two-day job to his satisfaction, although I forget whether or not China actually got the money.

At one point in the mid-1930s, we received word from our collaborators in England that they would probably shortly obtain the release from a Nazi concentration camp of Germany's best-known sinologist, a professor called Karl August Wittfogel. He had been incarcerated because, in addition to his academic position, he had been chairman of his local Communist Party organization. His British academic colleagues had fortunately discovered that his name was filed separately in the Nazi archives under his professorial and political occupations. Using the most common of all bureaucratic levers, bribery, they secured his release under his sinological identity. Both for his own security and because we Americans would be better able to find a place for Wittfogel to continue his work, he was to be whisked through England to our country.

He had been working on a monumental research project on China which was projected to involve the translation of source material on Chinese social, economic and cultural history. The material consisted of approximately 55,000 extracts, varying in length from a few lines to more than two-hundred pages, and covering the period from the establishment of the Han dynasty in the third century B.C. to the end of the Manchu empire in 1911 A.D. Carter, Lattimore and I played a prominent part in arranging a complicated sponsorship for the project, which involved the Rockefeller Foundation, the American IPR, the International Institute of Social Research (composed of refugee scholars from Nazi Germany), and Columbia University. Wittfogel arrived to find auspices and financing for him to start immediately on what was intended to be a long-term project.

This kind of work, which I used to call "social engineering," fascinated me. In this case, it paid off twofold, because not only did we successfully launch the project, but Karl August and I became friends. Or so I thought.

Thomas's second comment, after his remark about my flexibility, comes in his discussion of the McCarran subcommittee report (a reference to which appears in the early pages of this chapter):

> Even if reliable evidence can establish that an individual is or has been a Communist, can it be inferred that the individual must act as a Communist in all major activities? The McCarran Committee has given a positive answer in assessing Frederick Field's role in the IPR. In the words of the committee report, "Frederick Field was no less a Communist at his desk in the IPR office than when he reported to the Politburo of the American Communist Party, or handed in his column to the *Daily Worker*." Such an assumption seems logical. However, what does the record of the McCarran hearings and the IPR files have to say about Field's actions within the IPR? Certainly it would be very difficult to use Field's concrete actions in the institute in order to establish that he was using the IPR for party objectives. Field's writings for the IPR exhibit no political bias; neither is there any evidence he urged that a "line" be adopted by the *Far Eastern Survey*. Only in his attempt to merge the *Survey* and *Amerasia* can one infer a desire to encourage the IPR to take a more political stance. Even in that case, it should be noted that Field quickly dropped his proposal after discovering opposition from important members of the Board of Trustees, despite the fact that his heavy contributions to the institute seemingly would have given him a degree of leverage, had he decided to use it. Of note also is that no IPR trustee ever accused Field of injecting Communist Party views into the institute.

There follows part of the resolution passed by the American Council board of trustees in November 1940 with respect to my resignation offered the previous September:

> . . . Mr. Field joined the staff of the American Council in 1929. During his eleven years of service he has demonstrated an unusually high quality of leadership. The program of the American Council has expanded notably under his direction, partly because of his own untiring efforts, and partly because of his imaginative leadership in developing the cooperation of the entire staff . . . In this monumental work [*Economic Handbook of the Pacific Area*] his own research

abilities, together with his rare capacity for stimulating research on the part of his colleagues, were outstandingly exhibited. . . .

Throughout his connection with the Institute he has been most scrupulous and exacting in maintaining the highest objective standards for his own I.P.R. writings and that of his colleagues. He has combined personal modesty with the capacity to inspire high achievement on the part of others. He has been noted for his practical wisdom in counsel and amazing energy in action.

Under ordinary circumstances, I would not include statements such as those in my own book. Doing so would be offensive to me and to the reader. I make this exception simply because many of the assertions made about my IPR work by persons in high and conspicuous positions were so vile and unwarranted.

14

Red Hill

R ed Hill, the place I had in Connecticut, is an old, beautiful and close friend of mine. In fact, my relationship to the place was almost like a liaison with a woman. It involved the same first excitement, the many years of growing intimacy and deeper understanding, and finally the breakup for reasons not under my control. I loved Red Hill; I gave it a lot of sweat and energy, and it responded by giving me many, many years of pleasure.

Our relationship was based on the experience Red Hill gave me in the real things of life. Earth, trees, flowers, vegetables, are real; sidewalks, pavements, city noises and smells are far removed from reality. Calluses, stiff muscles, sweat, physical fatigue, are real; servants, luxuries, mansions, are tangential.

I have had some experience with reality versus abstraction from an intense study of an archaeological detail in Mexico, which has, oddly enough, for the context is so totally different, given me a clearer understanding of why Red Hill was so important to me. For a number of years, I worked on the designs found on pre-Hispanic clay stamps. I believe that all of the designs have meaning and that none is pure decoration. One way to interpret such designs is to work from a realistic depiction of the subject to a simplification of it and finally to a further abstraction that may have practically no resemblance to the original realist object.

Several centuries before Christ, for example, the Olmecs, a mother culture of later pre-Hispanic civilizations such as the Maya, depicted the snake. They designed it in realistic forms and in forms so abstract that they are difficult to recognize. In other words, some snake designs look like snakes and others do no more than suggest the idea of the snake by an abstract, symbolic form. If you draw the letter U, for instance, and then draw a simple straight line entering the open end of the U, you will produce a

134

design that appears to mean nothing. But if you know that to the Olmecs the U is a symbol, in this case a fairly clear ideograph, of a cave or an opening in the earth, say, a nest, and the line is a snake reduced to its simplest form, you will understand the combination to mean "a snake entering or leaving its nest."

The point is that abstractions are incomprehensible unless the person who views or experiences them is thereby reminded of the reality from which they are derived. To put it another way, the abstraction is void of meaning unless the real thing from which it comes is first understood.

From as far back as my early twenties I became aware of the degree to which a person's way of life could be distanced from those things that are real. My life was affected in two ways: by urban and country-estate living, for one, and by wealth, for another.

In many respects urban life is an abstraction from reality. Pavements replace soil. The nearest you get to woods are the logs that are delivered for the fireplace or an occasional walk in a park. Vegetables are bought in the market, not grown in the garden. Occupations are specialized, water is purified, neighbors are strangers, air is filtered, smells are of putrefaction rather than life. Urban living is a long way from nature.

The way I was brought up and the way we lived at 645 or High Lawn were as far removed from reality as possible. The essential thing was to do as little as possible for yourself. Everything was done for you. Servants prepared your meals and served them. The table was set, and the dishes were removed and washed, by servants. Someone picked your dirty clothes off the floor, and they reappeared cleaned, pressed and folded in the bureau drawer. Gardeners grew the flowers and vegetables. Chauffeurs went to the market to pick up the edibles that were not grown on the estate after the order was phoned in by the family's secretary. If a wall needed painting, a painter was hired. If a toilet went out of order, the plumber was summoned. If a bookshelf was needed, a carpenter put it up. If a shirt lacked a button, a nurse or maid sewed it on. Whatever was needed or wanted was bought; whatever had to be done was done by a servant or someone hired specially for the purpose.

I came to feel removed from the real things the world had to offer. I knew I must paint my own walls, cook my own breakfast, do my share of the dishes, cut my own firewood, dig the soil and seed my own vegetables. The opportunities of the city and the privileges of money require a foundation in the fundamentals of living. Doing it yourself is a neccesary preliminary to getting others to do it for you.

Two years after I returned from the London School of Economics in the early summer of 1928, I bought forty-odd acres of an unoccupied shoulder of a wooded Connecticut hill for $1,900. Those acres connected my rarified life with Mother Earth. That land and I had a long and endearing love affair. It put me in contact with real things and helped me to recognize the worth and worthlessness of some of the abstractions with which I normally dealt.

We called the property Red Hill, not in order to make it easier for J. Edgar Hoover to find me, but because it was so designated on a document that came with the property and because the many maples on the place resulted in fall colors which demanded some such title. The lovely site on a low southern New England hill overlooked a valley in which cows pastured and which was crossed by a country dirt road. A mile or so away were two farmhouses and their barns. In order to see the bottom of the valley, I had to clear trees away from the immediate front of the house and, in later years, more trees further away as they grew into the view.

In due course we added a small guest house well down in the woods and a swimming pool that could not be seen from the house, though the splashing could be heard. The pool for a while diverted airplane flights between Boston and New York, for we swam in the nude there. And since the view from the air was clear, commercial pilots detoured their planes a few miles to enjoy the sight. But it was the hedgehopping of pilots at a nearby army base that put a stop to those good times.

Betty and I started our life of weekends and vacations at Red Hill in a wooden shack consisting of a bedroom, a kitchen and what might flatteringly be called a temporary bathroom. That shack is where I typed most of *American Participation in the China Consortiums*, my first substantial piece of writing, and where my eldest daughter, Lila, spent a good part of her prenatal life.

We meanwhile became friends with a recently immigrated young Swiss architect, William Lescaze, and were inspired by his interesting ideas to begin talking about something more permanent. He had recently completed studies with Le Corbusier in France and had arrived on our shores with modern, even revolutionary, architectural concepts. They fascinated us, but what most intrigued us was perhaps the thought of trying them out in a conservative New England setting.

We saw a great deal of Bill as we discussed and drafted plans. The house was conceived from the inside out. How did we want to live? What were our interests? How were we going to use the house? There was not a word about how it was going to look until we had settled on what we were going to do with it on the inside.

We told Bill that we wanted to live informally—no maids, no butlers, no cooks, no fourth man. (In later years we occasionally relented and had a part-time housekeeper.) We wanted to live indoors and outdoors inter-changeably. Though we did not then know about the marvelous Japanese homes in which the transition from inside to outside is gradual, almost imperceptible, we had formulated the idea for ourselves. We were both pursuing intellectual lives and wanted space for lots of books and undisturbed study. The solution amused our friends. The house, when finished, had as part of the living-dining area two cubicles, just like the carrels of a research library; the walls were lined with books and desks were built into them. After many years these were removed to make room for children's activities.

The house, when completed in 1931, was a startling addition to the New England landscape. Built in what was then known as the "international style," it was the first private home of its kind in the eastern United States. It was made of steel, cement, cork and plaster and had not one piece of wood. Probably most astonishing of all was that a local carpenter, Charles L. Anderson, had built it. Upon first seeing the plans Lescaze had drawn, Anderson expressed the opinion that this was the craziest house anyone had ever wanted built. For his part, Lescaze had doubts that Anderson could do the job. Anderson had doubts the job was worth doing. Nevertheless, he read and followed the blueprints accurately, even though he was certain the building would collapse in the first storm. Twenty years later he admitted that the construction plan had been sound. The tug and haul between architect and contractor gradually grew into a sound working relationship and finally became mutual admiration.

The architectural journals gave the house full play, and *Life* gave it a four-page spread. It received so much publicity that on weekends during the first year busloads of architectural students would burst in upon us with sketchbooks in hand. We were pleased for Lescaze's sake. Our house was his first residential job in the United States (he had designed a bank building in Philadelphia), and the publicity did him no harm. He went on to a distinguished career as architect of important schools, private homes, broad-casting studios, office buildings and some of Manhattan's most functional and aesthetically pleasing skyscrapers.

The house gave us just what we wanted, a home that was neither large nor luxurious, at a total cost of around $35,000. It was comfortable, and it worked as we wanted it to. And it was an enormous if unconventional architectural success.

For many years I spent about every weekend I was in the United States at Red Hill; once in a while that actually came to fifty-two. Typically, I would arrive on Friday evening and leave at five-thirty on Monday morning. Daylight hours were spent cleaning and clearing the woods, cutting a large supply of logs for the winter fire, plowing and digging and planting the garden and tending it. Some part of the house always needed painting. To accomplish these feats I had a tractor with all kinds of gadgets, and sometimes I was able to cajole my guests from the city into lending a hand.

In the winter the snow took command. The approach to the house was a steep, curved driveway. Time and again on arriving late on a wintry Friday night, I would leave the car at the bottom of the hill, walk up the driveway, have a snifter of bourbon while the tractor engine was warming up, plow the snow on a trip down and up again, have another quick snifter to warm my own engine, march down the hill to the car and drive back up with companions and luggage. Winter was the season for indoor house painting and hauling fallen trees with the tractor, a time to do more reading and dart-throwing than we had time for in the warmer months.

During these years an important change was taking place in my private life. Betty and I had not made the success of our marriage that two decent and well-meaning people should have. I look back on our separation, which took place in mid-1935, with more than mere disappointment at this the most serious failure of my life. Certainly it was my first meaningful failure, and I was unprepared for it. It had an everlastingly deep effect on me.

How could this have happened to me? Everything had gone so well and so easily. I had been successful in attaining so many of the objectives I'd set for myself. I had overcome a shyness, a timidity or lack of self-confidence among my boyhood and adolescent contemporaries. I had learned a good deal about the sham of riches, the vulgarity and arrogance of the wealthy. Over and over again, I had experienced the soundness and genuineness of ordinary people. The value of learning, the discipline of work, the reality to be found in the earth, in growing things, had all become part of my life. I had developed convictions about the evils of our society and a passion to throw my energies into correcting them, a passion that I knew would remain with me all my life. Why, then, had I failed with Betty, whose importance equaled all of these things?

In the midst of emotional shock one does not think clearly. It took me a long time to figure out what had happened. There was, essentially, just one answer: I had worked, worked hard, at everything else; I had not worked at my marriage. And it had needed work, for I had entered it with an extraordinary lack of experience, extraordinary even for that day and for the manner in which I was brought up. If shy and timid are the expressions I use to describe my relations with the boys with whom I played and went to school, I have to say that with the few girls with whom I had any association—and they were very few—I was simply frightened, scared, petrified. I had felt at ease, relatively so, only with my cousins, Adele and Sheila. As I grew up, I learned to put up a facade so that my panic with females was not too conspicuous, but that act was hardly a substitute for experience.

It is very easy to blame one's parents for one's problems in adult life. And without doubt, one's parents should share the blame. But I believe that we must all learn how to cope with whatever problems our environment, including our parents, has given us. Not doing so means not taking responsibility for one's own life.

It was clear, in retrospect, that I had married Betty before coping with this particular and important problem. The marriage suffered and eventually collapsed because of this failure.

Another difficulty was that we were apart too often and for too long a time. I went alone to Japan and China on that second Asian trip for the IPR and later to the IPR office in Honolulu for several months. Betty was reluctant to leave her interesting job in New York and I was more conscientious about my IPR responsibilities than my marriage.

So Fred Field, for whom everything was going along so splendidly, suffered a sudden and severe injury to his pride. I was especially wounded because Betty departed to join my closest friend, Joe Barnes. A couple of years later, having somewhat recovered and having learned a little more about the complicated subject of the battle between the sexes, I fell in love and married again.

Through the IPR, in which her uncle, Professor Joseph Chamberlain of Columbia University, played a prominent role, I met Edith Chamberlain of San Francisco. We were married in February 1937. A year later, we had the pleasure of greeting my second daughter, Gail, but during her pregnancy Edith had unfortunately contracted tuberculosis. During her eventually complete recovery, which took a full year after Gail's birth, Edith was allowed to see her baby only at a distance. I cannot think of many things more traumatic than not being allowed to hold and play with your baby.

Throughout the depression that had followed my separation from Betty and the subsequent period in which I was climbing out of it, Red Hill and I remained faithful to each other. The place provided the perfect environment in which I could calm down, straighten things out, think more clearly, and enjoy life.

When I reached it on Friday evenings, I often didn't know who else might be there. A lot of friends knew that they were welcome whenever a bed was free and someone always seemed to be spending a vacation there. Friends would call me up in the city to ask if they could go up there for a few days, but by the time I arrived, I had often forgotten about their visit, and that led to a number of surprises. One occurred on a Saturday morning after I had arrived too late the night before to know who else was there. I awakened to the sound of splashing in the pool, but instead of going down to see who was swimming, I went to the kitchen to make breakfast. I was starting to eat when I heard the screen door behind me open and I looked around to find a perfectly beautiful young woman entering.

She said, "Hello, Fred, I'm Jane."

I said, "Hello, nice to meet you. I suppose you're the girl Steve just married." "Yes," said she, and sat down to nibble one of my English muffins. There would not have been anything unusual about this scene—if Jane had been wearing any clothes. But she had just stepped out of the pool and was stark naked.

This is indubitably a lovely experience for a young man, but it was not one to which I was accustomed. If it happened again today—I wish that it would—it would still be an experience to which I was not accustomed. On that occasion, I remember trying to appear nonchalant by keeping up a stream of conversation beginning with a remark that would ordinarily seem hackneyed, but in the circumstances was ill chosen. "You look familiar. I think I must have met you before." This in no way upset the young lady. She did not think we had met before, but it was quite natural I should have thought so. The year before, she said, she had been the Lucky Strike girl, and she had been seen all over the country on giant billboards in a clinging bathing suit. That was one of the nicest breakfasts I've ever had.

Another, rather different surprise also occurred while I was preparing breakfast after a late-night arrival. Some time before, a friend had telephoned to ask if she could use the house for several days and bring one or two friends along. On that Saturday morning, I supposed she was there, but I had no idea who her friends were.

Hearing footsteps, I looked up from the eggs frying in olive oil—a fad I enjoyed—to see a short, round man appear in the doorway. Hand extended, he stepped up to me and said jovially, "I presume you are Mr. Field." I said, "Yes, I am." And before I could make the great mistake of asking, he said, "I'm H. G. Wells."

That was a wonderful weekend. Wells was an agreeable, stimulating, undemanding guest. He was interested in my journey from right to left. He asked if I knew of others from prominent families who were traveling in the same direction. I described five or six friends who were working on progressive projects, none of whom, however, had gone as far as I had in becoming closely associated with the Communist Party.

"Will you," he asked, "invite them to be my guests at lunch next week and see if they can take the afternoon off from whatever they are doing so that we can have a long talk?"

I'm sure that if Mr. Wells were here he would forgive me if at this point

I digress for a moment. He would have been interested in the point that I want to make. When I say that the others had not gone so far to the left as I had, I do not mean to be critical in any sense. They all made very useful contributions through journalism, the struggles for civil rights and the backing of progressive ideas and individuals. It just so happened that I was the only one of this particular group who went on to embrace communism.

Others of my generation who were also born to riches and privilege took the political trip that I did. With a single exception, I did not know them at the time. I undertook the journey by myself. When we reached our political destination, we engaged in different types of activity, so that I never got to know any of them well, and most I never got to know at all. But I was aware that others were spitting the gold spoons out of their mouths.

The exception was Lement Upham Harris. I do not hesitate to mention him, as I would others who operated less openly, because for forty years he has been a proud and prominent member of the CPUSA.

Lem was also born to riches—a brokerage house that still bears the family name and the Plaza Hotel in New York, of which his father was a director. His family and mine shared the traditions and customs of the self-conscious old rich. Lem was a class ahead of me at Harvard and one of Osgood's closest college friends. While still in college, the three of us and our fathers took a fabulous trip to the Canadian Rockies. We made several first ascents of peaks around the Columbian Icefield, north of Lake Louise. In the 1920s, these peaks took a week to reach by packtrain, while they can now be approached in comfort by the new highways. Although our expedition was hard work, it had a luxurious aspect. Mr. Harris imported Joseph Biner, a mountain-climbing guide from Zermatt, Switzerland, and our father hired Edward Feutz, another climbing guide who had been brought over from Switzerland a few years before by the Canadian Pacific Railways and who now lived in the Swiss-populated village of Edelweiss between Banff and Lake Louise. These guides didn't make the climbing easier, but they did make it safer. Our names and climbs are recorded in the annals of the Alpine Club of Alberta and Saskatchewan.

Osgood thereafter stayed with the mountains, snow and ice, becoming a glacial specialist. Lem and I began our separate journeys to the political left. He became an expert on farm problems and spent many years in the northern Midwest and Northwest, studying, organizing and laying the groundwork for some of the most vigorous farm protests of the Great Depression and later years. Lem and I were separated by long distances, as well as by our respective specializations, so we saw little of each other during the years after college. But we kept in touch just enough so that I was aware that he had joined the Communists as an agricultural expert while I was approaching them from another direction. We were both surprised and pleased to find out that without any real contact with one another, we were nevertheless traveling the same road.

I wish Lem had been one of the group I invited to meet that eminent British liberal, H. G. Wells, but he was half a continent west of New York at the time. Those I did invite lunched with Mr. Wells and me at the Waldorf, and we lunched well. Surrounding our table as we sat down were several bottles of champagne. By the time we reached his upstairs suite, any lameness from which our tongues might have suffered had been cured. I have been unable to reach any of the others who attended in order to try to reconstruct our conversation that afternoon and my memory has given me little help. I remember only that our host wanted to know what was going on left of center in the country and we did our best to answer his questions. The only specific thing that comes to mind is that he said that he was on his way to Hollywood to see Charlie Chaplin.

For a few years after 1953, when I was living in Mexico, we used Red Hill for summer vacations. The rest of the year, it was well looked after by a good friend, Ellsworth Howe. He worked in a machine-tool factory in nearby Torrington and came to Red Hill for rest and nonindustrial air. His love for the place was almost as strong as mine; he was there after-hours, weekends and every moment that he could. When Ellie died suddenly of a heart attack, I lost a fine friend, and Red Hill, almost as if mourning his death and my long absences, gradually went to pieces. This process was hastened by the youthful vandalism prevalent in the 1960s. By that time I had also lost or given away a great deal of money and could not afford to maintain our home in Mexico and simultaneously prevent the deterioration of the New Hartford house and property. Finally, in January 1977, forty-seven years after I had bought that unoccupied shoulder of a wooded hill, I sold it for back taxes and two mortgages. Tears actually come to my eyes as I write about the end of my long affair with Red Hill.

Many people who live in the city say that they go to the country in order to get away. I went for a different reason—to find the reality of the good earth in order better to cope with the abstractions of city life and wealth. Today those pre-Hispanic clay stamps remind me that the way to understand an abstraction is to find the real thing from which it is derived and to trace the connection. You get nowhere and understand nothing by experiencing the abstraction alone.

"Out of reality are our tales of imagination fashioned."—Hans Christian Andersen.

15

Lessons in
Imperialism

The research and editing assignments I was given at the IPR took me deep into the relations between industrially unequal countries, principally the United States and China. During the nineteenth century and the first third of the twentieth, the United States had made notable industrial advances, whereas China had remained mired in feudalism, or its remnants. Forced by foreign powers to cede economic and political concessions at nearly all its vital points, China was, in fact, only a semi-independent state.

I had been introduced to imperialism at the London School of Economics though not specifically with respect to China. I had spent a year traveling in Asia, a year which included three months of field work in the Philippines on a specific aspect of relations between unequals.

Three books had given me a theoretical insight into what I was observing. One was *Imperialism*, by British economist T.A. Hobson, written in 1902; another was Lenin's *Imperialism, the Highest State of Capitalism*, 1917; and *Imperialism and World Politics*, by Columbia University professor Parker T. Moon, 1926. The first was an early socialist, the second a Communist and the third an academic investigator in a capitalist community.

That was my entire preparation in travel, research and reading when I undertook my first independent study of an important phase of American-Chinese relations. In 1929 the International Research Committee of the IPR asked me to make a study of American financing in China. I completed it in a year and a half, and it was published in the fall of 1931 by the University of Chicago Press under the title *American Participation in the China Consortiums*. It was a splendid assignment, from my point of view, for the subject had not been well covered in previous publications. The research required me to unravel a complicated story and led me to the major

143

official and unofficial sources on relations between the United States and China from 1900 to 1929.

In that period, I learned that the connection between the private banks in the United States, Great Britain, France, Germany, prerevolutionary Russia, and Japan and their respective governments was very close, the banks in fact being their countries' principal agents vis-à-vis China. Official government documents therefore told much of the story. But I also had an unusual opportunity to study private documents: I was given access to the minutes of the banking groups by Thomas Lamont of J. P. Morgan & Company, thanks to the intercession of Mr. Lamont's son, Corliss. Though Corliss was three years my senior, he and I had become friends while I was an undergraduate and he a first-year law student at Harvard. (As I write, this friendship has lasted well over half a century. For all that time we have moved in the areas occupied by the left, though usually in separate vehicles.) Corliss made the request of his father, and so I was given the privilege, a rare one, of examining these private bankers' files. Mr. Lamont's only condition was that I give him the opportunity to review the manuscript before publication. When I did so, he made two or three minor suggestions, and I accepted them.

Minutes of bankers' meetings are not frivolous reading, but these, beside being instructive, were more entertaining than I had expected. The secretary of the American group was Willard Straight, and he had written amusing comments on the margins and drawn caricatures of those attending. As his subsequent career indicated, he was not cut out to be a banker exploiting the miseries of the Chinese people. He married great wealth, and he and his wife, Dorothy, used it to further liberal ideas and causes. Herbert Croly of the *New Republic* wrote a biography of him; Willard's son for a time became editor of the magazine; and his daughter Beatrice became a well-known theatre and movie actress.

My book on the consortium was well received. As far as I know, it still provides the only detailed information on the American government's efforts to force itself into the China scene via a group of private banks. When Professor Charles P. Howland of Yale checked the manuscript, he suggested that I hold up publication for a couple of years in order to use it for a doctoral thesis under his tutelage. Although I gave the idea serious thought, I decided to turn it down because my enjoyable job at the IPR actually offered me better academic training than I would find at a university. I also saw no reason why a Ph.D. would enhance the kind of life that I expected to lead.

In preparing the book, I learned a great deal of the historical background of American-Chinese relations. Not only did the growing industrial-financial power of the United States and other countries impinge on the economic and political independence of China, it also presented China with well nigh insuperable problems in regard to modernization. I learned that the United States had been a latecomer on the Chinese scene. In order to wedge its way in, it had pursued an opportunistic policy of occasionally siding with the Chinese against the other foreign powers and occasionally with the latter against the Chinese. The United States never suggested that other foreign countries surrender their advantages; it objected only when it did not fully share those advantages. It was not concerned with the harm other foreign concessions would do to China but only with the harm they would do to America's current and potential commercial interests.

A short while after my study was finished, Carter and I agreed that the IPR needed a Russian specialist because the Soviet Union's position in the Far East could no longer be ignored. The job was a perfect one for Joe Barnes, who had actually begun to prepare himself for work of this kind when we attended the University of London together in 1927-28. A short time after Joe joined our staff, Doubleday, Doran, the well-known publishers, asked him to put together a symposium on the American effort in the Far East. It was published in 1934 under the title *Empire in the East*. All the contributors were members of the American IPR, though the book itself was not an official publication of the organization. IPR publications were limited to the field of research, and this book could more accurately be described as the application of research to policy. I was asked to write on the American financial stake in that part of the world. The nature of the symposium gave me an opportunity to break out of academic boundaries and to express my own opinions and conclusions, or, where I had none, to pose the relevant questions.

I was aware that many scholars devoted themselves to what was called pure research and that many others of a different cast devoted their talents to the popularization, interpretation or application of research. I wanted to participate in both aspects of knowledge, to dig out facts and to act upon them. I felt that fact-finding in itself was only the beginning of a process that needed to be completed by applying the findings to the lives we led. My point of view was not unusual, and I didn't dwell upon it until circumstances forced me to at a later date.

In *Empire in the East*, I went directly to what I thought was the essence of the question. In order to understand the significance of capital exports to the Far East, it was necessary to examine the economy which produced capital not used at home. If a surplus was produced that could not be absorbed within our own economy, then the availability of foreign markets for investments was essential. If, however, the surplus was a mere passing phase, or one subject to control, as wheat or cotton crops might be, then the American financial relation to the Far East would be susceptible to careful regulation. I realized that this distinction was not of merely academic importance, either to our country or to those which had been importing our capital. If foreign loans and investments represented a chosen policy of the United States, they could be expanded when socially useful and contracted when they threatened conflict. If, however, they were an integral part of our economic organization, the pressures to export capital would continue for good or bad as long as that organization remained intact. I was approaching the conclusion that if the effects of those financial exports were seriously detrimental to our own welfare and to that of the people of the East, they posed a major barrier to the continuance of a system of economy from which they inevitably flowed.

I was nearing a definition of imperialism that I was going to use from then on. I wrote in that chapter: "It is believed that the word [imperialism], though antagonistic to many persons, expresses better than any other those external relations of a nation which can be attributed to the operations of a capitalist system of economy." Further along I added, "Implicit in the use of the term is the suggestion that imperialism is an undesirable process and that it springs from a capitalist system of economy. Most of the studies devoted to expansionism support such a contention. . . . They differ as to whether doing away with imperialism simply means reform of the capitalist system from which it springs or a destruction of it." The crucial question was, "Is imperialism a characteristic of capitalism which can be dispensed with or is it part and parcel of capitalism?"

It was clear from what I wrote in 1934 that I inclined toward the "part and parcel" interpretation. That meant I was coming to the conclusion that if the evils of imperialism were to be eliminated, so must the system which gave rise to it.

Many years later, I am struck by the fact that although I came close to saying flatly that the United States could only contribute to a peaceful solution of the Far Eastern problem by ridding itself of its capitalist system, no one was disturbed or hinted that I was a "red" or an agent of the Soviet Union. The difference between 1934 and the postwar period, when I was called every bad name you can think of, was not so much in what I said or the position I took but in the places and the political climate in which I did it. There is quite a difference, I was to learn, in saying something under the banner of Doubleday, Doran and in "respectable" academic company and saying the same thing in the pages of New Masses or the Daily Worker. In 1934 the United States was in deep crisis. The economy was doing badly and important institutions of society had failed. There was, therefore, a greater acceptance of nonconventional ideas. In contrast, the postwar years were the aftermath of military triumph and a time when minds were closed. An intolerance of liberalism, to say nothing of radicalism, pervaded the atmosphere.

Empire in the East was well received; it was even recommended by the Book-of-the-Month Club. A *New York Tribune* editorial called it "a symposium which is vastly more than a collection of articles. It is edited: it has a kind of unity and cohesion; and thoughtful people, watching the rising storm clouds in the Far East, will find no other book from which they may learn so much. . . .There is nothing better in the field." The same newspaper gave our book a highly favorable review in its book section, as did the *New York Times*, the *Saturday Review of Literature* and other journals. The surprise was a long article in *Asia* of April 1934 in which George E. Sokolsky, the friend I had made in Shanghai, who was opportunistically jumping to the right (and not much later would berate me on every possible occasion), wrote, "Mr. Field's essay is really a brilliant discussion, not so much with regard to what the bankers did in China . . . but with regard to the inability of capitalism to survive without imperialism."

In 1934, Doubleday, Doran also published a 689-page book for the international body of the IPR called *Economic Handbook of the Pacific Area*, which I edited. In the preface I defined the book as "concerned entirely with material aspects of the vastly complicated and increasingly important economic problem of the peoples of the Pacific area." In a foreword, Newton D. Baker, President Wilson's secretary of war during World War I and, in 1934, chairman of the IPR, wrote the following:

> The *Economic Handbook of the Pacific Area* is the most impressive compilation of facts about the Pacific countries which has been attempted. Mr. Frederick V. Field of the Institute of Pacific Relations and his associates have gathered into one place the results of the latest surveys and studies upon the resources of the countries which border the Pacific basin, and have subjected these results to disinterested and expert scrutiny, so that in one book the student of the Pacific can find in statistical form practically all that is known about the facts which underlie the economic, industrial, and racial tensions in that area. The book is therefore indispensable to anyone who wants to base his thinking about the Pacific upon facts and has not the time to make for himself a laborious summary from sources widely scattered and often available only in languages which few of us command. . . .

The scope of the book is suggested by the chapter headings: Population, Land Utilization, Food Production and Consumption, Transportation, Public Finance, Capital Movements, Trade, International Mineral Products, International Agricultural and Textile Products, Weights and Measures, and Bibliography. There were 569 statistical tables, and the bibliography listed 318 sources.

For me the most interesting part of the long preparation of the book was the beginning of it. The Chinese, Japanese and American councils of the IPR were each invited by the international body to send a staff member to Honolulu so that the three could jointly plan the organization of the book. China sent Liu Yu-wan, Japan dispatched Saburo Matsukata, and I came from the American branch. Liu, who later represented Chiang Kai-shek's Taiwan government at the United Nations, had attended the same IPR conference as Tung Pi-wu, who later became president of the People's Republic of China. I remember Liu with greater pleasure as the young man who organized that sixty-four-course feast in my honor in Shanghai, the one at which I repeatedly bottoms-upped with all of the guests. A close friend, Matsukata was a forward-looking liberal and a descendant of a noble family of the period of the shogunate.

The three of us reached Honolulu at about the same time and made our first decision—to live together during our months in Honolulu. Of the multitude of decisions needed to complete the project during the next two years, this was the most difficult to carry out.

Although I had passed through Hawaii on my way to Japan, none of us had actually visited the island, and we knew little about it. But we learned some things quickly. One hotel after another, one boardinghouse after another, turned us down because Asians were not allowed in the better establishments. Hawaiian society was racially segregated. And it had not yet recovered from the notorious Massie case.

Mrs. Thalia Massie, the twenty-year-old wife of a U.S. Navy lieutenant, had claimed that she was criminally assaulted by five "natives," one of whom was named Joe Kahahawai. The nature of the accusations and of the trial that followed can be gathered from a statement made by Admiral William V. Pratt, then chief of naval operations. "On one side," he said, "was the failure of the native 'beach boys' to comprehend the moral standards of the whites; on the other was the failure of the white women to know the peril which lay in the attitudes of the natives."

While awaiting a second trial after the first was aborted, Kahahawai was required to report daily to the court. When he did so on January 8, 1932, he was lured into an automobile by a fake summons. After a wild chase, the police caught up with the car, which was driven by Mrs. Granville Fortescue, Thalia Massie's mother. It contained three live passengers and one dead. The live ones, beside the driver, were Lieutenant Massie and E. J. Lord, an enlisted man; the dead one was Joe Kahahawai.

After forty-nine hours of deliberation, what was known as a "mixed blood" jury found the trio and a fourth man guilty; they were sentenced to ten years of hard labor. Governor Judd of Hawaii immediately commuted the sentence to one hour. That hour was served in the Iolani Palace; at the end of sixty minutes they were freed. As a result, the racist nature of Hawaiian society came under the full glare of publicity. The unions, not the pious sugar planters or the pineapple growers or the other leaders of the upper classes, undertook a campaign of public education to rid the territory of its racism.

Eventually we found quarters in a decent bungalow hotel. Once established there, we had no more trouble. During the first weeks, I took care always to be on hand for meals with my two friends lest they should run into some unpleasantness in the dining room. After that, we forgot about our bigoted environment and got to work on the book.

Toward the end of the project, I went to London to complete those parts which I had undertaken to write on my own. They were the chapters on population, land utilization, food production and consumption, transportation, and the sections on coal, iron and steel, cotton textiles and wool. I was given full use of the fine library at the Royal Institute of International Affairs. Its secretary was my friend Ivison Macadam, whom I had first met at that student conference in Prague. The facilities included not only a desk and chair, an excellent librarian and the company of other researchers, but also tea and biscuits at both mid-morning and mid-afternoon.

My stay in London was cut short by the illness of my mother, then in her middle fifties. After my father wrote me that she was terminally ill with lung cancer, I arrived home to find her still well enough to accompany me to several Carnegie Hall concerts and some theatres, although these outings became increasingly difficult. Albert always parked the town car as near the theatre entrance as possible, but in those days, many chauffeured cars met their patrons, and we were lucky when he was able to find a place a block away. Those short walks, during which Mama leaned heavily on my arm, became more and more painful for her. Having shared the joys of many brisk walks in the country with her, I found those occasions dreadfully sad. For the final months of her life, Mama moved to Lenox. Her remaining days were not happy, although the visits of many of her friends did give her pleasure. Shortly before the end, Geraldine Farrar, who was long retired from opera, came to spend an evening with her old friend and admirer and sang some of Mama's favorite arias. Perhaps that was the best evening in the final year of Mama's life.

The last of the many things my mother gave me was a lesson in bravery that I shall never forget. Birth and death are the most important events of our lives, and yet we remember nothing about them. Our brains are too unformed to recall the first—although some analysts claim that something of the experience can be recaptured—and by the time death has taken place, our memory is no longer functioning. We do, however, know later whether or not our birth has been successful in regard to whether it resulted in producing mental and physical normality. Nevertheless, we actually make no contribution to that original event of our lives. Although we will never remember what happens at the moment of our dying, we do have the capacity to know how we approached it. We can, toward the end, live bravely, intelligently, with dignity and some understanding of our last experience. If we have lived through middle age, death occurs, barring an accident, after we have attained our full faculties and most of us remain conscious of the long or short approach to that final moment. If the end itself is not knowable, the approaches to the climatic cutoff of life are. The dying person must achieve satisfaction in knowing that he or she has prepared for the inevitable, just as for life's other climaxes, and has at least turned back the fears and the myths with which our society has so stupidly surrounded death.

I have no way of knowing the extent to which my mother understood the experience of dying. Her religious convictions and traditionalism must have given her strong support. With whatever understanding or beliefs she went through the experience, she did so with a dignity and bravery which her son can only hope to approximate.

While I was in London, my colleagues in New York, Russell G. Shiman and Kate L. Mitchell, had been completing their sections of the *Handbook*. In addition, Matsukata and another Japanese associate, Samitaro Uramatsu, and Liu provided a mass of statistics and translated material from their respective countries. Joe Barnes and his wife Kathleen had combed Russian sources. We all ended up with fingers blistered from slide rules.

Under the subheading "A Book That Deserves High Praise for the Concrete Knowledge It Discloses," the *New York Times Book Review* of October 7, 1934, devoted most of a page to elaborating what that headline suggested.

Counting the period at the London School, I had by that time spent a good part of eight years studying imperialism. I started with theoretical books and continued with travels in which I observed imperialism at work in various forms. I saw "coolies" being exploited and chained prisoners crushing rocks. I lived behind walls and barbed wire to "protect" me from the people whom I had come to visit. I was hated, spat upon, chased by barking dogs because I, a white foreigner, was assumed to be a running dog of imperialism. I stayed in foreign concessions where I "enjoyed" extraterritorial rights. I met foreigners who were advising corrupt rulers. In the Philippines, I studied a special case of exploitation. I was present as foreign troops marched into Manchuria and met practically no opposition because the invaders had already corrupted the local leadership. I then sat in libraries where I read, looked up data, made calculations and figured out what it all meant. I wrote one book, edited another and contributed to two others. By then I felt that I knew something about imperialism.

Imperialism, I concluded, was part and parcel of capitalism. Much later an acquaintance, Harry Magdoff, wrote a book (*The Age of Imperialism*, Monthly Review Press, 1969) in which he said, "Imperialism is not a matter of choice for a capitalist society; it is the very life of such a society." In other words, imperialism is an integral part of capitalism, and it cannot be eradicated without eradicating the system in which it is embedded. The word cannot therefore be correctly applied to any other organization of society. It does not belong in the political vocabulary of primitive, feudal or socialist societies but is characteristic only of capitalism. Other words and explanations must be found to describe the expansionist activities of other forms of society, such as the Aztecs, the Soviet Union or the Chinese Peoples' Republic. I found that Marxism was the only theoretical school of thought that had reached a precise definition of capitalist expansion, and this explanation was an important factor in my attraction to that discipline.

A fuller understanding of imperialism required a step beyond those I had already taken in my travels and studies. I needed to find out why capitalism inevitably led to imperialism. For that reason, I began to investigate one of the most difficult and controversial aspects of Marxist theory, namely, surplus value. Scholars have written thousands of pages for and against the theory. Although I was familiar with only a small part of the controversy, I could not find an alternative explanation of the imperialism that I had both observed and studied.

The Marxist theory of surplus value maintains that all production under capitalism produces a value over and above what is paid for materials and labor. This surplus is accumulated and is either withdrawn in the form of profits or reinvested. With the growth of monopoly, the accumulation of surpluses increases until the domestic market for reinvestment at attractive rates of return can no longer absorb it all, and the remainder seeks outlets abroad, where higher yields can be obtained. To sustain and expand this process, sources of raw materials have to be controlled, foreign social and economic systems must be shaped to the imperialist country's interests, and a never-ending struggle against rival imperialists must be maintained, often to the point of war.

As I saw it, surplus value could also operate in a socialist state as a method of accumulating funds for social services. The state would simply have to pay the producers less than the value of the goods and services they turned out and use the difference for the public weal. No uncontrollable internal pressure would exist to force a portion of the surplus value out of the country. A socialist society would be free to decide whether some of the surplus should be exported, how much, for what purposes, and when and where.

I thought that the United States and other capitalist countries were at a stage of transition toward socialism. An increasing portion of the accumulated surplus was going to the government in the form of taxes and a part of that portion was being returned to the people in a variety of social services. All tendencies in that direction should be encouraged. The industrial and financial monopolies, however, still called the tune. While our society was still a capitalist one in the 1930s, the cracks were showing. I wondered how the transition could be hastened and whether it could be completed by evolutionary means or only through a revolution.

The result of my lessons in imperialism was that I became convinced of an interpretation which was regarded as radical. I realized that I was continuing to move to the left and that, having come to a Marxist conclusion on one aspect of the social panorama, I had better find out what this school of thought had to offer on other issues.

16

Moving Left

So it was that during the first half of the 1930s I found myself moving away from what the Socialist Party represented and further to the left. "I found myself moving" is an indirect way of saying, "I was moving." Spanish-speaking people often express themselves that way. Instead of saying, "I dropped something," or "I broke something," they say, "Se me cayó," or "Se me rompió," some external force caused me to drop or break something. I take full responsibility for moving to the left; no one else called that turn. But in describing the move, I use the Spanish form because there was something inevitable and irresistible about it. Everything I had ever been or done or thought led in the direction I was then taking.

In the circumstances into which I was born, brought up and then educated, as well as the kind of work I fell into by accident and pursued by choice, my convictions came more from thinking than from sweating. This is one way to reach convictions, though not necessarily the best. My circumstances left me relatively free to choose my own path; my thoughts were not shaped by necessity. I was able to study, to look around, to ponder a wide range of ideas about the meaning and purpose of life and where I could do the most with mine.

I had a number of choices. My parents, for instance, had a wealthy bachelor friend who every summer had his chauffeur drive him from New York to Lenox in his Rolls Royce to visit us. This dry, unamusing gentleman had started somewhere low on the economic ladder and climbed high, so that when I knew him, he owned his own profitable insurance company. When I was in my middle teens, he informed my parents, without my knowledge, that he saw much promise in my future and hoped they could persuade me to go to work for him after I had completed my formal education. The prospect was that I would eventually inherit his lucrative business. My father, as I have already remarked, did not think that business was the proper way for a young man in my position to busy himself, and he never mentioned this matter of the insurance company to me. My mother, however, did believe her sons should go to work, if only because the discipline of office hours kept young men out of trouble. Her father, after all, had been an exceptionally successful merchant, while her indolent brother was a wastrel. And so she did tell me about the conversation and suggested that if I were interested, I should talk directly with our friend. In fact, I wondered why he had not talked directly to me in the first place. I decided that I was not interested, not because I had anything against business as such or the insurance business in particular, but simply because at that age I hadn't the vaguest idea what I wanted to do.

My step-grandfather, Henry White, who had had a distinguished diplomatic career, had married Nanan some years after the death of my grandfather. He spoke to me a number of times about choosing such a course for myself. I was fond of the man and listened attentively to what he said. In the *Harvard Yearbook* for the Class of 1927, I put myself down for "public life," so apparently some such idea persisted through college. Oddly enough, in the *Harvard Magazine's* summer issue of 1977, exactly fifty years after this declaration of intention, I am listed among others from my class "who performed distinguished national and international service" for my years with the IPR. My own feeling, however, is that while I cannot claim that all the aspects of my life have been exactly private, the public parts did not derive from the career I anticipated in 1927.

As I was finishing my undergraduate studies at Harvard, two of my prep school teachers talked to me about returning to the school to teach. For a while the idea intrigued me. Fortunately for the boys who might have become my students, I instead went on to my year in London and then to the IPR. I use the word "fortunately" seriously, because I never developed any talent for teaching. What little I attempted in later years was a dismal failure for those I tried to teach, as well as a disappointment to me, because I consider teaching one of the finest of all occupations.

In the early 1930s, after I had already been working at the IPR for a few years, I gave considerable attention to an offer which, had I accepted it, would have drastically changed the area of my interests, though not necessarily the political direction in which I was moving. The Crane Foundation, which had been established by a member of the family which manufactured the well-known plumbing fixtures, was developing a program to train area specialists who, upon becoming proficient, would almost surely find positions in the academic world or in the foreign service of government or in industry. I was offered the complicated area called the "Near East."

Although we talked in general terms of a five-year span, the training period had no time limit, and would reflect how long it took to learn the languages and to make oneself into a minor Aristotle for the area. The amount of the stipend would depend on one's living and educational needs. I had several long talks with the director of the foundation before deciding that I was well off working for the IPR and in the area of the Far East.

About this time, I was also interviewed by officials of Columbia Broadcasting to take over Edward Murrow's job as head of what I think was called the "Talks" department, because Ed was about to move up the ladder. The interview took place over several martinis at an expensive midtown restaurant, and one day I spent several hours at Ed's side while he was working to learn the nature of the job. Once again, when faced with an alternative, I found that I was enjoying my job at the IPR too much to make a change. Not that my decision was particularly important, because I don't believe the CBS people had been impressed by my martini-stimulated conversation.

Yet another possibility was a most improbable one. Ray Lyman Wilbur had been president of Stanford University before President Herbert Hoover brought him into the cabinet as Secretary of the Interior. I had seen a good deal of Wilbur because he had also been chairman of the IPR before he moved to Washington. With the defeat of Hoover in 1932, Wilbur returned to Stanford. A few years later Hoover asked him to recommend someone to act as his secretary during a trip he was planning to Europe. Wilbur thereupon got in touch with Carter and asked him to sound me out for the job. I was, at the time, becoming more and more involved with the Left, and realizing the inappropriateness of the suggestion, I told Carter that I did not think I should be considered further. The trip in question was the one during which Hoover had a much publicized interview with Hitler.

I continued my job with the IPR and continued to feed my curiosity. I wanted to find out why things worked the way they did. I wanted to know what came first, what followed, what was basic and what was superstructure. If God did not create, what did? If change and development did not come from heaven, what did cause them? Were the rich rich because they were better people? I had long suspected that there were other reasons. Were the poor poor because they were bad people? My limited experience indicated otherwise.

My exploration of Marxism was rewarding. I read a great deal of Marx and Engels and Lenin, and the letters, treatises and polemics of others. I was strongly attracted to the Marxist theory of imperialism—mainly the work of Lenin—and soon thereafter by dialectical and historical materialism in which I found an approach to the philosophical answers that I was seeking. There are no things in the world that are unknowable, it proclaimed, only things that are unknown. I liked that.

I made some notes at the time, and I still have them. Thanks to these, I can reconstruct what I learned then. Dialectical materialism regards nature as a connected and integral whole in which everything is related to everything else. It teaches that nature is in a state of continuous movement and change in which something is always growing and something is always disintegrating. The process of development passes from imperceptible to visible quantitative changes, which at a certain point become qualitative changes. When water is heated, it gets hotter and hotter until, at boiling point, it turns into steam. Internal contradictions are inherent in all phenomena of nature. All things have their positive and negative aspects. It is the struggle between these opposites that constitutes development and that at a certain stage turns quantity into quality.

The world by its very nature is material. This material world changes in accordance with the laws of movement of matter. To understand this process, there is no need to resort to an outside god or other spiritual concept. Such a material world is an objective reality which exists outside of and independent of one's mind. Matter is the source of sensations, ideas and thought; it is primary. Sensations, ideas and thought are reflections of matter and are therefore secondary—not in the sense that they are less important, but in the sense that they do not come first in the order of causation. The brain is the matter of thought; thought is the product of the brain. The brain, indeed, is the highest form of matter.

Our ability to know the material world has no limit. Our knowledge of the laws of nature is authentic knowledge and has the validity of objective truth. It is constantly advancing, and what is not known will gradually become known in the future.

Dialectical materialism seemed to me to be a comprehensive and understandable approach to the world in which we live. It provides the base for understanding how our society operates. The material life of society comes first, in the sense of causation, and social ideas and theories, political views and institutions derive from it. New ideas and theories come into being only after the development of the material life has posed new problems for society to solve. You would not expect industrial conglomerates to rise out of the Stone Age any more than you would expect Olmec mythology to arise out of the New York of today. Once set in motion, ideas and theories become potent forces for adjusting the structure of society to the demands made by the new changes in its material foundation.

Marxism uses the words "material" and "materialism" much more broadly than do its critics. The article on Marxism in the 1950 edition of the

Encyclopaedia Britannica, written by G. D. H. Cole (whom I select to quote because when I was first reading Marxism he was one of its clearest exponents), acknowledges that "Marx's materialist conception of history has often been misunderstood. It is far from being merely the doctrine that economic forces are predominant in the direction of social affairs, though this is involved in it. Still less is it the doctrine that individual men act only from material motives, and this is not even involved in it at all. . . ." It is the method of procuring the means of life, or in other words, it is the mode of production of material values, the way in which things are produced. The mode of production is made up of two factors: the instruments of production and the relations of production. The first are the tools and the second the organization of the people who use the tools. These relations include the slave system, the feudal system of serfs, capitalism and socialism.

Neither the instruments of production nor the relations between people remain static for long. The tools change as new inventions and discoveries are made. The relations of the people working the tools has to change accordingly. The social organization required to build a pre-Hispanic pyramid was different from that needed to build a modern skyscraper. As these changes take place in both the tools and the relations of the people using them, related adjustments are required in the whole social system, social ideas, political views and institutions. The mode of production of a society determines the society itself. Its ideas and theories and institutions follow the changes in the way it produces its material values. Whatever is man's way of life, such is his manner of thought.

Of the two factors, the first to change is the tools. Social organization does not change first so that a new tool can come into being. But after the initial impulse from the tools of production, the people using them then change the economic relations among themselves. If there is too much of a lag between the development of the tools and the organization of the people, conflict occurs, and it is resolved in a social explosion.

Some periods in history have produced particularly clear examples of the dialectic process. In the second half of the nineteenth century, for example, great changes took place in the vast prairie areas west of the Mississippi, in Texas and the regions north of it, The material factors affecting the changes involved a whole series of new developments and inventions. Among these were the building of the transcontinental railroads, the invention and mass production of barbed wire, improved methods of refrigeration and meat packing, such as the refrigerated railway car, and the invention of new agricultural machinery suitable to large-scale prairie farming. The people involved were, on the one hand, ranchers whose cattle the cowboys drove freely over vast stretches of land for feed, fattening, slaughtering and marketing or for reasons of climate. On the other hand were the farmers who were relentlessly pushing westward. Barbed wire made it possible for both sides to enclose their respective properties. The ranchers did so to protect their land from the advance of the farmers. The farmers guarded against encroachments of the ranchers' cattle. The railroads facilitated access to the new country. Refrigeration made it possible to locate slaughterhouses and meat-packing plants near the source and to ship the products back to the eastern markets. Farm machinery permitted the farmers to cultivate ever wider areas. In other words, the social organization of the prairie lands changed in response to technical advances, and both factors in turn influenced the federal government to pass legislation favorable to the new circumstances.

Consider three modern developments. Just a mention of atomic energy brings to mind the changes in our social organization which it requires. Another instrument of production, better called an instrument of non-production, is "The Pill," which is causing profound changes in our way of life. This new tool brings about a drastic change in our social habits simply because of its existence. A third example is the computer, the information machine. Its existence is changing the manner is which nearly every enterprise is conducted. Our social relations have had to adapt to the existence of atomic energy, "The Pill" and the computer just as in other times society's ways of doing things changed because man discovered how to make fire or invented the compass.

Several years before I became so immersed in Marxism, I had contributed a chapter to *Socialist Planning and a Socialist Program*. I have noted earlier that in expressing the general agreement among all the contributors, the editor pointed out that the United States then had the natural, technical and human resources to feed, clothe and shelter every man, woman and child in decency, security and comfort. But our resources were not being put to this use and could not be under capitalism. This task could only be accomplished under socialism. Socialist ideas, theories, institutions and conditions were already growing within our capitalist system in response to the rapid development of new tools. And they were growing in spite of the reluctance of certain elements of our society to accept the changes that the new instruments demanded. But these socialist tendencies were not growing fast enough. A thorough reorganization of the relations among people had to occur. If there was to be too much of a lag between the development of the tools and a corresponding social organization, the resolution would come by violent overthrow of the old relations. The hard fact of the matter is that those who resist those changes can only delay them but cannot prevent them from taking place. The changes are inevitable. The only choice is whether they will be permitted to take place peacefully or whether they will come through a violent social upheaval.

In the 1930s, I found the Marxist approach more plausible, logical and comprehensive than any other school of thought that I had encountered. It coped with priorities, causation and motivation. It described the relation of material to spiritual things, of matter to thought. It put our world into some kind of understandable order. I was also impressed with the fact that Marxist thought had little relation to the slanderous claims of its Establishment critics. Quite to the contrary, it was a serious philosophical approach to the great questions of our times.

My curiosity about the dialectical process led to a luncheon which, in retrospect, I find amusing. I had mentioned to Corliss Lamont my difficulties in understanding certain aspects of Marxism. He told me that he knew just the person to answer all my questions and invited me to join him and his friend at the Harvard Club. The friend turned out to be a colleague of Corliss's on the Columbia University faculty and a man erudite in the intricacies of the difficult school of Marxist thought. In an article titled "Why I Am a Communist" (*Modern Monthly*, April 1934), he had written that "truly understood communism does not involve the negation of democracy but its fulfillment." We enjoyed a long lunch with more talk than food. I pressed our guest with questions about the positive-negative-synthesis equation of dialectical materialism and came away from the meeting more than ever convinced of the soundness of Marxism.

Many of my contemporaries will remember the man who was enlightening me. He was Sidney Hook, a professor of philosophy who was making converts to communism in the early 1930s—and denouncing the Soviet Union and all it stood for in 1939. In the next two decades Hook would become known as one of our country's most prominent redbaiters, denouncer of Communists, a leading organizer of anti-Communist rallies, congresses and movements, a supporter of McCarthyism and an obedient servant of the Cold War. During twenty years of active participation in the Communist movement, I ran into other turncoats, but none so prominent as Hook. Nevertheless, at that luncheon, he helped me to become a Communist and, through my revulsion at his subsequent behavior, to remain one.

Unlike his Columbia colleague, Corliss has remained consistent throughout his life. He has never been a member of the Communist Party, and I do not believe he has ever regarded himself as a Marxist. He is and has been during all his adult life a philosophical humanist, as well as one of our country's outstanding fighters for civil liberties. As a leader in the innumerable and fierce civil rights struggles of our generation, few people have equaled his consistency and courage.

In 1978 Corliss sent me a Christmas letter in which he told me he was working on his own life story. He added that he was approaching seventy-seven and might not have much time left. My reply reminded him that less than two years before, we had had another Harvard Club lunch, just the two of us, during which he had informed me that he had just returned from a wonderful week of skiing at one of the western resorts and that he was pleased to find that he was skimming down the slopes as nimbly as ever. To his prowess at that youthful sport, I could only contrast my own relatively secure game of Ping-Pong. I assured him that from my observation he had plenty of time to finish his autobiography and even to publish a sequel. I urged him to work hard at it, for what he had to say and what his life has meant to my generation needed to be recorded.

His letter to me also gave me some information I had somehow missed. "When the McCarthy Committee got me cited for contempt of Congress in 1954," Corliss wrote, "there was quite a long debate about it in the Senate. At one point Joe McCarthy stated: 'Mr. Lamont is a man of great wealth. He was born with a silver spoon in his mouth. He has done more damage to this Nation than perhaps any other man in the country, with the possible exception of Frederick Field.' " In Corliss's opinion, that put us both on the honor list.

The surprising thing to me now, as I write in the last quarter of the twentieth century, is that Marxism remains the only great body of interpretation of modern society that has been produced in the last hundred and twenty-five years or so. Hundreds and probably thousands of books have attempted to explain capitalism, yet none of which I am aware has developed a comprehensive system of thought that includes causation and priorities and motivation or the relation of mind to matter or the connection between aesthetics and the material means of production. None has produced an explanation of how society works in relation to its material environment. Capitalism is without a philosophy. The Marxist philosophy and ethic, on the other hand, have been distorted and turned upside down by their critics. Nevertheless they remain as intact as a giant tree that for season after season has been pecked at by woodpeckers.

Much constructive criticism of Marxism has also attempted to develop and apply it to modern conditions. I have been especially interested in two areas in which it has been concerned. One I call the great analogy. The Marxist principle of social struggle and change and the passing from quantitative to qualitative or revolutionary change is essentially an analogy with what happens in nature. Water, for instance, changes qualitatively at its boiling and freezing points and metal is transformed at its melting point.

For a long time, however, I have been troubled by a too literal application of the analogy between science and society, between natural and social phenomena. At sea level, water boils at 212 degrees and freezes at 32 degrees. Metals melt at predictable temperatures. The application of dialectics to social phenomena is less certain. Revolutions, however, do not occur at predictable dates nor under precisely defined conditions. Social prophecy is an approximation of what will happen, not a detailed blueprint of events to come.

Earthquakes are also unpredictable at present, and they belong to natural rather than social phenomena. I expect, however, that this problem will be solved as scientists learn more about the circumstances under which earthquakes occur. Just as one can determine when water is about to boil by taking its temperature, so scientists will eventually learn to predict when and where earthquakes are to happen.

I wonder whether an analogous development will take place in our knowledge of social phenomena. Will social scientists learn enough about the process by which revolutions take place to predict when and where they will occur?

I do not have the answer, nor does anyone else. But many of us have from time to time in our political work wrongly thought we had exact answers to future events. We have attempted to foretell social changes as precisely as we have the point at which water will boil, and we have thus fooled ourselves and misled others.

It is obvious, for example, that the miserable social-economic organization of most Latin American countries must be replaced by a system of relations among people which is more in accord with modern instruments of production. Or, to put it in plainer language, these backward and obsolete Latin American societies must adjust themselves to the modern facts of life. The question is whether the changes will be permitted and even encouraged by the present powers-that-be or will have to come about through the violent overthrow of the existing system. What cannot be predicted in precise detail is the when, where and how of these events.

The second area that especially interests me is what happens in the dialectical process to the whole of society after the achievement of communism, which Marxist literature suggests is the "final" stage of social development. Marxism records five types of relations of production or five principal ways in which people have organized themselves: primitive communal, slave, feudal, capitalist and socialist. By inference, socialism will give way to communism, though to date there have been no communist societies. Each stage has followed the one preceding it through a dialectical process. The development of tools forced changes in the relations of those working them until quantity passed into quality, and feudalism, let's say, replaced slavery.

According to Marxism, the stage of socialism is eliminating the exploiters versus the exploited. The tools for producing the means of life and the organization of the people using the tools are coming into harmony. At the completion of this process the stage of communism will presumably be reached. My question is: What will happen then? Surely the dialectical process will not cease to operate. From communism, which will then be the positive factor, will its negative or opposite emerge? What will be that opposite? How, according to the laws of dialectics, can communism be the final stage of social relations?

We can afford to wait for the answer to those questions. But we cannot afford to wait for those who own and run our economy to learn to face the realities of the world. A capitalist society is well aware of the danger of earthquakes and is evidently taking steps to learn what to do about them. It seems incapable, however, of facing the realities of mass poverty, widespread undernourishment, environmental pollution, human cruelty, racism, and inequalities all through the social structure.

Apart from the two aspects of Marxism that I have discussed, the great analogy and the future dialectical development of society, there is a question raised by the location of the two great revolutions that have taken place during my lifetime. Marx and Engels anticipated that the adjustment between the tools of production developing rapidly in the nineteenth-century industrializing nations, England and Germany, and the social-political organization of the people of those countries would bring the English and German proletariat, the working people, to power before this would happen anywhere else. In other words, the revolution would take place first in England and Germany. They also predicted that this revolutionary change would not necessarily be violent. Industrial progress in those countries not only was polarizing the classes, but also welding the workers and their allies into organizations which potentially represented a majority of the total population and which were constantly gaining political experience.

Those predictions did not come true. The revolutions of the twentieth century took place in industrially backward countries whose industrial workers formed a minority. In China, indeed, the revolutionary vanguard was formed from the peasantry, backed, it is true, by the small industrial proletariat that existed in only a few of the cities. Looking up a Marxist reference some time ago, I found a source book published in the late 1950s, *Marx and Engels, Basic Writings on Politics and Philosophy*, by Lewis S. Feuer, formerly of Stanford University and later a professor at the University of Toronto. In it Feuer made an interesting comment. Referring to the revolutionary ferment in East Asia, he suggested that Marxist terms were filled with a new content. Capitalists were the Western imperialist rulers, the proletariat represented Asian people generally, and the class struggle became racial and national liberation.

In any case, both the Russian and Asian revolutions took place in countries and under conditions not envisioned by the nineteenth-century founders of Marxism. And the industrialized countries, England, Germany and now the United States, where the revolutionary movement should have begun, became the chief enemies and obstacles to the successful development of socialism under minorities in the USSR and China. In the early days of Marxism it had not been anticipated that the powerful industrialized countries would be the very ones to thwart socialism when it appeared on the scene.

It is therefore necessary to face the question whether the historical experience of the twentieth century invalidates the theories advanced by Marx and Engels in the nineteenth. Both Russia and China were, at the beginning of the twentieth century, way behind the industrialized countries in terms of the tools of production in use within their borders. Their respective revolutions, therefore, changed the form of their social organization before the instruments of production within their bounderies forced that transformation. Does this historical fact disprove the Marxist theory?

The answer, I believe, is that while it raises the question, it does not disprove the theory. By the time the Soviet and Chinese revolutions took place, the world was so integrated, so interconnected, that the Marxist theory of historical materialism could no longer be tested by what happened within national borders. The phenomena of advanced industrialization and technological development, the existence of a large, educated working class and the contradictions in the most advanced of the capitalist societies affected every part of the world. They affected all nations and all people regardless of national bounderies or different stages of development. Because of this complex interrelationship, which had become nearly universal, a revolutionary breakthrough could happen anywhere.

Among the factors that caused the breakthrough to occur in Russia and China were the quality of the revolutionary leadership combined with the despair of the peasants and workers and disillusionment of the intelligentsia; the weakness, inability and corruption of the rulers; the size of the two countries and their enormous human and material resources; and the momentary preoccupation of the potentially antagonistic countries, together with contradictions and confusion among them.

There is no question, nevertheless, that the when, how and where of these revolutions were not precisely predicted by Marx and Engels. They took place and have tried to maintain their momentum in a world whose technical development and integration could not have been anticipated in the mid-nineteenth century. To my way of thinking, however, none of this invalidates the theory of dialectical and historical materialism. Technological development inexorably impels societies to a socialist form of organization. What is difficult to predict is when and where the change will take place.

The Marxist system of looking at the world was first developed over a hundred years ago, and it has been adapting itself to a changing world ever since. As an over-all approach to understanding how the world functions, it has not been successfully challenged or replaced by any other philosophy.

It is one of the tragedies of our times that Marxism has been equated by ignorant and misguided people with evil. Marxism is not an evil. It is an intelligent philosophical explanation of how we live in relation to our material environment. It calls for changes in our society as technology provides the material base for change. It warns that if the dialectical process is opposed, it will nevertheless triumph, though at the cost of revolution. There is a fork in the road just ahead. One direction leads to violence and destruction, the other to peaceful evolution. For the life of me, I cannot see how there can be any question about which we should choose.

17

The Communist Party

My relationship with the American Communist Party started with our mutual interest in the China question. We were both concerned with the developing internal conflict between the Chiang Kai-shek government and the Communist forces which were dispossessing the landlord class and organizing revolutionary pockets in various interior regions. And we also cared about American Far Eastern policy, which was supporting the most corrupt elements of Chinese society and selling quantities of scrap iron to Japan's military while issuing demagogic declarations about peace.

While learning a good deal about eastern Asia, I had become convinced that the only way to stabilize the situation was to liberate the majority opposed to Chiang Kai-shek, which could only be done under the leadership of the Communists. They were the only internal group that both saw the situation clearly and was capable of taking and maintaining the revolutionary initiative. The corollary to this was that the United States should either maintain a hands-off policy between the contending forces within China, or, preferably, though far less likely, give active support to any and all democratic elements. For the United States to take a democratic position, it would have to support a united front of all those Chinese forces that would actively oppose Japanese aggression and simultaneously would have to put a diplomatic and economic stranglehold on those elements in Japan which were responsible for the mainland invasion that had begun in Mukden on that memorable September 18-19 of 1931. I found that the principal organized efforts in these directions in the United States stemmed from the American Communist Party.

I had been straining at the academic leash of the IPR. I did not want to devote myself to a purely academic life. I wanted to continue that type of work but to combine it with activities that derived from what my studies

165

were teaching me. I have already explained that I strongly believed the IPR should remain in its academic shell in order not to be destroyed. That scholarly purity could best be preserved by allowing those of its staff members who were so inclined to seek and develop outlets for their political convictions outside the IPR. I, at least, wanted the opportunity and freedom to express what I knew in political terms.

The CP was not the only institution to which I turned in what had become almost an obsession to see that the results of our research reached as wide a public as possible. I joined and became active in several other organizations that were "respectable" in every sense of the word. One of these was the Council on Foreign Relations, whose exclusive circles I was invited to join at the very time I was making my decisive move to the left. The Council was composed of those who considered themselves, with good reason, to be the brains behind American foreign policy and the trainers of our leading statesmen. The Council published then, as it still does, a distinguished quarterly called *Foreign Affairs*. Its headquarters was a former private home having a lot of wood paneling, and there, always in dinner jackets, we could meet and hobnob with leading foreign statesmen as well as exchange our wisdom among ourselves. At one of those formal dinners I was placed next to Allen Dulles, who later became head of the Central Intelligence Agency, and at another next to his brother, John Foster Dulles, who became U.S. Secretary of State and conceived that extraordinary policy called "brinkmanship." It will surprise no one to learn that, when I came upon bad times, I was summarily dropped from this august body without even the courtesy of a notice. I therefore cannot provide the exact date of my leaving, though it probably took place in 1950.

I also joined the Foreign Policy Association, a far more popular and liberal organization than the Council on Foreign Relations. The FPA counted among its much larger and more democratic membership a number of people who entertained doubts about the wisdom of Foggy Bottom.

In 1935 I became part of a small group that founded the Public Affairs Committee. There were six of us in the original group: Harold G. Moulton of the Brookings Institution, Luther Gulick of the Institute of Public Administration, Evans Clark of the Twentieth Century Fund, George Soule of the National Bureau of Economic Research, Raymond Leslie Buell of the Foreign Policy Association and I from the IPR. I made a smaller contribution to the success of this venture than the others; but the person mostly responsible for the splendid results was Maxwell S. Stewart, the organization's editor.

Our original statement—remember, this was 1935—said, "It is generally recognized that the United States is confronted with unprecedented economic and social problems. Although these problems have their roots in the past, they have come to a head with such comparative suddenness and are so complex that the American people appear to be in a state of bewilderment. New methods must be developed for transmitting the product of knowledge and thought to the people who in the last analysis formulate policies and control public opinion. . . .What is needed is a popular education program. If democracy is to be something more than a name and if this country is to avoid the pitfalls of dictatorship, a much larger proportion of people must attain an understanding of the nature of our economic, financial and social organization. . .and an ability to make an intelligent choice as to possible solutions."

Thirty-four years later, many years after my association with the organization had ended, I received its annual report and learned of some astonishing results. The total number of pamphlets distributed for the five years 1965-1969 was 10,826,971; three pamphlets published between 1935 and 1969 had topped a million and two more were just under that figure; altogether, 442 titles had been published. Among the big sellers were "The Races of Mankind," "The Facts about Cancer," "How to Tell Your Child about Sex," and "Building Your Marriage." Not a list of titles a Marxist outfit would have picked, perhaps, but pretty useful subjects nonetheless. I looked back at our original statement of purpose and realized that the Public Affairs Committee had been surprisingly successful in carrying out its mandate.

Those who experienced the early 1930s will recall the turmoil, the social unrest and the widespread disatisfaction with our traditional institutions caused by the Great Depression. It resulted in an uncountable number of personal rebellions which never congealed into politically threatening revolt against the Establishment, thanks to the political skills of President Roosevelt. Yes, there were plentiful protests, reforms, and ameliorative measures. Yes, our institutions were modified to take the force out of a potential political crisis.

Nevertheless, we had hopes and even expectations of achieving profound and lasting changes. Our expectations applied not only to the resolution of the domestic economic-social crisis but also the possibility of altering American foreign policy so that we would become aligned with the plain people of the world instead of with their oppressors. Nearly fifty years later, many of us still have such hopes, which have yet to be fulfilled.

The Communist Party, as I was to learn, was principally concerned with the enormous internal problems of our country, the effects of the Depression, the trade-union movement, the liberation and equalization of Negroes, the radicalization and politicalization of youth, poverty and unemployment. It was also concerned with supporting the Soviet Union and protecting it from slander.

During the early 1930s, I was primarily preoccupied with the Far East and American relations with that region. My general interest in social problems, which, at the end of my formal education, had brought me to the Socialist Party, had focused primarily on the Far East since my absorption in IPR work. Lord knows, the subject was neither narrow nor isolated from all of the others which plagued Americans at the time. My thinking, nevertheless, began with the America-China equation and from that moved to other problems, instead of the other way around. But this concern was enough to begin my contact with the American Communist Party.

The magazine *China Today* was already an ongoing publication when I joined the editorial board in July 1934, upon the invitation of the then editors. Here was my opportunity to draw political conclusions. I had known the other editors for some time and considered them first-rate people whose political ideas ran in the same channels as mine. I shall mention only three of them because their names have already been published and I can do no damage by identifying them again. I have already referred to Philip Jaffe, with whom I later founded the magazine *Amerasia*. T. A. Bisson was the Far Eastern expert of the Foreign Policy Association, and his writings were well known and highly respected. In his FPA work, Bisson maintained a high order of scholarship and what the Establishment calls "objectivity." (Objectivity in this sense means that you may describe in full detail the process of smashing your thumb with a hammer, but you must stop short of mentioning that it hurts.) I never had any reason to believe that Bisson belonged to the CP. Chi Chao-ting was a young Chinese who at the time was earning his doctorate at Columbia University with a brilliant thesis on large-scale irrigation in ancient China. A close friend of mine, Chi joined the international secretariat of the IPR at a later date and wrote several important monographs for it. He returned to China in the middle 1940s to take a high position on the staff of Chiang Kai-shek's brother-in-law, H. H. Kung. After the Communist take-over in 1949, Chi assumed an important post in the new government's financial apparatus.

On joining the editorial board of *China Today*, I was well aware that to all intents and purposes it was a Communist project. Some, though not all, of its editors were members of the American Party and others were either members or had close connections with the Chinese CP. The original editors had known me for two or three years and were familiar with my work and opinions. In inviting me to join them, they demonstrated their confidence in me, and, for my part, I joined them because I agreed with their politics and regarded them as able and honorable people. We met one long evening each week. Topics were assigned at the beginning of each month and at our subsequent meetings, we read aloud and criticized what each of us had prepared. I found these sessions to be excellent training in collective work.

My editorship lasted twenty-seven months. Although I took a pseudonym, by the end of that time my articles as well as I myself had become fairly well known among the Party leadership and some of the rank and file. I, in turn, had become acquainted with many members and officials. This building of friendship and mutual trust was a gradual process. Little by little, I became aware that I was becoming a full-fledged Communist and being treated as such. There was no decision, "Today I will become a Communist," but after a couple of years, I could look back and say, "Lo and behold, I have become a Communist."

In a spring 1950 session of the Senate subcommittee investigating Senator McCarthy's charges of Communist penetration of the State Department, Earl Browder, former general secretary of the CPUSA, was asked, "Did you know Frederick Vanderbilt Field as a member of the Communist Party?"

Browder answered, "I wouldn't be able to say definitely. I assumed he was, but I didn't know."

I was asked the same question the next day and avoided answering it by using the Fifth Amendment. Had I answered, I might have said: "I consider myself a Communist, although I don't now have nor have I ever had a credential showing that I am a member. Nobody ever said to me, 'Will you become a member of our organization?' I never belonged to a branch or a cell of the Party and I never paid Party dues. I made financial contributions to organizations in which Communists were interested, those groups that the public calls front organizations, but I did not give money to the Party as such. I suppose I am what the Party calls a member at large."

I would have liked to make that kind of statement publicly during the Cold War period, that time of the McCarthy madness. Those were days that Cedric Belfrage has aptly called *The American Inquisition* and Lillian Hellman dubbed *Scoundrel Time*. Why didn't I go public? A good many others may also have wanted to, but they didn't make such statements either. I think a great many well-meaning people mistakenly thought that we had something to hide, or that we were willfully defying the courts and the congressional inquisitors just for the sake of being ornery. That certainly wasn't the case.

If I had answered the question about Party membership, I would have been collaborating with the inquisitors' efforts to restrict freedom of speech, the right of assembly, the right to petition the government and other privileges that we presumably enjoy under the Constitution. In the legal sense, the act of answering a question validates its being asked. Neither

senators nor judges had any constitutional right to ask anyone whether he
was a Communist or a member of the Communist Party. People's political
opinions, just like their religious beliefs, are immune to inquiry, according
to the First Amendment. We may divulge our opinions if we so desire; the
matter is entirely up to us. But we cannot be forced to expose our private
convictions or to reveal our conscience.

The Cold War Establishment tried to nullify these constitutional rights
in every way that it could. The Smith Act made it a crime to advocate the
desirability of overthrowing any government in the United States by force
or violence. The anti-union Taft-Hartley Act of 1947 compelled all union
officers to sign oaths that they were not Communists. The McCarran Internal Security Act of 1950 set up the Subversive Activities Control Board
to force any organization with unorthodox political thinking to register, to
disclose its membership and financial affairs and to label itself subversive
on all of its printed matter. The McCarran-Walter Act of 1952, among
other things, removed deportation cases from the courts and turned them
over to special boards set up by the Immigration Service where ordinary
rules of evidence and procedure could be overlooked. All of these were
federal laws. And many states followed suit with their own repressive measures. During those Cold War days, the Establishment tried to narrow the
right against self-incrimination to such technicalities that witnesses practically had to be lawyers themselves in order to use it successfully.

I testified before one Senate committee that, under present circumstances,
the entire weight of the government and its various branches was being
brought to bear against all political thought, cultural expression and organizations which opposed the Cold War. I pointed out that a person could
not criticize the foreign policy of the government without being officially
castigated and publicly smeared. One could not, for instance, organize a
committee to advocate the opening of commercial and diplomatic relations
with the People's Republic of China without being branded disloyal. That
organization would also be placed on the subversive list by the Attorney
General and face persecution and possible prosecution.

All progressive-minded individuals, I felt, had to stand together in defense
of the traditional American right to free expression and organization, the
entire Bill of Rights and the inalienable right and duty to advocate policies
that they thought would bring about a lasting peace. The latter was then
of paramount importance.

In this context the question, "Are you a member of the Communist
Party?" became a principal weapon of the government in its attempt to
intimidate and terrorize its critics. If middle-of-the-roaders answered the
question negatively, reactionary fanatics would inevitably try to trap them

by associating them with others nearer the Communist position. Almost anyone who had any disagreement with the Cold War policy could be trapped simply by the assertion that the Communists held the same view.

It went like this: As the Communists were opposed to the Cold War, anyone who also opposed it or part of it found himself in jeopardy. To accomplish this, all the inquisition had to do was declare that communism was a criminal conspiracy (the Smith and McCarran acts)and then torment anyone who on any issue took a position similar to that advocated by the Communist Party. Pursue the practice to its logical conclusion: The Communist Party is against rape; *ergo*, to be safe, advocate rape.

These were the reasons I could not answer the inquisitors' questions regarding my Communist sympathies and affiliations. My economic independence made it easier for me than for most people to follow my convictions. There were others without that freedom who were forced by the Establishment to betray their friends and their beliefs. They deserve to be judged individually and according to their particular circumstances. Those who were *free* to make a choice and who then *chose* to be cowards were truly despicable.

The Fifth Amendment is a part of the Bill of Rights adopted in 1789. The pertinent section reads: "No person . . . shall be compelled in any criminal case to be a witness against himself." The struggle against the inquisitorial ecclesiastical and civil courts' practice of forcing testimony from accused witnesses was fought and won in England during the seventeenth century. Because of emigration, the Puritan revolution successfully planted the privilege against self-incrimination in the American colonies even before the battle was won in the mother country. It is a tradition as old and honored as America itself.

I did not encounter any significant harassment until more than ten years after I began my association with the Communist Party. I was left pretty much alone by the Establishment press. No sensational reports were published even when I resigned my staff job at the IPR to become executive secretary of one of the Party's prominent front organizations. There were a few unpleasant incidents, however. Shortly after the United States entered World War II, the FBI tipped off a couple of columnists that I had accepted a job offer from one of the military intelligence services. These columnists published nasty stories which created a public atmosphere in which the military had to renege on the offer, which, of course, was the purpose of the leak.

In any case, in the late thirties and during World War II, there was less harassment of the left than usual. That was a period of relative national unity in the face of a war which was first impending and then upon us. As far as I was concerned, until 1940, most of my time and energy went into my IPR work, and my political activity was largely confined to the evenings. I was not split in two by the combination because both my academic research activities and their political application primarily revolved around Far Eastern issues.

I was one of the many thousands who uncritically accepted the Soviet accounts of their political purges between 1935 and 1938. As a result of three public trials, which were attended by foreign correspondents and diplomats, some of the heroes of the revolution and of socialism were found guilty of treason and executed. We only learned of the untold number of other trials with similar results for untold thousands of lesser personalities many years later. The entire American Communist Party was taken in by this political outrage, and it was not alone. Many members of the Establishment were also fooled. The American ambassador, Joseph E. Davies, had attended the public trials, and he believed they were genuine. Even Walter Duranty, the *The New York Times* correspondent in Moscow, informed us that it was "unthinkable that Stalin. . .and the Court Martial could have sentenced their friends to death unless proofs of guilt were overwhelming."

It was not until 1956 that Khrushchev reported to the Twentieth Congress of the Communist Party of the Soviet Union the truth about what had taken place: countless thousands had been executed or imprisoned by Stalin under the pretext that they were "enemies of the people." That horror, Khrushchev told us, had been a deliberate hoax to eliminate the possibility of an ideological fight or even the open expression of dissenting views.

One day during the trials, I was asked to drop by the New York State CP headquarters where one of its high officials asked if I could cover a meeting of several Party cells being held that evening to explain the trials. "Okay," I said, "it's not quite in my line, but I've read the Party press on it and I suppose I can give the comrades some kind of report."

The meeting, held in a Brooklyn school, was attended by maybe thirty or forty CP youth. After I made my report—a simple repetition of what Party leaders had said in the press—I was questioned closely and persistently. The Party "line" had not convinced my audience, and these young American Communists were clearly uncomfortable.

"How, Comrade Field," one youth asked, "could this have happened in the Soviet Union? The explanations are not satisfactory." I remember my answer all too well. In fact, it frequently comes back to haunt me. The gist was this: "The only thing I can tell you is that because Comrade Stalin says so, we have to believe the trials are just. He has never let us down.

What he says must be true." My audience, as far as I could tell, accepted the answer.

I was then, as always, more concerned and more familiar with what was going on in China than in the Soviet Union, but when called upon to give an answer about a disturbing event in the latter, I unhesitatingly spread the gospel. Stalin was infallible; all my Communist surroundings told me so. So was Browder, although on a lower level of sanctity, and so were the other CP leaders. Whenever a newspaper headline proclaimed some startling event, we would ask the first comrade we ran into, "Has Earl said anything about this yet?" "Does anyone know what Gene thinks?" "What does Bill know about it?"

Participants in a political movement are expected to have respect for the wisdom of their leaders, though surely not to the extent of ceasing to think for themselves. But this was exactly what was happening to many of us. But in case any of my readers thinks that this situation was unique to the Communist Party, I want to remind them that precisely the same thing occurs in other political parties, especially during periods of stress such as the one that we were experiencing in the 1930s.

I might have become more involved in this "monolithism" if my work had not been so concentrated in the Far East. I worked in that field with a small group, first on *China Today*, then, after World War II, with GIs who had returned from the Philippines, China and Japan. We formed an informal CP Far Eastern Commission, of which I was chairman, and we kept in close contact with the Party leadership. We were directly in touch with events in China and other areas through publications, correspondence and visits, more so, I feel certain, than were the top functionaries. They, to my knowledge, never considered Far Eastern issues to be a matter of more than peripheral interest. I complained about that neglect and requested that it be officially discussed.

While I was able to pursue my principal work relatively independently, at the same time, I operated in a general atmosphere of Soviet infallibility. What Stalin said or wrote about nationalism or linguistics was more basic to the doctrine than *Das Kapital* because Marx, after all, wrote decades earlier and was subject to continuing interpretation. Stalin, on the other hand, was contemporary: he spoke literal truth. Without doubt, some of that awe of authority rubbed off on me. I was a good, unrebellious comrade.

But no matter how important those unfortunate errors and traditions in our Party were, they were hardly the whole picture of life and work in the CPUSA, most of which was positive and rewarding. We may have been surrounded by antisocialist and pro-imperialist enemies, but we were not such a small group ourselves. In the thirties and forties, the CP had perhaps as many members as belonged to the Socialist Party just after World War I, but the CP's membership was more cohesive, more militant and more disciplined. There was also the Communist Youth League and all kinds of alliances for specific objectives with community organizations, church groups, unions, Negro and other ethnic groups, liberals and intellectuals. Party members, in my experience, were among the better Americans. They made fine, warm and entertaining friends with a wide variety of interests, and, except for a handful of exceptions, trustworthy companions.

In those early years we were bound together both by the hostility of our political opponents and by the intensity of our own beliefs. We had faith in the importance and validity of our objectives. We supported each other with the strength of our convictions. We were utterly serious about what we were doing, devoted to our political mission and convinced that in the long run our goals would be achieved.

We were serious and hardworking, but we also enjoyed a comradeship having richness and variety. I found new facets of life. I was introduced to Bach by a group of comrades whom I saw socially. Driving up to northern New England one weekend, a long trip, I listened as my three companions, two men and a woman, all young, took turns whistling fragments of Bach's music and challenging the others to identify the piece. I was awed, impressed and envious. I knew nothing about ballet, classical or modern, and other comrades introduced me to this fascinating art. (In later years it became much more than an artistic fascination, for I am spending the latter third of my life married to a ballerina.) I knew nothing about off-Broadway theatre or music away from Carnegie Hall until comrades led me to them. Through friends I made in the Party, my cultural life broadened and deepened.

The picture of an American Communist that the Establishment has drawn is absurd. It depicts a secretive, conspiratorial figure who, most likely, has a bomb in his back pocket. He and his group are undoubtedly plotting to occupy the White House by force after they have destroyed the Capitol. If he's not that sort of ridiculous caricature, he is, at least, a strange, disgruntled, shifty-eyed un-American who, for a variety of psychological quirks, is against everything. That is not a picture of the hundreds of comrades whom I got to know. Nor is it, my dear friends, one of me.

Then there is the widespread myth that Communists are out to destroy everything. I spent twenty years as an active Communist and moved widely in Party circles. The only violence I personally experienced was practiced against me, not by me, in the course of attacks on picket lines, imprisonment and the expulsion of my wife from the country. The latter I consider a clear case of violence, and cowardly violence at that. Violence is not restricted to physical acts, but also includes psychological acts such as threats and blackmail which I suppose have been used against nearly every Party member. They were certainly used against me. For instance: "Field, if you don't answer that question, we'll cite you for contempt." "Field, if you do answer that question, we'll cite you for perjury."

During my lifetime, the policies of the CPUSA left no room for violence. Our country has found itself in a revolutionary situation only once. That was, of course, at the end of the eighteenth century, when it met the violence of its English oppressors with counterviolence and thereby achieved independence. The Communist Party has never done anything as idiotic as to advocate the violent overthrow of any American government. It has, however, dealt pedagogically with the subject of violence. Just as every American child is proudly taught the lesson of the heroic resistance to British violence by General Washington's troops, so every American Communist is taught that, given a hypothetical revolutionary situation in the socialist sense, the working class must be prepared, if necessary, to meet the violence of their oppressors with their own counterviolence.

When the gap between the developing tools of production on the one hand and the organization of society on the other becomes an intolerable burden upon the working class and the ruling class refuses to close that gap, then the call to arms becomes the only viable tactic left to the workers. In the words of the *Communist Manifesto*, the Communists must consequently "openly declare that their ends can be obtained only by forcible overthrow of all existing social conditions." That is the revolutionary doctrine of Marxism. In the present state of affairs in the United States the question of the use of revolutionary violence remains an academic subject. How long can it remain so? Will the reactionaries agree to the changes so desperately needed before conditions become "intolerable"?

For the reader who is simply interested in learning about the current practice of violence in the United States, however, there is no better way to start than by becoming acquainted with the history of the Central Intelligence Agency.

Were we Communists conspiratorial? Well, my section of the country conspired to elect some members of the New York City council, and we conspired to support the election of one or two members of Congress. But in both cases the Republicans and Democrats outconspired us by far. Along with others we conspired in many unions for better wages and fringe benefits, for honest union leaders and for stimulating and radicalizing the political outlook of the rank and file. We helped—I mean conspired—to unionize the employees of the federal government. We conspired to educate the public about the Far East and our government's policies there. We were conspiring all over the place. And so, fortunately, was almost everybody else in the United States—because that is one of the good ways our democracy works. A great many people were pressing their objectives in every walk of public life. Only when the Communists did it was it called conspiracy.

After World War II, the lives of members of the CPUSA became much more difficult. The country passed through ten to fifteen years of one of the most bigoted, narrow-minded, reactionary phases of its entire history. Liberals were hounded while radicals were persecuted and prosecuted. J. Edgar Hoover, surely one of the most despicable men ever to hold high public office in this country, was despicable both in his personal and public character. He and Senator Joe McCarthy, an ignorant, drunken homosexual—the latter reprehensible because he tried to hide it by persecuting other homosexuals—were among the most influential men in the country. The managers of the media, with a few isolated exceptions, were cowardly. The intelligentsia, with some notable exceptions, retreated to their ivory towers. Many liberals turned tail, and most kept silent. A few had strong spines. The Communist Party as a whole, and Party members personally, took a beating.

The Communist Party headquarters at 35 East 12th Street was a building remembered from the first visit. I don't know how it had been used before the Party occupied it nor how long the Communists had used it before I first became acquainted with it. It was nine or more stories high, ugly inside and out, neither ramshackle nor sparkling new. The *Daily Worker* was printed downstairs. The fifth floor was the headquarters of the New York State organization, and the ninth floor housed the national leadership. An extraordinary thing about the building was the apparent total absence of any system of security. I was there many times and became convinced that the lack of such measures was not only apparent but real. There were certainly no electronic devices. You could get out of the elevator on the ninth floor, and if nobody happened to be around to tell you whether Gene Dennis or Elizabeth Gurley Flynn or whoever was free, you could look around for them in all of the offices. The floor consisted of a number of plain, barely furnished offices which surrounded a large central room with a long table and chairs. That was where the governing body of the Party met.

I was asked to join some meetings of the national committee when Far Eastern questions were discussed. The talk was free; at these meetings there was no atmosphere of monolithism. At one—it must have taken place in the mid-nineteen forties—I gave vent to my major beef. Nobody in the leadership was giving enough attention to what was happening in China, to a revolutionary movement that was going to reshape the world. What was going on there was bound to have a great effect on Americans and on the country's foreign policy, I argued; we were not doing enough to prepare Americans for the eventual and certain success of communism.

I thought I had a clincher when I pointed out that I had been the only person, with a single exception, to write an article on Far Eastern affairs in the Party's theoretical journal, *The Communist*, later called *Political Affairs*, since the middle 1930s. Obviously, that was not the way it should be. (Anybody who wants to check that statement will find in the September 1937 issue an article by Lawrence Hearn, a pseudonym I occasionally used at the time.)

My beef didn't have much effect. What I was writing, they said, was perfectly satisfactory. They agreed with my analysis. Through me and the group of young veterans with whom I worked, they implied, plenty of attention was being given Asian issues. I was never satisfied on that point.

I was present at the meeting at which Browder was ousted as general secretary of the CPUSA. I remember it well because, on impulse, I did something that has since pleased me. Every once in a while, when I look back on my life, I'd like to go up to the Fred Field of a particular day and shake his hand. I said something to that effect when he joined the Socialist Party. The meeting at which Browder was denounced and fired was another. (There were other occasions when I'd like to take a swipe at him.)

As World War II was drawing to a close, Browder was developing a new thesis regarding the role which the Communist Party should play. In essence, Browder was calling for a postwar united front of all democratic elements to help the world recover from the holocaust and to prevent reactionaries from dominating the postwar political arena. The policy was directed to the domestic situation in the United States as well as to its international relations. The interests of the Communist Party were to be merged with those of all other political elements this side of outright fascists, reactionaries and imperialists.

Those who were not around during the international dispute that erupted over the Browder thesis may think, from this very brief description, that what he was advocating closely parallels the policy which several European Communist Parties, notably the Italian, Spanish and French, are practicing today. That is not so. There was a crucial difference. Browder's thesis included the virtual disappearance of the CPUSA. The Party had, in fact, been dissolved in 1944 and replaced by the Communist Political Association. Browder went further, suggesting that it abjure its political function altogether and become nothing more than an educational association. He referred to enlightened capitalism led by men of vision and intelligence. He was frankly impressed by FDR and the New Deal leadership. In essence, he was advocating class collaboration and the abandonment of an inde-

pendent Communist movement. The European parties today, far from considering dissolution, regard themselves as the nucleus, as Communists and
Marxists, of a progressive alliance that must take political leadership and
eventual power.

William Foster, in a letter to the National Committee, had sharply
criticized the extremes to which Browder was leading the Party, but he had
been persuaded to withdraw it in the interests of unity. But when the
Browder "line" was criticized in Europe, the Foster message was made public.
The Party leadership had made a grave mistake in keeping the internal
conflict to themselves until forced to reveal it by intervention from abroad.

Throughout my years of association with the CP, I was aware of ideological and personal infighting among the leadership, but only vaguely so.
Long before I came into the picture, the Lovestone-Foster struggle of the
middle 1920s had ended with the expulsion of the former and the election
of a compromise candidate, Browder, as general secretary and the elevation
of Foster to the chairmanship. All of us in or close to the Party during the
1930s were aware of friction between the chairman and the secretary,
friction that was both personal and political. I, at least, never became
involved or even concerned, because to all intents and purposes Browder
was the Party leader, popular and virtually unchallenged, and Foster was
an irritable elder statesman who had been sent upstairs.

Later, I saw a very different side of Bill Foster. At that time, in the later
1940s, he was preparing his *Outline Political History of the Americas*. When
it was published in 1951, the preface described its purpose as "a general
political history of the more than three hundred million people who make
up the many nations of North, Central and South America." Over the
years I had put together a fairly decent reference library on international
affairs, and it included basic Latin American material and a number of
current newspapers and magazines from that area. This library adjoined my
office at 23 West 26th Street.

Bill used to drop in once in a while to borrow material for his book.
While his young assistant was looking for what they needed in the library,
Bill would chat with me in my office. This was a small room containing,
aside from my desk and chair and bookshelves, only two other chairs. As
Foster's heart had been bothering him for some time, his doctor had ordered
him whenever possible to keep his feet level with or higher than his head.
So when he sat down opposite me, he would place his feet on the desk. I
had to dodge them to see his face. He was elderly and tired, but at the
same time amiable, informal and relaxed. I enjoyed the visits and was pleased
to see a side of him that no one had ever mentioned to me.

The other party to the dispute, Earl Browder, was physically inconspicuous. He was not outgoing or effusive, and certainly not a backslapper. Not that these characteristics are necessarily those of leadership, but in no other way on meeting him would a stranger have thought of Browder as a mass leader. He was a quiet person with an inward-turning personality. Someone has suggested that he was either shy or arrogant. I saw him quite a few times and observed neither characteristic. I remember him as a man who had the habit of concentrating on the matter at hand so that for long moments he remained expressionless, giving the impression that he was paying no attention to what was going on around him or even not listening to whoever was talking.

I found him less doctrinaire, more flexible, and easier in give and take than a good many others in the Party leadership. He spoke well, but was by no means a rabble-rouser. He was more of a lecturer, and he wrote the same way. Strangely, there were very few acceptable public speakers among the top Communists. Elizabeth Gurley Flynn was a notable exception. Browder, however, was effective on the platform only because what he said was well organized and those who heard him were his admirers, and therefore receptive.

I attended a few small meetings which Browder chaired. I had a political session alone with him regarding something he wanted me to do. At least twice, and probably three times, I spent evenings with him and his family at their home in Yonkers. Those evenings were informal, simple and middle-class. Browder's Russian wife was a cordial hostess who served good suppers. We talked about this and that, and later in the evening we went more seriously into what was happening in Asia.

I suppose that one could say that I knew Browder fairly well. I think that some of the characteristics that I observed help to explain his extreme divergence from the principal tenets of the American Communist Party or any Communist Party during the latter years of the war. He proved to be too flexible, too easy at the give-and-take of politics, too impressed with ability, which, not surprisingly, he also found in the camp of the class enemy. His personality kept him so aloof from his comrades in the Party leadership that, once started on a tangent, he traveled it for too long a time. Anyway, we don't see much backtracking in politics, on either the left or the right.

The alarm over the Browder doctrine was publicly sounded, not from within the American Party, but from Paris. Jacques Duclos, the head of the French Communists, wrote a blistering article in *Cahiers du Communisme* which accused Browder of surrendering to the capitalists and called on the American Communists to repudiate the fatal political error. William Foster, who had been Party chairman during Browder's leadership as general secretary, had opposed the developing Browder line all along. Because of Browder's popularity, Foster had not been able to make himself heard, but now he had his day in court.

I was invited by Eugene Dennis, who was to succeed Browder, to attend the February 13, 1946, meeting at which Browder's demise was to take place. The meeting was held in a small hall, and even then all the seats were not filled. I went to it alone, wondering why I had been asked. On entering, I saw several people I knew, and I sat down with them. We chatted about nothing in particular while waiting for the business to start. I happened to glance over to my right and saw Browder sitting alone. Noticing that the chairs on all sides of him were vacant, I said to my friends, "I'm going over to say hello to Earl." I did so and we shook hands. I didn't have the heart to leave. So I took the seat beside him, and I remained there throughout the proceedings. Though I agreed with the important political step that the Party was taking, I'm glad I remembered that Browder was a human being, a friend, a man I had admired and the leader of the CP during its most vigorous days. I believe I did a decent thing, and that is why I would like to be able today to meet the Fred Field of that February evening in 1946 to shake his hand.

I wish that what I am about to report were more a matter of amusement at the carelessness of much scholarship than an example of distortion of whatever goes on in the liberal-left sector of our society. But such errors, and many of them must be deliberate, are serious matters, for they permanently miseducate American youth. Perhaps that is what the Establishment wants to do.

An American history book that I keep on my desk is often useful for checking dates, the sequence of events, proper names and the like. But I keep my fingers crossed at its interpretations. The book is Samuel Eliot Morison's *Oxford History of the American People*. It is considered a standard history, and has apparently been very successful commercially. In the writing of this account, I looked up in Morison Browder's ousting as general secretary in order to check my own memory as well as the other sources that I was consulting. Here is what I found:

> For his continuing to preach friendly collaboration between the United States and Russia, which he had been ordered to do in 1941, he was contemptuously deposed in May 1945 by orders from Moscow. This caused all his lieutenants to weep and grovel for having "deserted the workers." Browder was replaced by William Z. Foster, willing to follow the "party line" wheresoever it might lead (p. 1048).

I wonder whether this passage makes any sense to anyone. It seems to imply that the American Communists ousted their general secretary because he preached friendly relations between their country and the Soviet Union. Morrison seems to be saying that Moscow ordered his dismissal because he advocated friendly relations with the Soviets. He is apparently informing his readers that American Communists decided in May 1941 to turn against collaboration with the USSR. A most extraordinary interpretation of history! Even elementary checkable facts are wrong: Browder's demise took place on February 13, 1946, not in May 1945. And Eugene Dennis, not Foster, succeeded Browder as general secretary. Foster was, in fact, elected chairman of the re-created CPUSA, the post he had held before the Party's dissolution.

Gene Dennis, who took over the general secretaryship charged with reconstituting and rebuilding the Party, was an altogether different type of person than either Foster or Browder. He asked questions rather than issued sectarian answers. I had always liked that heuristic method, from teachers, friends, bosses, political leaders. I saw it in McChesney, Earl Barnes, Carter— from all of whom I had something to learn. As far as I was familiar with it, Gene's role in the Party had been that of negotiator, unifier, a top functionary who tried to minimize personality clashes and to reason out ideological differences. His entire life, from early youth, had been that of a full-time, professional revolutionary. He had spent years as an organizer for the Communist International (the Comintern), many of them in China and other semicolonial areas, with long spells in Moscow as the CPUSA contact with the Comintern, and other years in California and the Midwest as an organizer for the American Party.

Some of this history, primarily the Comintern connection, was not known to me nor, as far as I know, to other rank-and-file members until very much later, when biographies and autobiographies of Party leaders began to appear. This secrecy was partly dictated by Moscow and accepted by the American leadership. Gene himself was also very close-mouthed about his own past. Fortunately, Gene's wife, Peggy, who like her husband was a full-time revolutionary, has written an autobiography from which we can learn much that we did not know or understand at the time. Her book is a revelation of the fine, courageous, selfless, devoted, highly principled life and motivation of many Communist functionaries and the miserable, petty, ill-advised, stupid, undemocratic goings-on that turn so many fine people away from what should be—and once was—the leading group of the American left.

Gene and Peggy and their second son, who was tiny then, spent a few weekends and short vacations at Red Hill, sometimes when I was there and sometimes by themselves. During those periods of relaxation, we talked no politics, I asked no questions about the Party, and Gene volunteered nothing about his past experiences. Instead, we enjoyed the lovely Connecticut countryside, ate well, relaxed in the pool and took advantage of the un-demanding atmosphere.

My political contact with Gene concerned Party work on Far Eastern issues. I consulted with him on my own initiative as often as I found it advisable, and once in a while I would receive a message that he would like to see me. Making dates to see him or anyone else on the ninth floor was not a formal undertaking. Usually, we just talked about what I was writing for the Party press, but on one occasion I remember saying to him, "Instead of my being a special or general member, why don't you let me become a regular rank-and-filer with credentials, an assignment to a local or occupational group and the financial responsibilities everyone else has?"

Gene gave me a direct answer: "It wouldn't be of any advantage to you or to the Party." I never again brought up the subject.

The *New Masses* was a weekly publication recognized by the public as a Communist journal, though it did not officially speak for the Party. From 1943 to 1947 I was one of its editors and a frequent contributor.

The *Daily Worker* was the Party's official newspaper. From May 5, 1944, to January 12, 1946, I wrote a weekly column on the Far East and Latin America under my own name. I have earlier mentioned *The Communist*, later called *Political Affairs*, an official theoretical journal for which I also wrote. And there was *China Today*, also previously mentioned, which had no direct relation to the Chinese or American parties but which was put out by a group of editors, most of whom were in or close to the CP and of which I was one.

From 1934 to 1948, when I was between the ages of twenty-nine and forty-three, I wrote somewhere in the neighborhood of one hundred and fifty articles for the Communist press. I was writing my head off during a good part of this period because I was also publishing in *Amerasia* and carrying out my responsibilities at the IPR.

Some of my articles dealt with Latin America, and I also wrote several on the 1945 San Francisco meeting to organize the United Nations, which Joe Starobin, the foreign affairs editor, and I covered for the *Daily Worker*. But most of my writing had to do with the Far East.

The articles on the Far East for the most part concerned the following broad subjects: (1) the problem of the internal unity of China's political and military forces confronted by Japanese aggression; (2) the fallacy of counting on the so-called Japanese moderates to check the military fascists; (3) the difficulty of achieving any kind of effective coordinated action between the United States and Great Britain in the Pacific area and later

the problem of making the war against Japan a coalition effort among those
two powers and China; and (4) the American government's policy from
1931 to 1941, which in effect helped the Japanese aggressors against the
Chinese defenders; and later, along the same line, its postwar policy of
politically and even militarily aiding the most reactionary Chinese clique
in its efforts to defeat not only the Communists but a whole series of
democratic groupings that had been formed in the course of the war.

Early during the American participation in the Pacific war, Roosevelt
sent General Joseph Stilwell to China to revive the Kuomintang so that it
would at least display enough energy to pin down the Japanese occupation
forces. Chiang, in fact, was retreating before the Japanese while storing the
war materials that the Americans were flying into China over the Hump
from Burma at great loss of life for what he hoped would be his postwar
battle against the Communists.

The personal relations between Chiang and Stilwell were the worst possible. That didn't matter as much as the fact that Chiang did not like the
situation into which the Americans were trying to push him. When, in
September 1944, Roosevelt urged Chiang to accept Stilwell as commander-
in-chief of all allied forces in China, Chiang balked and demanded Stilwell's
recall. There is no doubt that Roosevelt was absorbed in the European
theater of war, and paying little attention to China. But I have always felt
that there was more to the situation than that. His pre-Pearl Harbor policy
toward Japan, his evident ambition to have the United States replace the
French in Indochina after the war was won, and his ambiguous, fuzzy notions
about the internal situation in China have led me to believe that he simply
was unfamiliar with the Far Eastern situation. In any case, while the war
was on, his attention was focused elsewhere. As a result, he gave no intelligent political guidance to our actions across the Pacific.

Under pressure from Chiang, Roosevelt withdrew Stilwell in December
1944 and replaced him with General Patrick Hurley. Hurley speedily undid
Stilwell's work. Ably abetted by Ambassador Clarence Gauss, Stillwell had
been able to persuade Chiang to become a more positive force in the war.
The Stilwell mission had been an exception to the usual American role,
which was to support Chiang Kai-shek with no conditions attached. With
the collapse of the mission, United States policy reverted to the *status quo*.

The crisis over the recall of Stilwell brought China's disastrous internal
situation to the attention of most American readers for the first time.
Reporters from the leading Establishment newspapers visited the areas in
which the Communist armies were fighting the Japanese. As far as I know,
they all wrote glowing reports about the effectiveness of the Communist
strategy, both political and military.

In order to verify the date of Stilwell's recall, I turned again to Morison's *Oxford History of the American People* and read on, curious to see how the author treated those events. I was again startled to find extraordinary distortions, two of which I note here.

The first tells us, "The basic cause of the Pacific War of 1941-45 was the attempt of the United States to protect the integrity of China against Japan" (p. 1060). That was precisely what the United States had *not* been trying to do. Had it done so with any degree of success, it is quite possible that the Japanese military would have been stopped in its tracks and that there would have been no Pearl Harbor. Instead, the American government issued some rhetoric in China's direction and shipped vast quantities of scrap iron in Japan's.

Morison also informs us that "throughout the war Mao Tse-tung maintained a Communist government in North China, abstained from fighting Japan, and pinned down a large part of Chiang's army" (p. 1060). It is true that Mao was in the northwest during that part of the war in which the United States participated. The rest is false. Parts of the Communist forces were pinned down by Chiang, not the other way around, for he spent much of the war fighting his own people, not the Japanese. To say that the Communist armies abstained from fighting the Japanese is like saying that the sun rises in the west and sets in the east. If the author did not write that from inexcusable ignorance, what could have been his motive?

By and large, the American people during the early years of the war had been kept in ignorance of what was going on in China. The big news break came with the recall of Stilwell. The truth about China's internal disunity, Chiang's reluctance to commit Kuomintang troops to fight against the foreign enemy and the effective role played by the much smaller Communist forces burst upon an unsuspecting public. I took the occasion to do a little boasting about what my writer colleagues and I on the left had been doing all those years.

In my *Daily Worker* column of November 18, 1944, I wrote, "I doubt whether a single reader of the *Daily Worker*, the *Worker* [the Sunday edition of the daily], *New Masses*, the *Communist*, or any other Marxist newspaper or periodical, was caught off base when the floodgates of China news burst open." Those readers, I said, "formed a section of the American public which for years had been steadily informed and educated as to the actual events in China and as to their meaning." And I quoted from something that Browder had recently written. It seemed pertinent because of the astonishment with which most Americans received the China news.

"The highest contribution Marxism has to make to American life," Browder wrote, "is the introduction of science into politics. It is the substitution of the method of blind trial and error by the method of scientific theory which projects the new and unknown out of the old and known. It is the understanding of the world in motion, which makes possible the anticipation of that which has not yet come into existence, so that the human mind is not confronted with a constant succession of surprises for which it has no preparation." The "new and unknown" in China was, of course, the successes of the Chinese Communist movement allied with a variety of groups which had democratic tendencies. It was obvious that the shell of Chiang Kai-shek's regime, based in feudalism and unbelievably corrupt, was soon going to crack. When it did, in spite of American intervention on behalf of the doomed Kuomintang at all possible levels, those of us who for many years of close observation had been convinced of its inevitability were not surprised.

What do I mean by science in politics? What do Marxists in general, who use the term frequently, mean by it? It means, simply, that our thoughts, our ideas, our beliefs, our ideology must correspond to our observations and experiences. I have commented earlier on the difficulty of analytically observing social developments. Social phenomena are not as easy to observe and understand as are natural ones. The boiling point of water is more easily determined than the boiling point of social unrest. The difficulty, however, does not invalidate the process. Marxism is a laboratory manual for social investigation, a manual to be studied and carefully applied.

18

An American
Peace Movement

In a July 1951 Senate hearing, Edward Carter testified that he had once told me that by joining the American Peace Mobilization, I was making a mistake that I would regret for the rest of my life. Grant that my affiliation with the APM was not one of the most rewarding experiences of my life, it at least taught me some political lessons.

The APM was what was called a Communist-front organization, which meant that it came into existence through Communist Party initiative and that many Communists were active in it. In those days of the popular or people's front, however, the CP was successfully working with many non-Communists, so this peace movement was considerably broader than the Party itself.

Some time before the APM was formally organized, Earl Browder asked me if I would accept the executive secretaryship if it were offered me. At a private meeting he gave me his ideas on what a peace movement should be and what it should strive to accomplish. According to Browder, the movement should be as broad as possible and include community organizations, church groups, ethnic groups, especially blacks, those unions which were already close to the Party and whomever we could attract from the other unions like auto, coal and steel. These aims were, of course, common to all front organizations which wanted to reach out as far beyond the Communist Party itself as possible.

There was a great deal of peace sentiment in the country. Some of it was being organized from the Right on the grounds that a standoff would permit American imperialism to take over the job which Great Britain had previously done. In any case, these people felt that there was nothing to fear and a good deal to be gained from Hitlerism. In contrast, the Left wanted to organize the liberal, progressive, forces which opposed a war we believed would bring victory to one or another form of imperialism.

A large organizing conference was held in Chicago in the early fall of 1940. It was my first experience with a mass organization, and I was impressed. About five thousand delegates attended, and because they had been chosen by their union shops or locals, farm organizations, neighborhood groups, student clubs and so on, they actually represented countless more. Among the representatives were many top leaders of their organizations. The gathering was impressive not only for the substantial sector of the American public which it represented but also for its enthusiasm and devotion to the cause of peace. At the close of the conference, I was elected executive secretary.

My name was presented to the delegates and I was elected without discussion. They had evidently been told that I was to have the job. I stepped up to the platform to give an acceptance speech. I interpreted my platform appearance as simply a device to show my face so that the delegates would at least recognize me when I went about my work as their executive.

I was impressed by the gathering, but not by the manner in which I was elected. For one thing, it was an uncontested election. For another, I was not well known among the delegates and knew it. I had done no trade union work, or farm work, or community organization, and the majority of delegates didn't know me by sight, not to mention by any qualifications I might have had for the job. Moreover, just before I was nominated and unanimously elected to the executive secretaryship, someone else was similarly elevated to the position of administrative secretary. I had never heard of her and had not even been told that there was to be such a position. I did not know what relation between the two secretaries was intended. Were we to be equals or was I to be chief of staff as I had been previously led to believe? Who was to control the money-raising and the budget? Were we each supposed to check the other? These questions were never clarified. From the first there was personal friction between us and an unpleasantness that endured until the organization disbanded.

There is more to be said on this subject. In spite of its connections, its relations, a moderately successful united front movement and its own temporary suppression of long-term socialist objectives, the CP was still a minority movement. It was not widely accepted or respected, and its motives were held suspect by many Americans. A young man like Fred Field comes along from the outside, not an industrial worker, not a farm laborer, just a radical intellectual from a well-known family whose reputation rests only on his career as the executive of a bourgeois research-educational organization and his specialization in Far Eastern affairs. The problem for him in his Communist work is to what extent he earns his own way, merits the responsibilities he is given and how much he is used, exploited, displayed before the public as a facade, a front. From the very beginning of my association with the Party, I was well aware of this situation and conscious of the danger that it threatened.

One can be used in legitimate ways, as well as in ones which are degrading both to the exploiter and the exploited. Many of us have been in situations where lending our name or presence to a worthy cause is not only harmless but also useful and perfectly honorable. For example, another Party-inspired organization was the National Negro Congress, which promoted the Party line on black-white integration. I was regularly invited to its banquets, regularly showed up and was regularly placed at the head table. I was nothing more than a reasonably informed citizen who supported the organization's objectives. I was not a specialist in the field and in no way a leader in the movement. But if my WASP countenance at the head table was helpful— and I was often the only WASP to be seen there—I was glad to contribute in that small way. In our society, this sort of exploitation takes place all the time. It is an innocent practice. I have never had any objection to being so "used."

But there I was in the 1930s and 1940s, working with and in the Communist Party, which I was well aware did not have a reputation for delicacy in its handling of individuals. It had overriding interests and objectives and was not finicky in using people for its own purposes. That was not an unusual characteristic but one shared by most organizations. I identified myself with the Party's objectives; we were working with, not against each other. If my reputation and position were useful to the Party, well and good, as long as this exploitation was not carried to distasteful extremes. I had to be the judge of that. It was up to me to maintain a balance consistent with my personal integrity.

For that reason, I tried to stick to work in which I was confident I had something to contribute besides my pink skin and red hair and Vanderbilt background. My specialization, in which I felt I had some independent authority, was American-Far Eastern relations. And that is the area in which I did most of my Party work.

Taking on the executive secretaryship of the APM was well out on the borderline of doing my own thing. In fact, it came close to merely fronting for the CP. The nature of my "election" to the job had not been reassuring. During the nine months of the organization's existence, I was less comfortable intellectually and politically than at any other time in my long association with the Party.

The fact that I had no previous experience in this type of work concerned me little. I knew that when the Party undertook a major campaign, it assigned experienced personnel to all of the specialized activities that particular effort required. In the APM, we got all the help we needed in regard to publicity, publication, design, work, and promotion to accomplish our objectives among those whom we hoped to influence and organize. My job was pretty much to coordinate the work of others and to contribute whatever I could in the way of political brains. But while I had learned a good deal about the political forces at work in the Far East and the American Establishment's relations to them, I was not an expert on the European situation, which was where the war that concerned our movement was currently being fought.

From Chicago, I sent a long telegram to Professor Philip Jessup, who was then chairman of the American Council of the IPR. My wire explained that I felt strongly that the United States was becoming maneuvered into a dangerous imperialist war in Europe and that I thus felt obliged to accept the leadership which I had been asked to assume. I said that I feared that my new position would be misunderstood and misinterpreted in many sectors. In order to avoid harming the IPR, I hoped that my resignation as secretary of the American branch could take place immediately. Jessup and the other officers and trustees acted quickly and with great generosity. They accepted my resignation by giving me a six months' leave of absence without pay, while expressing the hope that I would return when my new work ended. I took the leave of absence in September 1940 and never did return to a staff job in the IPR. But I remained a member of its board of trustees until 1947, the eighteenth year of my association.

The APM existed for only nine months, but they were nine months of frenetic activity. We fought every step toward war and opposed every step against our democratic institutions that the preparation for war entailed. We petitioned, we demonstrated and we organized peace councils in over two hundred towns and cities. We attracted a broad coalition of progressive forces, including farmers, industrial workers, office workers, blacks, artists, young people, leaders of women's organizations and groups of senior citizens. We urged these recruits to build thousands of peace groups.

At the end of January 1941 we held a Working Conference for Peace, which was a meeting of leadership rather than one of the masses. Two hundred and twenty-five delegates in progressive organizations from twenty-seven states attended. Of these, sixty-four came from CIO unions and thirteen from the AFL.

On April 5 and 6 we held what we called an American People's Meeting at the Mecca Temple, which later became the New York City Center on 55th Street. This meeting resulted in a call to picket the White House, which brought our movement national attention, despite minimum and mostly derisive notices in the press.

The strong and widespread opinion in the United States against participation in the European war took several organized forms. There were conscientious objectors as there are against all wars. The other large groupings were the America First Committee and ourselves, though the Establishment press gave the former exaggerated attention and the APM the least possible. This unequal attention came about partly because we were just people, whereas the America Firsters included Charles Lindbergh, Sewell Avery of Sears Roebuck, Senators Burton Wheeler of Montana and Gerald Nye of North Dakota, Congressman Hamilton Fish of New York, the intellectual fascist Lawrence Dennis and David Lawrence of *U.S. News and World Reports*, as well as many other well-known personalities. The Hearst press and the *Chicago Tribune*, in particular, gave the America First Committee strong support.

Some of the America Firsters were isolationists, others were anti-Semites and the rest were near or outright fascists. What held them together was that they were essentially appeasers. Many of them were not only willing but anxious to settle on Hitler's terms. After the war was over, it was revealed that the organization had accepted financial backing from Nazi Germany.

Lindbergh was the only one of the America Firsters whom I had met personally. In late 1930 or early 1931, Jerome Greene, of the then important banking firm of Lee, Higginson and chairman of the American IPR, had asked me to meet him and Lindbergh at one of the downtown bankers' luncheon clubs. Lindbergh and his wife were soon to fly across the Pacific to Japan and China. In making his preparations, he had become appalled at the scarcity of useful maps of China. He needed precise information about potential landing sites in that country in case of emergency. Greene had apparently told Lindbergh that I was the person to put that information together for him.

With the help of Isaiah Bowman, director of the American Geographic Society, I assembled the available data. Later I was told that Lindbergh took the packet I had prepared with him on the trip. Curiously enough, Charles and Anne Lindbergh flew from Japan to Nanking, the capital of China, on September 18, 1931, the day the Japanese began their occupation of Manchuria and started World War II in Asia. That was also the day, as I have noted earlier, that I was on a train through Korea on my way to Mukden, the central point of the invasion.

I remember the lunch with Lindbergh well. My memory of what he looked like has, of course, been refreshed a hundred times, but that was my one chance to gain an impression of him as a person. He was natural in the sense of being unaffected in manner or thought, easy and outgoing, and very clear about what he wanted. He was modest, almost shy or diffident in the dictionary expression of "modest reserve." He was immediately likable.

I found it difficult during the America First period to believe that Lindbergh would have become a reactionary. I never had the chance to read or hear much about the development of his thinking, so I never understood his America First role. Lindbergh devoted his later years, however, to what he called "preserving our natural heritage." That pursuit, which is certainly one of the most honorable available to modern man, took him to the Philippines among other places. There he was one of the first visitors to the Stone Age Tasaday. In a moving foreword to John Nance's fascinating book about that primitive tribe, Lindbergh wrote:

> Sitting on a dry, stony hump in the living cave, cook fires behind me and the morning sun streaming in through mists and hanging vines, I thought of what qualities were missing in the ways of civilized man. Qualities of the senses manifest themselves in tribal areas—the feel of earth and bark and leaves, the taste of rushing water, the smell of embered chips, the sound of wind. A mother nurses her babe. Naked children play along cliff ledges. Youths climb up from the stream with fish, crabs, and frogs.

I like anyone who reacts with such love and understanding to the fundamentals of life—the fundamentals which are scarcely seen, felt, smelled or heard by urban dwellers any more. I was opposed to Lindbergh's reactionary political views, but I'm happy that my first and last impressions of him were such good ones.

The APM believed that the European war in those early stages was one between rival imperialists, the British Empire and the Nazi Reich. "While there may be some difference between the tyranny of Hitlerism and that of British imperialism," as Congressman Vito Marcantonio told Congress at the time, "that difference is one of degree, and the degree is so small as not to warrant anyone justly to say that this is a war between the democratic forces of the world and the Nazi forces of the world."

Hitler, unopposed, had annexed Austria in March 1938 and moved into Czechoslovakia in September of that year, with the acquiescence if not the blessings of the British and French prime ministers. Six months later, when Britain and France finally sensed that they were being deceived by Hitler, they made the futile gesture of guaranteeing Poland and Romania against aggression. This move would not have been futile if the Western Powers had accepted the Soviet Union's offer of partnership in the guarantee. They did not. The Soviets, thus finding themselves without effective allies in the containment of Nazi Germany, bought time by entering into a non-aggression pact with Hitler. In September 1939 the Nazis attacked Poland, and two days later Great Britain and France declared war on Germany.

This was hardly a people's war against fascism. It was a war between two systems of imperialism, one attempting to usurp the traditional position of the other, and the other trying to defend its domination of something like one-fifth of the world. This was not a war in which democratic America had a stake. It was a war in which an imperialist America had a vital stake.

The European equivalent to the Japanese seizure of large parts of China during the 1930s was the fascist attack on the legal Republican government of Spain. In the face of Hitler's and Mussolini's open and heavy involvement, the American government had declared an arms embargo against the democratic forces of Spain, thus helping to assure the fascist victory. It was therefore not surprising that we on the left took as a definition of the war aims of the American government an extraordinarily frank speech given to a convention of industrial and financial leaders by Virgil Jordan, president of the prestigious National Industrial Conference Board. As many readers will not remember those early days of World War II, they may be amazed at what an influential spokesman for American capitalism had to say:

> Whatever the outcome of the war, America has embarked on a career of imperialism, both in world affairs and every other aspect of life, with all the opportunities, responsibilities, and perils which that implies. The war inevitably involves a vast revolution in the balance of political and economic power, not only internationally but internally. Even though by our aid, England should emerge from this struggle without a defeat, she will be so impoverished economically and crippled in prestige that it is improbable she will be able to resume or maintain the dominant position in world affairs which she has occupied so long. At best, England will become a junior partner in a new Anglo-Saxon imperialism, in which the economic resources and the military and naval strength of the United States will be the center of gravity. Southward in our hemisphere and westward in the Pacific that path of empire takes its way, and in modern terms of economic power as well as political prestige, the scepter passes to the United States.
>
> Whatever the facts about this war have been or are now, it must be unmistakably clear to any intelligent person that we are engaged in it. Our government has committed the American community to participation in this war as the economic ally of England, and as her spiritual, if not her political partner in her struggle with enemies of the British Empire everywhere in the world, to help prevent, if possible, their destruction of the Empire, and if this not be possible, to take her place as the heir and residuary legatee or receiver for whatever economic and political assets of the Empire may survive her defeat."

The American Communist position was that the war should never have started. The forces that brought it about should have been contained from the very beginning. Hitler should have been restrained by an alliance of England, France and the Soviet Union before he became strong enough to precipitate war. At the very least, the United States should have supported the Spanish Republicans instead of cutting off their supply of arms and other forms of aid. Japan should have been contained way back in 1931 when the Pacific phase of World War II began. How? By supporting unity within China so that it could have successfully blunted Japanese aggression. That would have meant backing Chiang Kai-shek's government, but only on condition that it form an effective coalition with all the forces willing and able to fight the invader. It would also have meant, especially for the United States, stopping the shipment of scrap iron and other forms of military aid to the Japanese war party.

These policies were not adopted, either in the United States or Europe, until too late, because the influence of the imperialist and appeasement elements were stronger than those of the democratic forces. The good slogans and the great deeds came only after reactionaries had gone so far that they could not be stopped. The policies that had prevailed had strengthened the enemy across both oceans and had successfully prevented the internal and external alliances essential to weaken it.

In March 1941 I wrote and cabled Hewlitt Johnson, the Dean of Canterbury, a high official in the Church of England, inviting him to address our American People's Meeting in New York. The Dean had become internationally known as a socialist and as author of a widely read book on the USSR called *The Soviet Power*. He replied by cable that it was impossible for him to leave England at that time. In a long letter to me he outlined his position on the war. He felt it necessary, he wrote, to support the war effort in England because "I desire the triumph of socialism. . . .From our point of view we wish neither side to be completely victorious à la 1918. But least of all do we wish Hitler to win." Should England go down to defeat, "There could be little chance of proletariat radical change in Western Europe because the German armies could stamp it out as successfully as they have stamped out the armed resistance of the Spanish workers." If Hitler failed to win or if the war should end in a stalemate, "the German people . . . would revolt and a widespread European revolution would become a real possibility." The war did not end in a stalemate, and neither did the German people or any other in Western Europe revolt. The situation in the West was carefully controlled by what the Reverend Hewlitt Johnson had called "U.S.A. democratic capitalism."

I also corresponded with Theodore Dreiser at this time. He had written a book called *America Is Worth Saving*, and, in spite of his fame, was having difficulty finding a publisher. Dreiser got in touch with me in the late fall of 1940 because of my position in the APM, and I soon became involved in his problem. The book was a fighting defense of the American democracy of the Founding Fathers, the democracy defined in the Constitution and its Bill of Rights. It was a virulent attack on American monopolists and imperialists and a violent denunciation of the British Empire and all it stood for. The manuscript was loaded with libelous statements. This was not the only defect. It was also notably weak in its criticism of Hitlerism. This was not because Dreiser did not loath Nazism and fascism but rather because his venom against the British Empire consumed his attention. In documenting his case against the lesser evil, he neglected the greater one.

After some exchanges, I made it clear to Dreiser that the only way I could take responsibility for seeing the book published would be if he gave me a virtual power of attorney to excise from the manuscript all libelous or potentially libelous passages. To my astonishment, that is just what he did. On December 18, 1940, he wrote me a long letter from Hollywood enclosing a list of forty-nine probable or possible libelous statements which had been called to his attention by his lawyers, Greenbaum, Wolf and Ernst, the most distinguished of the firms dealing with the legal aspects of publication. "Messrs. Greenbaum, etc.," as Dreiser referred to his lawyers, had, for instance, written, "The charge that Morgan and Rockefeller control politicians is libelous." Under this Dreiser wrote, "This remark by a presumably intelligent firm of lawyers surely ought to be framed for posterity."

"Messrs. Greenbaum, etc." also called to the author's attention that it was probably libelous to say that Noel Coward exhales "the very putrid essence of English imperialist decay." Dreiser commented that he was willing to change that to "his work exhales, etc."

The first paragraph of Dreiser's letter to me read:

> I am afraid I cannot make it clear to you how truly grateful I am for your interest in and labor on and for my book. . . .It is true that you have the American Peace Mobilization at heart, but it does not follow that, personally, I am privileged to call on you for any service on my behalf or that personally you should be at such great pains to clear the path for my book. It might have been delegated to others far less competent than yourself, as I now clearly see. What gratifies me most is your clear grasp of the significance of the legal and conservative reactions to what I have to say and your individual willingness—in so far as possible—to mitigate or modify the same. So let me here in the first instance acknowledge—and gratefully—the services already offered—and plainly are willing to continue to render in connection with the solution of this problem of free speech and freedom of conscience as it shows itself in publication. Thanks and many of them.

A certain awkwardness in the way Dreiser expressed himself both in this letter and his new book reminds me of what Dorothy Parker had said of him ten years earlier:

> Theodore Dreiser
> Should ought to write nicer.

The reward for my efforts was that the publisher issued a special edition for the American Peace Mobilization. Perhaps I should never have become involved, for the book exaggerated the policy mistakes that the APM itself was making with regard to the character of the European war. Possibly I was too much impressed by the famous author to keep my political focus. I wonder if anyone else ever read the book?

I met Dreiser in person after the book was published. The APM invited him to speak to an outdoor meeting that we were planning in one of Washington's parks. The meeting was scheduled for a late afternoon, after government offices had closed, and he was to arrive in the morning on an overnight train. I had been warned that in order for the outdoor meeting to be a success, Dreiser should be kept away from the bottle during the day. Unable and unwilling to devote the entire day to keeping him otherwise busy, I enticed a young woman who was working in our office to do the honors. She hired a car, met the train, and went off sightseeing with the eminent gentleman. About an hour before the meeting, she reached me by telephone to say, "Everything went fine, except that when he got into the car, our friend pulled a bottle out of an inside pocket of his overcoat. And the bottle is now empty." We got a good crowd out for the meeting, but the main speaker was not as effective as he might have been.

The picket line in front of the White House was in itself a noteworthy political phenomenon. It was maintained without one minute's interruption for 1029 hours—or forty-three days and nights. I have no idea of the total number of participants. The strength of the line varied from a handful during the bleak early hours before dawn to several hundred during weekends. All kinds of Americans participated, but the backbone was always organized labor from the CIO and AFL. Progressive unions like the Fur Workers and the National Maritime Union, which in 1941 was progressive, sent their top officials to give leadership to their own rank-and-file participants.

There was never a break in discipline. Our rules were that the picketing was to be peaceful and that any attack from the outside was to be met by nonviolent resistance. The strikers for peace initiated not a single incident in all those long hours.

We were attacked several times by obviously organized raids on the picket line. These were usually manned by Marines. This greenhorn was marching during the first of these raids and I well remember the attack and the young uniformed men who suddenly came at us with their fists flying. It is not easy, especially for the inexperienced, neither to fight back nor to run. And it is surprising what a successful defense peaceful resistance can be. The attacks, it must be said, were not aimed at injuring us, which would have been counterproductive. Instead, they were intended to discourage and to intimidate us. They succeeded only in strengthening our morale.

Mostly, the crowds that watched or passed by were noncommittal and some were friendly. Many who had not come for that purpose stayed to join us. The Establishment press did its best to ignore us, as did the White House. From the first day, we had sent petitions in to the President, asking FDR to receive a delegation. We were consistently refused. Finally, about a month after we began, I was invited into the White House alone to talk with one of the President's aides.

Major General Edwin M. Watson, who was Roosevelt's military aide and also in charge of his appointments, received me, and we talked for perhaps an hour. He started on the wrong foot as far as I was concerned, and we thereafter never got in step. "Field," he said, "the President has asked me to tell you that he knows your family and your background. It's a fine family. Those people out in the street aren't your sort. You don't belong with them." Well, if anyone could find the quickest way to alienate me, General Watson had. The gall he had to sit in his plush office and hand me that crass snobbery disgusted me. I, of course, answered back with the obvious. I told him that those people out there were my people, my kind, my friends and my fellow Americans. I said I had every intention of sticking with them. They were the finest people I had known. The reader may gather that the interview was not a success. I asked again if we could send in a delegation to talk with the President. "No, he's too busy to see you."

I reported the conversation to my colleagues, and we went right on picketing.

The character of the war in Europe was changing rapidly. In April the so-called phony war came to an abrupt end—but we didn't recognize it at the time. Hitler invaded defenseless Denmark and then, with the help of the quislings, Norway. In May the Germans invaded Holland and Belgium with the most devastating and indiscriminate bombings yet known, and northern France fell shortly thereafter. Ordinary people were being killed by the thousands. And ordinary people were taking up arms against the fascists. A people's war, a guerrilla war was under way.

The Communist Party and its front organization, the APM, were slow to react to the change in the nature of the war. Not only should we have noted it and revised our policy quickly, but we should also have been able to anticipate, from the very nature of Hitlerism, what was bound to happen. In a long article in the July 23, 1951, *Life* with the disagreeable title "The Red's Pet Bluebood," I am quoted as saying ("Field says candidly," the article reported), "Looking back we made two serious mistakes. We misunderstood the nature of the war; it was a people's war long before we realized it. And we turned our propaganda too much on England and not enough on fascism."

Toward the end of June 1941, we did change our policy. But this change took place too late and under circumstances which made the motivation suspect. On Saturday, June 20, at noon, I climbed up on the White House fence, faced what was then a large picket line of several hundred and announced that this prolonged antiwar demonstration had accomplished all that it possibly could. It had dramatized our demands for a people's peace, for internal democracy and against participation in an imperialist war. As of this moment, the picketing was to come to an end. We sang, shook hands, kissed and embraced and went our various ways. We on the staff returned to our temporary office in order to close it. From there, I went straight to Red Hill in Connecticut for a good rest—and woke up the next morning to learn that Nazi Germany had invaded the Soviet Union.

There was only an accidental temporal connection between the Nazi invasion and the end of the picketing, though I suppose few believed that. The Lord knows how many times I was asked how we knew just the right time to stop an antiwar demonstration, especially for Communists. I didn't know; we didn't know. Obviously, the Russians were caught off guard. The fact is that I took the initiative in the decision to stop the demonstration for reasons internal to the APM.

The character of the European war had changed dramatically during the picketing. I wish that I could report that this change had been the reason for my initiative and for the backing that I received. In fact, it played a small part. We stopped because we were financially exhausted. After a long effort, we were finding it increasingly difficult to man the picket line. Unions and other organizations and individual friends had kept us going for seven weeks, and they, too, had reached their limits. Our direct expenses had been modest. They included rent for offices and the salaries of a small staff to perform the administrative tasks involved in maintaining a line for that length of time. The unions and other participating organizations as well as hundreds of individuals had paid the cost of their own travel and subsistence. We simply could not continue. The fact that we stopped just a few hours before Hitler invaded the Soviet Union was pure coincidence.

We kept the APM initials and changed our name to the American People's Mobilization. We did what we could to help prepare for our entry into the war, an event which by then had become inevitable. The war itself, to say nothing of the effort of Washington, was rapidly mobilizing the people. I do not believe our efforts added much except to set the record straight at that late date on where the Left stood.

On December 7, I was riding down Fifth Avenue in my car with the radio on. Just as I entered Madison Square at 25th Street, I heard the news. It was that "date that shall live in infamy." I suppose that millions of us had the same thought at that very moment: "My world has suddenly changed. My life has suddenly changed. Where and how am I going to fit into what has to be done?"

About two weeks later I was telephoned and asked to come right away to an office in mid-Manhattan. The man who received me—I forget his name—was experienced at finding people for specific jobs. Would I be interested, he asked, in going into one of the research agencies that furnished information to the civilian and military branches? He said that my IPR work was the kind of background they wanted and that Carter and others had recommended me. "Yes, of course," I answered.

That suggestion was cancelled a few days later in favor of something urgent that had come up. Would I go to Washington right away to be interviewed for a job in air force intelligence that had to do with the bombing of Japan? "Yes, of course," I replied.

Over a three-day period, I had several lengthy and searching interviews that the interviewing officers said were necessary because of my known left-wing views. I answered every question fully and frankly. I even submitted a list of every article I had ever written for Communist or Left publications. I was accepted by the officers in charge and instructed to buy a uniform, find a temporary place to live in Washington and take my physical examinations. Because I had been wearing glasses for some time and was worried that my eyesight might disqualify me, I went to my oculist with the problem. He advised me to hold off the medical examination for three days in which he told me not to wear my glasses, to read as little as possible but otherwise to lead a normal life. As a result, I got a headache and 20-20 vision on the test. The rest of the examination was no problem.

These preparations accomplished, the colonel who had been in charge of the questioning telephoned me to say that something had gone wrong. Could I please return to Washington immediately? I was not surprised, for in that day's New York papers two columnists had made the sensational discovery that the dangerous subversive, Frederick V. Field, had been offered a captaincy. They made it clear to readers who might not understand that my recruitment might put the whole war effort in jeopardy. The colonel in Washington told me that he regretted that somehow my commission had been held up somewhere on the outside but that there was nothing he could do about it. He asked if I would try to straighten the situation out myself.

I turned to my old chief and friend Edward Carter. With his usual abundance of energy and ability to move others into action, Carter got a number of influential people to intervene on my behalf, even though he disapproved of my recent APM activity. Among those he persuaded to look into the matter were Lauchlin Currie, an aide to President Roosevelt, William T. Stone, a State Department official and former president of the Foreign Policy Association, and Owen Lattimore, the best-known scholar on the IPR staff. Their efforts were in vain.

By then we were well into January 1942. My last birthday, in April of the previous year, had been my thirty-sixth, so that I was unlikely to be drafted. No one doubted that the FBI had blocked my commission and tipped off the two columnists to do the hatchet job. Having interfered once, they would do so again. I therefore had to acknowledge that I was barred from doing any kind of war work for which I was trained. During the next months, I discussed with a variety of friends the wisdom of enlisting as a private in the army. I had a strong inclination to do so because I was dismayed at the prospect of sitting out the war on the sidelines. To a man, my friends advised me against enlisting. Already there were indications of what would most likely happen if I did. A number of left-wingers had been put to work at cleaning latrines or similar constructive tasks. This category of war work certainly did not need further radical participation.

So, unwillingly, I did sit the war out. I was sure I could have done a decent job wherever I was placed, except on the latrine assignment. I was deeply disappointed. It appeared that the Establishment was really going to punish me for being a Communist. And if it did so in 1942, in an era when national unity supposedly included the Left, what were the prospects for the postwar period?

19

The Nineteen-Forties

I found myself in the middle of Latin American politics in 1943, ten years before I migrated to Mexico. The occasion was a convention of the leadership of the Confederation of Latin American Workers, CTAL according to its Spanish initials, which was held in Havana. On that trip I also met a famous American writer.

I attended the convention in several capacities. I was a fraternal delegate representing the Council for Pan-American Democracy, a Communist front organization, and a reporter for the *New Masses*. I was also supposed to be of some assistance to Jacob Potofsky, later president of the Amalgamated Clothing Workers and at that time chairman of the CIO Latin American Committee. In the latter capacity I was to see that this eminent trade union leader made no political *faux pas*, or at least that was my assignment from the American comrades.

Such a notion, however, had not been conveyed to Potofsky, or, if it had, he had not accepted it, for during the convention he never allowed me to get anywhere near him. I gave him no help whatsoever, to say nothing of advice. All the rest of the delegates, regular and fraternal, were housed in an adequate but far from plush hotel in the center of the city. Potofsky, however, had made reservations at one of the elegant beach resorts and appeared at the first meeting in an immaculate white flannel suit with matching shoes. After the convention, he and I returned to Miami on the same plane. When it landed, we were closeted in separate rooms with FBI interrogators for two hours. It was the most intense, hostile questioning I had ever undergone, and so it seems to have been for my partner. Potofsky was fit to be tied. He was so angry he was about ready to become a radical, an undertaking that would have required a long political trip.

Except for Argentina, which remained officially neutral, though effectively helping the Axis, the Latin American countries had in one way or another come to the assistance of the American war effort. Cuba, for instance, had declared war against the Axis in December 1941. It had provided facilities for United States air and naval bases, increased its production of war materials and helped the antisubmarine campaign. All of this under the leadership of Fulgencio Batista. During the 1930s, apparently opportunistically motivated, he had located himself well on the political left. Then, in the 1950s, under the prodding of Uncle Sam, he was to move as far to the right as the political spectrum goes. His domination of the Cuban scene lasted from 1933, when as an army sergeant, backed by intellectuals, professionals and students, he seized power, to 1959, when he fled the country before the revolutionary uprising led by Fidel Castro. In the 1930s and through World War II, Batista allied himself with the labor movement, largely organized and led by the Communist Party; in the 1950s he dissolved all political parties and became a fascist dictator. It was during his sojourn on the left that he appeared on the platform with the island's leading labor and Communist leaders to welcome the CTAL delegates.

On the evening of the opening meeting, the Labor Palace, which normally held 7,000 people, was jammed with nearly 10,000. I attended as the guest of Vicente Lombardo Toledano, the Mexican labor leader and chairman of the Latin American Confederation of Labor. In the 1930s he had made several visits to New York, and I had entertained him many times in my homes in New York and New Hartford and sat in on many of the private meetings he held with leaders of the American Left. His role in Mexican history is still debated. A complex man, he was in his manner the superintellectual, in his appearance the epitome of the comfortable bourgeois. Smoking his Dunhill pipe, dressed in his Brooks Brothers suit, he was the last person one would take for a trade union leader. Lombardo was an avowed Marxist and a clear and effective, if somewhat pedantic, speaker. The controversy about his historical role that can still stir up tempers in Mexico centers on the question of whether he had the political courage of his intellectual convictions.

The convention was a new experience for me. It was conducted in Spanish, which I understood imperfectly, but I didn't miss anything important because friends helped me out. Though a trade union gathering, the meeting was less concerned with wages and hours and benefits than with international politics, which in this case mostly concerned the war and the relations of the Latin American nations to the United States war effort. I was surprised to find that several of the labor leaders were senators or deputies in their own countries and that a large number of them were open Communists, and leaders of their respective Communist parties.

As I write, nearly forty years later, Fulgencio Batista is a dirty word in the vocabulary of any democratically minded person. His later years of cruel, oppressive dictatorship when he yapped at the heels of American imperialism were in sharp contrast to the man I saw, heard and shook hands with at that 1943 convention. When I first moved to Mexico ten years later and began to familiarize myself at closer hand with Latin American politics, I had to ask myself, "Is it possible that this is the same Batista?"

At that opening meeting Batista made a symbolic gesture that permitted no possible misunderstanding of exactly where he stood. In the row ahead of me sat Lygia Prestes, wearing mourning because of the recent death of her mother, a valiant Brazilian revolutionary. Lygia was the sister of Luis Carlos Prestes, the leader of the Brazilian Communist Party, and already a legendary figure. Born in 1898, he had been graduated in 1920 from military college as a lieutenant in the engineering corps. He became a captain two years later and then resigned from the army to devote himself to the Brazilian revolutionary movement. Following the defeat of a popular uprising, Prestes led a famous march of 15,000 antigovernment troops through the Brazilian jungle during the years 1925-27.

In 1935, Prestes led a broad alliance of Communists, socialists, students, trade unionists, professionals and even important sections of the army against the dictator, Getulio Vargas. Vargas then succeeded in destroying the movement. Thousands were imprisoned and tortured, and Prestes was sentenced to sixteen years of imprisonment, later extended by another thirty. When our convention met in 1943, he was still being held in solitary confinement.

At the time of our gathering, there could be no doubt whatsoever of what Prestes represented. There could therefore be no doubt about what Batista was saying when, at the opening session, he announced that he would be honored to be presented to Lygia Prestes. She was then escorted to the platform, and there she and Batista embraced.

The CTAL convention was hard work, for meetings were held morning, afternoon and evening. But because I had no official position or business, I enjoyed whatever free time I wanted to take. A friend of many years standing, Martha Gellhorn, was then living on the outskirts of Havana with her husband, Ernest Hemingway. I got in touch with Martha as soon as I reached Cuba, and she came to town to lunch with me on the second day. During the rest of the week, we met a number of times, usually at the apartment of a friend of Martha's, the attractive wife of the head of the FBI in Havana. Perhaps because she was attractive, I had no difficulty in adhering to the principle that thoughts of guilt by association should not enter my mind. It got a little bit sticky, however, toward the end of the week, when I was asked if I would object to stopping by a designated bar at a certain hour because the FBI chief himself wanted to meet me.

"Why?" I asked.

"Because he just wants to see what you look like," she answered. Fully aware that those political sleuths already had any number of pictures of me, I thought that answer unlikely, but having a yen to see what *he* looked like, I said that no, I had no objections to the rendezvous. We met and had a drink, and in ten minutes the confrontation was over. What did he look like? A recent Ivy League graduate. His organization got my finger-prints, which I carefully left on my highball glass, and I got a free drink.

Martha was and still is a staunch liberal. She has written some excellent articles and books about the most troublesome situations and most troubled spots of our generation. I have not seen her in a great many years, but once, during the McCarthy days, she took the trouble to write me a long letter pleading with me to think several times before continuing my asso-ciation with the Communists. At about the same time, I received a similarly motivated, well-intentioned and well-phrased letter from a first cousin, Douglas Burden, whom I had also not seen for many years, decades, in fact. At the time, I was too preoccupied and harassed to reply to either. I regret not having done so.

On two evenings a chauffeur picked me up at my hotel and drove me to the Hemingway home. It sat on a small hill with a spectacular view across the city to the harbor and ocean beyond. Those were strange evenings. I had never before met Hemingway, and the circumstances of this first meeting were not propitious. I had only recently read *For Whom the Bell Tolls*, a book that moved me and taught me a great deal about the Spanish Civil War. It had great literary and political importance, for Hemingway was writing honestly about a tough, nasty war, but some of my friends had criticized it because it mentioned Loyalist excesses as well as those on the fascist side. In any case, I was awed at meeting the author, but I was also cognizant of the fact that he was in the midst of this tiff with the American Communists.

I had been invited to arrive early so that I might enjoy the view before it became dark. As we waited the hour or so for supper, we drank a lot. Shortly, an unpleasantness occurred. Hemingway needed more ice. There were several young menservants around the house, and he called for one. There was no answer. He yelled. No response. Furious, he screamed. I dislike such scenes. I hate the idea of browbeating servants who, because of job insecurity and class position, cannot answer back. I should have said, as I was inclined to do, but didn't, "Look, you arrogant so-and-so, just tell me where the goddamn ice is and I'll be glad to get it for you." Fortunately,

Martha came running in to see what was the matter. She quietly summoned a servant and Mr. Hemingway soon had his ice.

He and I had two long conversations. Or, rather, I listened, opening my mouth just often enough to keep the monologue going. The subject for the first evening was clouds. That was appropriate, for from the veranda we could watch their changing forms and hues over a vast expanse of sky. The trouble was that Hemingway's description was highly technical. He knew the scientific nomenclature of clouds the way a horticulturist knows the Latin name of every plant, bush and tree. I found that monologue hard to follow. The second evening the monologue deteriorated: Machine guns were another subject in which I was unprepared. I thought clouds pretty, beautiful, fascinating; I thought machine guns dangerous. My knowledge of those subjects went no further.

In May 1977 the *New York Review of Books* published a searching criticism, by Wilfred Sheed, of three recent publications about Hemingway. As is customary in such long articles, the critic devoted a good deal of comment to the noted author himself. Two of Sheed's sentences especially caught my eye, because they express exactly and concisely what I was thinking of those monologues as the chauffeur drove me back to the center of Havana. "The clutter of expertise," Sheed wrote, "in, for example, *The Old Man and the Sea*, smothers one's imagination in a pile of fishing equipment. It is as if the author hoped to find his magic in the very names of the objects." The magic had not come across to me.

Only a year later, toward the end of World War II, the American Communist Party went through an ideological upheaval. In 1944, it was formally dissolved as a political party and formed itself into the Communist Political Association, a move which was reversed with the ousting of Browder as general secretary in February 1946. In spite of these tactical disturbances, the Communist organization and its members exhibited remarkable vigor during that period from 1944 to 1950, which saw the end of the Roosevelt era and World War II, the accession of Truman, the dropping of two atomic bombs on Japan, the breakup of the antifascist alliance and the emergence of the Cold War.

In this period I was not only involved, but deeply engrossed in a good half-dozen organizations. This hectic way of life sounds more fragmented than it really was, because the fragments were cemented into a whole by a common objective. We were trying to do our part to maintain what had been gained by the victory over fascism and to build upon it. And the reverse side of that positive goal was the incessant struggle against the repressive steps of our governing bodies. They were part and parcel of the Cold War, and they culminated in the national shame and disgrace of the McCarthy period.

I wrote my column for the *Daily Worker* until the early part of 1946 and remained an editor and writer for the *New Masses* into 1947. We formed the Council for Pan American Democracy during the war in an endeavor to bring the concept of democracy into our relations with the nations of Central and South America and the Caribbean. There lived in the New York area refugees from oppressive regimes in Haiti, the Dominican Republic, Chile and Argentina, to name just a few countries. These refugees, kept us informed of developments in their native lands. The Council reported these events, together with our own Establishment's relation to them, in a small sheet, most of which I wrote.

We formed a Committee for a Democratic Far Eastern Policy right after the war. The failure of the Chiang Kai-skek government to undertake any meaningful defense of the country against Japanese aggression during the whole period beginning in 1931 and its internal policy of repression rather than liberation had enormously strengthened the revolutionary movement led by the Chinese Communists. Many GIs returned from the Pacific theater outraged at the stupidity of the American government's continued support of the most reactionary elements in China, the Philippines and elsewhere. Recognizing the direction in which the Far Eastern situation was rapidly moving, we set out to influence American public opinion in order to bring pressure to bear on our own government for more realistic and forward-looking policies. Besides the returning GIs, we found strong support from many old "China hands," including those in the missionary field. Our executive secretary resigned her China YWCA job to join us.

One of the most rewarding personal connections I made during this period was with Brigadier General Evans Carlson. He had made military history as leader of "Carlson's Raiders." By developing guerrilla tactics far beyond anything dreamed of by his military colleagues, Carlson helped in recapturing Little Makin Island and Guadalcanal from the Japanese. He had learned his political and military lessons in the late twenties as a member of the American military intervention in Nicaragua. These lessons were reinforced during the two years spent as an official observer with the Chinese Communist Eighth Route Army in the late thirties. Carlson returned from the war in the Pacific exhausted and in poor health. He retired from the Army and settled in Southern California. He came east a few times, traveling cross-country in a dilapidated car, making frequent stops to talk with plain Americans and always anxious to find out what the Left was doing and thinking. We had long talks and became good friends. Finally, in 1947, his body gave out on him. Had he lived, he would have become an important leader of the American Left, one that was desperately needed.

Then there was the Progressive Party, which was built around the former secretary of agriculture and Vice President, Henry A. Wallace. In 1948, Wallace became its presidential candidate. I was involved—as who left of center wasn't?—but not in an important way. I was supposed to advise Wallace on Far Eastern policy, but I never did more to fulfill that responsibility than to have two private twenty-minute talks with him. I emerged from them with the feeling that I had accomplished nothing. Nevertheless, that third-party experience was perhaps the broadest, all-inclusive effort of the liberal-left forces in the forties, even though the election results were disappointing.

Of the left-wing organizations of that period with which I was closely identified, the Jefferson School was the most impressive and successful. It was founded in 1944 as a merger between the Workers' School, which was affiliated with the Communist Party, and the School of Democracy, which was started by a group of teachers who had been fired from City College and Brooklyn College after a witchhunt into so-called subversive activities in the New York City schools. The social engineer who put the Jefferson School together was an extraordinary man in the high leadership of the CP named Alexander Trachtenberg. I had known Trachty for a number of years, mainly as head of International Publishers, a well-run outfit that published Marxist classics and other party literature. During my contact with him over several pamphlets I wrote, I learned that he had been in the Czarist army during the Russo-Japanese War of 1905 and had personally blown up a railway bridge. I became fascinated by his experiences and personality. A short, rotund, heavily mustached man with unlimited energy, he was a staunch Communist who was always willing to give just an inch or two to the opposition. We got along well. It was Trachty who, a few years later, telephoned me at dawn one morning to tell me that the FBI was pounding on his door to arrest him. While the idea for the Jefferson School was being formulated, Trachty brought me into that institution on the ground floor, and when it was formally organized, I became secretary of the board of trustees.

We bought a sizable building on New York's Sixth Avenue at 16th Street, remodeled it and made sure that the elevator really worked. Howard Selsam, who had taught at the American University in Beirut for two years during the twenties, became director; David Goldway, executive secretary; and Doxey Wilkerson, who had just resigned from the faculty of Howard University, director of faculty and curriculum. We offered a program of over one hundred courses, the major emphasis being on economics, politics, philosophy and history, especially labor and Negro history. Other subjects were psychology, anthropology, literature, languages and art. There were also flourishing art and sculpture workshops, arts and crafts, a theatre group and even a chorus that gave Town Hall performances. At its peak, in 1947, the school had an enrollment of 5,100, and even two years later, with the Cold War intensifying, we still had 4,000. There were extension classes in many unions, for in those days many of the New York locals were under the leadership of the Left, and there were annexes in outlying neighborhoods, as many as fourteen at one time. The success of our school inspired the formation of similar institutions in Chicago, San Francisco, Boston and Harlem.

My role consisted in attending frequent and interminable meetings which thrashed out policy for the school. I also did some teaching, but it was these experiences that led me to my earlier remark that I never considered myself successful in that endeavor. With that exception, however, I have only the happiest memories of the Jefferson School and of the enormous effort so many of us put into it.

As the forties drew to a close, I was as active as I had ever been. But the activities that I thought might improve our world were soon rudely interrupted by the Establishment. Evidently, it did not approve what I was doing.

20

Things Warm Up

The series of confrontations between the Establishment and Fred Field began in April 1950 and continued until the end of 1953, when I finally left the country. Though there had been storms in my life before my exile—and there have been a normal number since—those three and a half years made the rest of my days seem as calm as the most tranquil New England pond. Events piled up on top of one another. They over-lapped. Some coincided. Each had its background in an earlier period and was related to all the others. These events come so close to each other chronologically that in telling about one of them, reference will inevitably have to be made to the others. The sequence could be confusing to the reader. The events were confusing to me.

Here, therefore, is a calendar of the main events. It should enable readers more easily to understand where, at any given moment in any event, we are. The July 1951 occurrences came within a few days of each other; they are listed in the order of their occurrence.

April 1950	McCarthy and my bank
April 1950	Tydings subcommittee hearing
September 1950	Senate votes FVF in contempt
February 1951	Seizure of IPR files
March 1951	FVF contempt trial
June 1951	Supreme Court upholds Smith Act
July 1951	Four CP leaders go underground
July 1951	Bail Fund hearing
July 1951	FVF goes to jail
July 1951	McCarran subcommittee hearing
April 1952	FVF released from jail

1953   Expulsion of my wife and our emigration

The above should keep the chronology straight as far as my more exposed life was concerned. Following the events I am about to relate, I pasted in a large scrapbook a stack of newspaper and magazine clippings that my wife had been keeping for me. With few exceptions, they came only from New York City papers and by no means from all of them. But the collection is sufficient to remind me today of that startling series of experiences.

The Senate hearings, the trial, the contempt judgment, and the jailing were all reported at length in the more conservative press and both at length and more luridly in the sensational papers. The *Journal American* became so excited that it printed one of its front-page four-column headlines about me in red ink. The *Post, News, Mirror*, and *Compass* at one point devoted their entire front pages to what was happening to this dangerous citizen. There were many photographs of me, whenever possible handcuffed or getting in or out of the Black Maria. The headlines called me a "Vanderbilt Scion," "Leftist Angel," "Red Angel," "Bail Fund Angel," "American Millionaire Communist," "Red's Pet Blueblood," "Left Wing Angel," and once in a while (though very seldom), I was called "Field." I never knew there were so many kinds of angels. The *Mesabi Daily News* of Virginia, Minnesota, one of the few out-of-town clippings I have, ran this five-column head: "He Dedicates Life to Biting Hand That Feeds Him." There followed a long article taken from the *Newsweek* profile of me. Through lack of enterprise, the editor missed a chance to give the piece a local slant. The great Mesabi range supplied iron ore to the steel mills of the American industrial northeast via the Great Lakes and the Pittsburgh and Lake Erie Railway, a Vanderbilt operation. At the time the article appeared, I still had a nice pile of stock in that railway line.

In this period, the most unpleasant thing to me personally was the publicity, something over which I had no control. Much that was written about me contained venom, a gloating over what at last was happening to that rich Commie bastard. I felt hatred from writers who didn't know me and never took the trouble to talk with me. They unscrupulously accepted whatever lies the FBI handed them and were truly running dogs of McCarthyism. None of them had either the slightest knowledge of the philosophy that I have tried to put forward in the previous chapters or the least interest in finding out what I—we—really stood for and why I was willing to run certain risks to achieve it.

Once the events of those two years began, I knew that there was no way out. Not that I was looking for one. I had gone into this thing with my mind and eyes open and fully understood what I was doing. I was well aware that life would get more difficult, and I was confident of my own inner strength. This was the climax to the political struggle to which I had committed myself many years before. I always knew that it was not a game, or a flirtation with the American left that I could break off at will. No, from the beginning it had been serious, and would always remain so. Honor was involved; there were too many political cowards around for me not to know the difference between honesty and opportunism. Other people were involved, people whom I admired and loved and to whom I felt responsible. Then there was that character, that friend, who had always been with me, the Fred Field with whom I had lived for this long with some feeling of pride, whom I had no intention of letting down just because the going looked rough in the immediate future. Most of all, I had the conviction that what I was doing was right.

Only a year or so before these dramatic events occurred, my marriage to Edith, which had lasted twelve years, came to an end. It had gradually fallen apart, for a number of reasons. The most important of these were long periods of separation as a result of my work and her slow recovery from illness, the changes which the illness caused in our personal relations, the hostility shown by some members of her family to our marriage in the first place, augmented by a real hatred of and embarrassment at my political activities, and my continued failure to work at my marriage as hard as I worked at everything else. We had good years together, however. Edith was a strong and adaptable person as well as a charmingly entertaining one. She weathered splendidly the stormy voyage on which I took her, from an unworried San Francisco life of comfort and wealth to the frantic, nerve-wracking existence of radicals in New York. She was wholly supportive of my Marxist beliefs and Party activities. And yet, along the way we lost our emotional dependence upon each other and found ourselves with a marriage lacking the qualities needed to hold it together.

In the end, it was I who wanted the divorce. I went to Las Vegas, and was utterly bored for six weeks. I gambled modestly in the evenings, read a lot, roamed the desert and surrounding mountains in my car, and talked to no one except two or three pit bosses and some managers of the Flamingo Hotel, where I was staying. These were interesting people with a background that was new to me. They were a part of the crowd Bugsey Seigel had put in to run his hotel and legal gambling operation. (Some had joined the staff after he was murdered.) With me they were straight and friendly. We established a relationship which I was to renew several times in the coming years.

Sharing the events that I relate in the following chapters was Anita Cohn Boyer, whom I married when a divorce decree put an end to my former marriage. It is commonly said by prison inmates that it is tougher for those on the outside than for the person serving time. I have reason to think that there's a good deal of truth in that remark. Anita and I had exactly one more or less normal year together, albeit a year of Party activity on my part and increasing Cold War pressures. Then, with the Tydings hearing, events began to crash down around us and to smash any hope of a normal life. Anita had gone through this before. Her former husband was Raymond Boyer, a professor of chemistry at McGill University in Montreal and a member of a wealthy, aristocratic French-Canadian family. After the war, Boyer had been convicted of breaching the official secrets act, and he had served a sentence in the penitentiary. It is true that they had already separated when this happened, but the experience was nonetheless a vivid and difficult one for Anita. She was naturally concerned, as I was, at the prospect of something similar disrupting her life again.

Another event in 1949 also affected me, though much less so. My father died at the age of seventy-nine. I have often thought that, for his sake, it was fortunate he did not live to witness the events that overtook his second son. Upon his death, his peers at the Grolier Club issued this encomium:

> One might well say, viewing his life in retrospect and with regard to the many changes that had come upon his contemporaries and the world at large at the time of his death . . . that, in all probability, we shall not have the exhilarating experience of seeing his like again. Sportsman, mechanical engineer, scholar, aristocrat, traveler, author and connoisseur, he was for all who knew him an inspiration. . . .

A portent of the tough events ahead showed up in the *New York Times* of the second of April 1950. In a speech to the United States Senate, Joseph McCarthy had exhibited photostatic copies of two cancelled checks totaling $3,500. They were made out to the American Council, Institute of Pacific Relations, and they were signed by Frederick V. Field. From reports in other newspapers, which gave the exact dates and the amounts of these checks, I was able to ascertain from my own records that these two checks had been drawn on the American People's Fund during the year 1943. That Fund was a tax-free philanthropic organization of which I was president. (As part of the Cold War oppression, its tax-exempt status was later revoked by the Treasury Department.) Before the Sons of the American Revolution on May 15, McCarthy brandished other checks signed by me totaling $6,500.

McCarthy discovered that ambassador-at-large Philip C. Jessup, who had for many years been prominently associated with the Institute of Pacific Relations, having at various times been chairman of its American section as well as of the international body, had been given a security clearance by the Atomic Energy Commission. McCarthy then informed Secretary of State Dean Acheson of the danger to American security represented by these donations from FVF to the IPR. The IPR had published in its biweekly, the *Far Eastern Survey*, one of the earliest reports on the Chinese Communist movement to appear in the United States. By McCarthy's extraordinary "logic," this indicated that the *Far Eastern Survey* was a tool of Moscow, and that proved the IPR was Communist. Jessup was responsible for all these terrible things. McCarthy, who had an elephant's delicate touch, described the *Far Eastern Survey* as part of a "three-horse team," the other two being the *Daily Worker* and *Izvestia*. Anyone energetic enough to look up the *Far Eastern Survey* in one of the larger libraries will be amused to find how academic—and, I am afraid, stuffy—it was.

In due course, the Chinese Communist movement triumphed. But Americans and their government had unfortunately paid so little attention to what was going on in China that when the Communists finally overthrew the government of Chiang Kai-shek it took this country over twenty years to grasp the significance of the event. The IPR should have been honored rather than harassed for pioneering information on such an obviously important happening.

How had my checks come into McCarthy's possession? That question troubled me. If he had obtained a few checks, might he not obtain more? And if he had checks, were any of my private papers safe? As answers, there were only limited possibilities: Either my house or office had been burglarized or my bank or the clearinghouse, through which all New York checks passed, had connived with someone who took the checks to McCarthy. After assuring myself of the improbability of the first and learning that the clearinghouse did not microfilm or record checks, I asked my attorney, Harold Cammer, to compose a letter for the bank's attention. He accordingly wrote the Guaranty Trust Company of New York (now the Morgan Guaranty Trust Company of New York), and in due course it replied that the checks had been subpoenaed by the House Committee on Un-American Activities and that it had no choice in the matter. The Guaranty *may* have had a legal loophole, but it had no excuse for not having voluntarily notified me of what it claimed it had been forced to do.

On April 28 I was testifying in Washington before a subcommittee of the Senate Foreign Relations Committee, accused of being an espionage agent of the Soviet Union. As a result of Senator McCarthy's sweeping claims that the State Department was peppered with Communists, the Senate appointed a subcommittee of its prestigious Foreign Relations Committee, to be headed by Millard Tydings of Maryland, to explore the accusations. On April 20, this group devoted four hours to hearing testimony from Louis F. Budenz. That was the day on which I was brought into the picture in a nasty way. Budenz's extensive testimony about me included the remark, "I accuse him here as a Soviet espionage agent who used money to influence the Institute of Pacific Relations." My immediate reply to this remark was published by the more responsible papers: "His [Budenz's] accusation against me is a shameless and slanderous lie. It is unfortunate that such a false witness should receive so much undeserved attention and that he should be cloaked in an aura of sanctity. Instead, he should be denounced for his depraved fabrications."

Budenz had been a member of the Communist Party for about nine years. During the latter part of that time, he had been managing editor of the Party's official newspaper, the *Daily Worker*. Precisely when I do not know, Budenz turned himself over to the FBI and became one of its principal and most inaccurate informers during the McCarthy period.

From the perspective of three decades, it is hard to believe that men and institutions and organizations of honorable and decent background should have taken Budenz seriously. But not only did the U.S. Senate, most of the nation's newspapers, and a large section of the public take him seriously, they spent millions of dollars and countless days and weeks airing and investigating the absurd charges of a professional liar. It is difficult now to believe the degree to which the country during those Cold War days was swept by hysteria. I did not enjoy being one of its victims. If Budenz said I was a spy, the best I could possibly hope for was to be considered an exceedingly dangerous citizen who was not to be trusted by anyone, let alone be given any position of responsibility.

For the hearings, the Tydings subcommittee had taken the largest of all the Senate committee rooms, for the purpose was not to discover the truth or falsity of the accusations but to give them the widest circulation possible. This was to be a show, not an investigation, and if I am not mistaken, these hearings were the first of their kind to be televised. My own appearance was televised, and when the session was over and the crowd had cleared away, the television people asked me to repeat the prepared statement I had read at the beginning of my testimony. That statement was shown to the public, not to give weight to what I had to say, but to exhibit before the American people a political freak who was trying to subvert the country's fine institutions with his millions.

I testified on April 28, and I was very nervous when the hearing began. There was a big crowd of what I supposed would be unfriendly people, though they did not particularly behave that way. I was seated at a table in the middle of the room with Harold Cammer beside me. In front of us stretched a long table at which the committee members sat. The television camera was to one side, and the lights seemed to come from everywhere, which is probably what they did. Tydings let me open with a prepared statement. By the time I finished, I felt composed. My voice had been pretty good, and I realized I could think under pressure. There was no shame in the position I was taking. The Senators were the ones who were making fools of themselves.

At the end of the session the subcommitte voted to recommend that I be cited for contempt of Congress. My only feeling was, "Well, here we go. They're really after me now. If they don't get me this time, they will the next, or the next. And there's nothing I can do about it except stick to my guns. Don't panic, don't give them any unnecessary advantage, don't get mad or impatient, don't let yourself be goaded. I'm guilty of nothing more than wanting peace in the world and a better society, and I have the right to fight for that in the perfectly constitutional way I have chosen."

The principal target of the Tydings subcommittee hearings was, in fact, Owen Lattimore, not Fred Field. Because, for a good many years, I had been standing close to Lattimore, Budenz thought to injure me, too. But it was Owen he sought to assassinate politically. Lattimore had been associated with the State Department, both in his capacity as adviser to Chiang Kai-shek and as adviser to Vice-President Henry Wallace on his trip to China. I was one of the persons through whom Lattimore was to be led to the gallows, because, as everybody knew, I was a spy, a traitor, a dangerous Red, an espionage agent of the Soviet Union and the organizer and leader of the Red cell in the Institute of Pacific Relations.

Budenz testified that he had never met Lattimore, didn't even know what he looked like. He did, however, know "Frederick Vanderbilt Field—a Communist whom I knew first as Comrade Spencer, and then later on as Mr. Field." The Spencer business is the giveaway here, for the FBI was a little careless about identifying the pseudonym I used in writing some articles in the middle 1930s. The name I actually used was Lawrence Hearn, but for some reason beyond my understanding the FBI creeps deduced it was Frederick Spencer.

I may be looking for more subtlety than actually existed in the FBI's anti-Red divisions. A pseudonym that didn't even have an F in it was a little too much for the brains of these federal sleuths. As a result of the FBI's easy solution, however, all the inquisitors questioned me about Spencer; not once was I asked about Lawrence Hearn, the pseudonym I had actually used occasionally. So I knew whenever I was questioned about Spencer that (a) the questioner had been coached by the FBI, and (b) the questioner himself had no independent knowledge of the matter. It was perfectly obvious to me, when Budenz identified me as Comrade Spencer, that he had been coached in his falsehoods by the FBI.

I knew Budenz. I had run into him several times at the Party headquarters but I had never done any work with him. He testified, under oath, that I had reported to the Communist Politburo, which he said he occasionally attended; that from the CP point of view Lattimore could be trusted; that Lattimore saw to it that Communists and the Communist line got prominence in *Pacific Affairs*, the journal of the IPR which Owen edited; that Lattimore was a Communist agent and the top architect of the State Department's Far Eastern policy. Budenz testified, in short, that Lattimore was a very important member of the CPUSA. It was true, Budenz admitted, that Lattimore had supported Finland when it was attacked by the Soviet Union and had praised the postwar Marshall Plan (which the Soviet Union bitterly opposed). But these actions could be explained because in order to cover their top agents, the Communists encouraged them to support certain policies that the Party opposed.

What was the connection between Lattimore and Field? They both performed their subversive activities through the supposedly respectable and influential Institute of Pacific Relations. They manipulated that organization so effectively that the American people were beginning to believe that the Chinese Communists were no more dangerous than "North Dakota Non-Partisan Leaguers."

Lattimore and I were colleagues on the staff of the IPR, and through that association we became casual friends. As editor of *Pacific Affairs*, he did an excellent job of publishing divergent points of view on the great Asian issues of the day. He was an internationally known scholar, without question one of the leading authorities on what can be called Inner Asia, that area which includes Outer and Inner Mongolia, Tibet and other sections of the Chinese hinterland or adjacent to it. At the time of the hearings he was head of the school of international affairs at Johns Hopkins University.

Owen is a witty, entertaining person, and he wears his scholarship lightly. On one occasion we both spoke at a meeting in Seattle, and San Francisco was the next destination. I had my car along and was going to make the long drive instead of going the sensible way, by train. Owen and his wife Eleanor kindly agreed to accompany me in the only Cadillac I have ever possessed. I had just outfitted it with blowout-proof tubeless tires, which were brand-new on the market. In three or four hours the first tire blew. In five or six, the second went. Toward the end of the afternoon—a Saturday, of course, when everything had shut down—the third and the fourth collapsed. We managed the next day's trip without food, for all the cash we carried had turned into rubber. Yet for hours on end during this discouraging and dreary journey Owen entertained us with a seemingly inexhaustible repertoire of songs, mostly ribald.

Life with Lattimore was not all political and academic. For a couple of years we worked in adjoining rooms at 129 East 52nd Street, the New York headquarters of the IPR. The rooms were more cubbyholes than offices befitting our exalted stations. They were enclosed by a partition that went only three-quarters of the way to the ceiling. Anything that went on inside could therefore easily be sensed outside.

One day Owen returned from a trip to Outer Mongolia with a gift for his next-door neighbor. He handed me a sizable white bag, telling me it contained Mongolian tobacco. As I was an enthusiastic pipe smoker, I immediately tried it out. It was good, a trifle dry maybe, but it had a pleasant flavor. We had both been smoking this tobacco for several days when a delegation of our women colleagues called upon us. They demanded that we quit. The tobacco stank, they informed us. "Naturally," Owen said, "it's camel dung."

Following Budenz as witness was Brigadier General Elliot R. Thorne, retired, former chief of counterintelligence for General of the Army Douglas MacArthur. General Thorne informed the subcommittee that Lattimore, whom he had three times investigated, was "a loyal American citizen and is in no way an agent of the Communist Party." Little attention was paid the general; he was testifying in the wrong direction, and not helping the committee.

When my turn came to testify, I said under oath that, "to the very best of my knowledge," Owen had never been a member of the Communist Party and never in any way had been disloyal to the United States. I also said that "under oath and without qualification or reservation of any kind," I had never been a Soviet espionage agent. Several State Department officials, Haldore Hanson, John S. Service, and John Carter Vincent, had been accused of being Communists by McCarthy. These men were real China experts because their reports had told the truth about China. They had foreseen the downfall of Chiang Kai-shek and the victory of the revolutionaries. The way to deny the truth, according to the McCarthyites, was to shorten the careers of those who discerned and revealed it. The way to do this was to brand these experts as Communists. I knew the three only by reputation; I do not remember ever meeting them. But I thought it important to do what little I could to throw a block in McCarthy's way. I told the subcommittee that to my knowledge none of them was a Communist or disloyal to the government.

In other words, I answered the questions that pertained to the Senatorial inquiry. The Tydings subcommittee had been set up to investigate Mc-

Carthy's charges that the State Department had been infiltrated by Communists. The four men whom I have just mentioned were or had been State Department officials. I was more than willing to answer questions related to them. The fact of the matter, however, was that the Senators didn't really examine me with respect to Lattimore or the three others. I made my statements with respect to them in my opening remarks. All the Senators were interested in accomplishing at my hearing was to smear me and then through other witnesses to establish my connection with Lattimore, thereby condemning him.

I refused to answer any questions with regard to my own political beliefs or affiliations or whether I knew a whole series of people who had no connection with the inquiry, including Browder, Whittaker Chambers, Alger Hiss and nine people connected with the magazine *Amerasia*. In all those cases I invoked the Fifth Amendment.

Admittedly, I was walking a tightrope. I was not going to incriminate myself by answering questions that would lead further into the endless territory of "Who do you know?" "What do you think?" into the land of the witch-hunt. On the other hand, I wanted to answer directly the accusations against the prime target, Lattimore, and the other three State Department officials. I thought I had succeeded. The chief counsel disagreed. He said that it was "obviously imposssible to develop a line of interrogation with this witness." And Henry Cabot Lodge, Jr., was horrified. "Here is the shocking spectacle of a man with every material advantage this country has to offer who refuses to help this committee do its plain duty," he said. The upshot was that the subcommittee recommended to the Committee on Foreign Relations that I be cited for contempt. That recommendation was passed on to the Senate as a whole, and I was so cited on no fewer than thirty-two counts.

The final report of the Tydings committee, which received a hundredth part of the attention given to its lurid hearings, found that McCarthy's charges of Communist infiltration of the State Department was "a hoax and a fraud . . . an effort to inflame the American people with a wave of hysteria and fear on an unbelievable scale." Nevertheless, great damage had been done by examining with such evident seriousness Budenz's transparent lies, in not exposing the FBI's complicity, in damaging the reputation of many individuals without giving them a chance to defend themselves, and in managing the whole so-called investigation for the maximum of publicity and the minimum of truth. Almost a year elapsed between my contumacious testimony and my trial for contempt. The nonjury trial was held in Washington, D.C., in March 1951 before federal judge T. Alan Goldsborough. I was ably defended by Harold Cammer and Joseph Forer, the latter a

Washington lawyer well known for his defense of civil rights victims. We sensed that the case was going favorably when Judge Goldsborough made such remarks as the one that it looked to him as if some of the questions had been asked Field "for the purpose of having his foot slip."

In his decision exonerating me, delivered the day after the trial, the judge contradicted the claim of the government prosecutor, saying there was no reason to suppose that I had not invoked the constitutional protection in good faith. He noted that Field "was charged before Congress with being a Communist spy and these charges were widely publicized. It was also charged," he added, "that he was a rich organizer of Communist activity. In that atmosphere he was called before a Congressional subcommittee. He knew he wasn't called before a Congressional subcommittee to be asked some simple question or one question. He knew he was called to be grilled."

"The court is of the opinion," Judge Goldsborough concluded, "that if the defendant had answered all these thirty-two questions in the affirmative—or in a certain way—it would have taken very little more evidence to put him in the penitentiary." Then he looked at me with an amused expression and observed that there were "honest Communists—naive Communists." These were persons who joined up in the belief that they were taking a step to benefit mankind. They were like the young lady who rode a tiger:

> They returned from the ride
> With the lady inside
> And the smile on the face of the tiger.

I did not think I was that naive, though I did agree that I was an "honest Communist." I thought that most of my comrades in the Party I knew were also honest Communists. But at that point I was not going to get up and argue with the good judge. I thought it better to leave the matter where it was. I congratulated Cammer and Forer and walked out of the courtroom a free man.

21

I Hold You in Contempt

I breathed more or less normally in April and May of 1951, but early in June the political air fouled again. In October 1949 eleven members of the National Committee of the CPUSA had been convicted of violating provisions of the Smith Act (formally known as the Alien Registration Act of 1940). Ten of the eleven were sentenced to five years in prison and fined $5,000; one, Robert Thompson, winner of the Congressional Medal of Honor for exceptional bravery in World War II, was given three years. They were granted bail totaling $260,000, which I, in my capacity as secretary of the Civil Rights Congress Bail Fund, put up. After the eleven lost in the Court of Appeals, their appeal was carried to the Supreme Court, which early in June 1951 upheld the constitutionality of the convictions.

In 1940 Congress had enacted the Smith Act, which, in its split infinitive wisdom, made it a crime "to knowingly or willfully advocate, abet, advise, or teach the duty, necessity, desirability or propriety of overthrowing any government in the United States by force or violence," or "to print, publish, edit, issue, circulate, sell, distribute, or publicly display any written or printed matter advocating" etc., the same, or "to organize or help organize any society, group, or assembly of persons who teach, advocate or encourage" the same, or to become a member of any such society, group or assembly "knowing the purposes thereof." Under this act, beginning in 1949 and lasting through the fifties, over seventy Communist Party officials were convicted in various trials.

By the summer of 1951 I had been associated with the CP for more than fifteen years. In most ways it had been a successful association. I had made close and loyal friends. We had worked together for years under strong outside pressure, and our confidence in each other had been cemented to withstand the stresses of the hostile world of the Establishment. That experience had begun during the depths of the Great Depression of the 1930s, continued through the period of the World War II, and had lasted by 1951 into the worst of the Cold War. I still felt that the CP was the principal organization through which I could work at the political level with some degree of effectiveness to combat the wrongs of our society.

The atmosphere of the Cold War was unpleasant, to say the least. You had to assume that your telephone was tapped, your mail opened, your private life spied upon and reported to the federal police. You didn't make a date by telephone to go to the movies without supposing that a reference to such and such a picture or such and such a restaurant would be interpreted as Aesopean language for some sinister rendezvous. I was amused at the recent flurry of excitement at the "discovery" that the FBI and CIA had long been invading people's privacy, opening mail, tapping telephones, burglarizing homes and offices, in short, flagrantly violating the law. All that was common practice in the postwar years, and all of us on the left knew it and protested it. No one in the Establishment paid the slightest attention.

I had personal experiences along these lines, though probably fewer and less harassing than many other comrades. One example of the surveillance to which I was subjected still seems somewhat amusing. In the late fall of 1949, I was in my office at 23 West 26th Street when I was notified by telephone of the arrest of the eleven members of the CP National Committee. When I was told of their bail requirements, I replied that I would immediately get in touch with my fellow trustees of the Bail Fund to get their approval, that I would then take a taxi to the Amalgamated Bank, collect the necessary bonds and from there, for security reasons, take a bus to Foley Square. I secured the bonds, boarded a bus just outside the bank on Union Square, and sat down with a satchel on my lap. In it were $260,000 in negotiable government bonds. Within half a block, a policeman was signaling the driver to pick him up. He boarded, looked around, and sat down next to me. When I left the bus, so did my companion. That was one time I was rather pleased my telephone conversation had been overheard.

Another episode was not so pleasant. On June 30, 1951, at six in the morning, the telephone at my bedside rang. Alexander Trachtenberg, a Party leader of the second-rank, without saying "hello" or "good morning" rapidly and in an agitated voice told me that at that moment the FBI was at his door. Would I immediately telephone the number he gave me to give whoever answered that information? I did so, having no idea to whom I was talking or why. All I said was, "Trachty just called and asked me to notify you that the FBI is at his door." "Thanks," a man replied and hung up. In a couple of hours it was on the radio that there had been another roundup, this time of the secondary leadership. One person on the list to be apprehended had left his apartment just before the FBI arrived. It seemed he had received a telephone call, duly recorded, warning him of impending arrest.

I had no particularly bad experience from this ever-present vigilance. It did, however, contribute to the jittery atmosphere in which we lived. One of the more unpleasant effects of the political situation as far as I was concerned was that in 1950 began a long period in which I was *persona non grata* to members of my own family. As we had not seen much of one another and had not kept up with what we were doing and thinking, I was not surprised. Yet I always hoped for a visit or a telephone call asking how things were, "Sorry you're having problems," "Is there anything we can do to help?" They did not come. More important, of course, was what was going on in our society as a whole. Families divided, neighbors became enemies, workers suspected one another; racism, always an ugly character-istic of the American people, became rampant; people mistrusted one an-other; the lowest profession, the informer, became an occupation glorified by the Senate, by the media, by Hollywood.

Some people, probably a good many conservative, well-to-do, upper bourgeois types, lived through those years unconcerned about what was going on, unthinking, unworried, unnoticing. They were so positioned in our social structure that the tragedy through which the country was passing left them unmoved and unmarked. But the heads of our government in all its branches knew very well what was going on. They were not the innocent dupes they pretended to be; they were not the hostages of the McCarthys, the McCarrans, the J. Edgar Hoovers, the bigots, the fanatics, the corrupted, who orchestrated those shameful years. They were their patrons, their pro-tectors, their "respectable" facade. That was the kind of America in which the Smith Act, itself the product of a degenerate society, was applied. I could think of nothing more useful at the time than helping its victims in any small way I could.

The text of the Smith Act says nothing about people who try to overcome the government by acts of violence. It speaks only of those who advocate or teach the duty or desirability of doing so, and of those who organize, not those who act. None of the defendants in the Smith Act trials was accused of making bombs, of securing military secrets, of training saboteurs. They were accused of (and ultimately sentenced to prison for) attending meetings at which a philosophical-political doctrine was discussed and taught.

The crux of the government's case was that this doctrine called for violent overthrow of the government under any and all circumstances. Did it? Is that what Marxism teaches? That is not what I learned from my reading or experiences. I became a Communist Party member not in support of such wildly irresponsible doctrine. I had become a Communist in the middle thirties, the days of the Great Depression, when the Nazis, Fascists and Japanese militarists were threatening the whole world, when as a result a political polarization was taking place among Americans. At that time, to put it broadly, one was either a profascist or an antifascist. The antifascists, whether they belonged to the extreme left, were right of center or at any of the positions in between, believed that in order to succeed in defeating fascism, they had to find a common political ground with all the others. To a considerable extent, such a common bond was forged and maintained during the Roosevelt years and helped to get the country through the war. When Truman became President at the end of the war, the unity began to break down. When it was completely shattered, we entered a fifteen-year period of anti-Red hysteria, and serious damage was done to our democratic institutions and traditions.

During the period of the antifascist front, the CP led the left sector. I have devoted a chapter to the Party's effort during the early part of the European phase of the war, the so-called phony war, in opposition to American participation. That effort lasted too long, and we put too much emphasis on British imperialism and too little on Hitler's Nazism. But after Hitler's invasion of the Soviet Union, and throughout the rest of the war, the Party played a unifying role. Although it wanted to continue to play that role, in the Cold War period of the second half of the 1940s and the 1950s its efforts were frustrated by the internal enemies of democracy and by those misled into believing that the way to strengthen democracy was to cut off its left arm.

With respect to the right to rebel and overthrow one's government, Communist theory closely corresponds to the famous statement in our own Declaration of Independence: "We hold these truths to be self-evident, that all men are created equal, that they are endowed by their Creator with certain unalienable Rights, that among these are Life, Liberty and the pursuit of Happiness." The Declaration continues: "That to secure these rights, Governments are instituted among Men, deriving their just powers from the consent of the governed." Then comes the pertinent passage: "That whenever any Form of Government becomes destructive of these ends, it is the Right of the People to alter or to abolish it, and to institute new Government, laying its foundation on such principles and organizing its powers in such a form, as to them seems most likely to effect their Safety and Happiness." A few sentences later, the thought is reinforced: "But when a long train of abuses and usurpations, pursuing invariably the same Object evinces a design to reduce them under absolute Despotism, it is their right, it is their duty, to throw off such Government, and to provide new guards for their future security." I am told that Marx and Engels were influenced by Thomas Jefferson, to whom these thoughts on the right to revolution are principally attributed.

In a speech in the House of Representatives on January 12, 1848, Abraham Lincoln emphasized the same principle: "Any people anywhere being inclined and having the power have the right to rise up and shake off the existing government, and form a new one that suits them better. This is a most valuable, a most sacred right—a right which we hope and believe is to liberate the world."

To me there was not only a right, but a need to teach such a doctrine in a country that had gone through the human horror of the Great Depression, that even in times of so-called prosperity had high unemployment, that after joining in the defeat of the fascist powers had embarked on a policy of Cold War, which it took no great prescience to envision might at any moment heat up—as in fact it did in Korea and Vietnam—and that might very well itself fall under despotic rule—which it came within an inch of doing under the administration of Richard Nixon.

I, along with Dashiell Hammett, Alpheous Hunton, Abner Green and Robert Dunn (the latter escaped our fate because of illness) had been asked to become trustees of a bail fund which the Civil Rights Congress had established to assist victims of the Cold War within the United States. Many of those aided were left-wing foreign-born residents whom the government was trying to deport. Indeed, the only deportation attempts were made against left-wingers. Among others aided were the CP leaders with whom we are here concerned.

Shortly after the Supreme Court ruled that their conviction under the Smith Act had been constitutional, those top functionaries of the Communist Party were ordered to surrender in order to begin serving their sentences. Four of the eleven, Henry Winston, Gus Hall, Robert Thompson and Gilbert Green, failed to show up and thereby forfeited their bail. And all hell broke loose.

I was not privy to the decision that four of the eleven were to jump bail and "go underground." The later explanation was that the Party anticipated a widespread seizure of functionaries, down to the local level, thereby wiping out the entire leadership. A few experienced officials had to disappear in order to prevent the complete success of such a wholesale raid. The survival of the organization demanded such a move.

As expected, I was immediately subpoenaed to appear in a federal court. Presiding over the case that July 5, 1951, was Judge Sylvester J. Ryan, and prosecuting was Irving Saypol. I had encountered my inquisitor once before.

In the late forties, we had both attended a function at Fieldston Academy just north of Manhattan. I was there because my oldest daughter was then a student at Fieldston and I suppose that Saypol attended for a similar reason. I remember very clearly being in conversation with Lila and a group of her friends when Saypol came over and interrupted. He said nothing more nor less than, "Field, I just want to take this opportunity to tell you that someday we're going to get you." I was therefore not too pleased to meet this patriot again under circumstances that were clearly unfavorable. From the first instant, it did indeed look as though his prediction was about to come true.

Believing that discovery of the whereabouts of the fugitives was the purpose of the hearing and its only legitimate purpose, I answered questions directed to that point. No, I had nothing to do with their disappearance. No, I had no idea where they were. Yes, I remembered having seen Gus Hall a few days before and Winston "some time last week." I said I had expressed "great concern and amazement" when I first learned the four were missing. Judge Ryan then informed me that by answering those questions I had denied myself the privilege of claiming the Fifth Amendment on other questions. (This was a very doubtful legal point, but in those days its validity was never questioned.) The hearing then moved on to its real objective.

Judge Ryan explained to me and the rest of his audience that he wanted the names of the contributors of the $80,000 that I had put up for those four fugitives—bail which had now been forfeited—because the names might lead to their whereabouts. It soon became apparent that extracting from me and my colleagues the list of contributors to the Bail Fund was the hearing's real purpose. Getting their names would not help discover the fugitives, but it certainly would expose the contributors. In the prevailing atmosphere of hysteria, that exposure surely would have caused the donors to lose their jobs and to suffer a multitude of other problems.

I answered certain questions about the contributors, thinking I could show the futility of further pursuing this line of questioning. I explained that we had received over three-quarters of a million dollars from several thousand contributors. Some had lent cash, others bonds. Several times I said that even if I divulged the names it could in no way help the court's effort to find the four. All the money and securities had gone into a general fund with which we had bought U.S. government bonds; there was no way to trace whose money was used to post that particular $80,000.

Mary Kaufman, the attorney for the Bail Fund, was in this instance also acting on my behalf—along with Victor Rabinowitz, who was my personal representative. Kaufman asked, "By what stretch of logic can this court hold that thousands of persons, who have contributed to the Bail Fund, but who personally have no role in posting bond for the four men, may have more knowledge of their whereabouts than a person brought in off the street?"

I produced our last financial report, which included receipts and disbursements but no names, hoping that would satisfy my inquisitors. It did not. It simply led to further questioning. Largely to protect myself and the many others available for the court's fishing expedition, I then resorted to the Fifth Amendment.

I refused to produce the fund's checkbook, certificates of deposit and the list of contributors. I refused to tell the court where the fund kept its records, when I had last seen them, whether Henry Winston was one of the contributors and whether I was.

For me the whole hearing had an air of unreality. When I agreed to become the secretary and main functionary of the Bail Fund, I had done so under certain conditions that were agreed to and strictly observed by all concerned. I was not only not to be the guardian of the list of contributors, but I was never to see it or to be told about it. I was not to have access in any form or manner to the checkbook or the accounts. I was not myself to contribute any money or certificates. Nor was I to have anything to do with raising the funds we required. My responsibilities were to attend and participate at meetings to decide when and how and for whom we were to post bail and then to do the posting myself.

I made these conditions to protect the contributors and myself from exactly the sort of inquisition that took place in Judge Ryan's court. I could openly and honestly have said that I did not know who the contributors were or who kept the books or where they were.

Things did not work out the way I had anticipated. The atmosphere was more devious and ruthless than I had expected. Even if I had said exactly what I have just written about the conditions I had made, I knew from experience that the FBI had a whole string of witnesses on call who would swear I was lying. They would testify that I did know who was on the list, where the list was, that I personally was one of the large contributors, and so on. They would be believed, and I would not. Perjury was a far greater personal risk than contempt. I had to assume that that was the way Saypol hoped "to get" me.

Aside from that reality, there were other people to consider—the bookkeeper, the fund-raisers, the accountant and the contributors themselves. It seemed much better to stop the Bail Fund witch-hunt with those of us who were its leaders. The court would get its victims, and reams of publicity. Saypol, his assistant Roy Cohn and the rest, momentary heroes of the

Establishment, would be rewarded with judgeships and fat attorney's fees. Several thousand good people, after losing some money, would be able to continue their normal lives, and our Bail Fund staff would not be exposed.

I think we were successful in stopping the hunt for names and names and more names. I believe we also maintained a sense of decency and an ethical standard in the face of a shamefully unjust search for lists and names. The hearing made it plain that the search for the four Communists was a pretext for damaging the lives of several thousand contributors. Losing track of the four fugitives had made the FBI look like a bunch of bungling amateurs. The agents of the Establishment were angry and looking all over for people to punish. In this case they got no further than the four trustees of the Bail Fund, and they didn't do us any harm we couldn't take in stride.

I have always figured that I had to live with myself more than with anybody else. This was no great discovery on my part, but, then, the commonplaces are often the most important. Otherwise, they would not be commonplace. If I needed to respect my friends, all the more reason to respect myself. My behavior had to be as consistent with my beliefs as possible. What I did had to conform with what I knew. The Lord only knows how many times I violated these principles, although I am aware of quite a few occasions when I took detours around what I knew to be right and rationalized how to live with my mistakes. On matters involving high political principles, however, I could not betray what I believed without being ashamed of myself forever. I have fervently hoped that the prominent actors and writers and others who ratted on their friends and comrades spent long hours over many years regurgitating their treachery.

The upshot of my lengthy and exhausting questioning that July 5 in Judge Ryan's court was that His Honor turned to me, and made some remarks to the effect that I had conducted myself courteously. Then he pronounced, "You are guilty in contempt of court and hereby committed to the custody of the Attorney General for ninety days, or until such time as you purge yourself." He gave me until next morning to see if I could either get somewhere with an appeal to a higher court or change my mind and confess all. Because my hopes and his were not fulfilled within the twenty-four hours, I was escorted the next day directly from the witness chair to the basement of the building. There a Black Maria was conveniently waiting to take me to the federal detention facility on West Street. On July 6 I spent my first night in jail.

I had a few more details to wrap up before settling down to serve my nine months—the three that Ryan had just given me and another six that were added a few days later. I got temporary bail several days after that first night and went to Red Hill to rest up. After I had been there all too short a time, I received a long-distance call from assistant federal attorney Roy Cohn informing me that the bail had been revoked and that I was immediately to report to his office. Because Red Hill is 115 miles by car from the city, I explained to Cohn that I would have to ask him to interpret "immediately" as something over three hours. His improbable answer was, "I want you here much quicker than that. Get in your airplane and you'll be here in an hour." I patiently informed him that I didn't have an airplane, never had had one and never expected to own one. Roy Cohn, some of my readers may recall, was the member of Senator Joseph McCarthy's staff who traveled through Europe with his friend, David Schine, in order to purge U.S. Information Agency libraries of subversive literature. Cohn is a man in whom in my opinion it is hard to find a redeeming quality; I have never heard anyone say anything good about him. But maybe that is because I have been fortunate enough not to have known the type that admires him. Four and a half hours later, after two or three bourbons and a good meal with friends who gave me a send-off, I reached Cohn's office. He was furious at having been kept waiting. According to the *Herald-Tribune*, "Within minutes [Field] was handcuffed, placed in a prison van and driven to Federal Detention Headquarters." The *New York Post* said I was asked by reporters whether I wanted to make a statement. "Field grinned and said, 'What the hell can I say?' "

By that time Hammett and Hunton had also been jailed, and Green, the remaining member of the Bail Fund trustees, was about to join us. But before his arrival, Hammett, Hunton and I were taken several times before a grand jury which asked us exactly the same questions that we had already refused to answer and for which refusal had been jailed. While these frequent interruptions to our peaceful life in jail were going on, I was escorted to Washington to appear before Senator McCarran and his colleagues. That performance I report in the next chapter. A correspondent of the *Daily Worker* kept better track of my busy schedule than I was able to. Under a headline which read "Torture by Testimony—The New Third Degree," he noted that on one day I arrived in my windowless limousine, the Black Maria, at the Federal Court House on Foley Square at ten in the morning, waited there two hours, went before a judge from noon to 12:15, went before the grand jury from 1:30 to 2:30, was returned to prison at 4:30 and at 6:30 was on the train to Washington.

As the grand jury considered my failure to answer those same questions I had been asked in Ryan's court contemptuous, it sent me upstairs to another federal court, this one presided over by Judge John F. X. McGohey, who ran through those same questions a third time. It was he who added six months to the three I had already received.

I never understood why this was not a clear case of double jeopardy. A minor point like that, I suppose, was of no importance in those days.

The New York press gave diverse impressions of me on the witness stand. The *Journal American* referred to "Field, a thin, ruddy-faced man wearing shell-rimmed spectacles, a grey suit and a red tie." The *Post* said that "Mr. Field took his banishment to jail quite calmly. He worked his thin, pinched face for a moment" after sentencing. The *World Telegram* wrote, "Field was red-faced and fidgety when Judge Ryan turned to him and said: 'The hearing is now closed and I adjudge you in contempt.' " The *Times* claimed, "Throughout the long, exhausting examination, the judge and the witness both maintained their self-possession, speaking courteous words in low voices, without gestures." To my knowledge, none of the papers noted the fact that upon sentencing me Judge Ryan complimented me on my conduct during the hearing.

No one will be surprised to learn that I got mighty little support in the commercial press for the position I had taken. The atmosphere was "Get the Commies and get them any way you can." I. F. Stone, of the *Compass*, however, came to my side. As I do not have many opportunities to quote something nice that was said in those days about the now middle-aged Fred Field, I shall include a couple of paragraphs of his long article:

> I take my hat off to Frederick Vanderbilt Field. The old Commodore might not like his descendant's associations but he'd certainly chuckle over his spunk. There was a healthy streak of anarchism in the Robber Barons who laid the foundation of American big business. . . .It's going to take more of that anarchistic streak to win the fight for liberty in America, and I'm glad to see a Vanderbilt carrying on the tradition. . . .what the government has to do as a government is one thing and what Mr. Field may have felt himself obliged to do is another. He had and has a moral obligation not to disclose the names of the good many people who supplied the bail funds of the Civil Rights Congress. The government has been trying to get those names for some time; the disappearance of the four convicted Communist leaders is only a new excuse. It wants the names for no good purpose.

Ted Thackrey, editor and publisher of the *Compass*, wrote a column referring to Stone's views of "the case of Frederick V. Field" and added his own comments:

> That Mr. Field is exhibiting a courage rare in our society is, I think, beyond debate; furthermore I concede that in view of the basis on which the bail funds were solicited and received and the virtual certainty that the government is unlikely to confine its questioning of bailbond contributions to the legitimate inquiry concerning any knowledge of the whereabouts of the fugitives, Field is acting in what he believes to be the best interests of the contributors.

If we had closed the doors to the hunters, we soon found that we had not locked them. The West Street house of detention was supposed to be nothing more than a way station to hold prisoners during their trials. When and if convicted, they were sent on to one or another of the permanent federal guest houses. We trustees, however, were held in West Street for many weeks while we were taken for repeated sessions with the New York State Banking Department at 270 Broadway. The Banking Department was seeking to determine whether the Bail Fund had been violating banking laws by accepting deposits without a license.

In this case we were dealing with a man who seemed to be straightforward. His name was Donald H. Aiken; he was the deputy superintendent of banks for the state. Our lawyers assured us that it was the century-old practice of the Department of Banks to treat as confidential all information submitted to it in the course of its investigations. Documents submitted to the department were immune from subpoena; its job was simply to protect the financial interests of all participants in institutions under investigation. They told us that those who had contributed to the Bail Fund could assume that the usual practices would prevail in any decisions that involved them.

We talked this over in jail among ourselves as well as with our lawyers on our frequent trips to 270 Broadway. Those trips were as absurd as everything else about jail. We would walk through crowded streets handcuffed to a guard in civilian clothes and climb into the building elevators where it was often difficult to prevent other passengers from trying to squeeze between us. A raincoat hanging over our arms would hide the handcuffs, but in the elevator the coat would often be jostled out of position—to the fright of the other passengers, who suddenly realized the dangerous company they had to keep until they could get off at the next floor.

On entering the department's offices we would be divested of the handcuffs and even be treated to the luxury of sandwiches. The Spanish word for handcuffs, incidentally, is *esposas*, which means wives. There is a lot, isn't there, still to be overcome.

We negotiated a settlement with Mr. Aiken. The Bail Fund had served its purpose; indeed, because of the political climate it no longer could function. One way or another, the government would continue its harassment in an effort to get the list of names. After what had happened, we would not be permitted to put up bail for political prisoners again. Considerable amounts had been lost through the forfeiting of bail on the four Communist leaders as well as in a previous case which involved Gerhardt Eisler. Eisler was a German who in 1949 became tired of waiting for a decision on long-drawn-out appeals of his deportation case and sailed to England, thereby forfeiting bail of $25,000. The best we could do was to make sure that as much money as possible was returned to the donors, a job that the Banking Department was authorized to do. With the losses already sustained, and the expenses incurred in the liquidation, the contributors by no means got back a hundred cents on the dollar. But at least they were no longer politically molested, and the witch-hunt over the Bail Fund was finally over.

22

The McCarran Hearing

On February 8, 1951, a truck backed up to a New England barn in Lee, Massachusetts, loaded innumerable cabinets of Institute of Pacific Relations files and drove off to Washington, D.C., where it delivered the lot to the Senate Subcommittee on Internal Security headed by Pat McCarran of Nevada. According to Edward Carter, who owned the barn and was also secretary general of the IPR, an investigator for Senator Joseph McCarthy named Don Surine, had previously stolen a number of documents from those files and turned them over to his boss. McCarthy then persuaded McCarran to secure a subpoena and take possession of the entire lot.

Neither Carter, his wife Alice nor anyone else was on the property at the time of the theft and removal of the files. The barn was located on a narrow, unpaved road that led off the Stockbridge-Lenox highway, on which there were only a few well-spaced farmhouses. The subpoena authorized service only on the owner of the barn, but because he was absent, it was served on the proprietor of an adjoining farm who knew nothing about the IPR or the contents of the barn. The barn was therefore entered illegally, apparently by the manure chute. The operation was a pure and simple theft perpetrated by McCarran's committee. During the long "investigation" of the IPR which followed, no officer of the organization was permitted access to those stolen files.

The officers of the IPR later testified that some time before the raid they had offered the files to the FBI, which examined them and found nothing to be concerned about.

The files were in that lonely spot at the time of the burglary because there was no room for them in the IPR offices in the city, and the officials of the organization assumed they were living in a law-abiding country. The files contained tens of thousands of letters and other documents that the

Institute had accumulated over twenty-six years. The correspondence ranged from the most businesslike to the most ridiculous.

I remember one letter I had written to a colleague the morning after taking the secretary of one of the richest women in the world to cocktails at the Gotham Hotel on 55th Street and Fifth Avenue. I was trying to persuade the secretary to recommend that her employer make a large contribution to the IPR. When I wrote the letter, I thought I had been successful, because the lady and I seemed to get on exceptionally well. A précis of the letter to my colleague—he was to continue the quest because I had to leave the city for several weeks—would read, "Give her five martinis." Now, when a communication of that sort is shown to you during a grand jury hearing, as this letter was shown to me in Washington many years later, as evidence of participation in a Red conspiracy, you don't know whether to take your inquisitors seriously or read to them from *Alice in Wonderland*.

The more serious and allegedly more incriminating letters included one written during World War II when the United States was allied with the Soviet Union. It suggested to someone in the State Department that he might be interested in having a talk with a prominent Russian academic expert on Asian questions who happened to be in the country. The letter was exhibited by the McCarran subcommittee as evidence that the IPR was infiltrating the State Department with Communists and communism.

It took McCarran's staff several months to go through the purloined files, not to obtain information, but to obtain names and more names. At one point in the examination of Carter, the subcommittee counsel, Robert Morris, read into the record eighty-one names, nearly all of whom Carter had testified had past or present connections with the IPR. Not unexpectedly, the list included such persons as Alger Hiss (already in jail, but at one time a distinguished member of the State Department), the group of foreign service officers whose reports on China had proved correct though contrary to what Washington officialdom had hoped would happen, and, of course, Owen Lattimore.

Would the reader be surprised if I said that the names of people like Newton D. Baker, Secretary of War during World War I, General of the Army George C. Marshall, currently Secretary of Defense, or Ray Lyman Wilbur, Secretary of the Interior under Hoover, all of whom had been officers of the IPR, were not on Morris's list? Nor did the subcommittee think it important to call to the public's attention the fact that the Institute had been financed from the beginning by the Rockefeller and Carnegie Foundations, the Rockefeller Brothers Fund and a number of the largest corporations in the country, and that their chief officers had served on the

IPR's board of trustees. Not a word was offered by the subcommittee to present a balanced picture that would have shown the IPR to be a thoroughly respectable (in the Establishment sense), influential, academic organization devoted to research and the dissemination of its findings.

The McCarran subcommittee began its hearings on the IPR in July 1951, five months after the raid on the Carter farm. Carter himself was the first witness. I appeared the next day, having previously been interviewed in a closed session by two of the subcommittee members. McCarran made a special arrangement with District Attorney Saypol to have me taken under guard to Washington for the public hearing, because I was then in jail in New York.

I found the hearing difficult, not so much because of the subject I was being asked about—I had become accustomed to interrogation—but because by early July of 1951, I was as close to physical exhaustion as I have ever been. The previous week's events had taxed my usually strong physique and temperament to the utmost. I had been judged in contempt of a federal court, put in jail, and released on bail, only to be returned to jail when bail was cancelled. The trip to Washington and the experience in its maximum security prison did not help. On the morning of the hearing I had been taken out of my cell at five o'clock for no reason at all—for no good reason, that is. I had tried in vain to sleep on the cement floor of the prison waiting room, and finally, five hours later, I was taken to the Senate Building. There, well protected between two marshals, I was whisked to the hearing room. After two hours of questioning, I had to swallow my pride and inform the Senators that I was tired out and could not go on without a rest and a sandwich.

Aside from my weariness, I knew that this time I was up against the real enemy. In comparison to McCarran, Tydings had been a knight in white armor fighting for liberty and decency. McCarran was the pinnacle of reaction, on a par with McCarthy, but less crude. He was the author of the McCarran Internal Security Act, enacted only a year before, which proclaimed communism to be a criminal conspiracy, authorized concentration camps for subversives, and established the Subversive Activities Control Board to force "subversive" organizations to register, disclose their membership and finances and declare their subversiveness on all published literature. If McCarran wasn't the devil himself, he was his surrogate.

I had no idea why I had been subpoenaed to appear before his committee—the previous private hearing had just fished around apparently aimlessly. Was this to be just another fishing expedition? Was it to be another attempt to trap me in the pitfalls of the Fifth Amendment? Or did this inquisition have some new gimmick that I hadn't heard about? All I could be sure of was that the hearing would not be searching for the truth. By authorizing the burglary in the Berkshires, the subcommittee had shown itself to be unscrupulous and lawless. Besides McCarran, its members included Homer Ferguson of Michigan, who turned out to be my most insistent questioner, and James O. Eastland of Mississippi, who was dressed in what one correspondent called "the vanilla-ice-cream-colored suit favored by Southerners in the Capital," and turned out to be my most unpleasant inquisitor. Joe McCarthy dropped in for a few minutes to see how things were going. It was not a pleasant group to face. On this occasion, Victor Rabinowitz was my lawyer and sat beside me during the interrogation.

McCarran opened the session with a lesson on the proper use of the Fifth Amendment and then launched into a short spellbinder on red-blooded Americanism more suited to a high-school oratorical contest.

"Mr. Field," he said, "I think those of us who come from the West are especially appreciative of the wonderful name that has been made in the history of America by your family. [He didn't explain why the family had a special appeal to Westerners and he didn't say whether he was talking about the Vanderbilts or the Fields, although it was obvious to which the old snob was referring.] It is a regrettable thing to me," he went on, "and to many others, that for some reason or other, best known to yourself, you seem to have perhaps for the time being forgotten the great achievements that were worked out by your ancestors and forebears."

The United States, he continued, "is today at the crossroads of its existence, for never has it been challenged by a more dangerous enemy." The danger would be somewhat alleviated, he felt, if I would tell "the people of this country in their most trying hour" everything that I knew. The committee, McCarran assured me, "is your friend." The committee "want to put you with your family in the fine history of your forebears."

I looked him straight in the eye and said nothing. I didn't think it appropriate to quote from Matthew Josephson's *Robber Barons* or to suggest that I didn't suppose the Commodore had ever done anything quite so grotesquely dishonest as swiping the files of a respectable citizen from his private residence.

The committee thereupon embarked on a lengthy interrogation about my marriages and spouses. Realizing how important this subject was, both to help my country escape the perilous danger in which it found itself and to rehabilitate myself in the eyes of the Vanderbilt family, I answered all of those questions to the best of my ability.

I was questioned about other matters that logically would seem to be off the agenda. There was the one, for instance, about my having registered with the Justice Department as an agent of the Chinese People's Republic.

In the early fall of 1950, I had received a cable from Peking from a very close friend, Chi Chao-ting, asking me for help. Chi had been my colleague sixteen years earlier on the magazine *China Today*. After the success of the revolution, he had become deputy director of the Bank of China. There was a problem about the use of funds deposited in the United States before the Communist takeover. It involved the Bank of China, the China National Aviation Corporation, and two Chinese postal and savings banks. Would I help? I cabled back, agreeing to help. I asked an able lawyer friend, Martin Popper, who already had experience handling the American affairs of socialist countries, to get me properly registered with our government as "attorney in fact." Popper was to handle the legal end of the matter himself.

Having started what I had been requested to do and having put the matter into competent hands, my presence was no longer required, and I withdrew from the arrangement in December of that year. It was also true that in November China had intervened in the Korean War, and Chinese troops were face-to-face in combat with American soldiers. I was strongly opposed to American involvement in that war, but nevertheless felt uncomfortable officially representing a country engaged in fighting fellow Americans. I suppose that consideration to some extent influenced my decision to withdraw. When the Senators badgered me on that point, I gave them that explanation.

Then they wanted to know why Carter had helped me, a person known to have Communist sympathies, when the FBI had blocked my military appointment in January 1942. They had questioned Carter and he told them he had supported me on the "honest conviction that I would give faithful service to the United States." They probably wanted to discredit his testimony through me. The Senators also wanted to know what officer or officers had been so eager to give me a commission. They obviously wanted to get their names, locate them these ten years later, and confront them with this direct evidence that they had conspired to overthrow the government of the United States by force and violence. I couldn't remember their names and I said so, and I was unwilling to guess "because it would be unfair to an officer to associate him favorably with me at the present time." I hope they all became generals.

Another matter that came up was my financial relationship to the IPR. All my inquisitors in those days assumed I had financed anything and everything with which I was associated. That assumption frankly got under my skin, for it was tantamount to saying that I bought my way wherever I went. Edward Carter cleared that matter up for the McCarran subcommittee before I got to the witness chair. He amused the Senators, who from my observation were not a particularly humorous group, by testifying that I was

not the "financial angel" I was reputed to be, but only a "minor cherub."
He calculated that the American branch of the IPR during its entire history
had spent about $3 million, of which I might have donated roughly $60,000.
I never made my own calculation, but informed the Senators that I would
not dispute Carter's figure.

During that hearing the Senators and I reached what seemed to me to
be the limits of the absurdities encountered in threading one's way through
what had become the technicalities of using the Fifth Amendment. They
placed before me a pamphlet which I had written for the Communist Party.

> SENATOR O'CONOR: Mr. Field, I have before me a booklet which is captioned
> China's Greatest Crisis, by Frederick V. Field. You are familiar with it since you
> are the author of it, is that not true?
> MR. FIELD: Senator, with respect to that question . . . I would like to invoke
> the privilege on the grounds that the answer might tend to incriminate me.
> SENATOR O'CONOR: At the outset I was merely intending to identify the
> Frederick V. Field as to whether or not that was you or another person, to your
> knowledge.
> MR. FIELD: I think I must invoke the privilege on that question.
> THE CHAIRMAN: You deny you were the author of it?
> MR. FIELD: I invoke the privilege. I decline to answer on the grounds that the
> answer might tend to incriminate me.
>
>   . . .
>
> SENATOR O'CONOR: Without giving support to the views expressed herein or
> without reaffirming them or in any sense taking any responsibility for the views,
> will you tell us whether or not this booklet was in fact published and distributed?
> I am not asking you for any connection you may have had with it other than
> just the fact of whether or not this booklet was in fact distributed. That is without
> asking you for a reaffirmation of the views or anything else related to it, just as
> to the mere fact.
> THE CHAIRMAN: The question is, Does he know whether or not it was printed?
> MR. FIELD: You have shown me a document. It has clearly been published and
> exists. I must acknowledge that.
> THE CHAIRMAN: Have you seen it before?
> MR. MORRIS: Have you seen it before?
> MR. FIELD: Mr. Chairman, I must respectfully decline to answer that question
> on the grounds the answer might tend to incriminate me.

In that case, I felt my questioners had some reason to feel exasperated.
If they had asked me, I would have agreed that the situation was absurd.
But I would have explained that the fault was not mine but rather the result
of the legal intricacies with which the courts had surrounded the use of the
privilege against self-incrimination. Had I answered, "Yes, I wrote that
pamphlet. It says so right on the cover," I would have opened myself up
to a whole series of further questions leading into my relations with many
individual Communists and non-Communists and with the Communist

Party, which the Smith and McCarran Acts had declared a criminal conspiracy. Because McCarran himself was chairing the meeting, I thought it the better part of wisdom to refrain from informing the committee that the Frederick V. Field who wrote that pamphlet was the same Frederick V. Field who was sitting in front of them.

Upon my plea of hunger and fatigue, the committee recessed, and I was escorted to a nearby room in which sat several women secretaries at their typewriters. No one said anything to me. I was placed at an empty table in the middle of the room, from which I could see one of my guards carefully keeping me in sight through an open door. A sandwich and a glass of milk revived me. I revived even more when Rabinowitz came in to tell me that there would be no further questioning because the committee had decided not to reconvene.

It was apparently evident to the Senators that while I had not answered a lot of questions, I had answered many others. McCarran told the press, "I don't think we'll cite him for contempt. He has enough trouble as it is. . . .We got more out of him than we expected."

The hearing had been unpleasant, but not as rough as I had expected. My frequent use of the Fifth Amendment was not challenged. About all the committee accomplished was to lay out on the record many of my activities. This, it seems, was exactly the object of the interrogation. William V. Shannon, the Washington correspondent of the *New York Post*, wrote a long article on the hearing for the *New Republic* (August 12, 1951) in which he suggested that interpretation.

Before quoting from it, though, I want to refer to other sections of that article in which Shannon referred to me as "the frustrated, unhappy, 'rich man's son,' " the "pseudo-scholar," a person so dependent on the "hard center of Party discipline" that if detached from it "Field's personality might well disintegrate," and so on. Not very nice stuff. As I remarked earlier, that kind of nastiness was the worst part of those 1950-52 experiences.

I thought that Shannon was better at political analysis than at characterizing Fred Field—and I hope my readers will agree. He presented an interesting interpretation of that day's hearing. It served McCarran's purpose, he wrote,

merely to get on the record the pattern of Field's past activities and associations. In this way, when liberals and other "uncooperative" witnesses appear before the committee, McCarran will be able to catch them with such questions as: Isn't that the organization Frederick Vanderbilt Field was a member of? Isn't that the magazine Field wrote for? or, Isn't that the same letterhead Field's name was on?

By using the genuine dark red of Field's past and present record, McCarran hopes to be able to color other men's records at least a dirty pink.

It's hard to believe now, so many years later, that I felt a sense of relief when I got back to the maximum security prison.

23

Guest of
the Government

Serving a jail sentence is a stupid, dull, wasteful experience. That much time is simply taken out of your life. You learn nothing useful or entertaining, though you do get to know a lot more about the mischief of life. An exception to a totally negative picture is that you learn about friendship. And I suppose you learn patience and to survive boredom. If you have to wait a few hours in line to get into the revival of *Gone with the Wind* or the Tutankhamun exhibit, you take it more in stride after having been a guest of the government.

My word on jail life doesn't carry great weight, because a nine-month sentence is short. You serve those nine months, however, with others who are doing two, five, ten or more years, and you catch on to what they are experiencing. I met a good many men during my brief months, and I can't remember a single one who you might say was moving upward, or undergoing experiences which might strengthen his moral fiber, make him a better person.

I was extraordinarily well treated by my fellow inmates, sometimes touchingly so. This was generally true of the political prisoners, or at least it was true of our Bail Fund group and the Hollywood Ten. But there were tragic exceptions. Philip Frankfeld, a victim of the Baltimore Smith Act trial, was beaten up in Atlanta; one of the "Eleven," Robert Thompson, had his skull broken by an iron bar wielded by a Yugoslav inmate who claimed that he had assassinated Communists in his own country. There were also a number of other less serious incidents.

Our treatment by the prison authorities was another matter. No one was treated "extraordinarily well," neither I nor anyone else. I, however, had nothing to complain about on that score. I was treated reasonably decently most of the time, yelled at two or three times and given small privileges two or three times. But many of my colleagues, particularly the national and state Party leaders, fared badly. All of the black political prisoners were segregated, as were all other black prisoners. Winston "lost his eyesight in prison as a result of neglect and a too-long-delayed operation by prison doctors," and Frankfeld "came out of prison shrunken and almost blind" as a result of harsh treatment by the authorities and the beating inflicted by other inmates. These quotations are taken from what, to date, must be considered the authoritative account of the outrages of the McCarthy period, David Caute's *Great Fear* (Simon and Schuster, New York, 1978). Caute devotes a whole chapter, entitled "Hell in Pittsburgh," to one of the most scandalous cases of prison brutality and judicial corruption, that of Steve Nelson, chairman of the Western Pennsylvania CP. "The Party's senior woman leader, Elizabeth Gurley Flynn," writes Caute, "already in her sixties, was locked up in New York City five times between 1951 and 1955." He quotes her as saying, "The vile language, the fights, the disgusting lesbian performances, were unbearable."

A few days after I was returned to West Street in July 1951, I was taken to appear before the McCarran subcommittee in Washington, D.C. It was a tiring experience. I traveled with a VIP as my protector, a captain of the prison guards. As we left the New York Detention Center in a taxi for Pennsylvania Station, he said, "I don't think we're going to need the handcuffs," and removed them. The taxi left us on the wrong side of the avenue so that we had to cross heavy traffic to reach the station. On getting out of the cab, I said, "You've done me a favor, let me carry your suitcase." We scrambled across the two-way traffic and inevitably got separated. I could see a worried look cross the captain's brow, but I waited for him to draw close to me. Once in the station it became obvious that we were being escorted. Groups of passengers dissolved before us, no tickets were shown or requested, and in no time at all we found ourselves in a compartment. The FBI agents, once again, were earning their wages.

The journey was uneventful except for an interesting conversation that lasted well into the night. I asked my companion what kind of joint the Washington jail was, and he answered that he happened to know all about it because he had served on a commission charged with making it escape-proof. Since it was so secure, he felt free to tell me some of the things that made it so. I shall not pass these secrets on, for who knows, one of my readers might one day be a guest of the government there himself. Well, I'll relent slightly. The walls were very thick and high. The steel highly tempered. They brought the bionic woman to Washington to test the results of their work, and even she couldn't bend the bars.

I slept fitfully because I was tense about the forthcoming hearing. The train made a special stop in the yards well outside Washington station to let this very important passenger off. And guess who was there at that very spot to greet him? Three FBI men. Their automobile was in the yard, too, only a few tracks away. We rushed through the early morning traffic to the federal jail.

"Get out of the car and walk to that door." Entering any modern jail happens exactly as you see it in the movies or on television. As you approach it, the outer door opens automatically. It closes behind you with the familiar click. There's another door in front of you, and after that still another. Then comes a long corridor with a uniformed human being at the end of it. Next, the fingerprinting all over again—how many of my prints do they have in their files?—and the showering.

The interesting part began when I was led to my cell. My block contained three floors of cells on one side of a large room where the inmates are herded for meals. As I entered this room, breakfast had just ended, and the prisoners were lining up to return to their cells. Everyone could see me, but not an eye seemed to turn nor an expression to change.

I soon learned that the prisoners had known from the papers that I was coming that morning; they knew a good deal about me. I was put in the last cell on the ground floor. It was the usual sort: a bed, a washbasin, a toilet, a chair and a small table, all clean. As the cells were in a row, you couldn't see from one into any of the others. You weren't allowed to talk, either.

Not ten minutes passed before a hand was awkwardly extended from the adjoining cell to mine. It gave me a pack of cigarettes. Matches followed. Five minutes later I received a pack of pipe tobacco. Then came a short written message which said, "Because you're new here, you'll be handed lunch in your cell. If you can't eat it all, flush it down the can."

Well, I was tired to the point of exhaustion. I was worried and, yes, scared about the next day's session with the senators. I was alone in a maximum security prison. And, then, suddenly, I was not alone. I had friends. They were helping me, and if they had started out that way, they were likely to see me through whatever problems I might have for the few days of my stay. So I lay down on the bed and slept soundly for two hours. When I woke up, I felt prepared to stand up to whatever was coming.

I learned later through prison sources that the leader of the inmates was a long-term major criminal, a former chief of a dope gang. He had sent word throughout the prison that when that guy Field showed up he was to be taken care of. And I was.

At West Street we were pretty free to wander around the corridor, talk and waste time while we endlessly swept and cleaned and painted the bars.

Meals were fairly informal, you could sit where you liked, serve yourself to no more than you thought you could eat, and you could talk to your neighbors. In Washington there were rules for everything and for every minute. But a stranger didn't know what they were. One of the rules, a strict one, was that you couldn't talk to anyone except during recreation or work. That evening, when we were let out of our cells—all cells opened electronically at the same moment—and I fell in line to march to the supper tables in the middle of that enormous room, I heard immediately behind me, "Don't turn your head." Whereupon the inmate in back of me explained, apparently without moving his lips, the whole supper routine.

I have no idea who these men were, why they were in prison, their names or anything else about them. But I do know they were certainly friends in need.

I got the same friendly treatment over and over again as I was moved from one jail to another, from one unfamiliar situation to one even less familiar. Considering my short sentence, I saw a remarkable lot of the federal prison system. After West Street and Washington I passed through the huge federal penitentiary in Lewisburg, Pennsylvania, through another way station, the juvenile facilities in Chillicothe, Ohio, and finally came to rest for several months in Ashland, Kentucky. I can't say I found any of them sufficiently attractive or their cuisines sufficiently tempting to make a voluntary return visit, even for old times' sake.

Most of the time I was in prison I took good treatment from the other inmates as a matter of course. I was grateful for it, but I didn't give it much thought. Toward the end of the sentence, I began to think about it a good deal; I have done so since. I suspect there were a number of reasons for it.

All inmates have one thing in common. They all think they are victims of a lousy society. All have been mistreated by the police, the judge, the jury. None would have found himself in this mess if society had treated him better. Parents were to blame, the boss was unjust, the foreman was a crook. Somebody else and something else were to blame. Maybe we didn't behave as well as we should have, but we got into this fix because everything worked against us. Life in jail is tough. We're not going to make it unless we stick together. I'll help you, you help me. The guards are a bunch of bastards. Together we can keep them out of our hair, but we can't do it alone.

There was a lot of common ground, but I think we politicals also had several special things going for us. We were prominent in the sense that our entrance had been heralded by a lot of publicity. Hammett was prominent in his own right as a famous author of the kind of books that had been read by at least some of the inmates. What made him universally known among the prison population wherever we went (Hammett and I were together for the whole of his sentence) was that at that very moment the radio was serializing Sam Spade's adventures. I was prominent for less deserved reasons. I was supposedly stinking rich, and I had had an inordinate amount of publicity, especially in the *News*, the *Mirror*, the kind of press that inmates were most likely to read. Hunton and Green had shared the publicity.

I think all the above played a part, though none of it was responsible for the kind of special treatment we sometimes received. The all-important thing was that, essentially, we were in jail for not ratting on our friends. The technicalities of the Fifth Amendment were mere details. That we were assumed to be Communists did not matter, we might as well have been dope peddlers who refused to give the police a list of our clients. We had not ratted, and so we had been put in jail. That was what counted. For that, anybody who has been in trouble with the authorities will give you a gold medal. We were good guys. We could be trusted. We were not only one of them, we were special. And so they took good care of us.

When you coop a bunch of men together in cells or cages, there is bound to be trouble. The only release is anger, and sometimes violence. No matter how much saltpeter is mixed in the food, you don't stop thinking about your girl. You go crazy with frustration, and you make it worse by thinking about it all the time. You are irritable from sheer boredom, especially in a place like West Street where the only thing to do is to sweep and mop corridors, paint bars and wonder what they're going to do to you next. West Street was the worst in this respect, because it was nothing more than a detention house for transients. There was no work schedule, no work facilities.

It's surprising how little trouble there actually was, at least while I was there. Somebody got hit on the head in the elevator one day. Two or three nights were bad because some dope addicts were put in straitjackets and moaned all night.

The most trouble I remember was caused when a teenage homosexual was brought in on a narcotics charge. I happened to be mopping around the reception quarters when he arrived, and I watched as he went through the routine physical examination and showered. The boy was pretty, with a beautiful girlish face, a boyish hairless body and completely feminine manner. The authorities made the mistake of putting him in one of the cages on the floor. That night the place was in an uproar. It was as if a bitch in heat had been caged with a pack of dogs. There was everything but howling, and no one would have thought it strange if that had taken place.

The next day the boy was placed in solitary, the only place where he could be protected from the other inmates. He was fed separately and taken to the roof for recreation at an hour when the rest of us were busy doing nothing elsewhere. Fortunately for all concerned, he was soon whisked off to some other jail.

Strange tales circulate about prison life. One such tale appears on pages 90 and 91 of Lillian Hellman's otherwise splendid book, *Scoundrel Time*. Hellman writes about an episode she says Hammett reported to her and which she claims "I like." It has to do with a Ping-Pong game in which Hammett and Jerome, one of the Communist Party's leading intellectuals, were playing against two other inmates, one of whom "had been arrested for murdering a federal agent." The game was then held up by a dispute between Hammett and Jerome, the former urging that the latter "should not expect honesty from criminals" and Jerome maintaining "the socialist necessity to believe in the reform of all men, the duty to show them the honest way." Play was resumed but after about ten shots "Jerome shouted across the table that the murderer had cheated again and that he was shocked. The murderer threw his bat across the table and advanced on Jerome with a knife. . . .As the knife was thrown, Hammett pushed Jerome to the floor and held on to the murderer with repeated apologies that hinted Jerome was not all there in the head. Peace was restored when Hammett made Jerome buy the knife-thrower two packs of cigarettes and take an oath not to play Ping-Pong again."

This is fiction. In my experience it didn't happen. Why the episode did not and could not have taken place as Hellman reported it will be clear when I describe how life in jail really was.

Consider the layout of the recreation facilities on the roof of the West Street jail. The prisoners entered by a stair that led from the top floor of the one-time Al Smith garage—for that is what it had been—directly into a cage which occupied most of roof. Outside the cage there was room for the guards to circulate and keep close watch on what was going on inside. The guards had rifles, as was customary when they were not in direct contact with the inmates. They would never have tolerated, even for two seconds, the kind of incident described by Hellman.

I have been in touch with three of my former West Street classmates, and we all agree that the incident did not occur. But as so often happens with exaggerations, there was a basis for the story. The real story is a more human one.

There was a former criminal in the jail, and he and Jerome had become friends. This man had spent fifteen years in the notorious Attica prison. There he had read everything he could lay his hands on, including the classics and some of Marx's writings. He completed his term. Then one day a friend asked him to drive to Harlem with him to collect a debt. A fight broke out between the friend and the Harlem man, the cops came and the friend beat it. Our man was picked up and sent to West Street pending a hearing. A bunch of fellow prisoners signed a petition on his behalf, a priest helped, and he was freed.

He and another inmate had played Ping-Pong against Hammett and Jerome, and the ex-criminal had become angry and thrown a bat across the court. There was no knife. There was a short flare-up, no big incident.

I had known Jerome for many years and had worked with him on several articles I had written for *Political Affairs*, of which he was editor. He was an admirable person, a man of unusual integrity. I don't like to see him painted a damn fool, and for that reason I deny the authenticity of the story told by Hellman. I have great respect for her moral and political courage and admiration for her as a writer. Hellman says she liked the story. I do not.

V. J. Jerome was one of the twenty-one so-called secondary Communist Party leaders also indicted under the Smith Act, seventeen of whom were arrested on June 20, 1951. Four were not apprehended at the time, and one was excused because of illness. The remainder of the male members were residing in West Street on my arrival there. During the first days of my visit I was put in a cage which already had nine or eleven occupants for its five or six double-tier beds—I forget which. All the others were members of this latest Smith Act roundup. I knew all of them and had worked closely with some of them for a long time. We made a congenial group in uncongenial circumstances. We were all commendably quick to learn to sweep, mop, and paint. Our long experience at teamwork had especially prepared us for mopping the long corridors. When done at its best, this task called for six participants working in perfect coordination. Three would assume the front rank with soap, disinfectant and water, and three would follow a few feet behind with dry mops and wringers. We should have gotten extra days off our sentences for the exemplary and cheerful manner in which we carried out this highly responsible task.

In looks and behavior, Jerome was the epitome of the intellectual. You had to know him well to realize that behind a serious facade lurked a dry humor. One day it burst through. When we returned from our frequent tours to various courthouses, we were always lined up naked before several guards. Each of us was commanded to "Open your mouth!" so that our mouths could be examined for caches of dope. "Spread your cheeks!" commanded the prisoner to turn his back to the examiner, spread his legs, bend forward and with his hands spread his "cheeks" to reveal another potential dope depository. On his first return from the outside, Jerome played the innocent. Upon hearing the order, he thrust his face right up to the guard, put a finger of each hand in his mouth and spread it in a broad grin. How could he be disciplined? Cheeks to such an intellectual were cheeks. As a result, he became famous.

I acquired some renown myself the first time I went through this degrading performance. When I had placed myself in the proper posture for the second phase, I peered around my left leg and, while gazing upside down at the guards inspecting me, remarked, "You won't find the fugitives there." That story spread through the prison system so fast and so far that when I reached Ashland, Kentucky, the first thing an inmate said to me when there were no guards around was, "Hey, you're the guy who . . . That was great!"

I have mentioned the cages in which we lived in West Street. The federal prison authorities had converted a truck garage into a penitentiary in the easiest, quickest and most economical way. They simply drove the trucks out and rolled cages in. Trucks neither required nor demanded air conditioning, even in July. Human beings did, but the authorities either paid no attention to our complaints or regarded criminals as somewhere between trucks and human beings on the ladder of evolution. We sweltered day and night.

After a week or so with my Party colleagues, I was moved to one of the smaller cages. It consisted of a runway leading into three separate cages, each with a double-tier bed and toilet. I shared mine with a very vivid personality, Abraham Brothman, who had been given a long sentence under the espionage statutes and was at West Street while his lawyer argued for a reduction of time. While I was still at that detention center, the appeal was won, and Abe went off to serve the remainder of his shortened sentence elsewhere. I recall his departure well. His secretary, who had been arrested with him, was then housed in the corresponding detention center for women, geographically a good distance away from us. Abe was a genius at gaining privileges and otherwise circumventing the rules. As he was a true genius as a scientist, he was always allowed to wander around long after the rest of us had been bedded in order to fix some wiring or other electronic device. Among the "extras" he enjoyed was a voluminous correspondence with his secretary. As was the custom, Abe was informed of his departure to another guesthouse only moments before he was to leave, just time to throw his toothbrush and razor and a couple of books into a paper bag. He didn't know what to do with all the letters he had received from the women's detention center. He couldn't take them with him, because the astonished authorities at the new place might be upset by such a flagrant breach of rules. The letters, moreover, were not of a kind that should be read by others. Abe's quick solution was to give the letters to Fred Field and let him worry about what to do with them. I spent the better part of that day shredding the pack into tiny little pieces and flushing them bit by bit down the toilet. I figured that if a trap for things of that sort existed somewhere in the prison's disposal system, I might as well make an awful lot of work for whoever was going to try to put those letters back into shape for reading.

By the time he left, Abe and I had become good friends. He was a wise and strong companion who helped me to adjust to prison life. Of all those I met during my prison days, he was the only one with whom I would have enjoyed a continuing friendship. Circumstances never made that possible.

In one of the adjoining cages in our little "apartment" was Morton Sobell, up from Atlanta in a futile plea for a review of his case. He had gone to Mexico with his family when the FBI began investigating his college class- mate, Julius Rosenberg. He had rented an apartment in Mexico City under his own name, though he had apparently done some traveling under an assumed name, a mistake as far as public relations were concerned. Mexican agents seized him in his apartment, beat him unconscious, and kidnapped him to Texas. There he was arrested by the FBI, which accused him of having had conversations with Rosenberg and held him under $100,000 bail. He was tried with the Rosenbergs and sentenced to thirty years for conspiracy to commit espionage.

Sobell had only recently begun serving his sentence when I saw him. While I was still at West Street, he was sent to Alcatraz, the most murderous of all prisons, and he remained there until public protest forced the au- thorities to send him to Atlanta for the remainder of his savage sentence. Sobell's punishment, after a scandously conducted trial in a political at- mosphere in which it was impossible to secure justice, was so outrageous that I was unable at the time to grasp its horror. I felt almost ashamed of my piddling nine months. Then and since, I have been bothered that my own troubles so absorbed me that I was incapable of giving any moral support to these other inmates. It was Brothman, on the contrary, who helped me. Sobell seemed so shocked and dazed by what had happened to him that the whole thing was still beyond his comprehension. He served his long sentence with exemplary courage. Years after I had gone to Mexico, he resumed an interrupted family life. I hope it has provided him some recom- pense for the long years of suffering.

Early one morning Hunton, Hammett and I were told we would be leaving right after breakfast. We packed—if that is the right word for stuffing a paper bag with the most elementary necessities—and boarded a large pas- senger bus. Letters painted on the sides identified it as belonging to the Federal Bureau of Prisons, but that was not its only distinguishing char- acteristic. The windows were barred, the driver's seat was protected from us by an iron grid, and in the middle of the seating section was another protected cubicle in which an armed guard sat. No nonsense was tolerated on that trip. You felt dangerous because you were regarded as dangerous— even though you might be Mr. Casper Milquetoast.

While crossing New Jersey, the bus broke down on the main street of a fair-sized town. We stopped opposite a high school just at the beginning of recess. The kids came pouring out and immediately surrounded our bus to look at all of us baddies. We must have been the best free show they had had in a long time. The girls hung around longer than the boys, which was normal, because while we may have been bad, we were also men, and that was just fine with us. We hadn't been that close to a crowd of blooming teenagers in quite a while. The guard and the driver, reinforced by local police, were beside themselves. They could do nothing about the girls, who were just doing what came naturally, and they couldn't do anything to us but tell us to shut the hell up. We calmed down at last when they threatened to close the windows. It took several hours for new parts to arrive and be installed. Meanwhile, our underground apparatus was organized and operating and we learned that the transmission had broken.

Instead of reaching Lewisburg, Pennsylvania, in the early afternoon as scheduled, we got there well after dark. Our stopover began with an unpleasant incident. We had been herded into a room with two chairs and a desk for the prison officials and no benches. We sat on the floor as roll was called, alphabetically. In our group of three, my name was called first. "Field?" "Yes, sir." Then, "Hammett?" "Yes, sir." Next, "Alphaeus." Dead silence. A little louder, "Alphaeus?" Not a sound. A shout, "ALPHAEUS" A quiet voice next to me said, "My name is Hunton." Alphaeus, if I haven't mentioned it earlier, was the only black among us. He won that battle hands down, for the official then said, "Alphaeus Hunton?" and my friend answered, "Present." The bastards we thought, the goddamn sons of bitches. And this is way up in Pennsylvania.

Hunton, Hammett and I were variations on a thin-man theme. Hammett, who had obviously modeled his famous fictional character after himself, was about my height but considerably sparer, if that was possible without becoming transparent. He was the oldest at 57, Hunton was 48, and I was 46 when we entered prison.

If Dash was physically conspicuous for his slimness, Alphaeus was notable for his enormous height. He was built like one of those basketball players who reach an arm up and flip the ball into the basket. His life, however, had not been that of an athlete. A graduate of Howard University, he had gone on to take an M.A. at Harvard and a Ph.D. at New York University. Then followed a long period of teaching at Howard before he came to work for the Council on African Affairs in New York. That was where I first met him and began to work closely with him on some of his organization's interests.

The Council on African Affairs pioneered the study of African struggles for freedom in the United States. Hunton came to it first as educational director and later became its executive secretary. In the preface to *Decision in Africa*, a book which Alphaeus wrote in the middle 1950s, Dr. W. E. B. Du Bois said of him, "He knows and appreciates the rise of socialism and sees in it the coming emancipation of the darker world from the exploitation of the white world." He was an admired friend, and I was dismayed that evening when I discovered that Alphaeus was not coming with us to Ashland. Instead, he was sent to an all-Negro prison. But on arriving at Ashland, I was glad we had parted company. The place was Jim-Crowed. The blacks were housed in separate cell blocks and sat at segregated tables in the mess hall.

The prison at Chillicothe, the next stop for Hammett and me, was actually for juvenile criminals. The atmosphere was so tense that it seemed always to be on the brink of violence. The discipline was iron. Not a word was spoken in the mess hall. You couldn't even make a sound as you shoved your knife and fork around your tin plate. Guards not only loitered on the edges of the room but also wandered through the spaces between the tables. It was there I experienced for the first time those electronic machines through which you pass on the way out in order to detect any metal object you might have swiped.

The cell doors at Chillicothe were not the usual bars—through bars you can at least see something, if only a wall—they were solid, with a tiny peephole that could be opened only by the guard from the outside. How, then, was it possible that, returning from supper, I found the *Saturday Evening Post* and the day's local newspaper just inside the cell door?

From Chillicothe to Ashland, Kentucky, is several hours' drive. As only three of us prisoners were making the trip, we went by private car rather than a bus. Two guards sat in front and we three in the back. The guards were perfectly safe as our movements were well restricted. Before we started the trip the three of us were lined up close together, Hammett and I on the outside. Between us was the third, a man being transferred from Atlanta, where he had served a long sentence, to Ashland for his final year. A single long chain was wound around each of us to hold us close together. We were handcuffed right hand to left with the links between the hands passed through the chain. We had just enough movement to light a cigarette or unzip our trousers.

At Ashland we were surprised to find that it looked from the outside like the local high school—except for a high surrounding wall with watchtowers at suitable intervals to prevent us from playing hooky. The illusion disappeared once inside, but this inmate kept trying to keep in mind that first outside impression.

A prisoner first entering the joint where he is to be a more or less permanant guest is first "broken in." We three were put in a special wing intended for this purpose, where we joined three or four others. In this case the blacks were not Jim-Crowed, for there were two in our small group. The point of the break-in period seems to be to see if you're going to be a troublemaker or a docile inmate, whether you're going to do as you are told or be a smart aleck, whether you're going to be finicky about your work assignments or accept what you're given, to see, in general, I suppose, what kind of guy you are. These were not difficult tests to pass. The provocations were obvious. The first morning, for instance, we were told to clean all the bathrooms in that wing. That fancy-pants with the Vanderbilt name was selected to do the toilet bowls. Did he fuss? Did he object? Did he tell the captain who gave him the assignment that this was obvious discrimination? No, he practically burst out singing "Waltzing Matilda" and proceeded to shine those bowls. If you had needed a mirror, you could comb your hair in them.

Having earned our Phi Beta Kappas in the break-in wing, Dash and I were assigned to a minimum security dormitory, while our partner on the trip from Chillicothe, for reasons unknown to us, went into a maximum security block. The dormitory, built by an architect who loved airplane hangars, housed eighty or a hundred inmates. There were four long rows of beds, the space between them being exactly that of the New York Times unfolded. There was a small metal table in that space, two drawers under the bed, and no chairs. At each end of the dormitory was a large doorless bathroom with showers, toilets and, in the center, a large round washbasin from which the water spouted out in the middle like a fountain in a public park, except that unfortunately, this one was not in a public park.

Dash saw too much of that dormitory. Instead of being given work in the laundry, kitchen, warehouse, carpentry shop or garden (yes, there were some flowers along the walks leading to the various buildings), he had the fascinating job of sweeping our dormitory. This he did cheerfully, using slow strokes, from morning to night. As we left for our jobs after breakfast, we would yell at him to get to work to clean up the joint for our return. Upon returning, the wits among us would purposely drop a cigarette or match on the floor and berate Dash for have done such a sloppy job.

We were standing in line for lunch one day shortly after we had arrived when Dash suddenly turned white as a sheet and staggered to a nearby bench. Concerned, I broke ranks and rushed after him. (For doing this I was sharply reprimanded.) He was simply dead-tired; his small store of energy was exhausted. He told me he suffered from low blood pressure, and that may have been true, but as I learned later, he had a long history of tuberculosis, and he did not talk about that. In his last years, he developed emphysema and, at the end, cancer. At Ashland, it seemed to me, he had no illusions that he had much longer to live. Though he did live until 1961, the authorities should not have been permitted to take five months (Dash got about a month off for good behavior) out of the life of a sick man.

I was aware that Dash had done very little, if any, creative writing after 1934, when he was forty years old. It was hard for me to understand how such an enormous talent could have simply ceased. He had had, as a matter of fact, only twelve years of productive writing; his first stories had been published in 1922. I asked him what had happened. Had he lost interest in writing? No, that was not it. From time to time he had tried to write again, but nothing had come of it. What was it then? I never got an adequate answer. Not that Dash didn't talk about it. He left the impression that he simply didn't know the answer. But maybe I was wrong; maybe he did not want to tell me or anyone else. Perhaps it was something very private to him. I suspect that he was so ravaged by ill health and too much drinking that his talent ebbed with his energy.

Hammett got along well with his fellow inmates. They were not strangers to him. He had been a Pinkerton agent and in his writing had brought a hard-boiled realism about crime to an enormous public. He knew what the bad ones were all about. He kidded the inmates unmercifully and sometimes, I thought, dangerously, for they were not a stable lot. But I was wrong. They took everything he dished out. He knew the men he was talking to. I am sure that living for a month or so with Hammett was the high point of their lives.

Dash and I never discussed our relation to the Communist Party. One didn't do that in those days. This was a carry-over, in some instances perhaps an absurd one, of our public fight to protect the privacy of every person's political and religious beliefs and conscience. Our forefathers had protected these very personal areas by putting the Fifth Amendment into the Bill of Rights and therefore into the Constitution. I assumed that Dash's connection with the Party was pretty much the same as mine, that is, what might be called a member-at-large. Years later, when *Continental Op*, a collection of Hammett's stories, was republished, I discovered in Professor Steven Marcus's introduction that "Hammett became involved, as did so many other writers and intellectuals of the period, in various left-wing and antifascist causes. He had become a Marxist: he had also committed himself to the cause of the Communist Party in America, and become a member of it probably sometime during 1937."

The Ashland inmates for the most part were serving sentences for petty crimes. A few, like the third passenger on our automobile trip from Chillicothe, had been transferred there after serving most of their long-term sentences elsewhere to ease them back into outside life. Some of the sentences, even for minor offenses, were long—five years and over for second and third offenders. We were in hillbilly country, an unforgettable fact because the radio blared hillbilly music from morning to night. A common offense was moonshining—if that relatively harmless vocation can be called an offense, to say nothing of calling it a crime.

Most of the hillbillies were illiterate; the one positive thing the prison did was to teach them to read and write. Most of them came in without ever having seen plumbing, and they did not know how to use it. I became a member of a small, informal committee in our dormitory to help these men when they arrived. Cleanliness is the cardinal rule of prison life. You can take a lot of discomfort in stride, but when scores of men are living together in close quarters, you cannot stand filth. We would literally teach these newcomers how to turn a shower on and off, how to soap themselves thoroughly, how to flush the can. For the first few days we gently saw to it that a daily shower became part of their routine. There was no problem. They quickly came to love these benefits of modern culture.

In fact, the expression "I never had it so good" was one of the prison jokes. We had among us a good number of inmates who in terms of bedding, plumbing and food had literally never had it so good. One young man— he could not have been more than twenty—had deliberately had himself rearrested after finishing his first term so that he could return to the safety and security of prison life. For a while I got fancy: for two packs of cigarettes a week this young man made my bed and saw to it that I got a set of the better pants and shirts that came out of the laundry. I used up my small allowance further by having a frame for an eight-by-ten picture of Anita made by an inmate who worked in the carpentry shop. This kind of self-indulgence was contrary to the rules, but for some reason no one ever called me on it.

A Ping-Pong table sat in the center of our dormitory. I played all that I could on weekends, when we had more loafing time, often with a Korean War resister from one of the religious sects, and I worked my way up until I got to be fair. I became good enough to win our dormitory competition, after which the winner of the maximum security blocks was brought over for the finals. I managed to skim through. That was fun. The tournament ended with a surprise. A delegation of guards, led by a captain, entered our barracks one Saturday, called for attention, and presented me with a pipe. I have received no complaints from the taxpayers.

As those things go in jail, I was given an interesting job assignment. I asked for the farm, but that was denied with the explanation that the farm was located outside the walls and was unprotected. I had received a lot of publicity, not exactly the kind to make one popular, and if it became known that I was working on the farm, I might be molested. In asking for that assignment I had emphasized that I wanted all the physical exercise I could get. So they put me in the warehouse at a job that kept me busy and healthy, with so much exercise that I stole naps whenever I could get away with it and enjoyed long siestas on weekends. I was one of three floor boys in a fairly large two-story structure adjoining the kitchen. A fourth inmate sat in front of the office typewriter all day and occasionally used it. (Dalton Trumbo of the Hollywood Ten had held the typing job shortly before my Ashland residency began. Years later, when I was seeing a good deal of him, I failed to inquire whether anything creative had come out of the many hours he sat in front of that office typewriter.)

Our job was to receive the goods coming into the warehouse, place them on the proper shelves and handle everything leaving the building. By now the reader may have learned enough about prison life to know that we also swept, mopped and dusted the place.

The warehouse was large because it serviced other federal penitentiaries as well as Ashland. We kept great quantities of prison clothes, shoes, blankets and gloves and whatever thousands of men use, tools and other prison equipment, and we stored all the food, fresh, refrigerated and pre-pared, that was consumed in our own prison. Every item was inventoried on records kept both in the office and on the shelves. Aside from the two main floors, there was a large walk-in refrigerator for meat and a sizable room where knives and other risky implements were protected from the inmates. That room was always kept locked.

We began the day by piling the kitchen's food order into large trollies. That task took us into the kitchen. There, every morning for many weeks, we each drank a huge glass of milk before it was watered down for our legitimate consumption at meals. Unfortunately, our illegal arrangement with one of the inmates who worked in the kitchen was discovered, and we were told to cut it out—or else.

The inmate who slept in the bed next to mine and with whom I had by then become good friends—he was in for taking a young woman across state lines for purposes of which society did not approve—was sent to the ware-house one late afternoon with a written order for something we were to deliver the next day. Noticing that the guard and my warehouse colleagues were putting an order together at the far end of the floor, my friend stepped into the refrigerator to find a nice chunk of ham to sneak into the dormitory. He asked me to please give him a signal when it was safe for him to come out. In a few moments the other warehouse guard, who was supposed to be in town, showed up. I became worried and then, as minutes passed, frightened; we would soon reach the end of the day's work, when the refrigerator door would be closed for the night. I thought, "This is a nasty situation, and I guess there's nothing to do but get my friend out and face a peck of trouble for both of us." Fortunately, by that time I had been working in the warehouse several months. I had an excellent work record and was on good terms with my bosses. I said to the guard, "Look, Mr. So-and-so, a few minutes ago an inmate stepped into that refrigerator and he must come out before we close that door. Can I tell him to come?" "Go ahead," he said and went into the small office with his back to us. I gave the signal, my friend walked out and nothing happened. That was a rare incident, the kind that gave you heart. Once in a while you realized you were dealing with human beings. There were also moments when you lost heart.

One such moment had its origin outside the prison walls. Under my mother's will the Guaranty Trust Company of New York (now the Morgan Guaranty), my father, brother and I were appointed trustees of the various trusts it established. One day I was summoned to the warden's office. Upon arriving there and seeing this gentleman for the first time, I was told that the other man present was a lawyer. He had some papers for me to sign. Neither man shook my hand, for that would have contaminated them. I was, however, asked to sit down in a chair with stuffing, a sure sign that something evil was about to take place. The lawyer informed me that he had a prepared statement of resignation as trustee of my mother's will and that the Guaranty had instructed him to get my signature to it. I was dispirited by the stupidity of my jail experience and disgusted at what I felt was the indecency of the bank's request. I was depressed, preoccupied with the strenuous job of keeping myself intact. I didn't even ask whether my brother had agreed to what the bank was doing. And I suppose the fact that I was never too interested in money matters had something to do with my signing. Later I regretted that I had given the bank such an easy victory.

After a few weeks of routine warehouse work, I was left pretty much on my own. I had found a few errors in the inventory, and when I called them to the attention of the bosses, they asked me to correct them and to look for more. I was even given the keys to the room with the knives and told to check that.

There was one unpleasant incident. I was working alone one day in the back of the downstairs room when I heard the guard say, "That man over there is Fred Vanderbilt Field." I looked up to find a woman and two men peering at me through the open shelves. I made no bones about being angry at this intrusion. I abruptly left what I was doing, went upstairs and sat in the warehouse office until the visitors left. The guard knew exactly what had happened. He didn't apologize—that would have been too much to expect—but neither did he call me down for leaving the job.

The work was relatively positive, not so much in itself as in comparison to the other aspects of jail life. Aside from that, I did what I suppose monks do. I shut myself in. To reduce my exposure to the outside world, I built a wall around myself. I never once went to the weekly movie. I didn't want to see or think about the outside until I was finished with the inside. I was scared that if I watched a sexy movie star for an hour and a half it would take a miserable week to stop thinking about her. It would be better not see her at all.

I allowed myself two exceptions, newspapers and mail. Anita had arranged for the *New York Times* and the *Washington Post* to be sent; and for several months I missed hardly a word in either. My mail was very limited; it came only from Anita, one or two letters a week. They were important, as were those I wrote her. In retrospect, I think they were too important. Inmates are prone to idolize their women and to create an imaginary relationship with them which is neither real nor human nor desirable. Who wants to love something ethereal? What are you going to do with an angel? I was no exception. I believe that the image which my troubled imagination made of my wife during those months in jail contributed to the breakdown of our marriage not long after I got out.

The visit which we were permitted once a month was as disturbing for me as it was pleasurable. Anita had to take the long trip from New York to Ashland (a trip which she could by no means manage every month) for the half-hour visit. At West Street we had communicated through a glass partition. In that respect, Ashland was better. We met in a large room furnished with chairs, which in comparison with our barracks seemed like Versailles. We could not sit next to each other, however, but only in facing chairs. And except for a chaste embrace upon meeting and parting, we were not allowed to touch. Even a fleeting contact of hands brought a frown from the guard. Here was one of the great stupidities of the American prison system. The denial of physical relations with one's wife caused unnecessary resentments, restlessness, bitterness and frustrations. One of the inevitable results was homosexuality. Fortunately, no one tried to involve me, but I was exposed to it, as is every inmate one way or another. One of the inmates we met during our break-in period had bored the hell out of me by talking for hours about the fiancée he had left and how sorry he felt for her and himself. A few weeks later, we heard from the next dormitory that he and six others had been put in solitary. He, it seems, was a queen, and he had got the others into trouble.

I was embarrassed by what happened to me at Christmastime when the regulations were relaxed and we were allowed to receive all the greetings sent us. Nearly everyone benefitted and received two or three cards or maybe as many as six or seven. But no one approached the munificence of my Christmas harvest. Day after day I received ten, fifteen, twenty cards or letters, until there were a hundred and eighty-five greetings cards covering the wall at the foot of my bed.

Things were relaxed on Christmas day. Our dormitory had a subdued gaiety. Because each inmate had been allowed one present from the outside, there were plenty of candies and sweet biscuits to go around. I am sure that some of the cheer was forced or pretended, but that was all right, too. What mattered was that the day was different from the others.

Now, long after it is all over, I am not at all sure that the extent to which I shut myself in was wise. I really fenced myself in thoroughly. Maybe it would have been better, easier, just to go along with what all the others were doing, such as going to the movies and reading novels. I denied myself all fiction because it was another image of the outside. Instead, I read hundreds and hundreds of pages of American history. I didn't read them as well as I should have, unfortunately, because I found it hard to concentrate. I wasn't taking notes, and I wasn't thinking about what I had read while doing other things. I didn't absorb as much as I might have had the circumstances been different. But, yes, some of it remained. Those comments I made several chapters back about the changes barbed wire, refrigeration, farm machinery and the rest brought about in the relations of farmers and ranchers in the American Southwest of the 1870s and 1880s originated in a history by Henry Steele Commager that I read while lying on my prison cot.

One spring morning—such a glorious time of year—I stuffed a few possessions into a couple of paper bags, walked to the front and changed into my outside clothes, which had been cleaned and pressed. I was stopped at the entrance by the deputy warden. He shook my hand and told me that I had done a good job in the warehouse. Then I spotted my black Jaguar at the outer gate and joined Anita.

24

Going to Mexico

For a year and a half after being fed and lodged by the government, I enjoyed more rest and relaxation and did less work than I had been accustomed to in the previous twenty-five years. Anita and I spent long periods at Red Hill restoring the somewhat neglected property as well as ourselves and also renewing those friendships still open to us. We soon realized, however, that we were not to be permitted a normal life; we were obliged to consider and then actively plan to leave the country. Our departure took place at the end of 1953. The reasons for considering the move were multiple, and one forced us actually to make it.

There was no political future for me, at least for the time being, and, probably for a long time to come. I don't mean a political future in the sense of a political career, for I had closed off that road long ago, but rather that I found myself blocked from active pursuit of the ideas and causes I had been trying to promote.

I had been particularly interested in advancing American friendship with China at all levels—commercial, cultural, and political. Not only was that objective now out of reach, as it was to remain for years to come, but my own efforts in that direction would be frustrated until the climate changed. I had no way of estimating when that might happen. I had become active trying to develop a more enlightened, democratic foreign policy vis-à-vis our Latin American brothers and involved in various civil rights domestic issues, of which desegregation was the most important. All of these were objectives requiring the widest and most nonpartisan support possible, and I had been so isolated by events that no one outside the Left would now have anything to do with me.

I had played a part in developing the Institute of Pacific Relations into a well-known, influential organization with a magnificent body of published research to its credit. The notoriety that had forced me into virtual inactivity had also, unfortunately in good part thanks to me, swamped the IPR. It was close to drowning, abandoned by most of its former benefactors.

I had been maneuvered into a position of uselessness by the McCarthy inquisition and by the effect of the inquisition upon people with whom I had associated for so many years. The academic group, a great many of my old friends, and others with whom I had always had at least a potential relationship had practically all ostracized me, and it would clearly be a long time before that situation changed.

Some of this ostracism went to absurd and unexpected lengths. Realizing that I would not be having more of the large fund-raising parties for which I had used my home at 16 West 12th Street—they had become checkpoints for identifying CP members and other radicals—we put it up for sale and selected an apartment in a new high-rise on the East River. When one of the city's largest real estate firms, management agents of the building, identified the new client, it refused to give me a lease. Friends in the business advised me that if one of the leading firms adopted that policy, the others would too.

Employment was also out of the question. There was no chance that any similar institution would give me a job of the kind I had enjoyed at the IPR for so many years.

I realized the futility of returning to the same political activities, or type of activity, that I had so hectically pursued since the beginning of the Cold War period. It was not that the activities themselves, and even less so their objectives, were futile. It was that I myself felt frustrated and boxed in. Through the Senate hearings and a principled use of the Fifth Amendment, I had been able to uphold certain ideas that I thought important, but I was not anxious for such opportunities to repeat themselves.

It was, then, a time to develop a new life, new interests and new occupations, and to do that it was necessary to change my environment. I was still able to make that kind of choice; most of my friends who had been caught in a similar situation were not.

The specific event that made our departure obligatory and even specified its date was the government's action against my wife. Anita was a Canadian citizen, and she had been married to a distinguished intellectual who had been involved in an even more difficult situation than I. He, too, had served a jail sentence. Anita, it seems, had consistently failed to pick solid Establishment husbands. During the preceding three years of our marriage, Washington had made no trouble for her. But shortly after I finished my jail sentence, the harassment began. It was obviously another way of harrassing me. A cowardly and cheap one, I thought.

Anita was ordered deported as an undesirable alien, not because of any activity in which she had engaged but because of the husbands she had chosen. We obtained the services of an able lawyer, Edward Aranow, who specialized in such matters, and he appealed the order. We secured several delays and even a reconsideration of the case. In due course we both appeared before the Board of Immigration Appeals in Washington. In the meantime we had been advised to follow the customary procedure and made a generous contribution to the political fortunes of a prominent senator: he assured us that his influence would arrange things favorably. His fortunes may have thereby been improved, but ours were not. Finally, the deportation became imminent, and Anita was told to be ready to leave the country at a moment's notice. Where to go presented little problem. Neither I nor anyone else who had had any kind of association with the Left could get a passport. As a result, we only had a choice of Canada and Mexico. We chose Mexico because of the climate—and because neither of us had ever been there. We went to El Paso, not one of my favorite American cities but just across the border from Mexico, to await the final reconsideration of the case. For a few weeks our life there was made reasonably pleasant through the thoughtfulness and kindness of an American vice-consul and his Mexican wife. Anita lost the appeal. She and her children took the train to Mexico City, while I returned to New York to settle our affairs and store our belongings for later shipment.

In December 1953, I packed Anita's tiny two-seater Simca with more than it could comfortably hold and set forth on my first trip to Mexico. In those days, there was no way to bypass Washington, D.C. In the heart of the city, I opened the right-hand window to ask directions. Upon receiving them I was unable to close it. Several hours in a repair shop failed to solve the problem and I departed behind schedule with a flimsy piece of cardboard to protect me from what by then had become a miserably cold wind. That situation prevailed until I reached Mexico, the cold blasts turning to temperate ones only when I passed into the milder climate of my destination.

I spent the last night before reaching Mexico City in Tamazunchale (many American tourists refer to it as Thomas and Charlie), a small, pleasant town in the Huasteca country at the foothills of the Sierra Madre. There was no gasoline there, and no one had any notion when a supply might arrive. On the poorly formulated but subconscious theory that someone up there or perhaps even someone down here would take care of such a damn fool, I started out at dawn the next morning with a dangerously low tank. The climb up the Sierra is spectacularly beautiful; in the early morning hours the vista is most glorious. The road is steep and tortuous. The Simca's small engine—when you opened the hood you had to look around to find it—worked on some unknown source of energy, for the gas needle was fluttering down to zero at an encouragingly slow rate.

Rounding a corner, I suddenly spotted a few turns ahead a long line of stopped cars, buses and trucks, and in a few minutes found myself at the end of a *cola*, literally a tail, that stretched as far as I could see and, as I soon learned, another kilometer or two beyond that. After half an hour, a couple of young men, perhaps in their late teens, came down the road to suggest that my car was so small I could pull out of line and work my way outside the *cola*. That meant driving between the line of cars on the right-hand lane and a decline of several hundred meters to the valley below. Off I went, fortified by friendly cheers. I doubt that such an outrageous attempt to get ahead of the line would today be greeted in such a friendly manner, especially if the perpetrator were a gringo.

Unless you count the chauffeur's jitters at the precarious position of the car, the journey along the ditch went without incident. The cause of the traffic jam was that two trailer trucks, going in opposite directions, had attempted a hairpin turn at the same time and had locked: neither could move backward or forward. The passage between the outside truck and what had now become a cliff seemed too narrow for even a two-seater Simca to navigate. It not only seemed so, it was.

Help and advice were immediately forthcoming. "*No se preocupe, Señor.*" I was told to drive slowly in low gear while three men pushed against the outside of the car to prevent it from slipping into the valley. We inched our way past the locked trucks. As I sailed away on the clear road ahead, I wondered where those men's feet had been while they were supporting the outside of my car. I did not go back to find out.

My initial experience of driving in Mexico impressed me greatly at the time but has since faded into the commonplace. With the constant driving over all these years, my heart has simply learned to function while in my throat.

I was excited by the scenery, which becomes extraordinarily dramatic and beautiful immediately south of the Texas border. I was delighted by the friendliness of the people. And not least, I was enthusiastic at the prospect of a new, unknown life. That episode of getting past the *cola* and edging around those trucks through a collective effort of the pleasantest sort was all that was needed to plunge me into an affair with Mexico.

I still had practically no gas. But I soon passed the summit and, having no problem of power brakes and power steering, cut the engine for a coast that must have lasted thirty or forty minutes. I found no gas at the first village down the mountain nor at the second. But at the second station I found a young American couple traveling in a ramshackle camper. We exchanged a few words of greeting, and they learned of my predicament, for by that time the tank was truly empty. They offered me a bottle of white gasoline they carried for a small camp stove, assuring me that an engine like mine would run on any kind of liquid. I found real gasoline before the contents of that bottle had run out. The trip into Mexico ended not only with a warm feeling for those young Mexicans at the top of the Sierra, but also with a reminder that my fellow Americans could be nice people too.

It is said that if one spends a few months in a new country and is open to new sights, customs and people, one can write a fairly acceptable book about it. But if that visit extends into years, many of those first impressions become blurred. Disillusion sets in. Doubts cast questions on those facts that at first seemed so certain. Freshness gives way to sophistication, and that yields to jaundice.

There is a good deal of truth to that point of view. I was eager, fresh, excited and energetically looking for the best in this totally strange country. And there was much to be found. Most tourists can attest to that.

As the Simca and I rolled down the long slope that leads from the north into the basin, the bottom part of which is Mexico City, I could see the snow-topped volcanoes, Iztaccihuatl and Popocatepetl, fifty or more miles away. The sight of those volcanoes can excite you for twenty-five years. I know, because I lived a thousand feet above the center of the city on its western edge. Every morning as I drove the children to school, I looked across the enormous expanse of the metropolis to see if those peaks way off to the east were sticking out through or over the clouds or smog. If I saw them, I started the day better off for it.

In 1953, Mexico City had perhaps half its present sixteen to seventeen million population. Its bourgeois section, its vast residential areas, the business and government centers, the innumerable churches and other colonial buildings—that part of the city where this descendant of the Commodore was still privileged to do most of his living—was beautiful. It was beautiful not in the North American sense, as I think San Francisco, Seattle and Minneapolis are, but rather in a European way—more like cities in France and Spain. It had fountains, statues, large boulevards and narrow streets, more small and large parks than we are used to, trees and flowers, and residences not packed against each other but usually surrounded by gardens. There was a nice mixture of colonial architecture, which can be very rococo, and modern, which can be international—in that it can be seen in Tokyo or New York or Berlin or Nairobi—or can have a distinct Mexican quality.

I love walking, even on city streets, and I saw much of bourgeois Mexico

City that way. The place stimulated me for many years, until it virtually ceased to exist as I first knew it. To describe more precisely what happened: smog, garbage, too many people with shattered dispositions, and hundreds of thousands of automobiles, buses and trucks finally took over. I was already there when the first traffic light was installed; it was on Avenida de los Insurgentes Sur. I wish there had never been a need for it.

The people were pleasant, interesting and helpful, even in the big city. They gave me the impression that they liked foreigners for other things beside money, though for that too—and why not? They were pleasantly eager to teach the visitor something about their language and customs. I was immediately confident that I could live a good life in this new country. But I had scarcely enough time to look around, to say nothing of becoming acclimated to my new environment, before I was summoned back to the United States.

25

The Lattimore Case

Early on the morning of September 3, 1954, less than eight months after I arrived in Mexico, two men from the United States embassy came to our apartment to hand me a summons to appear before the grand jury of the District of Columbia with certain documents pertaining to the Lattimore case.

The Tydings subcommittee had in the fall of 1950 cleared Owen of the charges made against him but not until after he had issued a scathing denunciation of its objectives and methods. His friends and colleagues were proud of what he said:

> I realize even more keenly than before that my obligation is to do everything I can, by the emphatic and conclusive refutation of these charges, to establish beyond question, beyond dispute and further challenge, the right of American scholars and authors to think, talk and write freely and honestly, without the paralyzing fear of the kind of attack to which I have been subjected. . . .

The Tydings subcommittee having allowed Lattimore to slip through its hands (after it roundly smeared him), Pat McCarran's subcommittee on internal security, which had already given me a going over in 1951, decided that its earlier hearings had accomplished absolutely nothing except to pollute the air and that it would once and for all make a name for itself by "getting" Lattimore. He had testified before that group in 1952, and the committee then handed the inquisitor's torch to the Department of Justice. Under the guidance of an assistant federal attorney by the name of Leo A. Rover, a grand jury handed down a seven-count indictment of Lattimore in December 1952. Five months later, Judge Luther W. Youngdahl of the U.S. District Court for the District of Columbia, a former governor of Minnesota, voided four of the principal counts. An appeals court agreed with that decision in respect to two of the counts, but reinstated the other two.

After the key counts in the government's indictment were dismissed, it decided not to go to trial with the remaining five. Instead, it reindicted Owen in October 1954, accusing him of lying under oath when he testified in 1952 that he had never followed the Communist line nor promoted Communist interests. In order to avoid another reversal, Rover then went to the extraordinary length of trying to force Youngdahl off the case. Youngdahl refused to budge, Rover failed in his efforts in an appeals court, and the government, which was under strong attack for attempting to intimidate the court, was obliged to announce that it would cease its efforts to try to unseat Youngdahl.

My brief appearance at the later stages of the case came a few weeks before the grand jury returned the second indictment. What I have to report about it does not pretend to throw new light on the Lattimore case, but it does provide evidence on some of my own activities that I have so far not dealt with.

Although the legality of the summons served on me was questionable because of my residence in Mexico, I decided, after consulting with Cammer, not to challenge it. As I don't like to fly, I asked the embassy to get me reservations for the train. When it became too late to make the grand jury date by train, the embassy informed me that they had no way of making railroad reservations and handed me an airplane ticket. Of course, that story was not true. Apparently, it was easier for the federal police to shadow me if I flew than if I went by rail. En route, the plane landed at Dallas, and as I went through customs, literally surrounded by FBI agents, I laughed to myself as I imagined them covering every station at which a train would have stopped.

I have often wondered what the FBI thought I might do. I had accepted the summons and agreed to go to Washington. Was I going to flee from Dallas? To go where? And why? Was one of the customs men a secret agent who was going to slip me a message from Moscow? Sometimes I conclude, for want of a better answer, that the FBI has too many agents and too little work, and so does this kind of boondoggling to keep everybody busy. Of course, I do not want my opinion in any way to damage the agency's chances of getting an increased appropriation when it next goes to Congress for its budget.

I had two long sessions with the grand jury on consecutive days. It was well along in the afternoon before the first day's questioning ended. Rover's words, before the jury and I were dismissed for the day, were addressed to me: "Field, if you don't cooperate with us better tomorrow than you have today, we'll cite you for contempt." With that threat in mind I thought that I had better telephone Cammer and review what had happened that day in order to figure out whether the threat had any substance.

On leaving the courthouse, I hailed a cab. It had to make a U-turn to go to the railway station where I knew there were a number of long-distance booths. As we were in the middle of the turn, a man rushed into the avenue to intercept us and jumped in the front seat. I suppose my shadow had thought that I was going to walk back to the hotel as I had walked from it in the morning and had been taken by surprise when I took a cab instead. Another chance at escape was foiled.

Once at the station I moved slowly in order to give my pursuer plenty of time to keep me in sight. The call to Cammer was reassuring. He explained that a contempt threat was some prosecutors' way of intimidating a witness.

During the final hour of the second day's session, Rover pulled something illegal. Unfortunately, I was not well enough aware of my rights to challenge him. No outsider, not even the witness's own attorney, is allowed in a grand jury room while testimony is being given. The law requires the sesson to be limited to the jurors, the witness, a court reporter and the United States attorney. In this case, however, two men were admitted. Each carried a large black loose-leaf volume with a great many pieces of paper sticking out, which evidently marked the pages to which they would be referring. The men were never identified, though they were obviously federal agents and the papers they were carrying were a huge file of my alleged wrong-doings. They remained while I was questioned and testified.

The summons calling me to Washington had instructed me to bring along eleven letters or copies thereof between Lattimore and me and two from Carter to me, all dated between 1935 and 1940, which was fourteen to nineteen years before. I informed the jury that I could not produce any of the originals because they had been stolen in 1951 by the McCarran sub-committee and that I didn't have copies because I had never kept IPR files of my own. But my lack didn't matter, because Rover, not surprisingly, had all the letters with him. I suppose that the thirteen letters were listed on the summons just to make it look important.

I had been called, I was told, in order to identify this correspondence, although the attorney turned out to have other matters on his mind as well. I was handed a letter and asked to read it and then tell the jury whether I had written or received it. All those questions I answered. For reasons I have already gone into, I refused to answer questions relating to my political beliefs or associations or questions leading into those areas, which is why Rover threatened me with contempt. But on the second day, when those two agents and the large black volumes came in, the session became an unabashed witch-hunt. For an hour I was bombarded with questions which had not the remotest connection with the Lattimore case.

I have in my files two partial lists of the questions put to me at that time. One, written on yellow legal paper, was jotted down hurriedly during the session; the second list, which must have been written after the session, is on the stationery of the Congressional Hotel where I was staying. The lists correspond closely.

Nine of the questions began in exactly the same way: "Have you ever been requested to act on behalf of the Soviet Union. . .," and then the nine endings: "by Budenz?" "by Browder?" "by any member of the American Communist Party?" "by any Communist of any Communist Party other than the American?" "by any diplomatic official accredited to the United States or to any other country?" "by any Soviet citizen?" "by any Chinese Communist?" "by any representative of the Chinese Communist Party?" "by Owen Lattimore?" To all those questions I invoked the Fifth Amendment. It was not difficult to imagine what could have happened if I had answered them instead. For example, had I said no to the one about Budenz, they would have had Budenz on the stand in no time at all, and he would have said something like this: "Yes, I clearly remember the occasion when I passed on to Comrade Spencer the message from Moscow in which Comrade Stalin asked him to come over to have tea with him." As a result, I would have landed in jail for perjury. There was convincing testimony on the record to show that the Establishment would believe absolutely *anything* Budenz said. I would not have had a chance.

I will answer those nine questions now. Actually, they are one question: "Have you ever been requested to act on behalf of the Soviet Union?" The answer is no. I was never so requested. At one time I did register as attorney-in-fact for the Chinese People's Republic at its request, but I was never asked to have a similar relation, or any other kind of relation, to the Soviet Union. And I was asked during World War II to contribute to Russian War Relief, but I would not call that "acting on behalf of the Soviet Union." I should explain that I never made the Soviet Union a major interest. For every book I read about the Soviet Union, I must have read twenty-five about China. I traveled to the Soviet Union and through it once, and never went back. Not that I lacked curiosity about developments after the revolution, but my major focus was always on China and the revolution developing there. I studied and became something of a specialist on aspects of American-Chinese relations, not American-Soviet relations. I don't believe I ever wrote an article on the Soviet Union as such, though on several occasions I wrote on the relation of the Soviet Revolution to the later

Chinese one. I read Lenin, Trotsky and Stalin and others for what they said on Marxist theory, not the USSR.

It is often assumed, mistakenly, that if you are a Communist you must also be a Russophile. You can be an excellent Communist and be oriented to a county in Arizona. Communist theory was originated by Germans living in England. It had its first large-scale application in the Soviet Union, where it developed both theoretically and empirically, but both in theory and practice Marxism has become a world-wide phenomenon. I chose to orient my communism to China. I found all those questions about acting on behalf of the Soviet Union wide of the mark.

The grand jury asked me several questions about my relations with Whittaker Chambers, the neurotic psychopath who, with the help of a future President, had railroaded Alger Hiss into jail and set Richard Nixon on the road to the White House. An ex-Communist, an ex-senior editor of *Time*, Chambers had obtained international notoriety by leading Nixon, in the dead of night, to his pumpkin patch, where he miraculously found State Department papers that he declared had been given to him by Hiss.

Cross my heart and hope to die, I never in my life knowingly met Chambers; and I doubt that I ever saw him. He had concocted a weird story about me. We had met. Where? In downtown New York on the corner of Chambers Street and one of its intersections. We had made a date for lunch. Where? The Vanderbilt Hotel. What did we talk about? A replacement for the leadership of a conspiratorial group in Washington, D.C., which had until recently been headed by a man whose name happened to be Field. And so on.

I remember subscribing at Harvard to a mail-order course called, if memory serves me, the Roth Memory Course. This was a method for improving your recollection by making associations with the thing or person to be remembered. If you met a Mr. Apple, for instance, you would be helped to recall his name by noting that he had red cheeks like an apple or hollow cheeks that looked just the opposite of an apple. To this day, if I should meet Mr. Apple again, the chances are good that I would step up to him and say, "Nice to see you again, Mr. Mellon." Not so, Chambers. He had apparently taken the Roth course and knew the system backward and forward. The only way he could possibly recall that fabrication about our meeting was by use of that series of coincidences he had invented.

While the defense was being organized for Alger Hiss's first trial, in 1949, I was asked to visit the offices of his New York lawyers to discuss the advisability of my testifying. The lawyers thought that testimony on the transparent trick by which Chambers had memorized the falsehood that we had conspired would be a convincing way to break down his expected testimony against their client. The idea was discarded, though, because my own public reputation was then becoming so bad that anyone on whose behalf I might testify would surely be condemned.

I was in jail in August 1951 when Chambers fabricated another total falsehood about me. He testified before the McCarran subcommittee that I was head of a Communist group that held meetings in 1937 at the home of my mother on Central Park West! Among those who attended, he said, were Joseph Barnes and J. Peters, the latter identified as a "Hungarian-born Communist leader." That testimony was not difficult to refute: My mother never had a home on Central Park West, and she had died October 15, 1934.

Other questions by Rover had to do with my relation with Laurence Duggan. Larry was the son of Dr. Stephen Duggan, founder and head of the Institute of International Education, an organization which before the war had pioneered scholarships for foreign students, an idea which proliferated in the postwar period. Dr. Duggan had been a trustee of the IPR, someone whom we on the staff got to know well. Larry and I had been classmates at Harvard, and for the last two years of our undergraduate lives we had shared with some others a suite of rooms in Massachusetts Hall. During the Roosevelt years he had a brilliant career in the State Department, quickly rising to assistant secretary in charge of Latin American affairs. Following the nationalization of petroleum by President Lázaro Cárdenas of Mexico, in March 1939, Duggan was sent to that country to negotiate the reimbursement of the expropriated American firms.

Larry and I saw little of each other after college, but every once in a while, hardly more than once a year, if that, we would meet for lunch, usually at the Washington Hotel in the capital. On one occasion I got him to come to New York to address a group of trade union leaders under the auspices of the Council for Pan American Democracy, of which I was an officer. At our lunches, which were social occasions between two old friends, I occasionally took up with him the problem that private institutions like the IPR had in securing authentic information from the State Department. I stressed the importance of opening up better channels of communication. I argued that from the State Department's point of view it was an opportunity to make known its objectives and methods as well as to learn the thinking of an interested and educated public. That was the way a democracy should work, though in those days it was not working that way. The State Department kept itself remote from the public, and the public had little confidence in the "cookie-pushers" who managed our foreign affairs.

In 1948 Duggan got into trouble, the exact nature of which has never been made known, at least publicly. The tragic upshot was that Larry, who by then had taken over his father's job with the Institute of International Education, died on December 20 in a sixteen-story fall from his Fifth Avenue office.

The government implied that I had something to do with the tragedy. When questioned about it before the Lattimore grand jury, I took the Fifth Amendment. An answer could easily have led me into dangerous territory.

The political connection between Larry and me, if one chooses to call what we talked about political, was no more than I have described above. I was aware that Larry's State Department responsibilities were with Latin America and not the Far East. He was, however, the only close personal contact I had in the department. I had met Stanley K. Hornbeck, the chief of the Far Eastern Division, but our relationship was distant and formal. Before taking such a matter up with Hornbeck, I wanted to know more about how the department worked, what were the possibilities of closer relations and what were the obstacles. That was all there was to the occasional talks Larry and I had over those Washington lunches, from which nothing ever resulted. I got Hornbeck to write an article for the first issue of *Amerasia*. I know that he followed the work of the IPR, and I believed that through Carter he gave us a helping hand once in a while, but I never pursued my ideas about developing closer relations with the State Department.

On December 26, six days after Larry's death, Attorney General Tom Clark broadcast that Duggan had told the FBI he had twice been approached in the late 1930s by people who wanted him to join a Communist espionage ring. Duggan gave the FBI that information, said Clark, during an interrogation on December 10, ten days before his death.

This story seems to have originated with Whittaker Chambers, but I did not know that until his book *Witness* came out in 1952. In it he spins a tale to the effect that the same J. Peters as above introduced Chambers to me in 1937 "for the express purpose of recruiting Duggan" for what Chambers refers to as an "apparatus." He repeats that we lunched at the Vanderbilt and that at the end of lunch he "watched with some amusement the casual way my millionaire comrade signed the chit." That gave Chambers's tale a quaint intimate touch. But the fact of the matter is that besides my not knowing or ever lunching with this storyteller, I didn't possess a credit card until several years after moving to Mexico, and I never enjoyed any signing privileges in any hotels or restaurants. Except for a couple of former speakeasies, I was an unknown customer to maitre d's and proprietors.

I spent that Christmas at Red Hill. While I was there, an FBI agent telephoned from New York to say that the Bureau wanted to question me about the Duggan matter immediately. I told him I would be returning to the city right after New Year's and would see him at his convenience. He set the date and time, the place to be the FBI office in the Federal Building. I agreed to the date, but said that because they wanted to see me, not I them, the place would be my office. On arriving, the agents were annoyed to find Harold Cammer, my attorney, awaiting them with me. They told me that Duggan had named me as the person, or one of the persons, who, as Clark had stated, had tried to involve him in an espionage ring. I didn't know about the Chambers story then; later, I realized that it had probably been Chambers, not Duggan, who had given that information. So I replied that such an accusation was impossible. Larry and I had been friends for many years, and he could not have given them such information. I told them that our meetings had nothing whatsoever to do with such a sinister idea. They pressed the questioning and I angrily told them that if they had somehow blackmailed Larry into making such a statement, I could understand for the first time why he had killed himself. "You must have hounded him to death," I said. I have had a good many contacts with the FBI and have found that their agents are well trained to keep their cool. On this occasion, the training forsook the two sitting in my office. One of them burst out, "Mr. Field, you don't like the FBI, do you?" I answered, "No, I don't." That was the end of the interrogation. I never heard another word about Duggan's alleged accusation.

I have no evidence, direct or indirect, to support my own angry suggestion that the FBI caused his death. But I have two reasons to believe that Larry never made such accusations against me or that if he did, he did so under unbearable pressure. For one thing, he was not the sort of person to lie about a friend or anyone else. Secondly, neither the FBI nor any other government representative or agency ever pursued the matter with me. If it had contained a shred of truth, it stands to reason that it would not have been so quickly dropped. I suppose that Chambers's story and the FBI questioning were one and the same thing. That is, Chambers probably invented the story and the FBI eagerly accepted it just as it had Budenz's lies. The Bureau then used the tale for its own propaganda purposes and abruptly dropped it when it was no longer useful.

Another unpleasant angle to the tragedy has occurred to me. Larry's rapid rise in the State Department took place while Sumner Welles was undersecretary. It was known that he had sponsored Larry's promotions. Sumner Welles was widely suspected of having been a homosexual; allegations to that effect had even appeared in the press. Larry was certainly not a homosexual but that would not have stopped the FBI from using his close personal relations with Welles to blackmail him. I would not put the tactic beyond that unscrupulous organization.

While waiting in an outer office to be ushered into the grand jury room the first day, my erstwhile friend, the German sinologist and Communist leader Karl August Wittfogel, came out of it and strode past me, obviously avoiding my eyes. Because I was to be the first and, as far as I knew, the only witness that day, it was somewhat startling to see that this man had preceded me. He could not have been up to any good, for much had happened since the mid-thirties when Carter, Lattimore and I, among others, had set up that long-term research project for the refugee from the Nazi concentration camp. I was not as surprised as I might have been, however, for soon after he settled down to work on the Chinese history project, things took an unexpected turn. Because he was ever so slow to produce, both the Rockefeller Foundation and we, his sponsors, began to worry. His politics also took an unanticipated direction.

Soon after Wittfogel's arrival in New York, I got to know him and his wife, Olga Lang, quite well. They invited me to their modest apartment near Columbia University on a number of occasions. I spent the first of these listening to Karl August elaborate on one of his principal interests, his theories on "hydraulic" societies and the social and political organization required to initiate and maintain huge irrigation projects (Mesopotamia and China were the examples I recall). On subsequent visits he began to rant against Stalin. He was not concerned about the trials of Russian dissidents or any of the other issues which were then dividing the Left, but about the theoretical point that Stalin did not support Marx's theory on the Asiatic mode of production. I have no idea what contrary theory Stalin held; the point struck me as fabricated for some purpose that I did not understand. In any case, Karl August soon saw to it that I and other Communist friends dropped out of his life.

Wittfogel completed only one section of the monumental Chinese history project. In 1949, and not before, there appeared a 756-page, large-format volume titled *History of Chinese Society, Liao*. This book, published by the American Philosophical Society with the aid of the IPR, was a history of the Liao Empire, which, from 907 to 1125, controlled the regions of modern Manchuria, Mongolia and the northwest part of what used to be called China Proper. Given the circumstances of our silent encounter in the antechamber of the grand jury, which was about to indict Lattimore, a short passage from Wittfogel's introduction to the book is specially interesting: "The oldest Western friend of the project, Owen Lattimore, brought to it his unique knowledge of Chinese frontier society and history. . . .He personally watched and scientifically supported our effort from its inception in 1935 until 1941 when he was appointed personal adviser to Generalissimo Chiang Kai-shek. . . ." Wittfogel also acknowledges help from Carter, Field and my IPR colleague Harriet Moore.

Wittfogel's anti-Stalinism widened to include anything and everything radical. By the time I saw him in the grand jury anteroom, we regarded him as an informer. He was making minor trouble for me and others, and directing a major effort against Lattimore, for whom he seemed to have developed a special vendetta. I have never fully understood this Wittfogel episode. Why had he turned against his benefactors? Did the government have some hold on him, something from his past in Germany, that caused him to go back on his own beliefs? Perhaps it had not been made clear when he entered the United States that he was a Communist as well as a sinologist. Possibly that fact had been kept secret and thus gave the government the leverage required to make him useful to it. Whatever it was, I was not happy to see him walk out of that jury room just before I was to enter it.

The second day, another acquaintance stepped out of the jury room as I was waiting to enter, but the circumstances were altogether different. This time we both stopped in astonishment. This was a real friend, one of the fine people with whom I had been associated, Harriet Moore, now Mrs. Peter Gelfan, my IPR colleague, the brilliant Bryn Mawr graduate whom Barnes and I had recruited. We had not seen each other for many years. Sobbing, she told me that Rover had treated her outrageously. She was so upset she feared she might lose the child she had been carrying for eight months. In a few moments she recovered her composure, and I could see that she was still a strong person. I was shocked, however, to find that Harriet, too, had been trapped in the Lattimore case.

At the end of the second day's session, the jury excused me. Those roses I was becoming so accustomed to were thrown around: Thank you for behaving courteously, etc. But this time I thought it a little too much. Rover followed me out of the building. Catching up to me, he put his arm around my shoulder. "Field", he said, "you comported yourself very well in there. I know that someday you're going to come to us and tell us your story." I held my tongue at this unctuousness and walked away. If he's still around, I hope someone will tell him to read this book. It's my story, and it's not the "please forgive me" one he expected. But, then, he didn't expect to lose the Lattimore case either.

It was the following month, October 1954, that Owen was reindicted on two counts of perjury by the same jury before which I had appeared. Judge Youngdahl, under attack by Rover, refused to disqualify himself and again dismissed the key indictment, a decision that was upheld in the appeals court by a tie vote. Thereupon, in June of 1955, the Attorney General, remarking that he saw no likelihood of obtaining a conviction, announced that the government would dismiss all charges and drop the case. Owen Lattimore's ordeal was over, and "the right of American scholars and authors to think, talk and write freely and honestly" was—at least in this instance—upheld.

26

In Mexico to Stay

My stay in Mexico got off to a fairly good start. With the help of friends, Anita had found a pleasant apartment on the Cuauhtemoc Glorieta. Two or three times a week I would walk from there down to the *centro*, the old section of the city where, centuries before, the Aztecs and then the Spaniards had set up their capitals. One went there for shopping, banking and dining. The Museum of Anthropology was just off the *Zócalo* where one could visit the Cathedral and the National Palace, which housed some of the great Rivera murals. The department stores had not yet built their branches, more glorified than the originals, near the residential areas of the rich and the new middle classes. I wrote to my friends how magnificent Paseo de la Reforma was with its eight central traffic lanes and four more side lanes. The center of the Paseo was separated from the sides by tremendous ash trees that had been planted during the French occupation almost a hundred years earlier. In recent years these great trees have begun to die from the smog.

I found every possible excuse to visit Teotihuacán, the series of pyramids, wall paintings and monumental sculptures, only an hour north of the city, dating back to between 150 B.C. and 650 A.D. George Pepper, an American friend in the movie business who had been blacklisted in Hollywood, and Dalton Trumbo of the Hollywood Ten introduced me to Tlatilco, a pre-Christian archaeological site on the edge of the Federal District. It was there I began the collection and studies which occupied so much of my attention in the ensuing years.

I found some fellow recorder players, too. Together we organized La Sociedad de la Flauta Barroca, and it soon became a major hobby. I had a great deal of reading to do in Mexican history and customs and in my new interest, archaeology. There were, moreover, language lessons, though I gavè them up too soon. I studied enough to get along in the markets and shops and among kind friends, but not enough to dominate the language. A combination of laziness and ineptness left me with limited Spanish distinguished by a heavy gringo accent. I read fairly easily, and my writing is adequate for messages, notes and letters to tolerant acquaintances, but I remain a failure when it comes to composing more formal letters in the roundabout, excessively courteous style of those who really know their Castilian.

In the 1950s about twenty-five American families had migrated to Mexico for political reasons and because of the economic consequences of pursuing left-wing politics. They had found it impossible to continue their interests or their careers at home. Some had arrived in Mexico on their last financial legs. We formed a congenial group. Our problem, socially, was to avoid seeing so much of each other that we would fail to become acquainted with the Mexicans among whom we were living. We solved that problem with varying degrees of success.

While I had left the United States physically, it remained my country, my home, my natural environment. I kept up with what was happening there as well as I could. When many of my old friends and acquaintances passed through as tourists, I found I could spend more relaxed time with them in Mexico than I had ever been able to do in the hectic circumstances of the life I had led in New York. I found it especially rewarding to renew and deepen old friendships and to make new friends of many former acquaintances. I had more time than ever before to read journals and to discuss and ponder world affairs. Even though I could no longer play an active role, I never felt that I lost touch with either the American Left or the fabulous and sometimes strange events in China.

Upon settling in Mexico, therefore, I quickly found a life full of activities, interests and friends. That part went well. All of that I enjoyed. But, unfortunately, those things are not all of life, and some of the rest went wrong.

At that time Mexico was in certain respects a booming country economically. Everywhere you looked there was construction: office buildings, homes, government centers, hospitals, schools. Dams and irrigation projects were under way in all parts of the country. New roads were being built everywhere you traveled. A new middle class was coming into being, and it was becoming a consumer of radios, televisions, automobiles, homes, shoes and clothes. Money was scarce and commanded high interest rates. It seemed sensible to bring some capital down for investment at a much higher rate of return than I could find at home.

That was a mistake. I was not a businessman, and never pretended to be. I had no personal interest in the business world, except to the extent necessary to provide a decent income. This consisted of my trusting the advice of friends, or, even worse, of entrusting them with the direct handling of my investments. I should have learned my lesson before I came to Mexico, but, alas, I didn't. In the thirties and forties, I had time and again listened to the advice of friends, putting my money where they suggested, never to see it again. I cannot point to a single successful venture. My friends were always sorry about their poor advice. Period. The same fate met every loan I was asked to make. I don't remember any ever being repaid.

There is no point in blaming friends for this state of affairs. I should have known better, or at least learned from repeated experiences. But I didn't. When I settled down in Mexico, I began the same financially suicidal business all over again. Looking back, it almost seems as if I had an obsession to lose money. I went into three business ventures and came out with three total losses. Not twenty-five or ten cents on the dollar. No, in two of them it was zero on the dollar, and on the third less than zero because I assumed responsibility for paying off the losses of a number of people whom I had persuaded to join in the investment.

At this point, in order not to depict myself as a charity case, I must state that I am doing fine on what is still left. I would not include this miserable financial story except to dispel the persistent myth that I am a very rich man. Besides, my business ineptitude is part of me and so part of my story.

To sum up the dismal subject: I started out in the 1930s being what I and most others considered wealthy. Since then I have given away approximately a third of the original fortune and lost another third. A third of what I once had remains—in greatly devalued dollars—in a trust fund I cannot touch, over which I have no control. For fifteen years a substantial part of the income has been devoted to paying off debts. I have no hesitation about revealing that from 1958 through 1976, my annual income varied between a low of $23,870 and a high of $37,700.

The other thing that went wrong was my marriage to Anita. It had begun its downhill course even before we were forced out of the United States and found refuge in Mexico. As far as I can make out—and who is really good at figuring out mistakes and failures?—it was thrown off course by the difficult period of my political troubles and ultimate jailing, and we were never able to turn it in the right direction again. Our marriage ended in divorce in July 1957.

I came to Mexico with an ingrained habit that stood out as conspicuously as if I had come with two heads. I am hopelessly, incurably punctual. In fact, the disease is so pronounced that I invariably arrive at appointments, whether business, social or even dental, ahead of time. I often feel that the characteristic makes me more noticeable in Mexico than does my New England appearance or atrocious accent. Needless to say, during two and a half decades, I have thereby wasted an enormous amount of time just waiting.

Which reminds me of Nieves Orozco Soberanes. When we began our life together, she was outstandingly Mexican with respect to punctuality. While I would be easing the car out of the garage to take us to a date, she would be starting to run the bathwater. My North American habits caused us embarrassing moments. We were invited to one dinner party, for instance, for eight-thirty, and at my insistence we arrived at eight-thirty, a heinous violation of Mexican etiquette. The host was still at his office, and the hostess had just stepped into the bathtub. I suspect that some of Nieves's friends quickly caught on to the uncouth manners of her new husband and invited us at least a half hour later than the other guests to even up our arrivals. Gradually, we have adjusted to each other's habits. I make a giant effort to be patient, and she makes a valiant effort to be on time. I always carry material to read while I wait, and this has resulted in a considerable improvement of my mind.

Nieves is an outstandingly beautiful person. She was born and spent her early life about fifty miles north of Mexico City in the state of Hidalgo, one of the truly miserable parts of the country. Her people are Otomís, a large group that inhabits a rough semicircle of terrain north of the Federal District. Since long before the Spanish conquest the Otomís have been noted for their independence from those who have tried to conquer or dominate them. With respect to one North American, Nieves has successfully carried on the tradition. The land she comes from is virtually desert; the only crop that grows readily on it is the kind of cactus that produces pulque, the national drink. With difficulty, a thin crop of corn and a few vegetables can also be coaxed out of the earth. Nieves's physical heritage from her parents is roughly a quarter Spanish and three-quarters indigenous.

At twelve, she was sent to the city to live with an aunt and uncle. In Mexico, aunts and uncles are not necessarily brothers and sisters of one of the parents, though they are included. Most aunts and uncles are what we would call cousins once or twice removed. It was the latter type of relative to whom Nieves was sent. This is a Mexican custom among poor country folk; the purpose is to secure an education for the children. In Nieves's case, and hers was not at all unusual, the "education" did not include schooling; it was actually sheer exploitation. The country child became the all-purpose servant of the city family. She cooked, washed, cleaned and took care of the babies.

In desperation, Nieves seized her first opportunity to escape. She had made friends with a young woman from a well-to-do family who was modeling for an Argentine woman artist, and through this friend she met the artist and began modeling for her. After some of the first drawings of Nieves were published in the newspapers, an effort was made to trace the model. Nieves tells me that when the reporters found the relatives with whom she had been living, the uncle informed her that they had denied knowing her and that henceforth they would disclaim any knowledge of her. They lost an all-round servant girl, and old-fashioned tradition prevailed. Young girls, or older ones for that matter, from respectable families were not supposed to pose for artists.

The Argentine lady sealed Nieves's fate by introducing her to Diego Rivera. At the age of thirteen, she began modeling for him.

Diego, as I hardly need say, was a remarkable man. He was large physically, humanly and artistically. I had met him briefly before I met Nieves, and in a way that I didn't like. His secretary, an aggressive Cuban woman, telephoned me shortly after my arrival in Mexico with the flattering message that Rivera would like to meet me. I accepted an invitation to visit his studio. Once I was there, the same lady sat me down and announced that Diego would like to paint my portrait. The fee, five thousand dollars, would be donated to the Mexican Communist Party. I didn't want any part of that arrangement. In the first place, I hadn't the slightest interest in having anyone, even so eminent an artist as Rivera, paint my portrait; in the second place, I could handle my political contributions by myself; and, in the third place, I didn't like entrapments. I didn't like them at all. All of this I conveyed sharply to the secretary. On my way out, I think only because to reach the street we had to go through the room where he was working, I was briefly introduced to the maestro.

After I was married to Nieves in April 1958, I saw Diego a number of times. The circumstances were sufficiently favorable for me to get a feeling for him as a person and in that way a better understanding of his art. His hugeness was always apparent. His exaggerations, which sometimes were just downright unabashed lies, matched the scale of his murals. His stories and opinions, his eating and drinking, were all gargantuan. Nieves told me that he and his friends, she usually among them, would often get in an old car and set out for some strange destination, often in search of archaeological finds. Almost invariably upon arriving at a site, a *campesino* would invite the group to his modest home and offer them pulque and whatever food the family had on hand. Diego accepted anything offered in the way of food or drink. When other local people would arrive, Diego would talk and laugh and tell his countless stories, and hours later the group would pick itself up, get in the car and resume the journey.

Rivera knew Mexico and the Mexican people, and they knew and understood him. He spoke their language and their thoughts. I am referring, of course, to the plain, ordinary Mexican, not the *politicos*. He knew them, too, but he was close to the guts of the country, not to its froth. When he painted those superb murals in the chapel at Chapingo or the political, historical ones in the National Palace or in the Cortez Palace in Cuernavaca, he was creating works that were purely Mexican and communicated their meaning to the ordinary citizen. The farmer or worker understands Rivera's work just as much as they understood the painter's talk in the farmer's *chosa*. He neither talked nor painted over their heads.

I think it's legitimate to say that on those occasions when Nieves and I saw Diego together, I felt, in one respect, rather superior. I had wooed and won Nieves, and Rivera had wooed and lost. I had not, at the time of the courtship, been aware of my competitive position, thank goodness. I learned about it afterward. Diego's campaign had begun when Nieves was seventeen. She had then married Jim Tillett, an English textile designer, and after that marriage broke up, Diego tried again. He found himself unmarried a while after I came to Mexico, and that is when his third and final pursuit of his favorite model was unknowingly thwarted by FVF.

It was not only Diego Rivera and Fred Field who thought highly of Nieves. The sentiment was shared by an unexpected admirer. One day, years later, as we were walking up a steep hill in Taxco, Marilyn Monroe turned to me and said, "You may know, Fred, that I'm not famous for my relations with females, but I must tell you that Nieves is one of the most beautiful women I've ever seen." Diego had been what might be called a responsible foster parent to Nieves. He took her under his ample wing and put her in the Academia de la Danza de Bellas Artes. There she was given a good secondary education and trained in both classical and modern ballet. To this day, she attends dance class five mornings a week, two hours a morning. If she misses a day because of some emergency, things are likely to go wrong at home.

During these years, music has been a major source of pleasure for me. Is there anyone who has heard a lot of music who has not at some point wanted to participate? I had sung soprano at school, which I had not enjoyed, and I had also sung in the glee club, which I liked. The piano had been a failure. I moved only six inches of a needed mile on the saxophone. When I was in bed from that leg I broke to end my three-day football career, I learned to play tunes on a pennywhistle. Even though James Galway can make one sound like a golden flute, it was hardly an instrument on which to launch a performing career. And so the many years passed, and I remained a totally vicarious musician. Finally, when I was forty-nine, I began the serious study of the recorder. An instrument which I bought in New York just before I moved to Mexico formed part of the cargo the Simca carried over the Sierra Madre.

Forty-nine is about the age one begins to think, or should begin to think, about getting old. I did not know as much about old age then as I do now, but I was aware that you had to prepare for it. I saw the terrible waste of elderly people in our society. So many have no place and no function. Many have nothing to do but to wait for the end. In their earlier days, they had neither the opportunity nor the motivation to develop interests that would keep them occupied in their later years.

One of the first things I noticed as I drove down through Mexico was that, at least among poor families, the old people were useful. They were needed. Even from the highway, I could observe that many of them were attending livestock, while many others were occupied with small children. Later, I learned that old people were respected for their experience; their advice was sought and followed. They were still a functioning part of society.

For the most part old people no longer play that role in our country. More often than not, they are shoved aside, relegated to old folks' homes or, if they are economically able, segregated in communities of senior citizens. The elderly are often a nuisance to their children.

Perhaps this may strike the reader as an elaborate way to explain why, at the age of forty-nine, I purchased a recorder and got to work on it. Performing on a musical instrument was one of the things I had decided to do in preparing for my old age. I also went into photography seriously. I joined a photo club where I learned developing, printing and enlarging—which I can return to whenever I have the time or desire to do so. And there were other pursuits, archaeology, for instance.

I chose the recorder because I had been told that it was an easy instrument to play satisfactorily. Nothing could be further from the truth. It is true that in a few lessons or a few do-it-yourself sessions you can learn to play simple tunes. But to play it well, to learn the great baroque classics of Bach, Telemann and Händel, or the modern idiom of Hindemith or Staeps, is not easy. Only a handful of great recorder artists like Krainis or Brüggen can play the recorder with facility and taste, and only a few amateurs can be called competent (a category of which I am not a member).

So why take it up at forty-nine, when it is too late to develop much technique? If I couldn't become a good performer, I could at least enjoy the by-products of working at it. The way to appreciate good writing is to try to write. The way to understand the works of the great painters is to study painting. The way to learn something about music is to work at an instrument, not necessarily in order to become an accomplished musician, but to train the ear, to feel the rhythms, to learn the problems of music, its history, its purpose and thereby to appreciate. Although I like music and had heard a great deal of it since early childhood, I didn't know much about it. I listen better and more critically now. Working at the recorder has been an extremely rewarding experience, one that has come entirely in my fifties, sixties and seventies. Fortunately, I have no rheumatic troubles and am able to continue struggling with problems of fingering, breathing and tone production. I enjoy playing in groups as well as alone, and, most important, I keep learning more about one of the great art forms.

Culture and politics are not different species but close cousins. One Christmas season in the 1960s, our recorder group was invited to give a concert of Christmas music at the American-Mexican Cultural Institute. This center, which is sponsored by the U.S. State Department, teaches English to thousands of Mexicans and does it well. It also presents free concerts and art exhibits to the public. We accepted the invitation and began rehearsing. In due course, our musical director submitted the program and list of performers at the Institute's request. I appeared in the general ensemble as well as in a quartet or sextet. A few days later, our director was notified that the program was just what they wanted, but there was one problem they had to take up with us. Because it would be embarrassing for an official government organization to have Frederick Field appear as a performer, would the recorder group please find a substitute. Such requests do not go down very well in Mexico. Our group replied that if FVF was not to appear, no one would. It took this stand, not because my recorder playing was indispensable, though I wish that had been a factor in the decision, but because Mexican organizations do not like to be dictated to by their imperialist neighbor. And they especially do not like it when it involves political imbecility.

Because the Institute had to put on some kind of Christmas function, it found a choral group to take our place. But nobody could find suitable Christmas music. I have a fairly good collection of sheet music, and the search eventually reached me. So I lent some pieces for the occasion and pasted on the face of each a notice reading: "This music is the property of Frederick V. Field. Anyone using it runs the risk of being found guilty by association."

While such stupidities occurred in the American backwater on Calle Hamburgo in Mexico City's Zona Rosa, some encouraging developments were taking place in the United States itself. I was able to experience one aspect of this change intimately. Every summer Nieves, the children and

I crowded into our car, filled the trunk and roof with luggage, and set forth for two months to some part of the country. We would go to northern California, where my daughter Gail and her family live, or to Minnesota, where Lila and her family have settled, or to the Northeast to visit friends and more family in the New York-New England area. In the early years, however, I drove a good part of the way alone and met Nieves and the kids north of the belt that stretches across the country from Arizona and New Mexico through Texas and the Deep South. I would not risk taking my Mexican wife to motels and restaurants in that dreadful belt of racial prejudice.

About 1962, early in the Kennedy administration, I began to notice a change. At the end of that summer, Nieves and the girls flew back to Mexico from New York for the opening of school. I drove home in a Jaguar. I was going through Louisiana when, near a small town just north of the Gulf, my car's valves blew. I spent a week, which included a hurricane, in a third-rate motel while at the other end of town the Jag's guts were removed and diagnosed and we waited for new ones to be flown from New York via Houston. The mechanic, a veteran of the Korean War, did the job in a barn behind his house with his seventeen-year-old daughter as his assistant. I hung around watching. We chatted and I learned something about the town, which had two high schools, one for whites, which the assistant mechanic attended, and one for blacks. Two years before, neither school had a swimming pool nor an adequate athletic field, so the town authorities appointed a committee, of which the mechanic was a member, to work out the solution. The outcome was that the white school was awarded the athletic field, which was to be used by the black students on certain days and for their games with other schools and the pool was built at the black school. The white students had access to the pool, but it was carefully pointed out to me that they would not use it. Twice during the week, a ramshackle car drew up with three or four black youth and the daughter went down the road to talk with them. Although she was allowed to do so, I was told that the blacks would not have been permitted to get out of the car and no interracial dating was permitted.

Many years later, that situation belongs to another era. But in 1962, I saw it as the breaking down of segregation. Things had begun to move. After that they moved pretty fast, though not fast enough. In any case, by the middle 1960s, Nieves and I and the children began our motor trips together and passed through that heretofore dreadful belt of America not only practically without incident but with increasing ease and pleasure.

27

Our Daughter Xochitl

The most profound of all my experiences during the latter part of my life concern our youngest daughter, born late in 1963. We called her Xochitl, a very Mexican name, which harks back to pre-Hispanic times, that period of Mexican history which most appeals to me. The word itself is Nahuatl, the language spoken (and in places still spoken) in the highlands before the coming of the Spaniards. In those early days Xochitl in her various capacities was goddess of art, of the dance, of music and of flowers. Nieves and I still buy plants for our garden from Xochimilco, which five hundred years ago was the garden of the Aztec rulers. Xochitl's heritage is impressive. We think that we named her well.

One June evening in 1980, I was alone with this daughter, then sixteen and a half years old. The rest of the family was away for the month and Xochitl and I had been going through the process of becoming reacquainted that should be experienced every so often. I had made supper for myself and helped my daughter prepare hers. A soap opera, telenovela, was showing. In Mexico these misrepresentations of life run well into so-called prime time, and in this not unusual case the show was so awful that we switched it off.

Xochitl asked me to read her the pamphlet we had brought home from her special school that afternoon. We went through it carefully, discussing the text, looking at the many illustrations and talking about those sections that particularly applied to her. I explained why she did not need to pay attention to other sections. At some point I said, "Xochitl ["x" is pronounced "s"], I don't know whether you realize it or not but you've done a remarkable job of adjusting yourself to your situation. And you've done much of it by yourself. Nieves and I have watched you very closely, but knowing that you had to work much of this out in your own way, we've

283

stepped in to help only when you seemed to get stuck or when the situation was unbearably difficult.

"Do you remember when you were a little girl, maybe about four or five years old? You used to go out in the street in front of our house to play with the other little girls in the neighborhood who were just about your age. It didn't work out for you. You stood around hoping to get into whatever game they were playing. But it was difficult because you couldn't keep up with their running and skipping and jumping around. And they didn't help you. They rejected you, if you know what that means. It means they didn't let you join them. You felt badly and came back to the house. This happened a good many times. Finally, you stopped trying to join the other children. Instead, you stood at the gate watching them play through the bars. Remember? You did that for a long time. Then, at last, you stopped watching the other little girls and you found ways to amuse yourself alone in the house. Remember?"

Nieves and I watched everything that was happening to this little girl. What difficult experiences she had to go through! How hard on her it must have been! She was too young for us to explain the situation, to tell her that there were some things that most other children could do that she couldn't, and to explain why this was so. She had to go through these experiences herself, she had to find her own way to cope with them, and then little by little, we hoped, she would understand and adjust to her condition. And so I asked Xochitl that evening, "Do you remember that bad time you went through while the other little girls were playing in the street?"

Xochitl looked at me with a puzzled expression. "*De veras viste todo eso? Supiste lo que estaba pasando?*" Did you really see all that? Did you know what was happening? Yes, I replied, we were very much aware of what was happening and we knew how difficult it was. I told her that we observed with admiration the way she gradually realized the situation, accepted it, and then found ways around it. She looked for things to do in the house that amused her and were within her competence. "*De veras se fijaron de lo que estaba pasando?*" Yes, Xochilota, we really did.

As a baby she had been slow to raise her head, slow to sit up and to crawl, slow to walk and talk. Later she had a tricycle, then a bicycle. But because Xochitl's sense of balance was apparently affected, she couldn't get the knack of riding. We gave her a croquet set one birthday, but that didn't work either; it was too difficult to get the mallet to strike the ball accurately. A lot of things we didn't get because we knew that they would bring no pleasure but only more frustration. For our daughter has serious problems.

Here and there they can be eased, lessened and compensated, but they cannot be eliminated.

Xochitl has cerebral palsy. She is the one out of every two hundred and fifty children born in Mexico with this affliction. In her dual citizen capacity as an American, she is one out of every three hundred and twelve children and adults with it in the United States.

That evening she and I once again went over what we knew about the affliction. What causes the condition? Technically, what is it? Can anything be done to alleviate it? Xochitl knows from her own observation that she is better off physically than a great many of her *compañeros*. She goes to a special school for children with cerebral palsy where some two hundred and fifty of them attend regular school classes and are given therapy. Many of them are permanent wheelchair cases. A few wear heavy braces in order to walk at all. Some have virtually no use of their arms and others of their legs. Most have speech problems, and a few suffer from deafness. There are several types of cerebral palsy, all having to do with the motor functions. Some of its victims move awkwardly. Others have conspicuous involuntary, uncontrolled movements. Others have a disturbed sense of balance and wear football helmets for protection against falls. And many have a combination of these problems. The majority have speech problems.

Xochitl walks, if somewhat awkwardly. She writes and usually eats with her left hand, for it is her right side that is more seriously affected. She has a serious speech problem, but her hearing, sight and intelligence are perfectly normal. She takes full care of herself, makes her bed and helps with the housework. For several years she wore a full body brace but does so no longer. She has had a series of operations on her feet and legs to give her more stability. They have been reasonably successful.

Cerebral palsy results from brain damage usually caused by an insufficient supply of oxygen before, during or just after birth and less frequently from childhood accidents. The damage is irretrievable.

Nothing we talked about that June evening was a revelation to Xochitl, because she was already well informed. What was important and helpful to both of us was the opportunity to go over the information together. In her school there is frank and precise talk with and before the children about their handicaps. They are given the facts about their condition. They are given encouragement, but not false hopes.

Aside from their physical handicaps, cerebral palsy children also face the problem of slower than normal learning development, not because they have less intelligence than other children but because of the unavoidable connection between motor and mental growth. A child who, because of motor problems, is slow to raise his or head to examine the small world of the crib or playpen, slow to sit up and experiment with the things within reach, slow to crawl and to acquire what is called hand-eye coordination— that child will also be slower to accumulate knowledge. As everybody knows, an important way to learn is by asking questions. This is particularly true in childhood. A child who has severe speech problems cannot ask questions, or can do so only with great difficulty. I have considerably more trouble understanding Xochitl than Nieves does. Xochitl has often in utter frustration given up trying to make me understand her, and whatever she wanted to ask me or to say remains uncommunicated. Because of the difficulty so many cerebral palsy children have in expressing themselves, they are likely to move through their schooling more slowly than other children.

Therapy should start as soon as possible. That requires early diagnosis of the child's problem. Doctors must be in a position to know what type of therapy is needed and where it can be obtained. The main therapy classifications are physical, occupational and speech, but there is a less definable form that may be as important as all the others put together. It has to do with the child's social environment, especially the family and the home. Love and acceptance are the most important factors involved in giving the child the most normal life possible. In this regard I think Nieves and I and the other members of our family have been successful.

In a society such as Mexico's, where ignorance, illiteracy and poverty are widespread, families traditionally hide and forget their abnormal children. City-dwellers often send the children to relatives in the country. They tend to lose interest in the child's development in the mistaken belief that nothing can be done to bring it into the mainstream of society. Our daughter was already over six years old when the first center for the specialized treament of cerebral palsy was founded in Mexico. Advanced work is still confined to Mexico City and is available only to a tiny proportion of the children who need special education and therapy. The doctors whom we consulted about Xochitl—and I believe they were the best to be found— were by no means prepared to advise us regarding the nature and place of treatment, to say nothing of diagnosing her condition. In the capital city, at least, that situation has since improved, largely thanks to the public education that has been carried out by the school which Xochitl attends. Even in the United States, where there is far more understanding and acceptance of all forms of handicap, the facilities for helping these children are few and far between.

One learns, as I have, that cerebral palsy children are normal human beings in every respect except where motor reflexes fail them. They are intelligent and observant. They have all the aspirations, hopes, desires, ambitions of nonhandicapped children. But they are unable to attain many of these aspirations, like Xochitl's wanting to play with her contemporaries in the street in front of our house, her longing to be accepted by them. They have to adjust themselves to that outlook. They see and feel and want so much of life that they cannot have. The least they deserve from their family, their neighbors, their society is to be treated with dignity and respect and to be accepted as the splendid, courageous human beings they are. The point of view that I have learned is this: I have problems, all kinds of problems, and so does everybody else. The difference is that these kids simply have extra problems.

I've learned much about life from Xochitl. I've learned about the adaptability of human beings, their ability to adjust, to compensate and to sublimate. The process of adjusting develops patience, courage and cheerfulness. Cheerfulness is an outstanding trait among the cerebral palsy children I've observed. It must be a kind of lubricant that makes the other things work. I've found that it is possible for someone to push into the background of consciousness what is difficult or impossible for them to do. I've seen the complete concentration required to move a finger or a tongue or to write or to comb one's hair or tie a shoe. I've watched two opposing urges: the dependence of one human being on others and that same persons's struggle for the maximum independence possible. I've learned how a person can ignore, not be upset, by the carelessness and thoughtlessness and even ignorance of others, the stares in the streets or in restaurants, the embarrassment or awkwardness of others on the occasion of the first confrontation and their confusion about what to say and how to act. I've noted that operations, therapeutic contraptions, doctors and hospitals can become a normal part of life.

I have seen the joy of little things, small pleasures and modest accomplishments, and the importance of steadfast cheerfulness. So I owe my daughter a great deal. I am wiser now than I was in 1963.

Xochitl will read what I have written about her, and in doing so I have faith that she will understand that I write with great love and admiration for her and for what she has done. She is a special person because she is handicapped. But she is also a special person because she is such a fine, brave and lovable one.

28

Reminders
of the Past

My life in Mexico may have been a new one, but it contained not infrequent reminders of my old one. In September 1956, for instance, I received a telegram from James O. Eastland, chairman of the Senate Internal Security Committee, instructing me to appear "in room 130-B Senate Office Building Washington at 10AM on Wednesday September 19, 1956, to testify in connection with matters now before the subcommittee." I had just returned from a trip to the United States to visit one of my daughters. I had learned that this most unreconstructed southern senator was attempting to connect Jacob Javits, the attorney general of New York State, then running for the U.S. Senate under the Republican banner, with the Red Menace by associating him with me. I had been unaware of it until that moment, but it appears that Javits and I had crossed the United States on the same train in April 1945 in order to attend the United Nations Organizing Conference in San Francisco. In those days you disembarked from the train in Oakland and crossed the bay to San Francisco on a ferry. The FBI had furnished Eastland with the information that Javits and I had been seen talking together on the forward deck of that ship. Confronted with this damaging information, Javits, according to the *New York Times* of September 6, 1956, testified, "I met a young man on the ferry who said something about the scenery or some ordinary expression of that kind, who was a college-boy-looking type of chap and described himself as Fred Field and said he was going to cover the U.N. conference for some newspaper work. And we exchanged some pleasantries that made no particular impression on me. . . ."

For my part, when thus reminded, I recalled exchanging a few words with someone as we both gazed admiringly upon that magnificent approach to San Francisco, but I had even less idea who he was than he had of me.

The upshot of this silly episode was that I didn't go to Washington. I didn't even reply to Eastland's telegram. Javits was elected senator, and the FBI got another A for effort, D for performance.

Another reminder of my former life occurred exactly two years later. Both my older daughters had come down from the United States to visit us, and we were spending a pleasant relaxed time together. Halfway through their scheduled visit, on the afternoon of September 6, 1958, a neighbor ran over to tell me that he had just received a telephone call (we had no telephone at that time) from a Mexican lawyer in the middle echelons of the bureaucracy with an urgent message for me. Orders had been issued by *Gobernación*, the government department responsible for foreign residents, for my arrest and deportation. The police had already gone looking for me at an apartment I had once occupied. I discovered later that a sympathetic friend in the government had removed my present address from my government file, leaving only the old one. I was to disappear, the message informed me, immediately, giving only my wife the location where I could be found for the next few days.

It can hardly be said that I fared badly. Lila and Gail and I motored to Cuernavaca, where we put my car in an inconspicuous place and took a room in one of the most beautiful inns in the world. The owner and staff had no idea they were harboring a dangerous fugitive. For two days we enjoyed the inn's exquisite gardens and internationally famous food. Then Nieves came down to say hello and to announce that a friend would be arriving after dark to move me to another location. The inn, it was thought with good reason, was not the best place to be if one wished to remain hidden.

That evening, after a delicious supper, a young man I had worked with in one of my ill-fated business ventures arrived and informed me that I was to follow him in my car to Acapulco. His father-in-law, a member of one of the government commissions, had placed his house at my disposal for the duration. Another "wanted" friend was already there. We arrived in the morning while it was still dark. My friend and I enjoyed this Mexican gentleman's hospitality for ten days. Then we received a telegram saying the coast was clear, so we returned to Mexico City and resumed our normal life.

Ten of us in all had been targeted for this round-up. Three were caught and immediately flown out of the country, never to return. The others, including myself, were luckier. They were warned of what was about to happen and managed one way or another to keep out of the way of the authorities. One jumped the fence back of his home as the police came in the front door, another joined me in Acapulco a few days later.

I have never found out what this was all about. The *Nation* in New York published an editorial suggesting that strikes and other disturbances in Mexico called for this sort of diversion. Our impression immediately after the event was that the American embassy was unhappy at the hospitality which the Mexican government had extended to leftists. It had thus brought pressure to bear upon *Gobernación*, then under the direction of a particularly reactionary minister, and persuaded it to issue the deportation orders.

My reaction to the episode was astonishment at the complexities of Mexican society. One branch of the government had ordered my expulsion while certain officials had saved me from arrest. Yet another official had offered his vacation house in Acapulco until the matter was resolved. I had known since my arrival in the country that Mexico was full of contradictions. I had never expected to be so deeply involved in them, or to be so grateful for their existence.

At about the same time a position which I had acquired in the academic world and which I esteemed was threatened. One of my stepsons attended a private primary school, and I had been invited to join its *mesa directiva*, its board of directors or trustees. My colleagues, all Mexican citizens, included two heads of prominent construction companies, an engineer, an architect, a lawyer, the manager of a large country club development and the part owner of an important manufacturing business. Because the school was new, the board met frequently and its members got to know each other well.

One day the chairman called me to ask me to come to his office as soon as I could. He told me that one of the board members had informed him and others that while at an American embassy function, he had been asked to make sure that I was forced to resign from the board. He had been told that I was *persona non grata* with the embassy and that my presence on the board made it impossible for the embassy to continue to recommend the school. That threat was so much nonsense. The embassy had never shown the slightest interest in our school and had certainly never recommended it to any one.

The chairman told me he would call an immediate special meeting to discuss the matter. I thought it would be better if I did not attend so that the other members could discuss the matter freely. No, he said, "You must attend. I want you to hear what is said." That afternoon I sent a letter of resignation to his office, saying I did not think the question should even be discussed because such political stupidities had no place in an educational body. Just a consideration of them might prove disruptive.

At the chairman's insistence, I finally did attend. The chairman explained what had happened in much the same words he had used with me. He deplored the interference of the embassy and spoke angrily of its arrogance in trying to influence the makeup of the board of a purely Mexican educational institution. He thereupon asked for a motion which would express, first, the board's complete confidence in me and its wish that I remain a trustee, and, second, the board's desire for the immediate resignation of the member who had demanded mine. The motion was offered and unanimously passed.

I had rarely received such heartwarming support, and I was grateful for it. I discovered a Mexican characteristic which I have since realized is always present, though seldom seen. When it is possible for Mexicans to do so, they will not take such arrogant dictation.

U.S. News and World Report carried a three-page feature on November 7, 1960, under the catchy title "Underground Railway for Reds Begins at U.S. Border." It claimed that "the colony of U.S. Reds" in Mexico numbered 400. That figure was made up, the magazine said, of "about 100 well-known American Communists who came to Mexico to escape attention several years ago during the anti-Communist hearings held by the late Senator Joseph McCarthy" and their dependents.

About twenty-five left-wingers plus their dependents would be a more accurate figure, and most of those were in Mexico for the simple reason that they could not find employment in the United States and they preferred not to have their families starve. In those days it was very much cheaper to live south of the border. Nearly all returned as soon as the political climate in the United States permitted them to resume their professions. I am one of the few who remained. I did so for several reasons. I enjoyed living in Mexico, I had become deeply interested and involved in archaeology and, most important, I had married a Mexican and we had two children who would remain Mexican citizens unless and until they chose U.S. citizenship.

U.S. News and World Report stated, "The colony of U.S. Reds takes care of the financial security of its members. It operates chicken farms, an ice-cream business and other enterprises." What an awful thing! To help each other. Frightfully un-American! Unfortunately, it was not true. Each family was working out its own solutions. It was true, however, that one valiant woman, whose husband was dying of emphysema, operated a chicken farm. I had nothing whatsoever to do with the farm and knew nothing of its finances except that I understood that she had made a go of the enterprise through very hard work. And, yes, it was true, there was an ice-cream business. I invested money in it as a business, not a philanthropy, and so did several of my American friends. The manager of the business used the income fraudulently. When we discovered the monkey business, we threatened him with public exposure and legal prosecution, and he left the country posthaste. We lost our shirts. Nearly all the other politically progressive Americans whom I knew wrote, opened shops, or developed businesses that carried them through their period of exile, and a few made modest fortunes.

The magazine article repeated the shopworn story: "The financiers of the outfit are identified by investigators as Frederick Vanderbilt Field and, until their departure, Mr. and Mrs. Stern." Alfred Stern was a Chicago businessman whom I knew after he had moved to New York many years ago; his wife was Martha Dodd, a well-known author and daughter of the American ambassador to Nazi Germany in the middle 1930s. According to *U.S. News and World Report*, the Sterns and I financed an underground railway for North American Reds, spies, traitors, and refugees via Mexico to the Soviet Union. We apparently cared for needy Communists, and we furnished documents "for bringing in new American Communists as business consultants." Instead of all this nonsense, a genuine investigator would soon have discovered that I was rapidly running short of shirts.

And there was also the Harold Lavine-*Newsweek* Affair. In March 1961 there was held in Mexico City a Latin American Conference for National Sovereignty, Economic Emancipation and Peace. The meeting was sponsored and chaired by Mexico's former president, Lázaro Cárdenas. It was not as great a success or as politically broad as its organizers apparently hoped, but it drew a large number of delegates from all over Latin America and hundreds of guests and visitors. The week-long conference was covered, though not lavishly, by the Mexican press. I had absolutely nothing to do with it, did not attend, did not talk then or since to anyone who did and gained my impressions of it solely from the newspapers.

However, the March 20 issue of *Newsweek*, on the stands by March 14, carried a scurrilous account of the meeting by its chief Latin American correspondent, Harold Lavine. It said, *inter alia*, that the Mexican government had "called in Mexico City's leading newspaper editors one by one and explained that by giving the conference any publicity they would simply be playing into the hands of Communists. They didn't make any threats; they didn't have to; the editors were only too glad to cooperate." My records show that on March 6 *Excelsior*, the leading newspaper, ran two full columns on the meeting and that all the papers carried something every day of the week. The coverage was not what an interested person would call adequate, but it was far from being the "blanket of silence" that Lavine reported.

Lavine wrote that he had spotted four Americans at the conference: a Dr. Holland Roberts, "a white-haired, middle-aged woman from California who refused to give her name," another nameless man who said he was a member of the United Electrical Workers Union and Frederick Vanderbilt

Field, "the millionaire refugee from House and Senate investigations on Communism."

I had had a lot of publicity, some based on fact, some based on half fact and half invention, and some, like this one, a complete and deliberate lie. I was angry. I had been angry before and done nothing about it. Protests to magazine and newspaper editors in those days were useless. But this time I had to do something. I was living in Mexico as the guest of the government, and if I was to stay, I had to conform to its rules. There weren't many. I could not work in a bar, I could not invest in any media enterprise and I could not own property within a certain number of meters of the coast. The important rule for foreigners was that they could not interfere in the internal affairs of the nation, and of course attending a conference on national sovereignty could be so interpreted. This time it was worth demanding a retraction from *Newsweek*. Lavine's article had put me in a precarious situation; many persons had been thrown out of the country on less evidence.

I therefore wrote a letter to the editor of the magazine demanding a retraction. In return I received a smooth Madison Avenue reply promising an investigation and later a short note stating that the author of the article had sworn to its truth.

As was customary among the American newsweeklies, the article had not been signed, and it was only at this point that through friends I discovered the name of the author. It took a bit of doing to find out how to meet him. I learned that a lady of whom Lavine was enamored was someone I had met and that she was about to throw a fiesta for something or other. Friends arranged to have my wife and me invited.

Lavine was a heavy drinker. When I met him at the fiesta, he was well on his way to proving this point. We behaved courteously toward each other as I went through the preliminaries. I soon informed him that I had not attended the conference and asked him where and how he had obtained the information that I had. His first answer was that he had seen me there himself. A little more pressing and he admitted that he had not attended but that the information came to him from a completely reliable source. What was that source? He couldn't reveal that to me. We stayed on that plateau for several more bourbons. But very late, the next morning in fact, Lavine finally told me that his information had come from the FBI.

That was not the end of this story which the FBI had fabricated and publicized through an irresponsible journalist. On March 16, 1961, Dr. Joseph F. Thorning of Marymount College testified under oath before a subcommittee of the Senate Committee on the Judiciary that I "was reported" to have been one of three Americans in attendance at an anti-

USA conference for national sovereignty in Mexico City and that we "actually attempted" to smash a reporter's camera in order to conceal our identities. Fascinating, isn't it, to watch a lie grow? And it was hardly reassuring to know what kind of person was teaching our youth.

29

An Indian-Summer Interlude

A bright star shone in my skies for a few days in February 1962. I had received a letter from a good friend, Martha Josefy, who lives in Connecticut, telling me that a friend of hers was coming to Mexico to buy furniture, ceramics, and textiles for a house she had recently bought. Her friend had never been in Mexico, spoke no Spanish, and would greatly appreciate it if I would help her when she first arrived. Martha went on about how she knew I was busy and did not like to be disturbed by every Tom, Dick and Harry who visited Mexico and needed help in doing this, that and the other, but this particular person about whom she was writing was especially nice and would not impose on me. Her name, she said, was Marilyn Monroe.

As I had no telephone in my office or home, I had to find a way for instant communication. A telegram would be much too slow, it would take several hours, and of course a letter was out of the question. I made record time to a friend's house some fifteen blocks away by walking, because public transportation could not be trusted on an errand of such importance. Fortunately, I found the friends at home and Martha on the other end of long distance. Speaking in the calmest voice I could muster, I told her that under the circumstances I was disposed to devote a few moments of my time to helping Marilyn.

Marilyn's companion, Mrs. Eustice Murray, was to arrive in Mexico a week early to line things up. I called on her and arranged to meet Marilyn right after her arrival. Mrs. Murray is an accomplished person in her own right. When she became a widow, she had gone into house decorating and also taken therapy training. In November of 1961, she had become Marilyn's part-time companion, chauffeur, housekeeper and sort of M.M. watcher at the suggestion of Marilyn's psychiatrist, Dr. Ralph Greenson. Things worked out well between the two women, and Marilyn shortly told Eunice of her ambition to have a house of her own and entrusted the companion with the job of finding one. Marilyn's idea for a house and for what was to go inside it was inspired by Eunice's own Spanish-style home, which she had decorated herself. Soon Eunice had moved in full time with Marilyn and often spent the night at her home. She was with Marilyn on the last day of her life and discovered her death that dreadful morning of August 5. Eunice wrote, with Rose Shade, one of the sympathetic and well-informed books on Marilyn, *Marilyn, the Last Months*.

I am writing about Marilyn's visit to Mexico partly because the glow of that bright star remains in my private heaven. In addition, she was an important person, and I would like to make a small, decent contribution to her memory.

Marilyn, as I was to learn, was notoriously late for all appointments, even the most important, but even she could not alter the schedule of the flight that brought her from Miami. She was taken to the Hilton Hotel, where a suite had been engaged through the good offices of Frank Sinatra. The next morning Nieves and I called on her and were greeted by Eunice. She explained that Marilyn was getting ready and would join us soon. We talked about what they were looking for in the way of furnishings, how many days we had and whether some travel could be included. Our conversation must have gone on nearly an hour before the bedroom door opened and Marilyn appeared.

When she came forward to greet us, the talk and beautiful week began, as well as one of the nicest friendships that Nieves and I have ever had. Marilyn was an extraordinary person. She was beautiful beyond measure. She was warm, attractive, bright and witty. Her politics were excellent. She was curious about things, people and ideas. She was open and frank and friendly. She was also incredibly complicated. The best champagne was sent up, which she and Nieves enjoyed—it is my wife's favorite beverage. I, made of less delicate fiber, stuck by bourbon, my traditional companion for celebrations.

As people do when they are getting acquainted, we talked about a little of everything and finally focused on how to go about buying the things that Marilyn needed for her house. Nieves and I thought that spending a few days in Taxco would be the best way to find the main furnishings. In her book Eunice writes, "The rapport between Marilyn and the Fields developed instantly. They had no sooner outlined their proposals than she exclaimed, 'It sounds wonderful. When do we start?' "

The local press had written an enormous amount about Marilyn's visit, and I had no idea how comfortable or even safe she would be in street crowds, shops, or, even worse, markets. I suggested we make a trial run to see how things went before undertaking the longer trip. We accordingly decided to go the next day to the Toluca market. Toluca is the capital of the State of Mexico, about an hour's ride from Mexico City. The market is a famous tourist attraction as well as being one of the largest meeting places for the exchange of goods and produce in the country. It covers several acres of open stalls, or *puestos*, usually covered with tentlike awnings. You can find anything from live pigs and turkeys to fine *serapes* and *rebosos*, ceramics and baskets. On Friday, which is market day and the day we were to go, there are hundreds upon hundreds of Mexicans of all types and classes, though mostly the poor, and a smattering of tourists, mostly *norteamericanos*, pushing and struggling to get through from one *puesto* to another.

Toluca is also well known for its skillful pickpockets. On a previous visit, I had found myself hemmed in on all sides. Suddenly I was pushed from the back, and so as not to fall forward into the people in front I threw up my arms. By the time I recovered my balance, aided by many hands, I didn't need to feel my pockets. I knew that I no longer had any cash, credit cards, driver's license, or residence permit. A visit to the Toluca market would indeed be a test.

To prepare for the trip, I turned to my close friend George Pepper, who had good connections with some of the moguls of the Mexican movie industry. He undertook to find out the advisability of as well as the procedure for procuring some kind of police protection. The upshot was that early the next morning two plainclothes members of the presidential guard showed up at my house, rather pleased at the job to which they had been assigned. While they breakfasted, Nieves and I went to the Hilton to pick up Marilyn and Eunice—and waited long enough to read all the morning papers, which that morning were full of M.M., before the lady appeared. That was the last time Marilyn kept us waiting. For the next several days, when we were traveling or back in the city, she was as prompt for appointments or meals as any other person. I concluded that in order to do something strange or new or to meet people for the first time, she had to prepare herself emotionally, and that might take an unpredictable length of time. When she gained confidence in those she was with and life became easy and informal, she no longer needed to psych herself up for the encounter.

We finally all gathered at our house, Marilyn and Eunice, George and Jeanette Pepper, the two guards and ourselves, and we set out in two cars, with walkie-talkies and pistols, for Toluca. The equipment could have been left behind.

The visit to the market was an experience for all of us. Marilyn had a reputation for wearing what can only be described as exceedingly sexy outfits—though for that matter she could have worn a flour sack and made it look like a costume for a finale of the Zeigfeld Follies. I had taken it upon myself the previous morning to suggest that she dress as demurely as possible, not so much to protect herself as out of respect for the Mexicans among whom she would be moving. In 1962 Mexican women were hardly ever seen wearing even the most modest slacks. Some tourists wore them, but they were conspicuous and considered in poor taste. When women's slacks and shorts and later miniskirts did hit Mexico, they did so with such suddenness, from the city to the smallest pueblo, that the landscape of the country seemed to change overnight. The movies and television and fashion journals had conveyed their cultural message.

Marilyn appeared that morning looking as innocent as anyone with that face and figure and disposition could. She had in her handbag a hideous wig and asked if she should wear it so that people would not recognize her. I expressed myself strongly against such an idea (a) because it would not disguise her, and (b) because I felt that the Mexicans as well as her host had the right to see her as she was. The wig did not appear again.

Marilyn's behavior fitted her attire. She was natural; she was not putting on a show for her admirers. A few days later I saw her under different circumstances. She had been invited to the movie studios where Buñuel was filming. There was mutual enjoyment on Marilyn's part and that of the Mexican actors at meeting each other; it was a pleasant occasion. On the way back to our car we had to walk quite a distance past studios and workshops. Word had got around that Marilyn was there, and our path was lined on both sides with actors and technicians. Marilyn and I were walking ahead with Nieves and George right behind us. As we progressed, I noticed a commotion, a sort of murmur from the onlookers. I glanced back at George and he winked at me. We exchanged places and I quickly discovered what was happening. Marilyn was putting on her famous fanny wiggle. None of that happened at Toluca.

The visit to the market was remarkable for a particular reason. The place was as crowded as I have ever seen it. Many hundreds of people were there; most of them were the poor who on market day came from near and far to sell what little they had to offer and to take back the few things they could purchase in exchange. The security guards later confirmed my impression that there was not a single person in that market who did not recognize Marilyn. Not one of them moved from where he or she was sitting, standing, working or talking. They simply turned their heads, smiled and watched her as she moved among them. No one reached out to touch her or to get closer. It was a display of personal dignity on the part of the Mexicans as well as respect for a beautiful foreigner whom they admired.

There were several groups of tourists. Most of them smiled and waved, and those nearby called a friendly, "Hi, Marilyn." Two groups of Americans, however, among whom some were brash and pushy, brought about the only occasions on which our security forces had to go on active duty. On the way home Marilyn told us how profoundly affected she had been by the dignified behavior of the Mexicans. It was something to which she was not accustomed.

Marilyn found a lot of things that she wanted. The guards, after the first few moments of stiff formality, began thoroughly to enjoy the excursion. Seeing that we were not going to have any real trouble, they refused to let us recruit youngsters to carry the purchases. They insisted on doing so themselves. By the end of our marketing, they could hardly be seen for the packages.

In Marilyn, the Last Months, Eunice wrote, "We had a wonderful light-hearted time of discovering colorful handcrafted items she could buy for her home, including baskets and linens, and a black-and-red-bordered wall hanging used later in the sunroom. . . .The trip to Toluca was a great success. Marilyn found the Fields easygoing, intelligent and thoughtful guides. . . ."

At that time I had a small Jaguar, a perfect vehicle in which to transport such a distinguished guest. The only trouble was that the engine was misbehaving. A mechanic, anxious to try out his boss's new grinding machine, had shortly before experimented with my car's valves. He had not been aware that infinite patience and many hours were required to replace them correctly and to achieve the necessary precision timing. The valves had consequently blown. The new set had been made for another make of car and did not have the hardness called for. During Marilyn's visit, the engine was rougher than it should have been; I was constantly worried that the valves would blow again. At such moments I felt more secure knowing that, should we be stranded in some remote spot, she still carried that wig in her pocketbook. However, we made Taxco and back all right. As a matter of fact, the Jag behaved well until about a week after Marilyn's departure, and by then, of course, a breakdown didn't matter.

By the time we reached that lovely mountain resort, Nieves and I had learned a good deal about Marilyn's recently purchased house. What was most important was that it was her first home, bought with her own money, and a place that she would furnish and decorate herself. She had no family, not a great deal of money, and very few real friends. She had been shamelessly exploited in Hollywood. Until very recently, her earnings had been modest. She was desperately lonely. This house was to be much more than a home. It was to help fill a large hole in her life. It was to substitute for a lot of things that she had either lost or never had. Arranging the house therefore became the most important thing on her mind. It had, she explained, the simple lines of a California Spanish mission; she wanted to equip it as far as possible with Mexican things.

Instead of going directly to Taxco from the city, we went a little further down the Acapulco highway to Iguala to visit William Spratling at his home, workshop, and pre-Hispanic museum, all of them combined in a series of connected structures. Spratling was the best-known silversmith in Mexico. As a young architect who had been teaching at Tulane University, he had come down to Mexico, fallen in love with it, and remained. He was single-handedly responsible for transforming Taxco from a secluded silver-mining town into one of the leading tourist attractions of the country and the center of silver design and artistry. Today a public museum in Taxco which houses his pre-Hispanic collection honors his memory.

Strangely enough, it was the furniture he had made for his own use that caught Marilyn's eye rather than the silver objects from his workshop. She arranged to have several pieces of furniture copied and sent to Los Angeles. It was lucky that we had stopped to see Bill on our way, for on telephoning for reservations we found that we had arrived on one of those unforeseen Mexican holidays. The hotels were completely filled. Bill phoned around among his friends and found rooms in one of the smaller inns, this one owned by another well-known silversmith, Antonio Castillo.

The place was called Los Arcos. Nieves and I returned to it several times, both because of the pleasant memories and the fact that it was an attractive, unassuming hostel, centrally located and serving decent food. On that first visit with Marilyn, we had three rooms around an inner second-floor patio, a location I well remember, for Marilyn was soon serenaded. Her first night in Mexico, before we met her, the Hilton management had taken her nightclubbing and she had, not surprisingly, caught the fancy of a nervy young man who had somehow later found out that she was going to Taxco. He had hired a mariachi band in Mexico City, put the musicians and himself into two taxis, and taken the three-hour trip. Not having any idea where Marilyn was staying, he had at first tried the larger tourist hotels until late at night he found her at Los Arcos. We had long before gone to bed and to sleep. According to Eunice Murray, it had been the first night in the months that she had been with Marilyn, and the only night in the last eight months of her life, that Marilyn had fallen asleep without a sedative.

We were awakened by a tremendous racket in the street below our windows. The first inkling I had of what was up was hearing Marilyn yelling out of her window, "Go home, you crazy Mexicans." I woke up Eunice and asked her what she thought I should do. The gist of her answer was, sensibly,

"What can you do?" I went to Marilyn's room and put it differently. "I'm pretty sure they want to come up to the patio. Shall I let them or shall I try to stop them?" She replied that it would be better if they didn't come up, but by that time it was too late. They were on the stairs and, as I quickly found out, in no mood to argue. The serenade took place. Everyone in the hotel woke up, but everyone took it in good spirits. Marilyn was skillfully polite without being encouraging. And when they left, she again went to sleep without sedation. If that pattern had only been established, she would not have died so soon afterward.

The shopping was successful. But one of the stores let her down by one inexcusable delay after another, so that many of the things never reached her before she died. Eunice reports, however, that this had not bothered Marilyn as much as I had feared, for she knew exactly what she had ordered and where it would be placed when it arrived and had had pleasure from the anticipation.

The people in the streets of Taxco were as dignified and courteous as they had been in Toluca. Two old women selling flowers came up to Marilyn and presented her with bouquets, and afterward, when I offered them something for their kindness, they said, no, the flowers were a gift. I don't remember a single person asking for an autograph.

There are Mexicans and Mexicans as there are Americans and Americans. Inevitably, we ran into the other Mexicans too. One of the store owners where Marilyn bought a quantity of things invited all of us to his house for tea or cocktails at the end of the day. Marilyn, mumbling something to me to the effect that she thought it was only polite to accept, said, "Yes, we'd love to go." The house was charming; it appeared that all would go well. It was built on the side of a hill, and we had entered on the uphill level where the living room, dining room, and kitchen were located. Suddenly and unexpectedly, the hostess, who was connected with one of the local schools, said to Marilyn, "I have all my school children down in the basement playroom waiting for you and I've promised that you would teach them how to do the twist." My heart sank, and Nieves looked fit to be tied. But Marilyn said, "Yes, of course, I'd love to."

On our way back to the hotel, I apologized, saying that I felt responsible. The one thing I had pledged to myself was not to permit anyone to exploit Marilyn, and then this unforeseeable thing had happened. Marilyn had taken it in her professional stride. "It was nothing. These things happen all the time, and the kids were wonderful." Well, I was sorry this had happened in Mexico.

A few days later we had another unfortunate event, this time in the city. Marilyn told us she had been invited to an evening reception in the home of a well-known movie actor and director. The reception had been described to her as being given by the industry as a whole. She begged us to come, though she explained that we would not be able to go together because the Hilton manager had asked her for the honor. We happened to have been invited anyway because Nieves had done pictures with these people for years and was still friends with a few of them.

Not many people were present. It was obviously a makeshift sort of affair. No one in the industry had had the gumption or courtesy to get up a really fine party to honor this visiting actress; this was a desperate afterthought. There was lots of drinking and a fine ranch-type folk singer. Finally, the host, who was holding a little package in his hand, called for silence and addressed Marilyn with a flowery though blurred speech. It ended with the presentation of the package, which, the host explained, contained a superb speciman of the art of the pre-Hispanic civilizations, a beautiful clay figure, an exquisite object which he trusted would forever adorn her new home. Marilyn accepted the gift, said a few polite words, and came over to sit by me to look at this lovely present. We unwrapped it, and I exclaimed, too loudly, "Christ, what a cheat!" It was a small contemporary ceramic figure which could be bought in any market in any part of the country for five to ten pesos.

The three evenings at Los Arcos we sat around our dining table talking, or rather listening, to Marilyn. She talked mostly about herself and some of the people who had been or still were important to her. She told us about her strong feelings for civil rights, for black equality, as well as her admiration for what was being done in China, her anger at red-baiting and McCarthyism and her hatred of J. Edgar Hoover. She said that at that much publicized party at the Lawfords where she first met Bobby Kennedy, she had asked him directly whether he and the President were going to fire Hoover. His answer, she said, was that they would like to, but at that time it was politically impossible.

She had good words for Frank Sinatra. She told us that he had taught her a lot about the problems of the black minority. She admired Kate Hepburn for her independence of the Hollywood crowd. She herself was not a partygoer; Marilyn said she seldom went out with the movie people, with whom she felt uncomfortable. Another subject was Carl Sandburg, one of her favorite people; she said a lot about what he told her about Lincoln but even more about his guitar and folk songs. She had much to say, and all of it nice, about Clark Gable, whom she had never met until *The Misfits*, which they had recently made together. This part of her conversation became almost mystic; Gable became confused with her own father, and when the talk was clearer, he was at least a father image. We heard about her orphanhood, the orphanage, the foster parents, her first and almost unknown marriage.

Her disappointments had been deep ones. She spoke especially about the miscarriages, her failure to become a mother and about her inability to make a good marriage with Arthur Miller. She seemed most of all to want to lead a private family life with a husband whom she loved and admired, children and a house in the country—all of the things she had almost but not quite achieved in Connecticut. We had the strong impression that she wanted to find a way to leave Hollywood and public life, that she had gotten a full gourmet meal out of it and now wanted to seek simpler, more lasting fare.

Marilyn talked at length about Miller, always with respect and kindness. It was she who had failed, who was not well enough educated, who had not read enough of the right kind of books and who didn't know a lot of important things. She luckily did not know about that frightful play *After the Fall* that he was writing about her, although she had unfortunately, according to Eunice, found out about a diary he had been keeping about their private life.

There was no question that the strong, dependable element in Marilyn's life had for many years been Joe DiMaggio. I have mentioned that she came to Mexico via Miami. She had taken the long way from New York in order to stop over for a few days to see Joe, who was helping out with the Yankees' early spring training. She had obviously enjoyed seeing him. She spoke at length about him and always with admiration and affection. With mutual admiration and affection and I think I can add a feeling of love, they had parted to remain friends. DiMaggio's devotion to Marilyn at the time of her death and during all the years since belongs among the great tragic romances of our time.

Back in Mexico City there was more shopping to be done. Bryna Prensky had a gallery specializing in young painters, many of whom were little known at the time. I took Marilyn there because she wanted some Mexican art for the new house. Bryna closed the gallery for the hour or so that we were there. She made no suggestions, nor did I. Marilyn picked out what she wanted. Weeks later, she sent word from Los Angeles that she was very happy with the paintings that she had chosen. One was a somber street scene in a Mexican pueblo by Migual Hernández Urban, another a still life of a thistle by an American artist, Nova Taylor, working in San Miguel Allende, and the third a back view of a nude by Hermosillo Rembrud.

The evening before Marilyn returned to Los Angeles, we had a farewell drink in her Hilton suite. As we left, she gave Nieves several bottles of her own favorite champagne. She walked down the corridor with us and we embraced.

During the next three months there was a great deal of correspondence between Eunice and me over the furniture and other things Marilyn had bought. Getting the suppliers to finish, pack and ship their orders turned out to be a stupid, detailed job. Fortunately, most of the purchases arrived while she was able to enjoy them.

On March 20 Eunice wrote, "The time has sped so swiftly and the many times Marilyn and I have referred to you in our daily conversation would indicate you are still with us . . . [Marilyn] has asked me to tell you she plans to write very soon. In fact she planned last week to spend one day as her 'Field day.' " Eunice also reported that Marilyn hadn't felt well after her return; she had caught some kind of bug in Mexico. I replied that such bugs were seasonal and come toward the end of the long dry season. "Tell Marilyn," I wrote, "to take good care of herself. If she needs a few days of complete calm and rest, now or any time, she will find the warmest possible welcome from Nieves and me. . . . Just tell her to come without publicity and to wear a nose ring . . . so that we will recognize her at the airport."

Martha Josefy, who had started this whole thing, wrote, "Marilyn telephoned to say how grateful . . . how wonderful Nieves and you were. . .in pleasure and help. I'm so happy it worked out well."

Nieves and I and our two children—the youngest hadn't been born yet—planned a trip to New York in July. Marilyn had told us that her apartment was always at our disposal, but we had not wished to take her up on that offer. We felt that for a family with small children to move into someone's apartment would be to take too much advantage, even of the best of friendships. But Marilyn insisted we make her apartment our headquarters.

We therefore spent two weeks in the middle of July at 444 East 57th Street. Soon after we arrived, Marilyn's friend Hedda Rosten, who kept an eye on the apartment in Marilyn's absence, telephoned to make sure we were comfortable. Hattie, the housekeeper, fed us, baby-sat for us and made us feel at home. Nieves and I slept in Marilyn's room with mirrored walls and ceiling. On the record player in the living room was the record which Marilyn had used to practice her famous "Happy Birthday to You" that she had sung the winter before in Madison Square Garden for President Kennedy's birthday. On the shelves were the books on philosophy, art and architecture with which she had been giving herself a late education. Hattie had been instructed not to let us pay for the food and liquor we consumed, but we found ways to circumvent that order. On our last day at the apartment, we called Marilyn to thank her. She was full of all kinds of plans and sounded as happy as when we had last seen her.

As soon as I got back to Mexico, on July 31st, I wrote Marilyn to tell her how much we had appreciated her hospitality and how marvelous Hattie had been. The letter ended, "Nieves asks me to send her love and . . . she also wants you to know that we hope you are winning your battles in Hollywood." I have never known whether she received that letter.

August 5 is Nieves's birthday. The evening before, a Saturday night, we had a small family party and opened the champagne Marilyn had given her a few months before when we said goodbye in the corridor of the Hilton. We toasted Nieves and then we toasted Marilyn. At noon the next day we heard on the radio that Marilyn had died early that morning. The bright star had gone out.

Later in the day I wrote a letter to Eunice which in her book she says she carried in her handbag and phrases from which ran through her mind at Marilyn's funeral. "Nieves and I are alone at home heartbroken," I said. I told her that after hearing the news, we had gone to my office in town to see if there was any mail and had found a letter giving us the latest about the successes and failures of the purchases and the plans Marilyn had for the future. "It is impossible to grasp the reality of what has happened. All we can think at the moment is that one of the finest women of our day is no more. The world and we needed her. . . ." Two weeks later Eunice wrote us, saying, "In my opinion Marilyn's sojourn in Mexico was the happiest experience in the last year of her life. . . ." I'm glad we had some part in it.

30

A New Interest— Archaeology

Thirty years passed between the Malinowski lectures at the University of London and my arrival in Mexico, thirty years in which archaeology was nothing more than a fascinating memory. I had had no opportunity to pursue it with either further reading or visits to sites and even museum exhibits. Therefore one of the most exciting things that happened to me in 1953 was to find myself suddenly exposed to one of the great archaeological areas of the world and in the midst of professionals and amateurs who were immersed in the discipline.

Was it the second or the third day after my arrival that I drove north of the city to the fabulous pyramids, paintings and scultures of Teotihuacán? Was it the third day or as late as the fourth that new friends took me half an hour from where we lived to Tlatilco, one of the most famous and prolific pre-Hispanic burial grounds of all Mesoamerica? Wasn't it about the end of the first week, surely not later, that I proudly placed on our living room table an exquisite small clay figurine which had been buried alongside a dead personage well before the birth of Christ and discovered only the day before?

That was the beginning of what became my chief occupation for the next twenty years. I cannot even count the visits that I have since made to Tlatilco, Teotihuacán and other sites. And I have placed literally thousands of archaeological pieces on our table to admire and study.

I began with a general interest in pre-Hispanic artifacts and gradually developed a specialized interest in clay stamps. During the first few years, I put together a heterogenous collection of examples of the successive cultures that had existed before the Spanish conquest in 1519. There were large and small anthropomorphic and zoomorphic figures, beads and hollow cylinders of jade and lesser stones for necklaces, bowls of every conceivable shape made of both clay and stone, fascinating decorated clay flutes, and those stamps about which not much was known. After a number of years of concentration on the stamps, I found that I had a very large and representative collection of them and after beginning my serious study of these objects, I probably had a larger and better one than anyone else had ever bothered to put together.

There were several reasons why I abandoned my interest in a general collection and turned to a specialized one. Collecting had become highly competitive. A growing number of private collectors, both Mexican and foreign, were vying with each other, and there was an increasingly flourishing illegal trade, handled mostly by *comerciantes*, to foreign countries. There were two results: prices skyrocketed and you frequently found yourself in unpleasant competition with friends and acquaintances. Because no one else was interested in stamps, I had the supply market to myself and therefore the prices remained relatively low. But the main reason for the concentration was that neither in the standard books on archaeology, whether written by Mexicans or by Americans, French or English, nor in various doctoral theses could I find a satisfactory explanation of what these stamps were. Why had they been made? For what were they used? What did they mean? I became curious, almost possessed to find some answers.

Another problem was that hungry bureaucrats congregate wherever there is value. Several collectors, Mexican as well as foreign, were held up virtually at gunpoint by rapacious government agents. I was one victim. I had a one-room office in the *Zona Rosa*, called the Pink Zone because it was or wanted to be considered halfway between a red zone and a white one. It aims to titillate visitors, particularly foreign tourists. I was there neither to titillate nor to be titillated. The zone had good communications with other parts of the city, and fine restaurants, and during the first years I was there, I was able to park my car in a street somewhere near my office. I worked alone and opened the door to whoever knocked.

One visitor presented credentials from the city treasury and pulled an absurd line about my having to pay taxes on the collection. We sat around and argued until we agreed on a present of two hundred dollars for his troubles. In the spring of 1970 when I opened the door to a determined knock, I was roughly pushed aside by three armed men, the leader with his hand on his pistol. Such rapacious hunger is not restricted to Mexican government officials, I should say. For in the middle 1960s, a personable young American and his girl friend called on me with a letter of introduction from a mutual acquaintance. They were also kind enough to bring with them a fine alto recorder that I had ordered long before. My music dealer had taken advantage of this couple's trip to Mexico to deliver the instrument. Unfortunately, I could not accept the flute because the young woman had tested it on the trip down and smeared the mouthpiece with lipstick. That stuff penetrates the wood and could never be removed. That annoyed me, but we managed to have a pleasant talk and they dropped in two or three times more. The day before they were to return to the United States, I invited them for lunch and did not go back to the office that afternoon. They did. When they left, their pockets were stuffed with about fifty small but well-chosen archaeological pieces. A few weeks later they sold the lot to a New York dealer who happened to know me. A year later the thief came back to Mexico, was arrested on a narcotics charge, and put in a provincial jail. He wrote me a letter asking me to bail him out. I did not reply. People who cheat me seem to have the unfortunate habit of thinking that they have thereby acquired a new friend.

The three *pistoleros* were a more serious matter. They carried credentials from *Hacienda*, the federal treasury. They said they had a truck around the corner to haul away my entire pre-Hispanic collection, which then numbered roughly three thousand items. They told me they would be glad to dismiss the truck if I would give them eighty thousand pesos, then worth sixty-four hundred dollars. I offered four hundred dollars, or five thousand pesos. It was obvious we had quite a lot of bargaining to do. It took us three hours to compromise—in their favor—on a figure of fifty thousand pesos or four thousand dollars.

We then entered the second phase of the negotiation: How was the money to be delivered? This discussion was taking place during midday on a Friday. That was when all such delicate transactions took place. If the victim didn't come across, he could be held on a fake charge *incomunicado* for seventy-two hours before being released on Monday morning. I would have no way to notify my family, lawyer or anyone else of my whereabouts or the nature of my predicament. They said they would come for the money as soon as the banks opened on Monday morning. That would be impossible, I said. I was short forty-two thousand pesos of the amount required inasmuch as I had only eight thousand in my account. "Then the deal's off," they said. "We'll get the truck." I suggested that that was no way to talk. My word was good, but I would have to borrow the money. That would take at least a week. I'd pay half a week from the next Monday and the other half at the end of the following week. We figuratively shook hands on that, though not literally, for while there hands were no longer on their weapons, I was not in the mood to make physical contact.

Only one of the men, the leader and spokesman, came for the final payment. After counting the cash, he sat down and made the following remarkable statement: "Sr. Field, I appreciate the way you have handled this. You are a man of your word. I have a small property on the outskirts of the city where on weekends I operate a pony-riding ring for children. The kids have a wonderful time. I know you have three little girls and I would be very glad if you would bring them out any weekend convenient for your family and I won't charge you anything."

The reader may have been wondering why I kept my word and made those delayed payments. Now he knows the reason. My children had never before been mentioned. How had he known about them? What more did he know about my family or my personal affairs? Immediately afterward, I reported what had happened to the highest officials I could reach. They told me I had done the only thing possible under the circumstances. They were sorry, but there was nothing they could do.

The government itself, of course, had nothing to do with these outrages. That one took place in the fall of 1970, at the end of a presidential sexenium when it is more than usually difficult to control the appetite of some of the more irresponsible members of the bureaucracy. That discouraging experience led me to abandon my downtown office for good and to lose altogether an already waning interest in further developing my collection.

It was a fortunate time to do so, because the next administration put an end to private collecting by passing a law giving the state itself a monopoly on the possession and traffic in pre-Hispanic artifacts. Private collecting virtually stopped. I had in any case already disposed of my best pieces. The new Museum of Anthropology had been built in Chapultepec Park in the early 1960s. I donated to it thirty-five of my finest pieces. I also agreed to sell the Museum at whatever price it set another hundred and twenty-three items of its choosing. I had, moreover, begun to trade off clay figures, bowls and even flutes, in which I was especially interested, for more and more clay stamps.

If you could afford to make your own collection, it was a good and quick way to become familiar with the artistic output of the ancient societies. However, when my collection began to get big, I felt uncomfortable about it. Beside satisfying my own interests, the justification for collecting was that, by and large, the private owner took better care of what he had than the public museums did. He was more likely than the public bodies to build up specialized collections, and in due course most of the private collections would become public property. Collecting was also a way of keeping material in the country which would otherwise have been sold abroad. A few years after taking up Mexican residence, I had made a will which left any archaeological material I might have to the national museum, but I canceled that clause ten or twelve years later because I was not happy with what had happened to other collections donated or sold to the museum. I decided it was better to bide my time until I could find a way to turn the pieces over to the public with a reasonable assurance that they would be properly safeguarded, exhibited and made available for study. The time did come, but much later.

I eventually found myself with a little more than three thousand stamps. Such a large collection gave me the opportunity to dig deep into that small corner of the archaeological map.

It is difficult to understand why the study of clay stamps had been neglected. Perhaps the reason was that they were relatively small or because excavators did not appreciate their importance and laid them aside in cartons unstudied. Possibly it was because modern archaeology was relatively new, and there were so many other studies to which the archaeologists gave priority. When I got started, only a handful of sources were worth looking up. A great deal of the work consisted of guesses, most of which would doubtless have to be discarded at a later date.

A pre-Hispanic stamp, or in Spanish *sello*, is of two principal types. One is a cylinder, sometimes hollow, sometimes solid, with a design on the surface. To make an impression of the cylinder, it must be rolled. The other type is flat. The design is backed by a handle which is usually pinched out of the soft clay but sometimes takes the form of the handle of an iron used to press clothes. This flat type is stamped on the surface to be printed just like one of the innumerable bureaucratic messages affixed to the back of a bank check. The great majority of both kinds are made of clay, a very few of stone.

The designs are the interesting thing. There is an almost infinite variety of them, from what appear to be (but probably are not) mere squiggles to realistic depictions of animals, especially serpents, some human figures and abstractions which represent symbols for such vital things in the lives of ancient peoples as water, earth, fire or fertility. Here, I thought, was one of their principal nonverbal forms of communication. If we could learn to read those stamp designs and understand their purpose and their meaning, we would greatly advance our knowledge of their societies.

Another fascinating thing about the stamps is their chronological and geographical spread. My collection, for instance, had examples dating back to roughly 1000 B.C. and forward to the early colonial period after the conquest, that is, to the middle of the sixteenth century. That takes us from the Olmec mother culture through the intervening ones to the final pre-Hispanic culture, the Aztec, and even a few decades into the Spanish. Geographically, the collections contained examples from the whole central belt, from the Gulf of Mexico to the Pacific. Conspicuously absent were the north, the part just below the Texas border, and, surprisingly, the south and southeast, Chiapas, Yucatán and Quintana Roo, the areas, that is, of the Maya civilization, where stamps were evidently not produced.

With a large number of stamps, I figured that I could study their meaning and purpose and make valid statistical calculations. From the beginning, I had a hunch that most of what I read about the stamps was wrong, because it did not correspond to what I was looking at every day. The standard works on Mexican pre-Hispanic civiliations contained only a sentence or two about these objects and reached a broad conclusion without documentation or even a footnote to lead one to the source of the statement. They declared that the stamps were used to decorate the human face and body. A few said that they were used to print textiles or designs on leather. There was one suggestion that they were used for the identification of private property or of goods for commercial trading.

Although I had more stamps in front of me than anyone else had ever had, neither I nor anyone else would ever find direct evidence to deny one theory or to prove another. We had the stamps themselves, but not the people who used them, none of whom had left us a definite clue. What I set out to do, therefore, was to consider all the circumstantial evidence, to weigh all the logical possibilities, and, principally, to become so closely familiar with the stamps themselves that they would speak to me. I thought that these designs could be compared to the print in a book. I had learned to read printed symbols represented by letters and words so that a book spoke to me. Couldn't I learn to read the message of those stamp designs?

That was my ultimate goal, but I didn't expect to go the whole way. I didn't expect to solve the historical secrets of those splendid civilizations. But I did hope that with a long period of concentrated study I might open a few cracks.

Between the time I started building the stamp collection and the day I donated it to the Mexican people, I spent ten years on that project. In that period I published two works: *Thoughts on the Meaning and Use of Pre-Hispanic Sellos*, in 1966, and in *Pre-Hispanic Mexican Stamp Designs*, in 1974.

I spent much of the time mulling over the problem. The various dictionary definitions of the word "mull" so aptly describe my method of work that I cannot resist the temptation to quote them: "to powder, pulverize, crush, grind, squeeze, or the like; to make a mess of; to muddle; to fumble; to work mentally, to cogitate; as to 'mull' over an idea" (*Webster's International*). Those three clauses in the middle—to make a mess of, to muddle, to fumble—are labeled "Obs. exc. Dial. Eng." Obsolete or not, they are most pertinent to my own experience.

The mulling business reminds me of what I learned from Graham Wallas, one of my lecturers at the London School of Economics. He wrote several books, two of which were important to me, *The Great Society* and *The Art of Thought*. In the latter he analyzes the process of thinking. He defines four overlapping stages: (1) a long and laborious period of preparation; (2) a stage of incubation in which the materials "lie in the back of the mind"; (3) the stage of illumination, in which the creative idea suddenly emerges into consciousness; and (4) the new ideas are given tangible form such as being put down on paper. That he calls the stage of verification.

These stages apply with extraordinary clarity to the processes of my archaeological study. During the first stage I collected objects. I handled them. I classified them according to provenance and culture. I prepared an elaborate card index broken down into seventy-seven design characteristics. I cleaned them. I even licked and smelled them to test their authenticity. And I searched the books to find out what they were, what they meant, how they were used.

In the second stage I fussed and fumed and did all those things that give meaning to that delightful word "mull," though with some emphasis on "to fumble." Perhaps Wallas's term "incubation" is more accurately descriptive. The ideas were incubating "in the back of my mind."

I well remember that the third stage came, as Wallas says, suddenly. He uses the word "illumination." At the time I remember thinking of it as "clarification," which is close, and also hoping that it was not further obfuscation of a complicated subject. Late one afternoon I was sitting at my desk doing nothing in particular, which is one of the things desks are for, and thinking that it was about time to go home. I suppose that, as usual those days, the problem of the clay stamps was somewhere in the back of my head. I was mulling. I remember saying to myself, practically aloud, "To hell with it. Get to work at the typewriter. Forget everything you've ever heard or read about these stamps and put down what you yourself know or think you know. See how it comes out." I wrote an outline that evening and next day filled it out to a memorandum of some fifteen pages. I liked it. I had confidence in it. It also disturbed me, because what it said contradicted the archaeologists whom I respected. The pros would ridicule this amateur out of existence.

I felt, nevertheless, that I was on the right track, so I made copies which I sent to archaeologists and museum people whom I personally knew, asking them to tear the memo apart. In my covering letter, I wrote, "I would really like whatever criticism, ruthless or otherwise, the piece calls for. My approach is one of being far more interested in the subject matter than in pride of authorship." To my astonishment, two weeks later I received a letter from Elizabeth Benson, curator of the pre-Columbian collection of

Dumbarton Oaks in Washington, D.C., an appendage of Harvard University, saying, "The paper is fine. The outline and the arguments are good and clear. We . . . would be interested in publishing this as one of our *Studies in Pre-Columbian Art and Archaeology* if it could be expanded and illustrated, and if you don't have any other plans for it." I pushed the wastepaper basket aside, my only other plan for the memo, and began expanding and illustrating.

Despite the lavish description I have given of my thought processes, I don't want to give the impression that I think I gave birth to anything world-shaking. Not at all. At best, I may have made a modest contribution to a tiny corner of the subject. I have dressed it up because the analysis of the thought process itself interests me. I was able to observe something I had been taught decades before in those same clear steps into which Professor Wallas had broken down the process. To be able to verify the analysis by one's own experience interests me, whether the process produces a mouse or a mountain.

My thesis about the stamps is that they were not made for facial or body decoration or for any of the other purposes which I have mentioned. No convincing evidence supports those notions, and much contradicts them. The stamps, in my opinion, were used for the same mythological, magical purpose that all the other symbolic paraphernalia with which the pre-Hispanic people surrounded themselves were used. If you print a clay stamp on your skin, the impression will come out quite clearly. I have done it on myself. But you can also use a violin as a percussion instrument by scratching or striking the soundbox. That doesn't prove that the violin was made for that purpose any more than the skin test proves the purpose of the stamps. In the case of the stamps, I think that the priests kept them in their possession, printed them on bark or cactus paper, and gave the common people that decorated paper to perform the magic required to alleviate their problems—drought, bad crops, barrenness—or to facilitate such pursuits as hunting or fishing, planting and harvesting. Very likely the printed paper was ceremoniously burned as an offering to the pertinent god, a custom still followed in remote parts of Mexico. I think it is very important that we learn to read the designs of the stamps, because understanding the symbols will lead us to the thought and structure of the societies that employed them.

I find occasional references to the Dumbarton Oaks monograph in the text or footnotes of what others write. The other volume, a large-format book of 222 pages, with 602 actual-size illustrations of the clay stamps, is a further elaboration of the theory introduced in the monograph. It sold "modestly but steadily," to use the publisher's words. Our local English-language newspaper, the *News*, gave the book a good send-off: "The drawings are excellent and the text superb." The illustrations are not drawings; they are retouched prints stamped directly on moistened blotting paper. But the thought and the rest of the sentence were so nice that I did not bother to send a correction.

My entire stamp collection is now housed, and part of it is exhibited, in the Alhondiga Museum in the delightful provincial capital, Guanajuato. I hope that many will enjoy it and that students and scholars will find it useful in continuing the investigation of pre-Hispanic stamps.

31

The Agenda
for Today's Meeting

The essence of democracy is the opportunity and willingness to act upon one's convictions. To make democracy work, everyone should turn his convictions into action.

What are some of the things to be done? What are the big problems that are facing those twenty-five children, grandchildren and great grandchildren to whom I have dedicated this book?

I don't pretend to offer a definitive list of the problems, but I can suggest some of them. To do so, I turn to two current publications, one of which has been read and commented upon by far too few and the other which has been read and discussed by many although not nearly enough. Both publications, or ones which are similar in content, should become part of the regular curricula of our school system.

In the spring of 1977 Jimmy Carter directed the appropriate branches of the government to undertake a study of the "probable changes in the world's population, natural resources, and environment through the end of the century" in order to provide information necessary to serve as "the foundation of our longer-term planning." The result, a voluminous work of three large-format volumes, was published in 1981 under the title *The Global 2000 Report to the President, Entering the Twenty-first Century.* It will startle the daylights out of a lot of people because it tells about the kind of world in which my children and theirs will have to live at the turn of the century. And that is not far away—though I can hardly expect to see it. Unless we all do something about it soon, and vigorously, it won't be a particularly pleasant or pretty world.

Between 1975 and 2000, the population of the world will increase from 4 billion to 6.35 billion, an increase of more than 50 percent. Of this growth, 92 percent will occur in the poorest countries, which at the beginning of the new century will have 79 percent of the world's population. In other words, of the world's 6.35 billion people, 5 billion will be living in the poor countries. These poor countries, according to the study, are most of Latin America, all of Africa, China, India and the remainder of Asia and Oceania; the industrialized or better-off areas are Australia, New Zealand, Canada, the United States, Japan, Western Europe and Eastern Europe, the USSR and a very small slice of Latin America.

In economic terms, while considerable improvement is projected for the less developed countries of Latin America, the heavily populated nations of South Asia will remain extremely poor, with a gross national product per capita of $200 in 1975 dollars. "The large existing gap between the rich and poor nations," the report informs us, "widens."

The forests of the world are disappearing at a rate of 18 to 20 million acres a year—that is, an area half the size of California—and most of this loss is taking place in the poor countries, which by the year 2000 will have lost about 40 percent of their present forest area.

An area the size of Maine is being lost to cropland and grassland each year. About our upper environment, the report tells us, "Atmospheric concentrations of carbon dioxide and ozone-depleting chemicals are expected to increase at a rate that could alter the world's climate and upper atmosphere by 2050." Acid rain threatens damage to lakes, soil and crops and "radioactive and other hazardous materials present health and safety problems in increasing numbers of countries."

The report further points out that between now and 2000, there will be a dramatic increase in the extinction of plant and animal species. Hundreds of thousands of species, something like 20 percent of all the species in the world, will be irretrievably lost.

The most serious environmental development will be an accelerating deterioration and loss of the resources essential for agriculture. "This overall development includes soil erosion; loss of nutrients and compaction of soil; increasing salinization of both irrigated land and water used for irrigation; loss of high quality cropland to urban development; crop damage due to increasing air and water pollution; extinction of local and wild crop strains needed by plant breeders for improving cultivated varieties; and more frequent and a more severe regional water shortages."

We live with more devastating problem than all the foregoing put together. We literally face the possibility of human extinction, the end of the entire human effort, the loss of all the accumulated human experience, the loss of all knowledge and all human records. I, as one out of over four billion individuals, endure the knowledge that my children and grandchildren and the great-grandchildren that are coming along may not complete their lives—not just one or two or three of them—but all of them. This frightening prospect is not just a philosophical possibility. It is a practical reality. Our political system is, seemingly with more and more frequency, putting the ultimate decisions in the hands of men or women intellectually incapable of comprehending these dangers and politically incapable of dealing with them. "To know and not to act is not to know." Well and good, but just turn that a bit: "To act without knowing may be the ultimate act."

In *The Fate of the Earth* Jonathan Schell writes, "The machinery of destruction is complete, poised on a hair trigger, waiting for the 'button' to be 'pushed' by some misguided or deranged human being or for some faulty computer chip to send out the instruction to fire."

It was we, the Americans, who first applied the principle of nuclear fission to human and material destruction. We remain the only nation to have done so. We lost the opportunity to atone for our guilt immediately after World War II by not unilaterally renouncing the further manufacture or employment of the atom bomb and by not destroying the atomic weapons we then had. Instead, we initiated the Cold War, one of the consequences of which was the race for nuclear superiority. The predicable result was that our alleged enemy followed suit. No American President, no American Congress, has had the intelligence or the guts to put a stop to this shameful process. And we, the American people, faced with an issue that can and should be answered by a simple yes or no, have become immersed in and bamboozled by the immeasurable complexity of the nuclear concept. We have protested all too feebly and have, in effect, thereby acquiesced in the growth of the horror which may now destroy us all.

Our present form of social organization has proved itself inadequate to cope with this new tool which scientists have presented to us. We are in imminent danger of allowing it to wipe us out and to prevent future generations from being born.

The socialist or socialist-aspiring sector of the world has joined this insane race toward mutual destruction. It has done so in response to our initiative. I urge that we proceed toward a resolution of this problem with the assumption that the socialist sector will respond to an initiative from our side to reverse the present suicidal course.

Without a doubt, the nuclear issue is the paramount issue of our day. Without a solution to this one, there will remain no humanity to concern itself with other issues. For this reason I urge that *The Fate of the Earth*— or another present or future text that expounds this problem with equal eloquence and passion—be made obligatory reading and study in our schools. It is clear to me that my generation has failed, and I am disposed to think that those now in their middle years will at best do no more than try to hold our rulers back from the brink. At the very least, let us do everything possible to prepare youth with the information, understanding and militancy required forever to remove from humanity this threat to its continuance.

Global 2000 concludes that "new and imaginative ideas—and a willingness to act on them—are essential." This is not a task that should be left to the heads of the great corporations, conglomerates and multinationals. By the laws of capitalism, as well as by their training and personal motivation, these leaders are dedicated to the making of profits. They may or may not be fine, outstanding and honorable persons, but their job is to make money. That goal is primary and has to be. And from long experience we know that what brings in the profits is not necessarily good for the nation or the world.

The profit motive, currently the fundamental mechanism for moving and regulating our society, must be replaced with a social welfare motive. Capitalism has served an historical epoch. It transformed feudalism to a industrial society. It brought with it bourgeois democracy. But it has served its time. The rapid development of the tools of production—and that includes the sensational development of nuclear fission and nuclear fusion—demands a corresponding change in the social relations of those who use these tools. Capitalism has become obsolete. It fails to meet the needs of all the people or even a majority of them. It is heavily responsible for the pollution of society and of the environment which is presaged by the *Global 2000 Report*.

There is a further point to be made regarding the concept "new and imaginative ideas—and a willingness to act on them." The theater of operations for what we have to do can no longer be limited to the village, the county or the state. The world has reached the point of contraction where the theater is not even just the nation, not even a nation as large as ours. The changes that must be made for survival go far beyond the capability of the United States or of any other nation. The big problems which now confront us are global and require a universal solution. Nothing better illustrates this than the issue of nuclear energy. Either it will be employed all over the globe for the benefit of men and women or it will forever do away with men and women. We have a clear choice. We must exercise it.

My Thanks

I realize that it is customary to put the acknowledgments at the beginning of a book. I am not putting mine at the end in order to be contrary. I am inclined to skip prefaces, acknowledgments, introductions and such front matter because I am anxious to get right into the body of the book. But if I have become interested in a book, I always read the end matter to see whether it contains information about the author, the sources and so on. Consequently, I figure that those who become interested in what I have written are more likely to read the acknowledgments if I put them at the end.

During the time that I have worked on this autobiography, a number of friends have been kind enough to read the manuscript at various stages. I thank them from the bottom of my heart for their helpful and sometimes insistent criticisms. I am not going to mention all their names. They know who they are, and their copies of the book will carry my appreciation. "Things," as we say, are indubitably better now than they were in the McCarthy days, but I am not sure that they are that good. This book makes me not just a supposed Communist but a declared one. Several of those who have helped me are young friends whose opinions I particularly valued because the only point in writing this kind of book was to address it to them. Several are working on their graduate degrees, others are awaiting university appointments or promotions. Still other are established in the professions, and they should remain there. Let them prosper and gain their promotions without being hindered by guilt by association.

I have never before done autobiographical writing, except for that youthful socialist venture in the 1920s. This is a different business from trying to explain the relations of American bankers to the prerevolutionary Chinese government. I am therefore most grateful to two experienced editors who became my friends in the process of advising me. In the early stages of trying to give the story some shape, Mary Heathcote was immensely helpful. In the latter stages, Adolph Suehsdorf gave me innumerable suggestions on how to fashion a still rough draft into a publishable manuscript.

Harold Cammer, to whom I have several times referred in the previous pages, has been my close friend as well as attorney for a great many years. He has seen me through a good many troubles. Throughout the preparation of this book he has been a most searching and insistent critic, constantly urging me to improve my work. That is one of the better parts of friendship, for which I am deeply grateful.

Somewhere along the line, I got in touch with Susan Ann Protter, my literary agent, who conveyed to me the notion that she would have an easier time selling the opus if I did this, that and the other to improve it. I took her advice and thus improved the MS. When I turned the book over to Lawrence Hill, I asked him to send me any suggestions that he might have. Both he and his editor, Donald J. Davidson, responded to this request with constructive suggestions.

I hope that I have sufficiently succeeded in following the guidance of all these good people so that the outcome in some measure rewards their efforts.

I want, in addition, to thank Nieves and our young daughters for tolerating the author through the long time it took him, to the neglect of many of his home responsibilities, to get his thoughts and experiences down on paper. Sometimes, when for long periods I was mulling over the less pleasant parts, my moods undoubtedly reflected those events. All I can offer them, aside from my thanks, is that because of their patience they will have a document from which better to know their husband and father.

I would never have written this account of my life if it had not been for the late Charles Small. For years he urged me to put my experiences and ideas on paper. I was not the only one, by any means. Charlie felt that the Left had made an important contribution to American life during the generation to which we both belonged. He knew it would be largely ignored or misrepresented by Establishment historians and that therefore as many as possible of those who had participated should record what they had done and why so that future generations would at least have a body of published material from which to get a more balanced view of those decades of war and crisis and violence. It was he more than most of the rest of us who should have written an autobiography. But Charlie was so busy working on his friends that he never got around to doing the job himself.

He was among the finest individuals I have known. He was a great person and an exceedingly simple one. Charlie devoted his entire life to the selfless pursuit of everything and anything that would make the United States a better place for those who do its work.

It is customary to thank the hard-working, loyal and indefatigable typist who produced those hundreds of clean pages the author turned over to the publisher. The only appropriate comment I can make with respect to the typo-filled pages this typist delivered is that in producing them and their several discarded antecedents he finally learned to use a third finger.